FRIENDS OF SIR ROBERT HART

To Jean
with love

Mary Tiffen

FRIENDS OF

SIR ROBERT HART

THREE GENERATIONS OF CARRALL
WOMEN IN CHINA

Mary Tiffen

In association with

TIFFANIA BOOKS

Copyright © Mary Tiffen 2012
First published in 2012 by Tiffania Books
Orchard House, Tower Hill Road, Crewkerne, TA18 8BJ
www.tiffaniabooks.com

Distributed by Gardners Books, 1 Whittle Drive, Eastbourne, East
Sussex, BN23 6QH
Tel: +44(0)1323 521555 | Fax: +44(0)1323 521666

British Library Cataloguing in Publication Data
A catalogue record for this book is available from the British Library

ISBN 978-0-9570353-0-0

Typeset by Amolibros, Milverton, Somerset
This book production has been managed by Amolibros
www.amolibros.com
Printed and bound by T J International Ltd, Padstow, Cornwall, UK

Dedicated to the memory of my aunt,

Kathleen Fawcus Newton, née Carrall, born in Sir Robert Hart's residence in Peking on 20 April 1883, died in Poole, Dorset on 5 February 1971,

and her daughter, my cousin Keeve, née Newton, born in Winnipeg, Canada, on 6 August 1913, died near Dungannon, Tyrone, Northern Ireland, on 19 January 2011.

Without the work of Kathleen in collecting material on our family history, and of Keeve in conserving her mother's work, this book could not have been written.

ABOUT THE AUTHOR

MARY TIFFEN read history at Cambridge University, but after a PhD at the London School of Economics, made her main career in examining the social and economic aspects of agricultural change in Africa and the Middle East. She is best known as the leader of a team examining change in Machakos District, Kenya, 1930 to 1990. The resulting book, with its then and now photographs, showed the change from degraded almost treeless land to carefully cultivated terraces as population grew sixfold. It helped change thinking on the relationship between population growth, poverty, and environmental degradation – see <www.drylandsresearch.org.uk>.

In this retirement work she examines her own family background, finding a fascinating story of her connection over three maternal generations with an outstanding Ulster man who was head of the Chinese Imperial Maritime Customs from 1863 to 1908.

Her main previous books are:

Mary Tiffen, *The Enterprising Peasant: A Study of Economic Development in Gombe Emirate, North Eastern State, Nigeria, 1900-1968*. HMSO, London, 1976.

Mary Tiffen, Michael Mortimore. and Frances Gichuki, *More People, Less Erosion: Environmental Recovery in Kenya*. John Wiley, Chichester, 1994.

CONTENTS

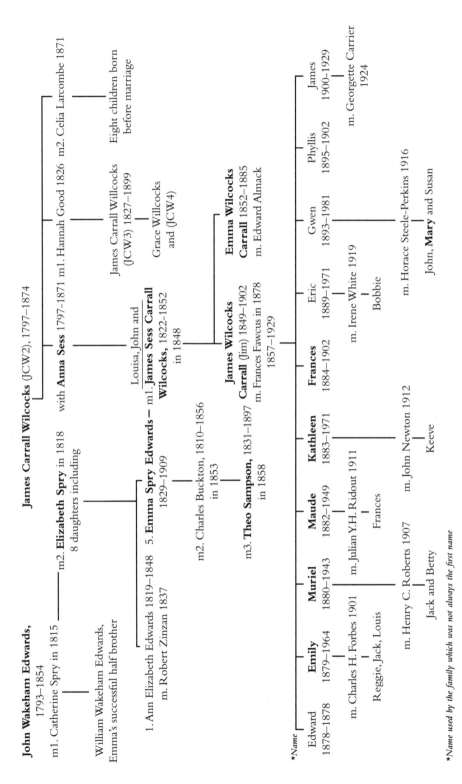

John Wakeham Edwards,
1793–1854
m1. Catherine Spry in 1815 —————— m2. **Elizabeth Spry** in 1818
8 daughters including

William Wakeham Edwards,
Emma's successful half brother

1. Ann Elizabeth Edwards 1819–1848
m. Robert Zinzan 1837

5. **Emma Spry Edwards** — m1. **James Sess Carrall**
1829–1909   **Wilcocks,** 1822–1852
                                                in 1848

m2. Charles Buckton, 1810–1856
in 1853

m3. **Theo Sampson,** 1831–1897
in 1858

James Carrall Wilcocks (JCW2), 1797–1874

with **Anna Sess** 1797–1871 m1. Hannah Good 1826 m2. Celia Larcombe 1871

Eight children born
before marriage

James Carrall Willcocks
(JCW3) 1827–1899

Grace Willcocks
and (JCW 4)

Louisa, John and

**Emma Wilcocks
Carrall** 1852–1885
m. Edward Almack

**James Wilcocks
Carrall** (Jim) 1849–1902
m. Frances Fawcus in 1878
1857–1929

Edward	**Emily**	**Muriel**	**Maude**	**Kathleen**	**Frances**	Eric	Gwen	Phyllis	James
1878–1878	1879–1964	1880–1943	1882–1949	1883–1971	1884–1902	1889–1971	1893–1981	1895–1902	1900–1929

m. Charles H. Forbes 1901

m. Julian Y.H. Ridout 1911

Frances

m. John Newton 1912

Keeve

m. Irene White 1919

Bobbie

m. Horace Steele-Perkins 1916

John, **Mary** and Susan

m. Georgette Carrier
1924

m. Henry C. Roberts 1907

Jack and Betty

Reggie, Jack, Louis

*Name

*Name used by the family which was not always the first name

Figure (i) Family tree, main characters emboldened.

xi

LIST OF ILLUSTRATIONS

Facing page 142

Facing page 174

Facing page 238

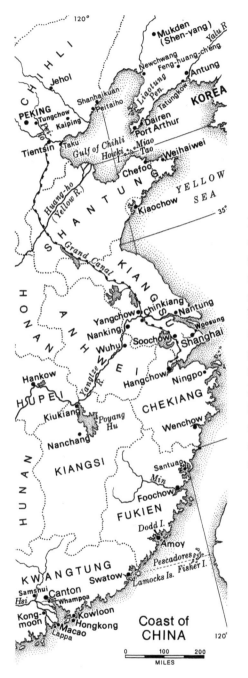

Figure (ii). China coast, as at 1868–1907 (Fairbank et al. 1975, frontispiece).

CHINA AS KNOWN TO THE BRITISH IN THE NINETEENTH CENTURY

For most of the years this book covers, the Wade-Giles system of romanising Chinese names was used and these are shown in he map. I use these throughout in both text and quotations, for Canton, Peking, Chefoo and Amoy, but give the Pinyin form at first mention. In other cases, I have used the Pinyin system for names and places in the text, as it is usually sufficiently similar to be clear. The two spellings of places and rivers are shown overleaf.

WALES-GILES TO PINYIN CONVERSION

Wades-Giles	Pinyin
Amoy	Xiamen
Canton	Guangzhou
Chefoo	Yantai
Fuchow	Fuzhou
Kiangsi	Guangxi
Kwantung	Guangdong
Macao	Macau
Manchuria	Manchow
Matsoo	Matsu Tao
Moukden	Shenyang
Pearl River	Zhu Jiang
Peitaiho:	Beidaihe
Peking	Beijing
Port Arthur	Lushun
Shantung	Shandong
Taku	Dagu
Tientsin	Tianjin
Tongku	Tanggu
Wei-hai-wei	Weihai
Whampoa	Huangpu
Yangtse	Yangzi
Yellow River	Huang He
Yunnan	Kunming

Two persons frequently mentioned are:
    Li or Li Hung Chang, now Li Hongzhang,
    Yeh, now Ye Mingchen.

FOREWORD

In his 1891 play *Lady Windermere's Fan*, Oscar Wilde famously wrote that 'between men and women there is no friendship possible', and the modern reader might believe this to be a commonplace assertion of the period. How could there be friendship when Victorian men and women lived such divergent lives that historians use the term 'separate spheres' to describe their segregation, as if each gender inhabited its own discrete world? And how could any platonic affection exist when society kept such a close watch for any hint of sexual immorality, particularly from women? Certainly, a friendship which violated the complex rules of Victorian propriety was a risk to the reputation of the woman (and sometimes the man) engaging in it; this was the subject of Wilde's play. Yet under certain circumstances, even intimate cross-gender friendships were considered harmless.

In this book, Mary Tiffen has used family papers and extensive archival research to unearth the story of the remarkable women of the Carrall family and their friendships with Robert Hart, administrator extraordinaire of late Qing China. We are given a cracking tale of expatriate life, rich in detail, as bold, bright women far from home pushed against the onerous restrictions imposed by Victorian notions of femininity in pursuit of fulfilment. For this reader, though, the greatest joy of this book lies in what it shows us about relationships between Victorian men and women. We see them as spouses, as lovers, but most refreshingly, as friends; and the core of the book lies in the deep emotional connection between Hart and three generations of Carrall women.

Both Hart and the Carralls knew from experience the cost when society considered a connection between a man and a woman to be unacceptable. They remained, however, optimistic about the potential for friendship, and the friendship they shared was not simply possible but life-changing. Robert Hart was for over forty years the preeminent European in China, and his good opinion could secure prosperity as surely as his censure guaranteed disgrace. Hart's friendship with the Carralls helped to transform the family's fortunes, as they overcame the taint of illegitimacy to achieve success and respectability. Though less readily apparent, the Carrall women influenced Hart in return. Hart believed that both China and the West would benefit from a stronger Chinese state and from closer diplomatic ties with the West. His views echo those expressed by many of today's politicians, but they earned him criticism as well as praise from contemporaries. Throughout his frenetic career, Hart's affectionate friendships with women seem to have been a source of strength as he doggedly charted his own course through a half-century of turbulent Chinese politics.

Queen's University Belfast has rightly supported publication of this book. Hart's conduct immediately after graduation was not auspicious; the university's decision to nominate him for a diplomatic post in China pulled him out of a post-graduate year of drinking with disreputable friends. But Hart recovered from this to become one of the university's most distinguished alumni, and after his retirement was appointed Pro-Chancellor. It is to be hoped that this book will help to introduce this brilliant, dedicated and sometimes sentimental son of Portadown to those unfamiliar with his achievements. Instead of finding an account of a great man doing momentous things, though, readers of this book will get to know Hart in a much more personal way: through precious glimpses of the interior world he shared most especially with his female friends.

Dr Emma Reisz
Lecturer in Asian History, Queen's University Belfast

PROLOGUE — NOW AND THEN

The dead call to us out of the past, like owls calling out of the dark.
They ask to be heard, remembered, understood. (Richard Holmes)[1]

Links with the Past

I am the lucky possessor of 'interesting relatives with singular names doing remarkable things at auspicious times and in exotic places'.[2] I have known from childhood that my mother, née Gwen Carrall, was born in China at Chefoo, Shantung (now Yantai, in Shandong), in 1893, and that her father had served under the Ulster man, Sir Robert Hart, as Commissioner of Customs there. After my father was posted to Hong Kong in 1938, I had visited Chefoo with my mother in the summer of 1939. We had gone to nearby Weihaiwei (now Weihai) for a break from the damp mists of Hong Kong. She found there were still steamers to Chefoo, and decided to take me to her childhood home.

Some memories of that visit as an eight-year-old have stayed with me. One is of struggling ever upwards through a large garden to a house then occupied by the Japanese commandant. (The Japanese had occupied Chefoo during their war against China, which began in 1936.) He made us welcome and showed us round. The second is of going in a rickshaw, passing Japanese sentries on the outskirts of the town, to a cemetery on Temple Hill beyond. My mother and I were accompanied by her old amah,[3] who had continued to tend the grave of my grandfather. On the way back I apparently fell asleep, and my mother told me the amah had explained to the sentries that I was overcome by the solemnity of a visit to my ancestor! These memories were all I had to guide me when I made a diversion to Yantai, during a holiday in China in 2002, one hundred years after my grandfather's death. The manager of the local branch of the China International Travel Service took me to the

Building Archive office, to locate the site of the cemetery on Temple Hill, and showed me round the former Settlement Hill, where my grandparents had lived. Some of the older houses remain — one being an interesting museum — in what is now a public park. The house of the Commissioner of Customs is gone, and by its old top gate there now stands a memorial to the Chinese who died during the Japanese occupation.

British women and children were evacuated from Hong Kong to Australia in 1940. My father, fortunately for him, was posted to India a fortnight before war was declared on the Japanese, after their attack on Pearl Harbour in December 1941. We rejoined him there, and we only returned to England in December 1945, without him. I did not immediately know that my parents' marriage was effectively at an end. It is only in writing this book that I realised that I shared with my mother and aunts their experience of returning to a little known homeland and an amorphous class status. Like them, I was a middle-class child coming to terms with comparative poverty, and the need to help my mother to earn a living, after a childhood in which my parents had operated at the higher levels of colonial society.

I learnt about my great-grandmother, née Emma Spry Edwards, the first woman in our family to live in China, after our return, from her grand-daughter, my Aunt Kath (Mrs Kathleen F Newton, née Carrall). She also told me that Sir Robert Hart, head of the Chinese Imperial Maritime Customs 1863–1908, had promised Emma to give her son a post in that service if he learnt Chinese. Aunt Kath was a woman born tragically out of her time, but despite her troubles she remained fresh, enthusiastic and fascinated by China. In her seventies a Belfast reporter wrote 'I had [Hart's] portrait painted for me...by a lady who seemed unaware that she herself was an admirable and fascinating subject'. (Aunt Kath and her daughter both married into Ulster families.) Hart was her godfather, and Kath visited him in 1900, the year of the Boxer Rebellion, during which she kept a diary. She is a main character in the second half of this book. She was our family historian, preserving many family records, but she never discovered why Emma, who had married a James Carrall Wilcocks in 1848, registered their son, born in 1849, as James Wilcocks Carrall, making her descendants the Carralls of this book.

Learning that I was the fourth generation of my family to have been in China led me to choose Sino-British relations 1830–42 as my special subject when I read history at Cambridge, 1949–52. However, my husband's work abroad in the British Council meant I made my own career mainly in the Middle East and Africa, becoming a specialist in social and economic development. It was only after I finally retired in 2001 that I started looking into my maternal family history. The 2002 trip was part of this, and I reported on it to cousins. Keeve, Kath's daughter, then sent me Aunt Kath's collection, apart from some materials on Hart which she had previously donated to Queen's University, Belfast (QUB), where Hart had studied. Other cousins provided photograph albums.

The Hart Connection

Delving into the family of my grandmother, the Fawcuses and Specialls, occupied me for a considerable time, and it was only in autumn 2006 that I began writing up Aunt Kath's 1900 diary which included her visit to Sir Robert Hart, just before he was caught in the siege of the legations during the Boxer rebellion. I then found that Professor Robert Bickers of Bristol University was organising a conference on Hart and the Chinese Imperial Maritime Customs in February 2007. He kindly invited me, and I took with me Kath's 1900 diary, two photograph albums and the Chinese scroll presented to my grandfather in 1900 which I had inherited from my mother. These intrigued many of the participants, while for my part I realised what a key role Hart had played in China's first tentative steps to modernisation and participation in global trade. The Chinese Imperial Maritime Customs which he headed was China's first modern bureaucracy. This unique organisation was staffed in its upper echelons by westerners from all the nations trading with China, headed by a Britisher responsible to the Chinese Government. In the diversity of its staff it resembled a modern international organisation or large business. Its responsibilities extended to harbours, light-houses, statistical data collection from trade to health to meteorology, and later to a modern postal service. It sponsored two high-level institutions for Chinese wishing to study western languages and sciences. In addition, as a trusted Chinese civil servant, Hart played an important mediating role in several international crises, as he was able to understand both the foreign and the Chinese viewpoints. I saw that the materials I had would be of interest to far more people than my immediate family.

Dr Richard O'Leary, then of QUB, invited me to explore the Hart collection held there, including Keeve's donations, known as the Irons' gift.[4] Amongst the latter were Hart's twenty-three letters to Kath, 1896–1907. The Senior Subject Librarian, Deirdre Wildy, had also unearthed a box from the then unclassified Hart collection, containing letters which Kath, her mother and two of her sisters had written to him during 1902–03, when they returned to Europe after my grandfather's death. There was also a letter from my great-grandmother, Emma Spry Edwards, showing that she had corresponded with Hart since she first met him in 1858. One letter from Hart to Kath revealed that Emma's daughter, another Emma, had visited Hart and his wife in Peking in 1875, and that he had regarded her as a great friend. Thus, there was an amazing three-generational friendship between Hart and the Carrall women.

Hart lost all the letters he had received before 1900 when his house in Peking (Beijing) was fired in the Boxer rebellion. His diaries were saved, and had been donated to QUB by his great-grandson in 1970. On that first visit I studied the ones covering 1882–3, when my grandparents stayed in his house, where Aunt Kath was born. I could see that the warm, generous personality so often concealed by his IGship, as my grandmother put it, was revealed more fully in his letters to my aunt than in his diaries. The cantankerous, prejudiced boss depicted by one of his Commissioners, Paul King, is in contrast to the experience of the Carralls.[5]

By early 2008 Deidre Wildy had obtained a grant and got the whole Hart collection catalogued. On my next visit I found over one hundred more letters, one of which showed that my grandmother had corresponded with Hart since her stay in his house in 1882-3. Meanwhile, Bristol University had scanned the Chefoo albums for its digital collection of European photos of China in the nineteenth and twentieth centuries. Besides making these available on the web, the high quality scan helped me to upgrade some faded and acid-marked photos for this book.[6] I was the lucky possessor not only of an interesting family, but of a treasure trove of first-hand material on their thoughts and emotions, appearance and actions.

Hart: Relations with Women, Family and Staff

I found that as I researched these lives two themes were emerging. The first concerns Sir Robert Hart himself. This book cannot do justice to his major achievements, nor discuss the full range of a complex character. I concentrate on his relationship with women and family, which also impinged on his relationship with his staff. His relationship with women introduces my second theme, the nature of the Victorian family and the social conventions which upheld it, in its two forms, legal, based on marriage, and illicit, where there were children, but no marriage.

The factual writer is constrained by the availability of the evidence. After 1896 my grandparents and aunts can speak for themselves, to develop the family theme. Letters, diaries and hand-written reports are quoted in italic, as a reminder of an age which predated the typewriter as well as the computer. They can be *heard*, in the words of Richard Holmes at the beginning of this Prologue, but while the eye-level view gives insight into feelings, it is also blinkered and partial. I try to make the writers *understood*, by presenting some of the background events and the social conventions governing family life at the time. Here I have the advantage of being the intermediate generation between then and now. Some of those conventions and limitations on women were still in existence when I returned from India to England as a fourteen-year-old in December 1945. Hence, I also allow my own voice to be heard.

Hart's relationship with women and family changed as he matured from hot-headed youth to disappointed *pater familias*. His conscience, underpinned by the religious teaching of his youth, gave him both an imperfectly followed ideal of sex only within marriage and a strong Protestant work ethic. The latter impelled him to use the great intellectual gifts with which he had been endowed for work that would not only support his family but also achieve good outcomes for those he had undertaken to serve.[7] (Normal ambition and desire for wealth and recognition were also present.) His youthful emotions required not only sexual satisfaction but also companionable friendship, but his work and his isolation in the narrow society of expatriate Peking gave him little opportunity to find the woman who could meet both needs. Three chapters on his life, correlating with the three generations of Carralls whom he knew, thread through the book. The tension between work goals and emotional needs gave rise to intermittent depression, even as a young man. In middle age it almost broke him. In a lonely old age the third chapter shows him still haunted by the fruits of his youthful relationship with a Chinese girl and disappointed by his legal children and by the limited outcome of his hopes for China. His voice can be heard through his diaries and letters, enabling the reader to judge him for themselves, but the chapter closes with my own view of him in his relations with women and as an employer.

My first-hand material on the Carralls is unevenly distributed. For the first two generations I had only a few photographs, Hart's diaries, some memories written down by Aunt Kath, a glimpse of Emma's second husband from British consular archives, and the writings of Theophilus Sampson, her third husband. Sometimes I was able to supplement these by eye-level views from other contemporary observers. The first three chapters explain how and why Hart, my great-grandmother Emma and her third husband, Theo Sampson, arrived in China in 1853 and 1854. Chapter One takes Emma from a clean little Devon town to a London slum and, after an ill-fated first marriage, to a China mired in civil war. Chapter Two takes Hart from Ulster to China, where he met Emma and Theo Sampson in 1858 and became head of the Customs in 1863. It ends with his marriage during leave in 1866 to a respectable Irish girl, which he hoped would solve his struggles between sex and conscience. Chapter Three shows how the penniless Theo arrived in Whampoa in 1853 and developed various successful careers. These chapters introduce the family theme, for Emma's first husband, my great-grandfather, was illegitimate, which multiplied her troubles when he died, and Hart had an illicit relationship from 1857 to 1864 with a Chinese girl, resulting in three children. Chapter Four describes the disintegration of Hart's marriage and his nervous breakdown, through a combination of factors which included his admiration for intelligent young women like Emma's daughter, Emma Carrall, who visited him in 1875, and the re-immergence into his life of his illegitimate children. (There was also an attractive Mrs Glover.) Chapter Five follows the early career in the Customs of my grandfather, Emma's son Jim Carrall, his marriage to Frances Fawcus, their time with Hart in Peking in 1883 (where Frances, but not Jim, earned Hart's affection) to Carrall's successful re-establishment of his reputation by his conduct during the vicious French attack on Fuzhou in 1884.

The Carrall letters that I found in Belfast and my aunt Kath's 1900 diary form the basis of the second part of the book. Chapters Six to Ten give an insider view of a legal and loving Victorian expatriate family, at a critical period in both their own lives (the daughters were growing into young women) and that of China, 1896–1911, during which their relationship with Hart was particularly intense and continuous. Kath's view is supplemented by that of her parents and sisters. We can, like Hart, share her schooldays, a visit to him in Peking, the Boxer rebellion of 1900, and the emotions evoked by a marriage, a broken engagement, the death of the bread-winner and a difficult resettlement in the home country, 1902–11.

The letters illustrate the extraordinarily intimate relationship which Hart was able to enjoy with the daughters and wives of his staff or associates, at a time in his life when he had disciplined himself to keep this within the bounds of friendship. These friendships helped him to endure the loneliness brought about by the breakdown of his legal marriage and the trials caused by his children, both legitimate and illegitimate, from whom he was physically separated. His responses to the Carrall letters show his sympathetic understanding of young people and their mothers. In Chapter Eleven he confronts his failures as a father in the last years of his life, using, in his words to Kath, the 'opium' of work, to combat his loneliness and sadness. Demanding new work included taking on the internal taxes on trade, forming the modernised postal service for which he had long struggled, and helping China to preserve its unity in the face of European and Japanese land-grabbing and the mortal weakness of the Manchu dynasty that he was serving. The chapter also discusses his personnel management. His devotion to the good of the Customs meant that he always bore in mind a man's ability to do the job, whether or not he liked him, or his wife, on a personal basis, and that he did not allow a bad first impression to stand in the way of later promotion if this was justified.

The Carrall family was not the only one to enjoy Hart's friendship. His staff's seventieth birthday address in 1905 expresses this:

> We therefore ask you to accept, on behalf of close upon ten thousand men of all ranks and nationalities, their most sincere and heartfelt wish that you may be spared for many years of health and happiness, not alone to those who know you only as a Chief, but also to those — and they are many — who have reason to regard you as a personal friend.[8]

This is from the men. What this book reveals is that in many cases their wives and children also regarded him as a trusted personal friend.

The Victorian Family, Legal and Illegal

Before passing on to the story it may be helpful to describe the Victorian family. The legal family was, and had been for hundreds of generations, the basic building block of society. It provided for the passing of values, skills and knowledge to the next generation. Life-long marriage was the foundation by which society ensured that a man took responsibility for his children, and protected his wife during what could be forty years of child-bearing and child-rearing. (My grandmother Frances had her first child in 1878, and her youngest reached the age of eighteen only in 1918. She died ten years later.) However, by family the Victorians meant a unit larger than that of parents and children. Importantly, it also included grandparents, aunts and uncles, and more tenuously, cousins. In the all too common event of a parent dying, the surviving spouse depended on this wider unit for help — typically financial help from male members and caring help from female members. The social insurance provided by the extended family was, however, only as good as the number of successful males in it. Having sons was important, for a good son knew he should help his mother and sisters, especially if they were left in distress when their father died.

The state was too poor to provide social security. In Britain the minimal help provided through local taxes by the poor law provisions could bankrupt middle-class traders, professionals and craftsmen in times of economic depression when the numbers of poor increased and such taxes rose in step, as one of my Fawcus ancestors found to his cost in the 1840s. However, society had reached a stage of prosperity which made it possible to specialise roles within marriage. Most middle-class women could concentrate on feeding and clothing their husbands and children, maintaining hygienic standards to keep them healthy, nursing them when ill, providing primary education to their children and keeping family networks alive through correspondence and entertaining, without at the same time having to mind the shop, or assist their husbands in other ways to meet the man's primary responsibility for providing the family income.

Given all this, marriage was a step to be taken seriously, in consultation with the rest of the family, and until the age of twenty-one, only with the parents' explicit consent (the father normally, the mother if he had died). The serious responsibilities which a man was implicitly undertaking meant that no girl should encourage him, by her behaviour, to get so far as a proposal if she did not intend to accept him. No man, once accepted, should run away from these responsibilities by failing to proceed to marriage, especially if he called himself a gentleman. Two Carrall family dramas illustrate these situations.

We all know about the second-class status of women at this time, who only gradually between 1850 and 1900 got some control over their personal assets, and some access to higher education and a career. We consider less often the flip-side to the concept of legal, life-long marriage — the disgrace attached to producing children outside marriage. This was an all too common experience, since the only secure, widely-known method of birth control was abstinence from sexual relations. Bastards, as they were called, had no automatic claim either to their father's help or to his name. Many men, including both Emma's father-not-in-law and Hart, did provide financial help, but they lived separately from their children. Harriet, in Jane Austen's *Emma*, knew nothing about her father, though he paid for her keep. Such fathers were not present to provide the love, care, guidance, encouragement and discipline which a man could give within marriage. A legal father may be away from his family for months, even years at a time, because of his work or war, but this is different, as I can testify from my own experience, from finding out that your father has voluntarily walked out on you. A father's death has to be borne as courageously as possible, but love remains. It is his desertion that causes bitterness.

Illegitimate children were therefore the disgrace of an irresponsible man as well as of the woman, and a threat to the whole of society, since they were less likely to be reared as responsible, ethical citizens. Bastards passed on bad blood. (We would say they had a family background less conducive to a good upbringing, although not making this impossible.) The disgrace passed down the generations. In 1947 and 1959, Aunt Kath, trying to find out more about her grandfather, had her letters ignored because the Wilcocks receiving them did not wish to have anything to do with the illegitimate branch of the family.[9] Hart, in his seventies, was still dealing with the consequences of his illicit youthful relationship and the possibility of blackmail.

The normal legal family faced special challenges when its head lived outside the home country. First, for parents, expatriate life involves tensions between home country and country of residence, separations from elderly parents and often, from children who needed to be educated at home. Second, there were particular hazards in nineteenth-century China, not only from civil unrest, widespread in the 1850s and exploding again in 1900, but also from an even higher risk than at home of death from disease. Third, there was the challenge of readjusting to life in the home country whether by retirement (as with Hart) or even more harshly, as in the Carrall case, because of the premature death of the bread-winner.

Expatriate families were not exempt from the more normal challenges parents face as children grow up. The mores of the time created tensions between parents and young people over love affairs in a far more acute form than today, as both Hart and the Carralls found. New tensions were appearing from the aspirations of some women, including my great-aunt Emma and my aunt Kath, for an independent career. In the final chapter, after considering Hart's relationship with women and family, I add a short personal postscript on the problems still facing society in supporting the difficult parental task of bringing up a caring, ethical next generation, without the benefit of the religious ethos that guided Hart.

Acknowledgements

I am grateful to Professor Robert Bickers at Bristol and Deidre Wildy at QUB for help and advice from start to finish of this book. Bristol University's website is an invaluable source of information on Customs personnel. Catherine Ladds, then of Bristol University, kindly collected material on my grandfather during a visit to the Customs archive in Nanjing. Stimulating discussions with her and Dr Richard O'Leary, then at QUB, helped me to improve my knowledge of the Customs background. Dr Emma Reisz, Lecturer in Asian History at QUB gave much valued help in the final stages. As an alumna of the London School of Economics it was invaluable to be able to use their wonderful library with its helpful staff. The internet has enabled me to contact fellow family historians listed in the bibliography, to find nineteenth-century authors and to contact scholars studying Chinese and Western interactions all over the world, for whose encouragement and pointers I am indeed grateful. Amongst these are Professor Hans van de Ven of Cambridge University, Professor Fa-ti Fan at the State University of

New York at Binghamton, Professor John Carroll at Hong Kong University, Frances Wood of the British Library and Dr R G Tiedemann. The comments of Susanna Hoe and two anonymous reviewers have been genuinely helpful in making revisions.

On the family side, Keeve's contribution has already been mentioned. I am only sorry that she died just before this book was completed. Aunt Maude's grandson, Lennox Harvey-Jamieson, provided two albums of photos taken in Chefoo. William Forbes-Newton, Aunt Emily's grandson, provided photos and some memories of her, as did Andrew de Candole, Aunt Muriel's grandson. The notes to some chapters show help from many others with whom I share an ancestor, or whose own ancestors met mine at some point.

I am also grateful to my old friend and colleague Margaret Cornell, who edited the books I wrote while at the Overseas Development Institute, and who volunteered to work through my first draft. Mistakes made later are my fault, not hers! My daughter Jenny, her husband Jason and my son Martin made comments from the point of view of their generation, which were extremely helpful. Diana Brown provided assistance at various points. I found an excellent producer in Amolibros. My husband, Brian, has been enormously patient in dealing with the distractions of authorship, and I thank him for his love, consideration and domestic support.

CHAPTER ONE

EMMA SPRY EDWARDS GOES TO
CHINA IN 1853

'...we had 37 shot in our residence, one of which, a six pounder, passed within but two inches of the head of my wife, & as near to my youngest child.' So wrote Charles Buckton, the second of Emma Spry Edwards' three husbands. How did a young woman from Devon find herself on 29 December 1854 in a houseboat on the Pearl River (Zhu Jiang), in the middle of a battle between the gunboats of the Chinese Emperor and the ships of rebels? How did she subsequently become a lifelong friend of Robert Hart, who became head of the Chinese Imperial Maritime Customs? And why were her children called Carrall, when she had married a Wilcocks? The answers lie in the social status of her first husband. It is a complicated story but needs to be told to show why the Carralls were in China and the perils of illegitimacy

Emma's Devon Parents

The Edwards family owned and farmed land in the South Hams, a fertile area of rolling hills and small villages in Devon. As only the eldest son inherited land, younger sons and their offspring, like Emma's father, John Wakeham Edwards, born in 1793, looked elsewhere for a living. He became a surgeon by a seven-year apprenticeship, starting at about the age of fourteen. His master, an older practitioner, would have also taught him the use of common drugs, such as laudanum (opium), and the advantages and disadvantages of alcohol to deaden the pain of the cut.[1] Thus armed, surgeons dealt with the consequences of fights, accidents, obstructed labour in women, kidney stones etc., operating in their own homes or those of their patients. They were often also consulted about illnesses. The remedies they concocted and sold were an important source of income.

In 1815 the young surgeon, aged twenty-two, married Catherine Spry. In 1817 they had a son, William, but Catherine died a few months later. The following year John married her older sister, Elizabeth Spry (see Family Tree, page xi). With Elizabeth he had eight daughters and a son. As a woman's chief security lay in her family, especially if her husband died, the ratio of daughters to sons in this family was to prove unfortunate. Elizabeth's first children, including Emma, their fifth daughter, were born in the village of Chillington. The family then moved a few miles to Kingsbridge, where Emma was baptised in the Parish Church in June 1829. She was the only one given her mother's maiden name, Spry, which she used in her signature most of her life.

Today, Kingsbridge, the main market town of the South Hams, is accessible only by narrow country lanes to the north or via the ferry at Dartmouth to the east. Then, the many-branched Kingsbridge estuary provided water routes to nearby villages and more distant towns. The 'salubrious' town had piped water from the nearby hills, a gasworks to provide lighting, and many small shops and workshops. White's Directory shows it had about 2,000 inhabitants in 1841 and 3,000 in 1851, when it boasted five surgeons.

The intense competition for patients brought John low; the *London Gazette* records his bankruptcy on 26 July 1839, when he is described as a 'druggist , dealer and chapman' which suggests he sold other things besides medicines. He recovered to be described as 'surgeon' in the 1841 census , which shows Emma, aged 12, living with her parents and five of her sisters in Duncombe Street, on the corner of the elegant Fore Street (Figures 1.2 and 1.3). One servant suggests only modest prosperity, and that their mother gave her daughters a practical knowledge of cooking and household skills. There was no assistant to steady patients when operations were undertaken without anaesthetics, to pass the implements, and to mix the medicines prescribed, and neither of John's two sons was at home or living locally. Since John Wakeham Edwards is recorded as having taken on a female apprentice, Susanna Stone, age thirteen, in June 1817, it seems likely that as his daughters entered their teens, he taught one or more of them to help him, training them up and then despatching them out to find work if they had not married.

Emma's older sister Catherine was absent from home in both the 1841 and 1851 census. The poorer middle-class families could not afford idle daughters.

Education for girls was bad in the early nineteenth century. The 1841 census shows no governess. Middle-class girls in families unable to afford one were taught by their mothers or older sisters. Emma enjoyed books, but had scanty knowledge of history and geography, even when this concerned the Spry family. She treasured letters from her mother's half-brother, William Spry, a midshipman on Admiral Rodney's ship at the Battle of the Saints in 1782, near Dominica in the West Indies, but was inaccurate on its location and the significance of the French defeat.[2] Her letters to Hart show she was pleased that her grand-daughters received a far better education in China at the end of the century.

The sons would have been educated at a school that provided a foundation in Latin and mathematics. By the 1830s surgeons were amongst the best educated men in Britain. Their studies were far more taxing than the degrees offered at the unreformed Oxford and Cambridge, and demanded at least four years of lectures and practical work before taking the examination for Membership of the Royal College of Surgeons (MRCS).[3] We will meet later in China former surgeons like Rutherford Alcock and Robert Bredon, who rose high as administrators in their respective services after ceasing to practice. Emma's half-brother William, aged twenty-three, got his MRCS in August 1840. His friend, Robert Zinzan, who was a few years older, had married the oldest Edwards girl, Ann Elizabeth, in the bride's church at Kingsbridge in August 1837, after gaining his MRCS. The twenty-year-old William crammed his signature in as a third witness (not legally required), as if to show that he had introduced them. As was to be expected, her father was the first witness, and he delivered her first child, Lavinia, in Kingsbridge the next year. (Lavinia was later to follow Emma to China.) Emma's own marriage was to be significantly different.

Aunt Kath remembered her grandmother as loving nature and poetry. After Emma's death she found amongst her possessions *The Book of Gems*, an illustrated poetry anthology that came out in three volumes in the late 1830s. Emma had marked up verses in a poem by Gray:

Figure A. Carrall's gown, worn by his great grandson, Lennox Harvey-Jamieson.

Figure B. The blue button on the hat indicates he was a Mandarin of the third order of rank.

Figure C. The order of the Double Dragon. With the hat, now in the possession of Rodger Harvey-Jamieson.

Figure D. Yantai in 2002, from the primary school on Temple Hill.

Figure E. The fishing harbour in 2002, adjacent to the old Customs jetty. To the rear right is the promontory, with its modern lighthouse.

Figure F. The beach southeast of the promontory, near the site of the CIM schools (now a naval academy), where summer visitors (now from China and Korea), still enjoy the bathing.

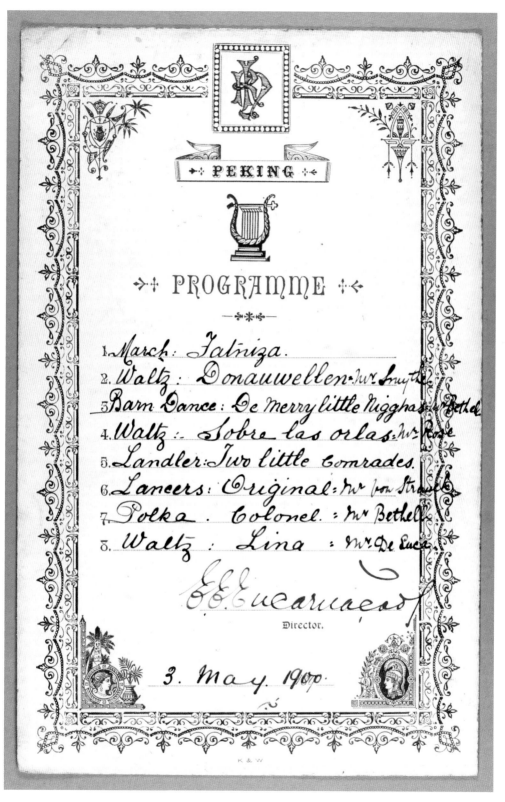

Figure G. The dance programme, with Maude's partners' names written in (Ca-s06).

Figure H. Scroll 2 (Chinese order right to left) now in the possession of Jim's great-grandson Rodger Harvey-Jamieson.

Figure I. Cabin class menu on the Bingo Maru, kept in Maude's album, with an odd mixture of French and English (Ca2-105).

Figure J. The author visiting Chefoo (Yentai) in 2002. A fine road and bund now runs from the old Settlement Hill in the background to the Naval Academy now on the site of the Chefoo CIM schools.

Ah happy hills; ah pleasing shade!
Ah, fields beloved in vain!
Where once my careless childhood stray'd
A stranger yet to pain

The next years of her life were to be marked by a complete absence of happy hills and pleasing shade.

London and Emma's Marriage to Whom?

In 1842 Emma's father moved to London. He appeared in January 1843 as a competent medical witness in a case at the Old Bailey, describing himself as a surgeon at 66 Wardour Street. An unknown crisis must have driven him to leave his deep family roots in the South Hams and move to Soho, a stinking London slum, where families shared space with animals, slaughterhouses and grease-boiling dens. The sewers were decaying and the cesspits under their houses unemptied.[4] The same crisis may have caused his son, William, to move in 1842 to Antigua, in the West Indies.[5] His father, who had funded his expensive education, lost the son who could join him in his practice and help the family as he aged. (The younger son, John, probably at school in 1841, failed to qualify, and died in a lunatic asylum in 1868 as a mere medical assistant.)

Medical knowledge was still primitive. Dr John Snow pinpointed a suspect well in Soho only in 1854, showing that cholera came from drinking polluted water rather than breathing bad air. In 1847, Dr Ignaz Semmelweiss, a physician in a Vienna hospital, found that death from childbed fever, common amongst women giving birth in hospital, could be greatly reduced if students and doctors washed their hands between autopsies and examinations of women in labour, but it was many years before his ideas were accepted. The realisation that many diseases were spread by germs, which could jump from person to person by various mechanisms, came still later.

Even so, the many doctors who had qualified by education and examination after an 1815 statute could show that they probably knew more about drugs and diseases than a man who, unlike them, had no letters after his name. The move to London was disastrous financially. On 6 June 1846 the *London Gazette* records John Wakeham Edwards in the Debtrors' Prison, petitioning for release on grounds of his insolvency.

(An 1838 Act allowed insolvent debtors to go free if they handed over all their assets to a Provisional Assignee). He is described as 'late of 36 Green Street, Stepney', to which he had evidently moved, and as a 'Surgeon, Apothecary and Accoucheur'. Effectively, he was bankrupt. It seems possible that his son-in-law Robert Zinzan, living and practising in Edmonton in 1845, and who had moved by 1848 to Hackney Road in what was then the outskirts of north London, had leased a surgery and dwelling at 87 St Martin's Lane where his father-in-law could re-establish himself. Emma, now fifteen, possibly eased family finances by becoming an assistant to Robert Webb. He is recorded in the 1851 census as Robert Webb, MRCS, LCA, aged 31, General Practitioner, living with his wife at 266 High Street, Poplar. Like Emma, he was born in the small village of Chillington, so he must have known her family. He was also a friend of her brother-in-law, Robert Zinzan.[1] Emma probably only got board and pocket money. The Edwards daughters did not become nurses, for this was a low-class, disreputable occupation: we think of Dickens' Mrs. Gamp in *Martin Chuzzlewit*. There were no training institutions for nurses in England at the time. Florence Nightingale contemporaneously fought an unsuccessful battle with her wealthy upper-class parents to be allowed to study nursing abroad.

By 1848 Emma had got to know James Sess Carrall Wilcocks. He was a printer and publisher and lived across the river in York Road, Lambeth, but his works were in the Strand, not far from St Martin's Lane. We can safely assume that Emma's parents investigated his background. They would not have liked what they found. James avoided the public calling of banns for three weeks prior to the wedding by paying for a marriage licence on 27 April 1848. Emma was 'upwards of nineteen'. James made an oath that he had obtained the necessary parental consent (Figure 1.4) but he gave her father only the legal minimum three days to receive the information and object.

The wedding took place on 30 April in the bridegroom's parish, St John's, Waterloo. Emma gave her address as High Street, Poplar. The first witness was Robert Webb. The second witness was John Blake, husband of the groom's sister, Louisa. There was no parental witness, particularly unusual where the girl was a minor. Aunt Kath was sure Emma had married without her father's consent. Photography was at its beginning at the time of her marriage, but later portraits suggest a strong-minded woman (Figure 1, a and b). Once she had set her heart on marrying James, she would not easily be deterred, even if she had known the reason for the probable parental opposition.

The happy early days of marriage were immediately saddened by the death of her sister. Zinzan sent the notice of Ann Elizabeth's 'deeply-regretted' death to *The Times* of Monday 22 May 1848 from 87 St Martins Lane. Unable to manage his four children without his wife, he seems for a time to have shared this surgery and dwelling with his father-in-law. By 1851 he had moved out of London, leaving two children with his mother-in-law and two with his own mother. The separation of male and female roles was a matter of practical necessity. Husbands worked far longer hours than today, and the work of women in keeping a family and house clean, and its inhabitants fed, clothed and educated, without electricity or machines, was labour-intensive.[6]

The 1851 census shows that James employed twenty men at his works. They could afford an experienced domestic servant, Mary Murphy, a twenty-eight-year-old Irish widow. (Emma's mother, with three unmarried daughters and two grandchildren at home, had only an eighteen-year-old girl to help out.) It looked as if Emma had done well for herself. Their son was born on 24 September 1849 at 48 York Road, Lambeth. It should have been a time of family rejoicing, with a proud father promptly registering his first-born son. This did not happen, for there was a problem over his surname.

James's probable father was a wealthy Exeter merchant, the second of a line of five fathers and sons named James Carrall Wilcocks. I will refer to him as JCW2 to distinguish him from the James who was Emma's husband.[7] His mother was Anna Sess, from a poor working-class family in Moretonhampstead, Devon. Their relationship lasted at least six years. Their first children, Louisa and James, were baptised with the Wilcocks name in Exeter in 1819 and 1822 respectively, though only marriage could legally entitle them to it.

By 1825 JCW2 was twenty-eight. His father had made him a partner in the family business, and may well have urged him to find a wife of good social status and to produce a legitimate heir. JCW2 married Hannah Good in London in January 1826 and a legal JCW3, their only child, was born in Exeter in 1827. I think JCW2 first made provision for Anna Sess and her children. It seems likely that he arranged for the annuity which continued to her death, and told her that she could use his middle name, Carrall, to disguise the fatherless state of her children.

Unfortunately, in what may have been an emotional farewell, he also got a third child on the way: John Carrall was born in 1826 in Anna's home town, Moretonhampstead. (Robert Hart later made the same mistake.) In the 1841 census the nineteen-year-old James appears as a Carrall, living with his mother Anna Carrall, and his younger brother John Carrall, fifteen, as lodgers in Lambeth, London. The social stigma of illegitimacy and its attendant security risks explain our family tradition that Emma's parents opposed the marriage.

By 1846 JCW2's legal marriage was in trouble. We know this because an 1857 Act made divorce possible for the first time, under strictly limited conditions, and in 1858 *The Times* recorded Hannah's application for judicial separation, citing JCW2's adultery with Celia Larcombe. Hannah stated that though they had had only one child they had lived together affectionately as man and wife till the summer of 1846, when he refused to cohabit with her any longer. She did not proceed on to a divorce.

It seems probable that JCW2, though he despatched his first children to London and did not live with them after his marriage, felt a responsibility for them until they could earn or marry. In the 1840s, no longer caring what Hannah thought, he acknowledged them publicly again. James's sister, Louisa, who married John Blake in 1844 and James when he married Emma in 1848 both named their father as James Wilcocks, draper, and gave their surname as Wilcocks. This must have been with his sanction. It is also likely that JCW2 provided James with start-up capital for his printing and publishing business, and that he paid the fees for the decent education and apprenticeship that this career required. Anna could have afforded neither on her own, while JCW2 could afford to have his portrait painted (Figure 1.5).

There is no evidence that JCW2 ever returned to Anna Sess, who in 1849 was fifty-two. By then he was involved with the twenty-six-year-old Celia Larcombe. A crisis was provoked when Celia produced in Exeter on 6 September 1849 the first of their eight children, Alfred James Carrall Wilcocks — just three weeks before Emma gave him a grandson. The 1851 census shows he provided Celia with an annuity and a very decent establishment in Exeter. His will (from which only Celia's children benefitted) demonstrated that she had a strong hold over him, and tolerated no rivals to her own children. When their first child was born JCW2 probably told Anna Sess's children to stop using the Wilcocks name forthwith. James' younger brother, John, married on 20 October

1849 as John Sess Carrall. The priest inserted dashes in place of his father's name and occupation, clearly revealing his shameful fatherless status. Emma's husband could not so easily give way. He would have wanted his own son's legality made crystal clear by registering him with the surname on the parental marriage certificate, but if JCW2 had provided the finance for James's business he would eventually have had to submit. Children should be registered within six months of birth, and it was Emma who finally did so, on 7 March 1850, naming both her son and his father as James Wilcocks Carrall. James used this name in the 1851 census.

As a sad footnote to this story, Anna died on 27 November 1871 in the home of her grand-daughter. (She had helped John Blake to bring up his children as Louisa, in a fit of madness after the birth of her sixth child, had committed suicide in 1858.) The death certificate was later officially corrected to substitute 'Anna Sess' for 'Anna Sess Carrall' and 'Annuitant' for 'Widow of James Carrall a Draper'. The only person with a strong motive to require this was JCW2, who had finally married Celia in March 1870, just a week after his legal wife Hannah died. If he had a living wife at that time, this marriage would be invalid and he could be convicted of bigamy. Anna had to be disowned and disgraced after death — striking evidence of the lifelong shame and grief that an illicit relationship could then cause.

Widowhood and Remarriage

In April 1852 Emma's husband died. She was a widow at twenty-three, and three months pregnant with her second child. In her distress and confusion she did not register the death, so the cause is unknown. Central London cemeteries were full so 'Emma Wilcocks' purchased a grave at Highgate Cemetery on 10 April, and her husband was buried as James Sess Carrall Wilcocks on 17 April 1852. This suggests that JCW2 provided the £10 or more required for the private grave. He was sufficiently grieved by the death of his first son to restore his name and give him a decent burial.

The only well-off man in Emma's own family was her half-brother, William, but a letter to Antigua would take months to reach him. Emma's father was too poor to help. In the 1851 census John Wakeham Edwards described himself, aged fifty-seven, as a general practitioner in medicine. He had probably lost the speed and dexterity needed for surgery without anaesthetics. The London Medical Directory of 1852 specifically states that he was in practice prior to 1815, to explain the absence of qualifications. He seems to have resorted to illegal activities. He was at Central Criminal Court, Old Bailey, charged with procuring a miscarriage of a woman by use of an instrument in 1850. Due to the absence of the prosecutrix he was found not guilty, as on two other similar charges. Women would not have liked to confess to an illegal abortion. He may already have been showing signs of mental disturbance for on 3 August 1854 he died at St Luke's Hospital, which catered for the insane. The immediate cause was general paralysis for three months. Those who could afford it cared for their sick at home rather than put them in the filthy hospitals catering for the poor. St Luke's was cleaner than most, only because it earned donations by attracting spectators to come and watch the inmates' odd behaviour. Emma's father was buried at Highgate Cemetery in a common grave, shared with other paupers. Emma's mother had no money for a private grave.

William did return temporarily from Antigua to help his mother and sisters, combining this with gaining his Fellowship (FRCS) in 1856 and his Licentiate of the Royal College of Physicians, Edinburgh, in 1860. A reference to his son in a letter she wrote to Hart in 1900 shows Emma always kept in touch with him and his family. He may have had a photograph (then still an expensive novelty) taken of Emma's mother and sent to Emma (Figure 1.6) together with one of her sister Catherine, who went to Antigua with him. The inscriptions on the back show that Emma treasured these. Figures 1.1b and 1.6 show Emma and her mother at the same age, and their physical resemblance, but her mother looks battered by fate, while Emma stood erect despite the many blows she suffered.

In 1852 the pregnant Emma could not wait for William to appear. She had to beg help from her husband's father, help that would be more niggardly than in the case of a legal relationship, for her son did not carry the family name. Her daughter was born six months after her husband's death, in Lambeth on 24 September 1852, in Anna Sess's lodgings. Emma registered her promptly, a month later, as Emma Wilcocks Carrall. On 18 January 1853, in Liverpool, she married Charles Buckton, twenty years her senior, who described himself as a merchant. She and her Carrall children then sailed with him to Whampoa, the port of Canton (Guangzhou) in China. While the Sprys had a history of migration to the West Indies, China was an unknown land, where she would be far from friends and relatives, but she had few options. Almost the only jobs open to women then were as servants, for which employers preferred unmarried women or childless widows. With two young children, she was not going to get many marriage offers.

She signed the marriage register as Emma Wilcocks. This, I think, suggests that JCW2 had a hand in introducing the pair. (His legal wife, Hannah, came from the same part of London as Buckton's parents.) My aunt wrote that her husband left Emma with only £300 and that her father gave her no help. My guess is that JCW2 provided this sum. Once married and in China he need feel no further financial responsibility and she would be far from his new family.

Buckton probably did not tell Emma (or JCW2) much about his finances. When he married his first wife in 1841 at St George's, Hanover Square, he was commander of the *Algerine* but he was later dismissed. In 1847 he was declared insolvent in Hong Kong. In 1850 Charles Buckton, ship's chandler of Whampoa Reach, was advertising for sale a soda water machine, nearly new, with bottles, corks, oil of lemons and all necessaries. A second-hand machine does not suggest a substantial enterprise. When his wife died he returned to London, to give their children into the care of her parents.[8] Emma's £300, which by the law of the time he would control, was an attraction which enabled him, amongst other things, to buy some expensive china. While Emma had little option but to accept him, she may have appreciated the education and flamboyance which, as with her first husband, show up in his signature (Figure 1.6).

The China that Greeted Emma

A little history is necessary to explain how Emma soon afterwards found herself in a houseboat under bombardment by opposing gunships. British and other foreign merchants had been trading with China since the late seventeenth century. However, foreign trade was limited to the single port of Canton, on the Pearl River. Merchants resided in their 'factories', combined residences and offices. These were outside the walled city, which they were not allowed to enter, and they could only deal with a specified group (Hong) of Chinese merchants. On the British side, the monopoly of trade was initially held by the East India Company which also effectively ruled large parts of India. The larger European sailing ships could come up only as far as Whampoa, some ten miles downstream of Canton. Goods were transhipped up or down in smaller vessels.

Tea from Canton was in increasing demand in Britain and, by the late eighteenth century, tea duties constituted about ten per cent of British tax revenue. However, as there was limited demand in China for British goods, the tea had to be paid for in gold or silver. Opium could be grown in India, and was in demand in China, first as a medicine and then, as more and more was shipped by the East India Company in exchange for tea, as a recreational drug. In 1834 the East India Company lost its monopoly and more traders joined in the China trade. The Chinese government officially banned opium imports, but it suited all parties to ignore this most of the time and to continue to trade in it on offshore islands. The Chinese authorities finally took effective action in 1839 by seizing and dumping a large quantity of opium. The British Foreign Secretary, Palmerston, retaliated with military force against this 'confiscation', leading to what is now known as the First Opium War. The defeated Chinese agreed in 1842 to open five 'Treaty Ports', where British consuls and traders were to be allowed to reside permanently, and to the trial of any miscreants amongst British citizens in British consular courts. They also ceded the barren island of Hong Kong to the British. In addition, there was a most favoured nation clause, by which any concessions later made to other nations should extend to Britain. The French and Americans followed this up with their own similar treaties and, as both also secured the rights of their missionaries to preach Christianity, this right also applied to British missionaries.

Opium was not mentioned. In practice it continued as an illegal trade from the offshore islands. In practice also, the legal trade in Canton was still based at the factories, since the Viceroy, Ye Mingchen (called Yeh in British reports), continued to refuse foreigners entry to the city. This remained a bone of contention. The Chinese saw China as the centre of the world. Foreign countries were tributaries, their inhabitants described by a word which, to British indignation, could be translated as 'barbarians'.[9] The Imperial authorities in Peking refused to have any direct dealings with Westerners, delegating all matters concerned with their trade to their Viceroy at Canton. (A Viceroy supervised two or more provinces, each with its own Governor.[10])

Internally, the Manchu Qing dynasty, itself foreign to the majority Han Chinese, was failing. Most peasants lived on the edge of subsistence in huts of mud and bamboo. Law and order were deteriorating as traditional self-policing in towns and villages was no longer backed by an efficient military. Pirates were active on the Pearl River. Discontented groups coalesced in the 1850s, especially amongst the poor southerners in Kwantung (Guangdong) Province, of which Canton was the capital, and the Kiangsi (Guangxi) region to its north. This Taiping revolt lasted for fifteen years, its leader preaching a form of egalitarian Christianity with Chinese characteristics. As the rebels controlled more and more territory, the Imperial revenues fell. The unpaid Imperial troops lived by plunder, oppression and extortion. Thousands of people were killed in the battles and their aftermath of executions.[11]

We can imagine Emma's first glimpse of her new home from a description by Lt. James D Johnston of the US navy, of his trip from Hong Kong to Canton in 1860.[12] After the rough sea voyage round the stormy Cape of Good Hope, taking some three months, she would have been glad to pass the barren rocky hills dominating the entrance to the river. Then she would have seen bright green rice fields appearing in the more level countryside, and little villages, sometimes with a pagoda. The broad river was thronged with large and small boats, perhaps reminding her of the Kingsbridge estuary, but the experienced Buckton may have warned her that some of the junks, with small guns projecting over the side, could host pirates.

Johnston describes Whampoa as having:

> four distinct settlements in the neighbourhood of the anchorage… . Immediately abreast of the spot where we dropped our anchor, there was a collection of small wooden tenements which had the appearance of standing on stilts, knee-deep in the water. [This collection of rickety buildings, he said, comprised 'Bamboo town']. Numberless sampans, with their bamboo covers, were fastened to the piles upon which the houses are elevated, and served as the abode of a large number of families. Just above this unsavoury and pestiferous collection of houses, which really resembled dilapidated bird-

cages more than any human habitations, there was a small collection of brick buildings crowded together on a narrow street running along the river bank, at the upper end of which several docks for repairing ships had been constructed, and this place, which is situated on Dane's Island, I understood to be Whampoa. Two of these docks are lined with stone, and kept in excellent condition, being capable of admitting vessels of the largest class. [Buckton's houseboat would have been in this area]. Opposite to these, on the low island of Whampoa, is another settlement called 'New town' where there is a small collection of Chinese shops and sailor boarding-houses, and where, also, the market for foreign shipping is situated. In the rear of this, and some three miles distant, is a walled town which is now known as 'old Whampoa' [He later visited it, was impressed by its two-storey brick houses, two ancient temples, and air of prosperity, but] we saw numbers of female children hobbling through the streets in a manner that it was painful to witness.

The rest of the town would have compared badly in its amenities with the smaller Kingsbridge of Emma's childhood.
Johnston remarks

the style of residence adopted by a majority of the foreigners engaged in mercantile or professional business...consists of the hull of some old vessel, covered over with a roof of shingles or boards, and fitted up internally as nearly after the manner of a house as practicable. These floating dwellings are denominated Chops, [derived from the Chinese word for number, as on a licence]. and my experience on board the one occupied by the American Vice-Consul at this place — Henry P. Blanchard, Esq., — was certainly calculated to produce the most favourable impression as to their capabilities in the way of affording personal comforts, and the most liberal display of hospitality on the part of the occupants. The lack of suitable houses on shore, and the greater security of property against the thievish propensities of the lower class of Chinese, with other considerations of a political nature, render this mode of living far preferable to a residence in town.

In 1851 there were only a handful of permanent British residents in Whampoa: the Vice-Consul and his constable, three shipwrights, two surgeons, a master mariner, a ship's chandler (Buckton) and a clerk. Most foreigners lived at Canton and Harry Parkes, then Acting Consul at Canton, in his annual return for 1856, showed 110 English residents and 124 Parsees and others (the Indian community under British protection was generally referred to as Parsee). Parkes also noted that 161 ships came in, with 4,757 men, and 164 went out.

Besides the British and Indian populations, there were Americans, Germans, Dutch, French, and a good sprinkling of Portuguese, who had the small territory of Macao (Macau). The little British community was divided by class: ladies and gentlemen, and lesser men, such as craftsmen, clerks, soldiers, sailors, and constables. Buckton would have been trying to maintain his status as a gentleman, as a former master of an East India Company ship, but Emma would have found few other 'ladies'.[13] Johnston does not mention any women as present at the dinners he enjoyed on Blanchard's chop. The only reference I have found to other British women in Whampoa was in December 1856, when female relatives raised the alarm when the father of Cooper, the master shipwright at Whampoa, was kidnapped from the top of his chop. Young British Vice-Consuls could not afford wives and the Foreign Office provided only mean bachelor accommodation for this rank. The American Vice-Consul's main occupation was trade, so he could afford a better houseboat than that of Alex Bird, the British Vice-Consul in Whampoa. Bird had two small rooms as his office and accommodation, above the below-decks prison cells for noisy drunken seamen. This was replaced in 1853 by an old chop-boat, from which he barely escaped when it sprang a leak one night. He was granted sick leave, understandably suffering from nervous irritation and mental depression, in 1854. The Foreign Office then acquired the *Alligator*, large, old and dirty. Charles Winchester, Bird's temporary replacement, grumbled that it was expensive for a bachelor to maintain.

Emma is not likely to have made friends of Chinese women. While her little boy could play with the local Chinese boys, and pick up the language from them, Emma would have found the poorer Chinese women busy working, and the more leisured ones restricted in their movement by their bound feet, rarely leaving their houses except when screened in a sedan chair. One can imagine that Emma would have been glad to get to know the surgeons, as a reminder of her father and half-brother. One of them, Bruce, had an MRCS from Edinburgh.

During the trading season the place was crammed with ships, and the Vice-Consul and his Constable would be hard put to it to maintain some sort of order, amongst several thousand merchant seamen full of spirit (in both senses). Whampoa usually had a British naval steamer, which could go up to Canton if necessary, and the Consul could call on a frigate and steamer at or near Hong Kong. (The trade was worth protecting: it was estimated to bring India an annual revenue of £3 million, and Britain some £6 million in the early 1850s.[14]) The seamen provided plenty of work for the surgeons and probably made excursions to the market unpleasant for Emma.

The Whampoa Battles of December 1854 and March 1855

Throughout 1853 and 1854 successive British Consuls and their interpreter staff in Canton were reporting the increasing disorder in the province, with a degree of sympathy for the justified grievances of the population, moderated by their anxieties about the effect on trade. In June 1853 Consul D Brookes Robertson included a report by Parkes, then his interpreter, of two or three thousand bandits in the northwest of the province, and other robbers in the northeast. In his statistical report he blamed their activities for the decrease in imports of £112,675 and in exports of £1,584,524 compared with the previous year.[15]

By December 1854 the rebels were in effective control of Whampoa. Robertson included in his political memorandum of 8 January 1855 an account of the large rebel fleet which passed through foreign shipping and attacked a fleet of nineteen government junks anchored below. He reported that many foreign vessels were struck by shot, and one or two people on board were injured. He attached an account from Emma's husband, Buckton, one of those affected:

> In forwarding to you the enclosed accounts of damages sustained on the 29th December last I have named as small an amount as will cover the losses I sustained; taking into consideration that I have now two vessels that I must repair & give up all storage for a length of time, as the period at which the repair can be completed

*is uncertain & no Chinese will undertake the risk without my
personal superintendence & protection.*

[He says he has not made any claim for personal danger,
despite the thirty-seven shots received, as quoted at the
beginning of the chapter.] *Furthermore, we were nearly sinking
on the ensuing night from damages received. I had to remove our
goods at night by which we lost more than can at present be
ascertained.*

Buckton gave the letter, with a detailed claim for repairs and losses
totalling $3,821, to Vice-Consul Alex Bird at Whampoa, who forwarded
it on 11 January to the Consul at Canton. The repair of his houseboat,
the two storage boats and the small gig were estimated as somewhat
under $1,000. His loss of property shows something of their style of
living.

Cabinet Maker's Work

1 Plate Chest	$20.00]	
1 Dining Table	$16.00]	40.00
1 Chair	$4.00]	

Sundries

2 new canvas Side Curtains	$10.00]	
8 Panes of Glass	$3.20]	28.20
New Matting for half the roof	$15.00]	

Private property destroyed by shot in dining room

1 Dinner Service	$60.00	
1 Breakfast do [ditto]	40.00	
1 pr Cut Glass Decanters	9.00	
1 Cruet Stand	12.00	
1 Argand Lamp	14.00	
1 Barometer & Thermometer	6.00	41.00

In Pantry & store room

7 tumblers & 5 wine glasses	
4 Bottles Porter 3 do Ale 7 do Sherry	
& 4 Port Wine}	10.25

5 do Brandy		16.00	
1 water filter		12.00	
1 oil cloth table cover, new matting			
& sundry repairs		50.00	88.25

On the storage junk *Magnet*, he had lost

Broken on board	*8 Bottles sherry*	6.00
	3 do Liqueurs	2.25
	10 tumblers	12.50
	3 decanters	12.00
	8 Bottles Curry Paste	8.00

A second storage hulk contained a case of four dozen bottles of pale ale. He then added $2,500 for personal inconvenience. The common currency for trade was the Mexican dollar, worth at the time about a fifth of the British £ sterling. The total claim, $3,831, was approximately £766.[16]

The chop appears to have been a fairly commodious residence, unlike that of the unfortunate Vice-Consul Bird. The liquor shows that, like the American Vice-consul, Buckton could entertain his guests liberally! The loss of the water filter was important, for it removed some of the harmful bacteria that their supply contained. Whether Emma knew that drinking water should also be boiled, we do not know. One hopes she had learnt the habit of taking liquid, like the Chinese, in the form of tea. She had evidently learnt a new style of cooking, using the bottles of curry paste. The *Argand Lamp* would have been sadly missed. It was an improvement on the ordinary oil lamp and gave out six to ten candle power, enabling her to read or sew in the evening.

The incident provides a nice illustration of bureaucracy at work. Vice-Consul Bird passed the claim up to Consul Robertson in Canton on 11 January, specifically saying he was making no comment on the amount. Robertson wrote back to Buckton on 17 January saying that the $2,500 for personal inconvenience required explanation. He needed a surveyor's report for the repairs. Regarding personal effects: *'you charge for total loss. It is impossible they could have been utterly destroyed — you must furnish a list of articles damaged'*. Then the matter could be referred to HE [His Excellency] Sir John Bowring (who had become Governor of Hong Kong and Superintendent of Trade in all the Treaty Ports in April 1854) for adjudication. Buckton replied immediately.

Whampoa, 18th January 1855

Sir

I have to acknowledge the receipt of your letter of yesterday & in reply, beg to place before you the following personal inconvenience.

In consequence of the damage done to my property I am obliged to give up any idea of storage of goods — for which purpose the Vessels are intended, until such time as they are once more in insurable repair — this item being a loss of $400 to $500 per month & the vessels will not all be in order for at least three months, as few persons can be got to work on them during these disturbed times, & then only upon double Wages, & without any guarantee as to time, & then the work not done so well as it would be in peaceable times.

*In consequence of the leaky state of my Chop Boat, from firing shots into, & alongside of her, the Vessel was on the point of sinking at three o'clock on the morning of the 1st Jan*y *& I had to remove my wife & family at that hour without waiting for them even to dress. In the confusion occasioned by having to employ stranger boats to remove my Household property, I lost many valuable articles which I can never recover, & would not have lost for ten times their intrinsic value, & I consider that in stating only $2,500 as personal inconvenience, that I should not cover it, were I to have placed the sum at double the amount & I only reduced it to this amount to make the more certain of its ready payment. With regard to the total loss on the Dinner & Breakfast Services, I certainly cannot put them down otherwise. I brought them from England with me two years ago, & they are valuable & good so long as they are perfect: — I cannot replace any portions that are lost, but what remains I am ready to give up on being provided with a complete set as they were — from the Dinner Service I have had broken, a Cheese Stand, 2 Covered Dishes, 1 Hot Water Dish, sundry Flat dishes & plates. From the Breakfast Service 2 Hot Water Plates, Slop Basin, various Breakfast Cups, Coffee Cups, &*

several egg cups etc, & thus, neither Service is of its original &
proper use.

With respect to the parties who fired the shot, it would be difficult
in such a state of Excitement as we were in to say truthfully, who
were the chief aggressors. I can only say I received shot from both
parties, & I leave the matter in the hands of those whose duty it
was to disperse such an armament, so destructive to British life &
property: — and can only say that any pecuniary remuneration will
be totally inadequate as a recompense for the danger we have been
placed in.

Enclosed I beg to hand you the Survey Report you require.

The china services were an important sign of his social status. The
Yamen of the local magistrate was probably one of the brick houses
on the narrow street that Johnston describes as running along the river
bank. Buckton would have had business dealings with him.

The survey report was signed by D Gow and Theoˢ Sampson, who
each received a survey fee of $8. Theophilus Sampson, who became
Emma's third husband, was the Constable at the Vice-Consulate. The
two men confirmed Buckton's claims on the damage, and added that
the chop got so shaken, losing its calking, because the fighting vessels
had lashed themselves to it, to steady their boats for firing their cannons.
No wonder that Emma was sheltering her little daughter on her lap
during this terrifying episode. It is nice to see that Buckton referred to
the child as his own.

Robertson duly forwarded this report to Bowring. He called attention
to the large item of $2,500 for personal inconvenience.

I confess it appears to me immense; but unquestionably his
family was placed in a position of great peril, and his property
in great danger by the acts of the belligerent parties. The claim
is supported by survey certificate and the amount for repairs
estimated by a Chinese carpenter. I could refer them for re-
certification by the Public Surveyor, Capt. Cleveley; but I
hesitate to incur further expense as the Chinese authorities will
certainly repudiate the claim, if made to them, on the grounds
they were not the attacking party, and to obtain compensation
from the rebels will be all but hopeless unless enforced by
measures highly inexpedient just at this moment. I therefore fear

*the chances of Mr. Buckton obtaining compensation are rather
remote.*

Robertson's files do not report the contemporary actions of his
superior, Sir John Bowring, Governor of Hong Kong, and Superintendent
of British trade for all China. While Robertson believed that *'there is a
great deal to be done with these people if you keep on good terms with them'*
Bowring, Consul Rutherford Alcock (who succeeded Robertson in May
1855) and Harry Parkes (Alcock's interpreter, who succeeded him as
Consul when Alcock went on sick leave in July 1856) were known to
think that the only way to deal with the Chinese was to stand firm on
every point in British rights, no matter how insignificant.[17]

Earlier in 1854 Viceroy Ye Mingchen had refused Bowring's requests
for a personal meeting to discuss treaty revision, but by early December
he was desperate enough at the rebel success to appeal to Bowring to
send British naval ships to save Canton. Bowring, under cover of
protecting British persons and property, responded (after Christmas was
over) in person, going with visiting Admiral Stirling up river, in company
with US ships. They arrived in Canton on 31 December, 1854, the rebel
fleet dispersing before them. The Viceroy showed no gratitude and,
when Bowring asked to see him in the city, he sent only a sub-magistrate
to attend him in the consulate, at the factories outside the walls. This
snub helps explain Bowring's later actions.

Any relief Emma felt at the sight of the foreign warships was as
temporary as their visit. Throughout February Robertson was
reporting the increased control of the rebels over Whampoa, and
their intention to set it up as a port and to blockade Canton. On 22
February he wrote:

> *I should be most unwilling that we should get in collision with
> these people but I cannot but mark the rapid advances they are
> making towards carrying out their threat of a blockade & their
> consequent contempt of Your Excellency's notice that such will not
> be permitted.*

Robertson thought that there would be no effective action against
the rebels, but Ye Mingchen surprised him. The Imperial naval
commander informed him that on 3 March he intended to attack rebels
at Blenheim Reach just below Whampoa, and on 7 March Robertson

heard heavy firing all day. Robertson forwarded a report by Acting Interpreter Pedder on 13 March 1855:

> *Since the middle of last month, the band of insurgents whose HQ was at Whampoa as also other bands in different parts of the province have been pillaging, burning & slaying...driving people in the neighbourhood to resist if they could.... The Governor General* [his title for Ye Mingchen] *called up the people of the country between Whampoa & the river to cooperate with the authorities & about 35,000 trained men were placed at the disposal of the government.* [These would have been the local militias many Chinese gentry had established to protect themselves and their tenants.][18] *The Government had a flotilla of small gun boats which drove back rebel vessels which were abandoned on shore, and was able to reoccupy forts in rebel hands. The Government captured upwards of 1,200 men on 6th 7th & 8th — who will be executed — & a great number must have been killed, 7–8000. Signed W M Pedder. True copy C. T. Jones.*

Robertson cannot have been alone in feeling '*a load of anxieties taken off my mind*'. The battle of the gun-ships at Blenheim Reach was horribly near, and Emma knew that her family had now twice narrowly escaped death. She was prompted to take her religion more seriously than she had done previously. Her children had never been baptised, and might not qualify for heaven. On the next visit by the young Consulate chaplain from Canton, the Reverend Henry Gray, her daughter was christened in Whampoa, on 24 April, 1855.[19] My grandfather was not, Gray possibly considering him too old for infant baptism but not old enough to make his own promises. Over the next years Emma's faith was to grow, sustaining her through other tragedies that lay in store.

Buckton seems to have been able to resume normal activities, and to support his friends. In April 1855 he provided a bail bond 'for the sum of $50 for Charles S Pryde, a US citizen charged with felony, to guarantee his appearance before the [US] Consular Court for Whampoa.[20] But he had still not received compensation, as, naturally, Bowring had referred all the papers to the distant Foreign Office in England. Buckton tried again with Robertson's replacement, Rutherford Alcock. He felt aggrieved because Admiral Stirling had made the rebel leader pay a large sum in compensation for the loss of a boat,

the lorcha S. Cuthbert[21]*...that merely flew the British Flag though
owned by a Chinese...(as I know by having calculated the amount
at his request and which sum was weighed by my Comprador)* [his
Chinese interpreter and agent]*... . It having been proved
subsequently that no money was due on account of the lorcha
being engaged in trafic* [sic] *that was not allowable, and that the
cash was paid into the Government fund in consequence, I beg
respectfully to suggest the payment of so fair and just a claim as
mine might be liquidated out of the sum...*

*Having a large Family to support in England, such a loss as I
have sustained, even by the detention of repayment, has been a
source of the greatest inconvenience, as it has prevented me
remitting such moneys as I am owing for goods, to supply me in
needful stores required in my business.*

The Death of Buckton and the Arrow War

As all the papers had been sent to England, it is unlikely that Buckton
had any luck before he died aged forty-six on 15 June 1856, on board
his chop, in Whampoa anchorage. He is described as a store-keeper.
Consulate death certificates did not require the cause of death. The
informant was the Constable, Sampson. There is no comment on his
death in the consular files, or on the plight of Emma and her children.
The next information we have of her is her marriage to Sampson in
Hong Kong Cathedral in August 1858, two years later. The small
Whampoa community would probably have helped the widow by the
customary whip-round, for Buckton left nothing, dying in debt. The
Hong Kong Government *Gazette* carried a notice of a second and final
dividend of six per cent being paid to his creditors on 26 November
1859. His creditors may have held off until his widow remarried. Till
then, she faced again the problem of how to support herself and her
children.

Emma had certainly left Whampoa by December 1856. In October
that year the Chinese had detained a lorcha, the *Arrow*, captained by
Thomas Kennedy, and imprisoned its crew. Parkes, now Consul in
Canton, protested. Bowring and Sir Michael Seymour, the British
Admiral, were in agreement in using the incident to enforce the treaty
rights believed to enable Consuls to have direct access to the government

officials in Canton, and British citizens to enter the city. Their case was weakened when it transpired that the registration of the *Arrow* in Hong Kong had expired, and still more when Ye Mingchen sent back the twelve members of its crew (though not in the public manner demanded). On 27 October, Seymour began firing at the city wall and specifically at Ye's Yamen within the city. He and the American Consul marched through the Yamen with marines before withdrawing. Desultory firing continued, with life in the European factories just outside the city becoming more and more uncomfortable. The ladies of the Consulates departed for Hong Kong. On 13 December Parkes cleared his office and reported that the remaining twenty-seven merchant vessels, and most of the British community, had departed for Whampoa. The following day the foreign factories were burned down, with one of Parkes' assistants being killed by a falling wall. Sampson was told to take the body to Hong Kong with the office archives. As Seymour was unable to maintain his two ships outside Canton any longer, on 16 December, from on board H.M.S. *Coriander*, Parkes advised the remaining British residents including those at Whampoa to leave with what property they had left. The kidnapping of William Cooper, father of the master shipwright there (referred to earlier), underlined the dangers, and Parkes thought that by 29 December 1856 '*nearly the whole of the foreign community had gradually removed away for Hong Kong*'. Trade with Canton came to an end under a continuing British naval blockade.

These warlike activities, often called the Second Opium War, were not popular at home. Palmerston, now the Prime Minister, was defeated in the Commons on the issue, but won the election of March 1857. Palmerston knew that Bowring's judgement was at fault in choosing the *Arrow* as the bone of contention, and he appointed Lord Elgin over his head to take charge of relations with China, with instructions to go to Peking (Beijing) to ask for reparation of losses and complete observance of the treaties in future. He was to work with the French, who had a justifiable grievance over the execution of a priest in 1856. Elgin was promised 2,500 men, but was told to use force only if necessary. In fact Elgin felt obliged to send some soldiers back to India because of the outbreak of the mutiny there, and this, together with delays by the French envoy (who preferred to come out by the long sea route) meant that he could do nothing immediately. People in Hong Kong were fearful, for the almost uninhabited island of 1842 now had a small

British community living amongst eighty thousand Chinese immigrants. Its Bishop commented that *'they felt exposed, not merely to the ordinary danger of a foreign residence, but to the cup of the poisoner, the knife of the assassin and the torch of the midnight incendiary'*. A baker had put arsenic in bread delivered to Bowring and other leading citizens, but got the dose wrong, making them ill rather than killing them. Many in Hong Kong were firmly behind Bowring, and resented what they saw as Elgin's dilatory tactics. Elgin remained by preference on his steamship, the *Ava*. To cheer people up, he took the *Ava* up the Canton river for a picnic. The day was fine and almost all the ladies of the colony (who were greatly outnumbered by gentlemen) were present. In the evening they danced on deck by the light of Chinese lanterns to music provided by the band of Admiral Seymour's flagship, the *Calcutta*. I like to think that Emma was among the party.

It was only in December 1857 that Elgin demanded that Ye Mingchen agree to the complete fulfilment of the treaties, including the admission of British subjects to the city of Canton, and compensation. If the Viceroy accepted these and the French demands, the blockade of Canton would be lifted. As he refused, on 15 December the British and French fleets moved up river with 5,679 armed men. On 5 January 1858 the city was entered and Ye Mingchen and his senior officials captured. His subordinate, Pih-Kwei, indicated that he had opposed Ye Mingchen and was installed as governor in his place, supervised by a tribunal of three allied Commissioners, Parkes, Holloway of the Marines, and Martineau for France, with power to approve all his proclamations and to try all cases in which a foreigner was involved. The blockade was lifted on 10 February, and life began to return to normal in Canton, and traders to return. In April 1858 Robert Hart became the Commission's Secretary. Sampson was its Head Clerk and Cashier. The action now moved north, with successes, failures and interludes of negotiation. The culmination was an attack on Peking, and the burning of the Imperial Summer Palace, which led to the Convention of Peking in 1860.[22]

Marriage to Sampson, and Meeting Robert Hart

Emma had taken her time in selecting her next husband. We know she had a choice. In his diary of 23 August 1858 Hart wrote: *'Sampson went to Hongkong today to meet Mrs. Buckton* [Mrs. Brickton in the printed version] *and her two children. Mrs. B. is the lady Jones used to be so 'spoony' about. Sampson now goes to espouse her.'*[23] C Treasure Jones was the student interpreter who made the file copy of Pedder's report of 13 March 1855, quoted above.

Hong Kong Cathedral records show Emma and Sampson were married by licence on 26 August (Figure 1.7). The witnesses could not be identified. It could be significant that the officiator, Charles John Armistens, the young Chaplain of the Royal Naval Hospital ship, *Melville*, felt justified in taking up a lot of room on her wedding certificate, almost squeezing out the groom. This makes me wonder if Emma had supported herself by helping out on the naval hospital ship, and had thus come to know him as a friend. The witnesses may also be naval officers, for they do not appear in Carl Smith's records of Hong Kong residents. The naval personnel suffered relatively few battle casualties but were dying from typhoid, dysentery, malaria, etc. The Whampoa surgeons and a husband with long residence in Asia, would have given her some useful tips in dealing with these, to supplement what she might have learnt from her possible assistance to her father and Robert Webb. This is speculation, but it is in line with Aunt Kath's comment in her memoir of Emma on the 'liberation' that the East afforded expatriate women. Florence Nightingale in the Crimean War, 1854-6, had just made it acceptable for 'ladies' to act as nurses. A young woman who registered her son and bought a grave for her first husband, without asking a man to do this for her, is likely to have sought a means of supporting her children independently if she could, at least until that interesting young man, Sampson, was in a position to marry her.

When Sampson brought her to Canton she met Hart, his boss, and began the friendship which was to last for the rest of their lives. Hart recorded their first meetings:

> *Thursday 23rd September 1858. Sampson brought up his wife today: pretty little step daughter.*
>
> *Monday 27th September. Went with General & ladies to Western Suburb Temples. Mrs. S. a very nice lady.*

My aunt wrote that Emma was one of the first white ladies to enter Canton, her grandmother probably telling her of this occasion. Emma and Sampson were still enjoying their honeymoon, though both suffered interludes of illness. Hart recorded: '*Saturday 9 October 1858. Sampson laid up: Fever & new wife. The little step-daughter told a number of the officers the other day that papa and mama go to bed every day for an hour or so!*'

Emma recalled that time in a letter she wrote to Hart in November 1900: '*In 1858, the Canton garrison days, I had inflammation of the lungs. Our quarters faced north, & we had paper windows which did not keep the rain out, since that time I have suffered from lung trouble and spit blood...*' Probably, like Hart, they were housed in Ye Mingchen's old Yamen, or what remained of it after its bombardment in 1856. While the chop at Whampoa had required glass panes to repair its windows, wealthy Chinese officials still used oiled paper. In its isolation, a country once technologically ahead of Europe had fallen far behind. Emma's illness was very probably pulmonary tuberculosis, caused by inhaling infected droplets, not by the damp. It was present in Canton, as in Britain. Emma was strong enough to get over the initial attack, but recurrent bouts would follow. The disease can have side-effects on the reproductive system and is still a common cause of infertility in India.[24] Despite Sampson's best efforts, she had no more children.

Emma was the first of the Carralls to become a friend of Hart, a friendship that, as her surviving letters to him of 1900–1 show, lasted more than forty years. We know little of how it developed, as Hart had reasons to cease keeping a diary for the remainder of his stay in Canton.

CHAPTER TWO

ROBERT HART BUILDS A CAREER IN CHINA AND HASTILY FINDS A WIFE

Hart's Ulster Origins

Robert Hart was born the first of twelve children in 1835 in Portadown, Armagh. The earliest photograph we have is one sent to Emma Sampson, shown in Figure 2.1. His father, Henry Hart, a strict Methodist, had a grocery licensed to sell spirits, and was a partner in a small distillery which burnt down. He did better as manager of a distillery at Culcavey, sending his son to a private school in Hillsborough nearby, and, at eleven, to the Methodist school in Taunton, England. Horrified when the boy returned to Belfast at the end of the year without the promised escort, Henry transferred him to the Wesley Connexional School in Dublin, 1848–50. He paid extra for drawing and French lessons, as well as the standard Latin, Greek and mathematics. At the age of fifteen, in 1850, Robert entered the newly established Queen's College in Belfast.

All Ireland was then part of the United Kingdom and Robert Hart referred to himself as Irish, British and, occasionally, English.[1] The terrible Irish famine of 1845–9, caused by the failure of the potato crop, was in full force. However, the north was already striking a contemporary travel writer, Henry D Inglis, as very different from the south. The majority religion was Protestant rather than Catholic and many of its people had close ties with Scotland, leading to a dominant ethic of hard work and careful control of expenditure. Hart felt guilty over time wasted in reading novels to the end of his life. The economy was much more diverse than in the agricultural south, with many small industries. The linen industry in particular was expanding. Belfast was a rapidly growing city. Full of mills, with scores of tall chimneys, the demand for labour meant that wages were much higher there than in the south. Few people had large incomes from rents or interest, but most earned a sufficiency by hard work. Inglis contrasted the way merchants in the south spent their profits on pleasures, while the tradesmen of the north 'mind their business, accumulate capital, employ it in some wholesome enterprise, and give employment'.[2] The rising prosperity at home, due to railways, steam power and factory production, meant that Hart saw these as the way out of the poverty and famine he was to encounter in China.

His religion, so deeply imbued in childhood, also brought joy and delight in music. Long afterwards in China he wrote in his diary:

> *Sunday 27 December 1863: This morning, lying in bed half asleep,*
> *I almost heard the choristers in Hillsborough church singing 'Oh*
> *be joyful in the Lord,' to the anthem-air they use there on*
> *Christmas mornings.... . Oh dear! Oh dear! When shall I again*
> *attend service in that church? How I shall delight in going there.*

Like Emma Sampson he retained from childhood a love of the countryside and of walking and riding. His mother was a farmer's daughter. The sixteen-mile return trip on foot to the nearest town, Lisburn, was commonplace. His diaries in Canton and Shanghai are peppered with references to evening walks or rides when he gloried in fine skies and rural greenery.

This was an unlikely background from which to join the Foreign Office, then the preserve of the younger sons of the upper class, where connections to an influential superior (interest) helped promotion.[3] But although British social life had strong class distinctions, education, united with hard work, could provide an upward route. Hart grasped this early. In his diary on 24 December 1863, soon after he achieved the headship of the Chinese Imperial Customs, he wrote:

> *I have got on without aid, without interest, and without asking*
> *for anything! My aim at school was to be first of my class: at*
> *college to be first too: and in China...my aim has always been to*
> *understand and fit myself for the head work of whatever*
> *department fate attached me to.*

At Queen's College the curriculum was modelled on the Scottish universities, providing a broader general education than Oxford or

Cambridge. In addition to the traditional Greek and Latin, logic and metaphysics— philosophy, in modern terms — it included modern literature and languages, science, physical geography, law, and political economy (which included statistics). Hart won two gold medals, one for literature and one for logic and metaphysics, and prizes in other subjects. The political economy texts of the time were Adam Smith, David Ricardo and John Stuart Mill, convincing him of the advantages of free trade and specialisation. He was interested in the contribution of science to improved technology. He became friends with James Brazier, briefly at Belfast as Assistant to the Professor of Chemistry.[4] They kept in touch by letter after Hart left for China and three of Brazier's sons joined the Customs.

Hart graduated in spring 1853 with first-class honours, and gained a senior scholarship in Modern Languages and Modern History for a postgraduate year leading to an MA. He was undecided what career to follow. But in March 1854 the Foreign Office decided it needed more student interpreters to serve Britain's growing trade with China, at the attractive starting salary of £200 p.a. Each of the four Irish Queen's Colleges was asked to nominate a man with linguistic ability, but not a mere linguist. The Belfast College chose Hart out of many applicants. On 13 April 1854 he was appointed; in July, he was in Hong Kong after a seven-week journey out by the Cairo route.

In Hong Kong Hart began keeping a diary and on 31 December he explains this sudden move:

> No year has as yet been so remarkable as this one… . How little I thought when sitting in the Primitive Chapel…listening to Dr. Urwick's Lectures on China…that I sh'd have personal experience of that strange nation… . But I fell into bad company…and accepted the appointment partly to get away from the scene of my misconduct — partly to keep from having to decide between the Law & the Gospel: and here I am in China! Perhaps it is in answer to my prayers of May 1853; if so, I am in my providential path, and God will make me a blessing! God grant it for Christ's sake! Amen.
>
> This year has given me great knowledge of the world in many respects. In the early part of it I was led into scenes of vice and wickedness which I always had shunned before. Associating with

gay ladies, I became quite a gay young man. My former habits of
study and application had become tedious, intolerable, &
distasteful; and deeply did I drink of the cup of sinful pleasures.

He was encouraged in that care-free life by one of the two Swanton brothers with whom he shared digs. The elder, William, *'was a good steady man of twenty-three'*. The younger, a friend from his Dublin schooldays, had become *'rather a character...I accompanied him once or twice to the Theatre, and then to the Billiard Table. I...rushed into everything that was exciting, in order to stifle conscience and give loose to the lusts and desires of the flesh'*.

For three months his gold medals were in the pawn shop, financing his new way of life. *'But God saw fit to punish me...the effects of the abuse came on, and for several weeks I was confined to Bed...when I was told that...I had been unanimously selected by the Council of the College.'*

He recovered sufficiently to receive the appointment in London, but between that time and leaving for China four weeks later, felt so weak that he was obliged to leave Ireland *'...perhaps forever — without bidding good-bye to one-half of my friends and acquaintances'*.

Coping with a Strange World and Lovely Women

Thus an immature nineteen-year-old arrived in Hong Kong, where his first diary opens on 27 August 1854 *' "roughing it in the bush"...Victoria, the capital of Hong Kong, — the residence of Merchant Princes etc. etc.'* compared badly with Belfast. His long entry the next day, Sunday, set himself high standards. The purpose of the diary was to *'note down how the day has been spent, so that faults may be more clearly seen and the means of improvement devised'*.

He was posted to Ningbo — Ningpo as he called it. On 14 September he boarded the sailing vessel *Iona* for Shanghai. Stormy contrary winds delayed its arrival till 7 October, the vessel almost running out of food. (Steamships were shortly to change all that.) Here he met Bowring, there as Superintendent of Trade for all the Chinese ports, and some of his superiors in the consular service, Thomas Wade, Horatio Nelson Lay and Rutherford Alcock, who were to be important in his later career. Ten days later, he made the two-day boat trip south to Ningbo.

Ningbo had long been an important centre of Chinese internal trade.

The map on p. xvi shows it was situated near the terminus of the Grand Canal leading to the northern cities, and surrounded by waterways to the Yangzi. However, it was losing ground to Shanghai. In 1854 the long-term foreign residents, apart from Portuguese from Macau, were a dozen American, French and British missionaries, the British and Portuguese consuls and a few merchants. These scattered foreigners had plenty of opportunity to observe Chinese life and pick up the local dialect, for there was no foreign quarter. Hart, however, had to study the official tongue, Mandarin, by hiring a teacher who spoke no English. For many months he lacked even the dictionary he had ordered. His own books, misdirected in Hong Kong, took a year to reach him.

His superior in Ningbo, during the absence on leave of the Vice-Consul, was John Meadows.[5] Hart lived with him for his first week. On his first working day, 20 October, Meadows took him round to meet the most important members of the foreign community, including the head of the Roman Catholic mission with whom Hart proudly managed several minutes' conversation in French. The next day Meadows introduced him to the Chinese authorities.

On Friday 27 October he moved into his own quarters within the consulate, and hired a servant.

> How very lonely I have been today!…Not a soul had I to speak to (that is in English), until half past four: and then it was by a mere chance that I met Mr. Meadows at his boat. With my teacher from 9 ½ until 1 p.m. Dined at three. My servant is a very stupid fellow — he brought me fish after…all the other dishes.

On Sunday 29 October he went to the interdenominational service that the Protestant missionaries shared, and made a long entry in his diary: 'My Companion in the Consulate is a very free thinker; and I may act as I like without fearing rebuke from him. He keeps his Chinese <u>wife</u> (he calls her, we w'd say mistress) and I may do the same. Here is a great temptation'. This led to a long reflection, part of which was:

> My salary would not support an English wife: such a person is considered a great 'bother' out here: delicate — sickly, demanding great attention, medical care, and numerous servants etc.…Now some of the Chinese women are very good-looking: you can make one your absolute possession for from 50 to 100 dollars and

*support her here at a cost of 2 or 3 dollars a month [he paid his
cook $4]...Is not my state a very trying one, full of temptation —
and that too of the most enticing kind?...But if I believe it is very
wrong so to act, and if I fear to do so, I sh'd give up such thoughts
as well to avoid sin as to cease from making myself miserable.*

Giving up the thought of what was common practice at the time
was not easy. His diary is full of his struggles with his conscience, with
prayers for God's help, intermixed with periods of calm content in the
knowledge that God loved him. He was held back from the equal
availability of casual sex by fear, for he knew its possible penalties. It
was not till 2 December that he was able to write:

*During the last two or three days an event has happened of the
greatest importance to me! The illness from wh' I have suffered
since the end of last January, and from which I have so long
wished for relief, seems to be about to leave me. In another week I
hope to be quite well: and on Christmas day I hope to enjoy a good
glass of Punch...*

The small community boasted two medical missionary doctors who
may have advised him to steer clear of alcohol as part of his recovery
programme from what I assume was a sexually transmitted disease.
After an all-male festive dinner given by Meadows on 18 December, he
woke next morning with *'a most horrible headache'*, and very ashamed
of the song he had written in his diary in preparation, to be sung to
the tune of Auld Lang Syne. This concluded:

*Then as we're far from English joys — girls — concerts — balls
  — and plays —
The best of Chinese Customs blend with good old English ways —
Love native Lassies — smoke cigars — drink wine — good toddy
  brew —
The fault's our own if we don't enjoy some life at Ningpofoo
At Ningpofoo, my friends, at Ningpofoo —
There's what may make life charming, even here at Ningpofoo.*

Meadow provided an uncommon example as he treated his Chinese
companion entirely as a wife. He asked the young man to act as Executor
of his will, by which he intended to leave her all his property. Hart

always behaved courteously towards Mrs Meadows, who spoke no English, and could not host the dinners Meadows gave. The missionary community showed him that a wife could be not only a charming hostess but also a partner in her husband's work. On his first day Hart had been introduced to the elder of the two Misses Dyer who were assisting in a mission school for Chinese girls. Her younger sister Maria was to occupy his thoughts a great deal in the next few months, but at this first meeting:

> I made a fool of myself here I think. I remarked to Miss Dyer that the Chinese language was a very uninteresting study. 'Do you think so?' said she. 'I think it very interesting — the Ningpo dialect at least.'...I am surprised to find the ladies such students and such proficients in the colloquial of the District.

Missionary wives worked as teachers or gave other assistance in missionary work. In Britain he would not have met women students or married women working at a profession outside their home.

The missionaries provided his chief relief from loneliness. He met them every Sunday at the morning service, and he was grateful for the books they lent him. On Tuesday 31 October Mr Cobbold (of the English Church Mission) called and particularly enquired if Hart had his own apartment. On hearing this was so, Cobbold said: ' "So much the better, very glad to hear it." From this I am inclined to think that he fears contact with Mr. Meadows will tend to...tincture me with his German rational views on theological subjects.' In later discussions Hart learnt that Meadows believed in God, but not in a common descent from Adam and Eve, and came to respect his honesty and integrity. At a later stage he too began to move towards the more critical view of parts of the Bible advanced by the German theologian David Strauss.[6]

The same day he received a note: 'Mr. Hart Esq. Can you come tomorrow evening and take tea with us. Yours truly, M.W.M.' This struck him as very poor style. Why both Mr and Esq? Who was M.W.M.? It had come via Mr Martin's coolie, but there were two Mr Martins, neither with the initials M.W. He guessed, correctly, which wife it might be and wrote back formally presenting his compliments and expressing the pleasure he would feel in accepting the invitation. He had an excellent evening with an amiable American lady, who had also invited Mr and Mrs Nevius. They played musical instruments and sang, and the cakes were delicious.

However, it was a reminder that if he was to advance, one day he must have a wife who had learnt or could learn the elaborate rules of etiquette which governed invitations, calls, precedence at table etc.

Such pleasant suppers occurred only every three weeks or so, and in between he was lonely and uncertain whether he should have come to China. It was not till 15 February 1855 that he got letters that were replies to ones that he had sent. Their different dates show that the mail service was slow and erratic: '*1. From <u>Dada</u> — dated <u>16 October</u> in reply to my first letter (3 August) from Hongkong: 2. from <u>Wm Swanton</u>, dated 26 Oct, 3. from Mary* [his sister], *dated 1 November, in reply to mine of the 11 September...*'.

No wonder he felt isolated!

Despite the loneliness, he did not altogether enjoy having to put up Lay and another young consular officer, when they arrived unexpectedly on 22 November 1854, with Sir John Bowring. He had to give them his bed while he slept on his chair. They left two days later for three days up country, and then returned for another six days. Hart's comments were: '*I have been put to some expense entertaining them...they succeeded in making me as idle as they were themselves, so that for the last fortnight I have made but very little progress in my Chinese Studies.*' Even at this early stage, work came first! He also noted: '*Lay I do not like so much as I did when in Shanghai. He treats the Chinese in so insulting & unkind a manner as to irritate me very much.*' He had already learnt better ways from his Ningbo associates.

Loneliness meant that he could almost give way to the desire for marriage. On Friday 8 December 1854 he recollected that:

> *on Tuesday last I took tea with Mrs. Goddard. Her eldest daughter is a very nice girl, about fourteen or fifteen years of age...she pressed my hand very palpably when I was bidding her goodnight...almost made up my mind to propose two things to Mrs. Goddard:* [to marry her now or later]*...So very lonely am I! So much do I wish for something to love and to be kind to — so great is my longing for some companion who will love me.*

At dinners he intrigued to get seated next to Miss Maria Dyer but without success, for his hosts knew he could not afford to marry. On the one occasion when he could have proposed privately to her on a walk he was in such a commotion that he failed to find words.

He learnt instead to be friends with the untouchable married ladies, stopping himself from recording a forbidden thought about Mrs Nevius on 17 December: *'If — but no!'* On 2 January 1855 he simply enjoyed his conversation with this charming lady at dinner. Helen Nevius and her husband John (aged twenty-two and twenty-five respectively) were both engaged in missionary work, she as a teacher. On 2 February after tea with them he wrote *'This society certainly does me good.'* She was to remain a friend for life, though illness took her from Ningbo for some part of his time there.

llness was a constant hazard. Mrs Goddard, whose daughter had so affected him, was returning to America, her husband having died of typhus. Hart twice mentions Mr Nevius being in bed with erysipelas — an acute spreading infection of the skin and underlying fat, now easily cured by antibiotics, but then painful and dangerous. On his first round of visits he noticed how often the conversation turned to 'fever and ague'. Ague, as in Shakespearian England, was malaria. Its connection with mosquitoes was unknown. In May 1855 Hart was writing of them as a nuisance, but without concern: *'Just now a lot of Mosquitoes are playing about my head. There's no use in attempting to kill any — 'their name is legion.' Today I put up my <u>Mosquito curtain</u> — I should have done it three or four days sooner.'*

Childbirth was also hazardous. In January 1855: *'Mrs. Gough was <u>confined</u>: the child had to be cut to pieces in her womb, as it was overgrown, Mrs. G. is going on well.'*

Hart himself remained remarkably healthy, recording only a couple of bouts of diarrhoea and fever, despite the unhygienic state of the Consulate. The Foreign Office had refused money for a well, or even for jars to catch roof water, so the water supply was presumably the adjacent pond. This hosted malarial mosquitoes in the summer, when it often overflowed into the house, and the summer smells from the nearby shallow graveyard were an added discomfort.[7]

Meadows got himself into trouble on Christmas Day 1854 when a Portuguese, Vulpino,[8] beat up one of the Consulate's Chinese staff. Hart, hearing of this, fetched Meadows (who had been paying convivial Christmas calls on merchants). The enraged Meadows ordered his staff to arm themselves with sticks, took his pistol and set off for Vulpino's house, where the staff proceeded to beat him up. Hart managed to prevent severe injury (for *'Mr. Meadows was very much excited'*). Meadows

Figure 1.1a. Top left: Emma Spry Sampson, circa 1875, aged forty-six.

Figure 1.1b. Top right: Emma in October 1892, aged sixty-two (Ca. S10).

Figure 1.2. Bottom left: The junction of Duncombe Street and Fore Street, Kingsbridge, in 2008. The Edwards' house was probably the one near the car.

Figure 1.3. Bottom right: The King's Arms in Fore Street, the main social centre of the town, with an Assembly Rooms.

the Proceeding of the said Matrimony, according to the Tenor of such Licence. And he further made Oath, that he, the said

Appearer

hath had *his* usual Place of Abode within the said *District of*

Saint John Waterloo

for the Space of Fifteen Days last past. *And he lastly made Oath that he hath obtained the consent of John Edwards the natural and lawful father of the said minor to the said intended marriage.*

James Ss/ Carrall Wilcocks

ORN before me.

Figure 1.4. Top: James' oath on his application for a licence to marry, 1848.

Figure 1.5. Bottom left: James Carrall Wilcocks 2, 1797–1874, Exeter merchant, painting now in the possession of Paul Wilcocks.

Figure 1.6. Bottom right: Elizabeth Edwards, née Spry, born 1792, in her sixties.

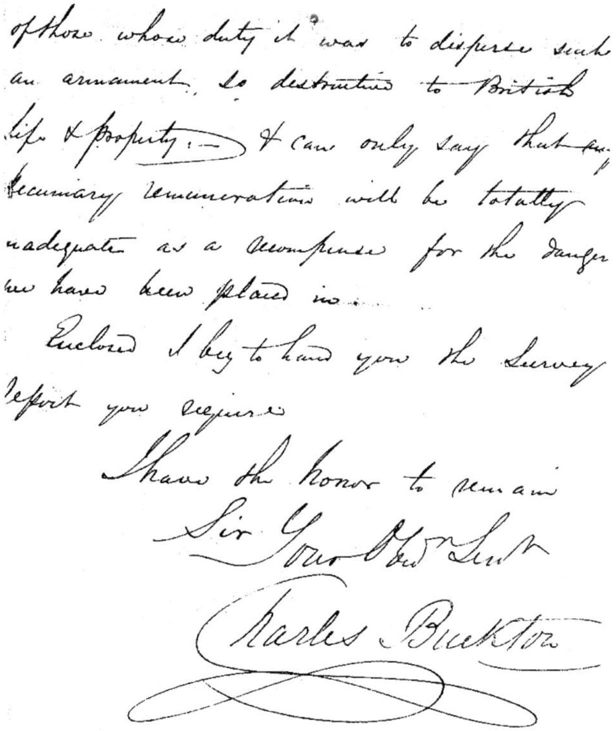

of those whose duty it was to disperse such an armament, so destructive to British life & property: — & can only say that any pecuniary remuneration will be totally inadequate as a recompense for the danger we have been placed in.

Enclosed I beg to hand you the Survey report you require

I have the honor to remain

Sir Your Obd^t Servt

Charles Buckton

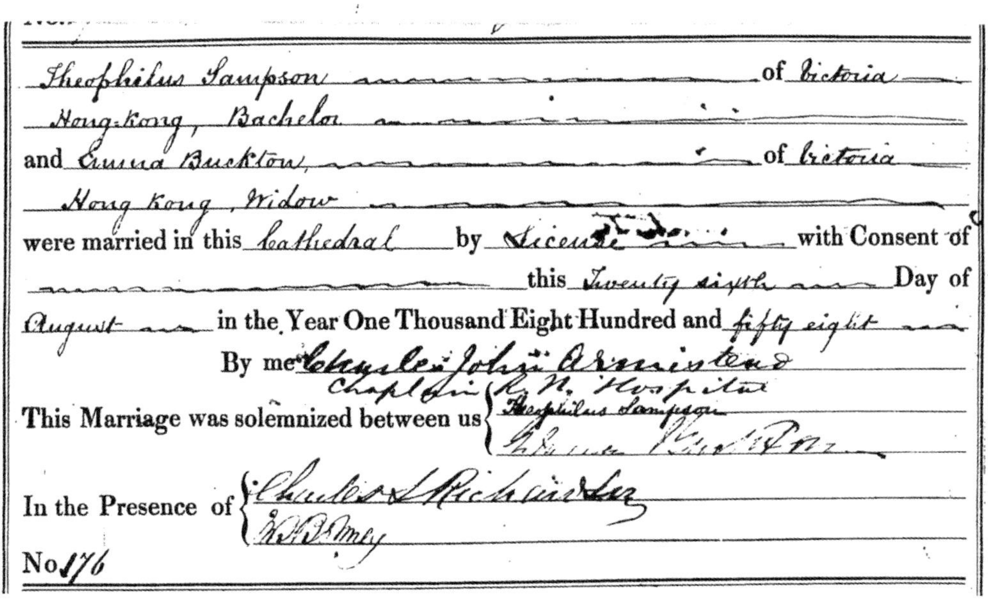

Theophilus Sampson of Victoria Hong-Kong, Bachelor

and Emma Buckton, of Victoria Hong Kong, Widow

were married in this Cathedral by Licence with Consent of ——— this Twenty sixth Day of August in the Year One Thousand Eight Hundred and fifty eight

By me Charles John Armistead Chaplain R. N. Hospital

This Marriage was solemnized between us { Theophilus Sampson / Emma Buckton

In the Presence of { Charles S Richardson / W. H. Pomey

No 176

Figure 1.7. Top: Charles Buckton's second letter and signature.

Figure 1.8 .Above: Marriage certificate of Emma Buckton and Theophilus Sampson, 1858.

Figure 3.1. Top right: Theo Sampson in 1874.

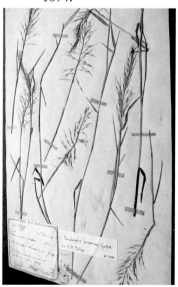

Figure 2.1. Top left: The young Hart in Canton, circa 1861. Copyright of Queen's University Belfast, Sir Robert Hart Collection, MS 15. Part of the Irons gift, it would originally have been given to Emma Sampson.

Figure 3.2. Above: Part of Sampson's Canton grasses collection held at Kew Gardens, where it is still being consulted. It shows the labour involved in being a 'collector and presenter'.

Figure 3.3. Left: Christchurch on Shamien, and the shady riverside walk. (Photo taken circa 1895, when Emma's son Jim was Acting Commissioner, Canton.)

Figure 4.1. Top left: Emma Carrall, taken in Hong Kong, probably just before her visit to Peking.

Figure 4.2. Right: Emma Carrall, aged twenty-four, and her mother, Emma Spry Sampson, in London.

Figure 4.3. Left: Even in 1900 a Peking cart was not the most comfortable of conveyances (Ca01-118).

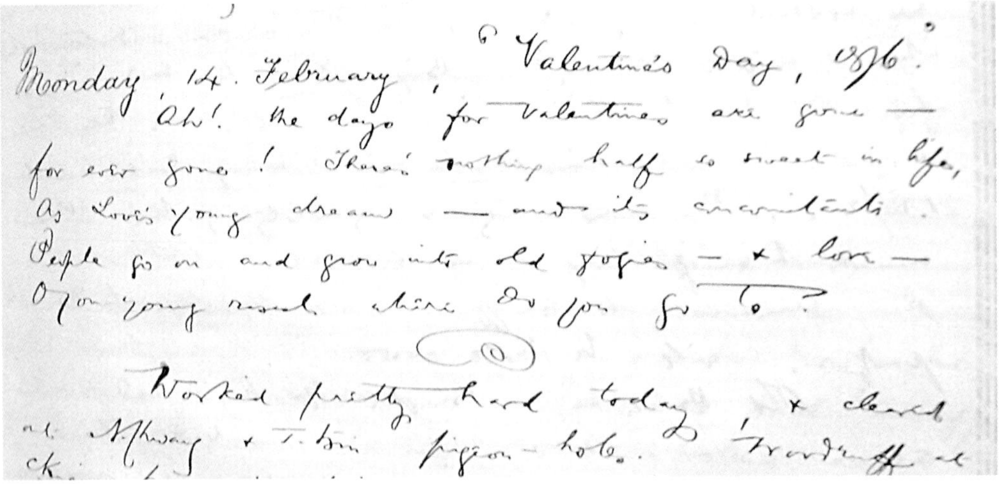

Monday 14. February , 'Valentine's Day, 1876.'
'Ah! the days for Valentines are gone —
for ever gone! There's nothing half so sweet in life,
As Love's young dream — and its concomitants.
People go on and grow into old fogies — & love —
O you young rascal where do you go to?

Worked pretty hard today & cleared
at Athway & T...... pigeon-holes. Trouddruff at
ck...

Figure 4.4. Top: The entry for 14 February, 1876.

Figure 4.5. Left: Hart, Hessie and their two children, Evey and Bruce, 1878. It was probably taken at Bad Ischl, Austria. Copyright of Queen's University Belfast, Sir Robert Hart Collection, MS 15.

Figure 4.6. Right: A mother's memorial.

Figure 5.1. Top left: The young Jim Carrall. The back is inscribed 'For Father and Mother, with James' love. China, 1 Oct. 1870' , two days after his twenty-first birthday. (Hart later referred to the handsome young man he remembered from 1869.)

Figure 5.2. Top centre: Frances Fawcus, nearly eleven, in August 1868.

Figure 5.4 (a). Top right: Grace Wilcocks, Leamington, 1876.

(b). Middle left: Jim Carrall, Hamburg 1876.

Figure 5. 5. Middle centre: (a) Frances Fawcus.

(b) Middle right: Her teacher, Rachel Speciall, circa 1872.

Figure 5.6. Bottom right: Frances in 1877, aged twenty.

Figure 5.3. The Fawcus family in 1860. The boys had been in a cricket match that day. Jim's friends, Jack and Arthur, are standing at either end of the back row. Frances is the three-year-old sitting on her older sister's lap. Two more children followed (courtesy of Lindsay Stilwell, descendant of Evans Fawcus, the young boy on the left).

then ordered Vulpino to be given thirty-five lashes before releasing him. The Portuguese consul naturally complained, and Meadows was in trouble with his superiors. In March he was demoted, and ultimately resigned, becoming a merchant in Tientsin (Tianjin). More happily, a boat arrived that day with a *'kind loving letter from dear Mamma'*, written on 31 August in which he was told of his sister Teresa's marriage. This failed to get an approving comment.

On 1 April 1855 Dr Charles Winchester replaced Meadows as acting Vice-Consul. On 8 June Hart quoted him as having commended to Sir John Bowring the way Hart *'superintends the reports of shipping made to the Chinese Customs and exhibits zeal and intelligence in discharging the duties of an Assistant'*...also *'making highly satisfactory progress in Chinese'*. On 4 July 1855 he was officially appointed Assistant and his salary was increased to £270.

Hart was now staying with Captain Patridge, who had given him a bedroom for the summer. Patridge, a colourful character, was the Ningbo agent of Jardine Matheson & Co., the largest trading company in opium and other goods on the China coast, and his house would have been the best available in Ningbo. Hart's entry on 29 July 1855 is:

> *The last four weeks have passed very pleasantly, my health is excellent, and with depression of Spirits I am little troubled. I fear when I go back to the Consulate for the winter, I shall feel the loneliness very much. Enjoy the present, however, & let the future look out for itself.*

This is the last entry till March 1858. Knowing Hart, he probably took advantage of this stay to learn from Patridge the mechanics of the China trade.[9]

It was just as well to enjoy the present, for in 1856 Ningbo was suffering from the general disorder in China at the time. Cantonese pirates were pursuing vengeance on the Portuguese community, their rivals in the opium trade, and massacred many of them. The chance arrival of a French warship drove them off before the attacks spread to other foreigners. Hart also suffered an emotional upheaval that year:

> *...in 1856, I was as near getting married as any man ever was that didn't get married...but the young lady's papa did not think me rich enough, — the affair was knocked on the head — and in three*

*months…she was married to another man…I got over it quickly
too — in one way: but I immediately took an immoderate dose of
Byron, thought I had been harshly dealt with…and began a life of
dissipation the thoughts of which make me now disgusted with
myself… . From that slough I, however, gradually emerged…*

This was in a letter to his fiancée, Hester Bredon, a few days before
their marriage.[10] He did not tell her of another girl in his life.

Ayaou

The first few pages of Hart's next surviving diary are torn out. The
entries begin on 3 March 1858, in Canton. He had been transferred there
early in 1858 as Second Assistant soon after the city was taken by the
British and French forces and the Viceroy, Ye, removed. In April Hart
became Secretary and Interpreter for the Allied Commission effectively
governing the city, with a salary of £1,500 p.a. He was working with
Harry Parkes, the most active of the three Commissioners.

The new diary reveals a different man from the one in Ningbo. He
was still going to church regularly, but he was also enjoying a much
more diverse social life. The Allied forces in Canton were organising
races, theatricals, card games, etc. and there were many dinners and
outings. He could enjoy rides out into the country, once conditions had
settled down, as he could afford a horse and groom. Struggles with
his conscience are markedly absent.

Katherine Bruner and her colleagues thought that the change was
due to Captain Patridge's comprador having supplied him with a
Cantonese girl from 'a proper but lower-class background' and that his
years with her, 1857–1865, 'gave him his fill of romance', and made
him happier with Chinese culture and his career.[11] I think the change
began earlier, with promotion. From the arrival of Winchester on 1
April 1855 he had been doing more responsible work. He was a man
for whom the satisfactions of work with a useful purpose and where
his merits were acknowledged always came first. From April to July
1855 his diary entries had already become much shorter and more
infrequent than they had been earlier. He acquired Ayaou in Ningbo
in 1857, at least eighteen months after his move into Patridge's house,
possibly after a reminder of the dangers of 'dissipation'. A later reference

suggests she was then about sixteen. She went with him to Canton but the more confident and happy note of diary entries, which starts in Ningbo, probably derived more from his promotions than from her company, which, in 1858, he was ready to quit.

Though taking a Chinese mistress was common, those in the consular service were expected to hide it discreetly. Ayaou was at first living in his quarters in Ye's old Yamen.

> *20 May 1858 Achih* [his steward] *told me today that last night about 6 o'clock two officers entered my house, and were only got out after considerable trouble. Ayaou took refuge in back apartment and was not seen.*

> *26 May 1858 Ayaou two months* _____

The blank signifies her pregnancy. The normal practice was for the expatriate then to terminate the arrangement with a suitable payment. As Canton was becoming very unsafe, Hart despatched her to Macau, and began negotiating her parting settlement.

> *Monday 26 July 1858. Sent Achih to Macao today: sent $20 to Ayaou.* [This was for her monthly living costs; she had probably had a similar sum when she first left.]

> *Sunday 15 August 1858. Modest request from Ayaou for $700 or at least $200 — 'no can' !!!*

> *Thursday 16 September 1858. Went out this morning alone for the first time the last four months.* [Canton was safer again.] *I went to see Ayaou who came back from Macao the night before last. Demands $200. I must cut the connection.*

This shows that, after the unpleasant incident on 20 May, he had housed her in a separate establishment.

> *Sunday, 19 September, 1858: Gave Sampson a cheque on O.B.* [Oriental Banking Corporation] *for $100 and drew $59 of this month's pay. Paid Ayaou $125: I understand this closes the connection.*

> *Monday 20 September...Ayaou went to Macao today.*

It sounds as if Sampson knew about Ayaou. He was willing to provide $100 in cash to help Hart. He may have been an intermediary with Achih in the negotiation for he was well-acquainted with local customs.

On Wednesday 22 September Hart found it *'very hard work getting through the evening. Went to see Ayi near NE Gate.'* His remedy for missing Ayaou was to get a replacement, which he finalised the next day, the same Thursday that Sampson had introduced him to his wife, Emma. He settled with her in two sorts of dollars *'$100 & $22 Ch:'* He called himself asinine but took full advantage:

> *Friday, 24 September 1858. Ayi brought to the house in Pagoda St.* [presumably where he had housed Ayaou].

> *Saturday, 25 September 1858.* [After another visit to Ayi] *met Mr. P.* [Parkes] *on my return and was considerably taken aback.*

> *Sunday, 26 September 1858. Again Ayi...*

After that there are no more mentions of Ayi. In November he was made Chinese Secretary to the new British Consul, Rutherford Alcock, who, unlike Parkes, was not a master of the language. Hart was at once given a lot of work. He had to move out of the Yamen, being no longer in the service of the Commission. He took temporary quarters first on one chop and then in *'the new "Consulate", Vacher's old chop. Very filthy'.* On 5 December he was *'horribly uncomfortable...living in such confined space & having another person sleeping in the same room'.* This would have made it difficult to keep visits to a Chinese mistress private.

The diary stops again on 6 December 1858. Very possibly Ayaou returned to show him their daughter, named Anna, who would have been born in December 1858, and this led to his taking her back. The sight of their first child is for many men is a transforming event in their lives. He certainly associated with Ayaou again, for they had two sons born around May 1862 and August 1865, but she and the children probably continued to live in a separate house, in Canton or Macao. In a Statutory Declaration made in 1905 he stated that he met this Cantonese girl in Ningbo in 1857, and that she came with him to Canton. He continues, with vagueness over the dates, that

> *I left her then at Macao and though she continued to be...paid $30*

*a month…we never lived together afterwards and very rarely
met…*

*In 1866 the connection was dissolved and Ayaou was then
presented with $3000 when she surrendered her children to my
agent and herself married a Chinaman… . While in China, I
believe I only saw Anna twice or thrice, Herbert once and Arthur
never. Ayaou was a very good little girl…*[12]

$3,000 whether Chinese or Mexican, was far more than the usual
parting present. Hart also said that when he had the children sent to
his lawyer in England in 1866, he provided £6,000 to be used for their
benefit. The interest would have amply covered their living costs and
they were initially brought up by the wife of the book-keeper at a London
firm with which he dealt. In a similar declaration in 1910 he added that
the £6,000 had long since been divided between them, as it had been
intended to help launch them into the world.

I think the children were probably kept out of his way, to reduce
the heartbreak of the final parting that he knew was the price he had
to pay for his increasingly successful career. Unlike John Meadows, Hart
never regarded the arrangement as equivalent to a marriage. But the
way he spoke of Ayaou to the end of his life, and the large sums involved,
show that their relationship must have deepened after Anna's birth. There
is no other way to account for the contrast between his casualness in
1858, when $200 was too much for a parting gift, and the much more
costly arrangements of 1866. The best of their time together was
probably while he was in Canton, 1859–61, for after that the travels
imposed by his career would mean less frequent meetings.

The Beginnings of Hart's Customs Career

In 1859 the Hoppo, the official in charge of Customs collection, was
concerned by the diminishing revenues he was able to transmit to his
superiors in Peking, and by the extreme difficulty of collecting the duties
on opium. (The trade had been legalised in 1858, and the duty on it
was eight per cent as compared with the regular five per cent on other
goods.) Alcock, who had previously been Consul in Shanghai, suggested
to him that he should adopt the Shanghai solution — a foreign-supervised
Customs service. The Chinese authorities liked this idea, and asked Hart

to set it up in Canton. Lay (who was now in Chinese employ as Inspector-General of the Customs, based at Shanghai) also approved. At the end of June 1859 Hart resigned from the Consular service and became a Chinese civil servant, first as Deputy Commissioner of Customs and later as Commissioner in Canton. The British government approved as it thought the new Customs arrangements were in the interests of orderly trade. The British belief at this time was that free trade was in the interest of all parties, provided competition was fair and there was good order. The China trade at the time met neither condition, with some merchants seeking illicit advantage by smuggling goods in and out, others by giving bribes to pay less than official duties, while pirates created uncertainty and huge losses. An efficient, honest Customs Service would mean that all parties paid the same duties, and the revenues could provide resources for keeping order, on sea and land. With British, American and French backing, the system was also being adopted in other ports.

All this was against the confused background of the continuing Taiping rebellion, the allied attack on Peking which resulted in the acceptance of the Treaty of Tientsin in 1860, the death of the Emperor in August 1861, and court rivalries over who should take charge of his infant son by the concubine, Cixi. Cixi emerged as the winner and was to dominate China for the next forty years as the Empress Dowager. Very conservative, reluctant to change, she nevertheless secured something of a dynastic revival. Prince Gong (or Kung, as Hart wrote his name), was appointed head of the Tsungli Yamen in Peking, an office which for the first time handled centrally both the Customs and the general foreign relations previously delegated to the Viceroy of Canton. Hart was to work with him over many years. On the military side, there was Li Hongzhang (usually Li or Li Hung Chang in the diaries), who saw the need for modern industries and training to strengthen military capacity. Both Hart and the German Commissioner of Customs in Tianjin, Detring, establish close ties with him.

The Tsungli Yamen confirmed Lay's previous appointment as Inspector-General, but Lay immediately applied for sick leave, sailing for England in March 1861 before a reply could reach him. This was typical of the disrespect that Hart had first noticed in Ningbo. Lay left George H Fitzroy at Shanghai and Hart from Canton jointly in charge of the Customs. As Fitzroy had no Chinese, it was the younger man, Hart, who went north to Peking to take Prince Gong's orders. The members of the Tsungli Yamen found his careful, polite explanations of the mechanisms of trade and customs collection far superior to Lay's hectoring manner. He was there during June 1861, then in Tientsin and other new northern ports to establish the new Customs operations, and back in Peking for September. Sir Frederick Bruce, Lord Elgin's brother, was now British Minister in Peking and reported to the Foreign Office:

> *without the presence of Mr. Hart and the knowledge he possesses of Chinese financial arrangements.... . I do not think I could have worked out in detail at Peking, the Treaty of Tientsin, and it is to him and his European assistants that I must now look to overcome the ignorance and perverseness of the Chinese Provincial Officers.*[13]

It was one thing for the Treaty to state that new ports should be opened to foreign trade, but another altogether to put this into operation and to make that trade fair and orderly. Hart was now based at Shanghai, but was travelling a good deal during Lay's absence, 1861–63, opening Customs offices at new ports, and appointing and instructing staff.[14] This reduced time for rest and relaxation with Ayaou. The birth of Herbert around May 1862 shows that they had been able to meet in the autumn of 1861. The gap in his diary which lasted till April 1863 suggests that he was still seeing her when he could up to that point, but he may never have taken her to Shanghai, which was frequently in danger from the Taiping rebellion.

Hart was also corresponding with Lay over the order for a flotilla of small armed steamers for China, to suppress piracy and rebellion. (It became known as the Lay-Osborn flotilla, Osborn being its commander.) In April 1863 Lay returned to China, with the flotilla, and resumed the office of Inspector-General. However, Lay's ideas on how the flotilla should be commanded were completely at variance with those of the Chinese authorities. Put briefly, he wanted himself, not any Chinese official, to have the final authority over it.

Hart expected trouble from the day he first met Lay after his return. His diary resumes on 9 May 1863:

> *Met Lay...he is greatly changed, anglicised in fact to such a degree that I fear his task with the Chinese will be very uphill work. He'll not meet their views, and he will insist on his own: he will*

dogmatise and not explain...I sh'd not be surprised to see
everything in a grand mess.

In June he was with Lay in Peking, for difficult negotiations on the management of the fleet and other Customs matters. Lay made a trip back to Shanghai in July, and was away a month. The summer pace was leisurely and Hart had time for an entry in his diary on 25 July 1863 which shows both his pride in his progress financially, and his loyalty to his family. He lists his pay rises since the day nine years earlier when he had landed in China, first from £200 to £270, then in 1858 from £500 to £1500, and in July 1860 (on becoming Commissioner of Customs in Canton) to £2500 p.a. *'and now, in July 1863 it is £3300 and more. Not bad that! And during the last four years I have sent home as a present to my Father £3094.15.10, and to my sisters and cousins £461.12.3: in all, £3556.8.1 stg'*. The gifts show him helping his family in the way expected of a successful man at the time, in both Britain and China (and as is still expected in many cultures today). As a young man he was pleased that in the Chinese Customs he no longer had British income tax and Consular Superannuation Fund payments deducted from his salary, but the absence of solid pension arrangements for the Customs officers and their widows caused trouble later for his staff.

When Lay returned to Peking at the beginning of September, he sent Hart back to Shanghai to take the place of the Commissioner there, who had died. Lay's considerable demands now included powers to allocate the revenues the Customs brought in, and a palace in Peking for his residence, while he had still not met the Chinese request for a proper account of the money spent on the armed steamers that they had ordered. In November, the Yamen dismissed him, Sir Frederick Bruce raising no objection.

On Sunday 29 November 1863, at breakfast in Shanghai, the twenty-eight-year old Hart received a despatch from the Tsungli Yamen, with several enclosures. He finished his meal, and *'as usual, read my morning chapter* [in the Bible] *and prayed'* before opening it. It contained his appointment as Inspector-General, and a letter from Bruce begging him to accept, which he did.

The New Inspector-General

On 23 December, he was feeling depressed, because of time wasted, etc., but cheered up as he wrote that his success was due to his own hard work from youth (as already quoted). He then listed his objectives as Inspector-General (IG) The first was to whip the Foreign Inspectorate into shape, getting good people as commissioners and office men, and seeing that all did their work properly, so that the merchants had no cause for complaint and the Imperial receipts were swelled by the increase in trade. Objects 2, 3, 4 and 5 were concerned with getting to know China better, inducing friendlier feelings towards foreigners, and finding out what products of Western civilisation could most benefit China, and in what ways beneficial change could be introduced. Object 7 was to support the noble work of preaching the Gospel. Number 6 was '*I must set a good example, in conduct, to all my subs* [subordinates]'. Though unspecified, this to his mind meant trying to dispense with a concubine and all forms of illicit sex (though he remained tolerant of such activities by young subordinates, if carried on discreetly).

The first objective was to a man of his temperament the easiest, though it entailed hard, detailed work. An American Commissioner, Edward Bangs Drew, described how he created uniformity at all offices, calling for full lists of their employees, then classifying, ranking and grading them, with appropriate rates of pay, and issuing regulations and instructions for each. He wanted each man to know clearly what was expected of him, and then be held strictly to executing it. Customs staff were divided into two categories: the top grade of Indoor staff (who came to be recruited through the London office after a nomination from Hart), and a lower grade of Outdoor staff, such as the tidewaiters (who met incoming ships on the tide), who were mostly locally recruited from expatriate seamen or others already on the China coast. With James Campbell, who had been in the Audit office of the Treasury in London before joining the Customs under Lay in 1862, he set up systems of accounting which Campbell taught in each office. Hart not only put Campbell's expertise to good use but also enjoyed his company, for Campbell was no mere accountant and had attended both Paris and Heidelberg universities. The accounts were summarised in Peking for the audit department to bring to him each Saturday. Hart also worked out the reporting required on work done, money collected and staff performance, so that he could see who deserved promotion. Drew insists on the thoroughness and durability of this early organising work, which enabled Hart to deal smoothly both with the expansion of the service and with time-consuming international crises where his advice was sought by both sides. Drew cites the Sino-British crisis in 1876 and the Sino-French virtual war of 1884–5, both the background of later chapters.[15]

The first example of crisis work was in January and February 1864. Li Hongzhang had put General Gordon in charge of a force of mercenaries under Western officers, known as the 'Ever Victorious Army', which he was employing to assist in putting down the long-running Taiping revolt.[16] Hart spent three weeks searching across freezing marshes for Gordon's hideout, to get him to continue his successful campaign, despite Gordon's wrath that Li Hongzhang had executed some rebel leaders, despite knowing that Gordon had promised them safe conduct. There were reasons for this, and Hart was able to assist in the re-establishment of relations between Li and Gordon.[17] The crushing of the Taiping revolt provided the internal peace without which trade could not flourish. Hart agonised in April entries in his diary over whether he was doing the right thing in supporting the Imperialists, but concluded that the Taiping were equally bad in their behaviour, but did not have the organisational capability of his Manchu employers, whom he could hope to influence by his advice (his object 5). However, the incident gave him more understanding of the unwillingness of Lay and Osborn to leave the final authority over the fleet in Chinese hands.

As to objective 6, he had begun on a new path as soon as the possibility of his promotion became clear, in September 1863 when he left Lay in Peking. On Sunday 6 March 1864 he wrote:

> It is six months today since I started on [the proper path]: many inward struggles, but no outward giving way in the direction I most feared. I have felt quite happy during some time back…. But such happy seasons are necessarily ephemeral, and the fight and struggles will have to be gone through afresh…. I feel rather lonely, and I wish very much I had a wife…

It looks as if at this stage he was missing Ayaou both as a sexual outlet and as a companion — but it was sexual satisfaction that felt most urgent. A few days later, on 9 March, he acknowledged 'my besetting sin, "womanising" has worried me day after day...I find it almost impossible to refrain from indulging in imagination in those pleasures which I have strength enough to refrain from outwardly'.[18]

On 23 July 1864 he congratulated himself that his reveries about women were becoming shorter and less engrossing, but alas, on 6 August, 'Temptation to get a concubine is very strong...nothing bothers me so much, as my liking for women. It is, however, more than a year since I even touched one.'

'More than a year' suggests that he was with Ayaou before going to Peking with Lay in the summer of 1863, and that while he was there, he realised what his future might be, and determined to clear the decks for a suitable marriage by formally ending the relationship. Most expatriates in China would have made a small payment, and have expected the children to be re-absorbed into their mother's extended family. Hart evidently felt that if they remained in China, they could embarrass him and his future wife. He accepted financial responsibility for his 'wards' and let them bear his name, but, born outside marriage, they were not, in the Victorian sense, his family, entitled to his presence and affection. He wanted them brought up in Britain. He needed a trustworthy intermediary who knew Cantonese customs. It could not be a Customs employee. The whole matter was so secret that he did not even mention it in his diary. I think his thoughts turned to Sampson. He was still in close touch him, his wife Emma and her enchanting daughter. Diary entries in Peking on 21 June 1864 recount that the 'dear little girl' had sent him her photograph and that he had sent her a note in reply on 24 June.

Hart returned to Shanghai on 4 November (having successfully resisted temptation from the Chinese girls next door) and was astonished by the brilliance of the new gaslights on the Bund and in the Club. On 9 December he left for Hong Kong, the journey, as he noted, taking only sixty-nine hours under steam. He then went straight on to Canton. His references to the visits he made show that he had become intimately acquainted with the expatriate intellectuals there who were seeking a better understanding of Chinese civilisation during the undiarised years, 1859–1861.

While in Canton, on 20 December 1864, he received a letter from his mother: 'Mama writes of a Miss Breadon, [sic] and speaks of £5,000 [the money he could expect her to bring]... . The desire for a pleasant *fireside increases, but that for matrimony wanes.'* His desire for matrimony might have waned after seeing Ayaou, but soon re-established itself. On 10 January he was planning to visit Hong Kong to make 'sundry arrangements' before leaving the south. The next entry, 15 January 1865, showed that this did not result in an intended meeting with Dr Wilhelm Lobscheid, *'so that I had to leave undone the private business I was most anxious to have got arranged'*. Sampson was well acquainted with Lobscheid, an unusual German missionary, and may have suggested that he could arrange the despatch of the children to England. It seems likely that on what Hart intended to be a farewell visit in December 1864 he negotiated the deal with Ayaou, but, like JCW2 on a similar occasion, he also seems to have made her pregnant again, thus delaying any plan for the immediate removal of the children. In the August 1866 letter to Hester Bredon quoted earlier he said, *'I have for the last two years at least led a blameless life'*, but this passed over the probable accompaniment to his last meeting with Ayaou.

On 25 January 1865, during the Chinese New Year holiday, he listed four wives he had called on in Canton and *'had a very pleasant gossip in each place'*. They included Emma Sampson and a Mrs Happer (of whose daughter more later). He was again reminded of the compensations of a good marriage. On his birthday, 20 February 1865, he wrote:

> *Thirty, and still unmarried; the sooner I plunge into the connubial state, the better. If I don't do it during the next four or five years, I must for ever leave it alone. I fear my ten weeks' stay at home at the end of this year will scarcely suffice for inspiring — though an hour is enough for me to fall in — love.*

During this time he was somewhat fearfully questioning whether every word of the Bible was inspired by God, according to the traditional doctrine of 'plenary inspiration'. In August 1864 in a long entry he concludes that it is allowable to approach some elements critically, and by January 1865 he inclined to rejecting plenary inspiration, while *'in dread lest, through my desire to do sundry things which early teaching...has made me regard with an amount of dislike that is superstitious, I may be led to view the truth through other than neutral glasses'*. He was conscious of the link between religion and morality.

He kept no diary from 25 February to Sunday 7 May 1865. His summary of that time shows that he was touring the southern ports, arranging staff matters and their housing and briefing Chinese officials. It included another trip to Hong Kong, 22–24 March. During this he probably concluded his 'private business' with Lobscheid successfully. He certainly left the place in a happier frame of mind and with a better impression of its modern improvements than was the case in January.

He had returned to Shanghai by 1 April 1865, but left on 20 June, once again summoned to Peking. His return south was constantly delayed by the Chinese authorities. At the end of October 1865 they asked him to make Peking his headquarters and his home, the very thing they had refused to Lay. He did not obtain permission for a home leave till early 1866. The despatch of his children to his lawyer in London in 1866 must have been arranged by letter, on the basis of the plans laid during his earlier visits to Canton and Hong Kong.

Courting Hester Bredon

That winter he had been rather intrigued by a Miss Lowder, who was staying with Rutherford Alcock, who had succeeded Bruce as British Minister. On 1 January 1866 he wrote: *'Every time I see her I like her better. But I doubt whether we would suit each other and I must therefore avoid haste & be prudent.'* By the end of the month the young lady had made it abundantly clear that she was not interested, thus making it urgent to find a wife during his leave. Before departing he left instructions for some modernisation of his Chinese house to make it more comfortable for such a person, by installing glass windows and wooden floors.[19]

Being Hart, he also used the visit to forward one of his work objectives. The Yamen was sending a retired official with his accompanying son and servants, to visit Europe as an official sightseer and reporter. Hart provided two young Customs officers, one English and one French, as his interpreters and minders (a job they found difficult). Hart hoped that this might be the first step in persuading the Yamen of the usefulness of establishing China's first diplomatic missions abroad. (This was not achieved till 1877.)

The large party left Peking on 2 March 1866. They visited the pyramids in Cairo (which by this time could be reached by train from Suez) and arrived in Marseilles on 2 May. Hart spent only a day in Paris (where he left the Chinese party) and after a night in London (which would have been an opportunity to see his lawyer and finalise arrangements for Ayaou's children) he crossed to Ireland for two weeks with his parents at Ravarnet and visits to his friends and married sisters. He then returned to London to arrange the Chinese visits in England. The *'virtuous affection'* he sought could not be found as he rushed around town. Back home on 25 May, he was ready to seek family help. His entries in his diary during this time were brief, which he excuses and explains in a long entry on Sunday 15 July:

> *for the last three months or more I have been in a whirl of excitement,*
> *& have felt it almost impossible to think: I c'd neither criticise the*
> *past, nor plan the future, & I experienced an equal impossibility*
> *in respect of a conscious process of thought in the present.*

This was his state when he called with his aunt on the eighteen-year-old Hester Bredon and her mother, on 31 May. She was the daughter of his aunt's doctor, who had died a fortnight earlier. His aunt had already sent him her photograph, which he had received — and liked — just before embarking from Shanghai. At their third meeting, on 5 June, a four-line entry describes his proposal, her acceptance, and her mother's approval, subject to consulting Hester's elder brother. Hart had asked her if she *'could find it in her heart to come to China with me'*.

Unlike the due consideration marking his approach to Miss Lowder in Peking, there was scant investigation of her qualities as a companion or as a cosmopolitan hostess. Her make of piano gets mentioned, but not her musicianship. A letter written to her in August shows he did not know whether, like him, she enjoyed country pleasures more than urban ones, since they had only met indoors, in town. He assumed, rather than knew, that she would meet his need for an understanding, sympathetic friend. In a letter to her on 24 July he told her how much he desired to: *'have you always at my side, to talk to you about every occurrence — and to feel, whether you spoke it or not, your sympathy in all my affairs!'* For her part, Hester was able to accept him quickly, partly because her family had prepared the ground, but mainly because he provided a gateway to a wider world she wanted to explore. Her old home would now be associated with the death of her father. Her brother, Dr Robert Bredon, gave his assent a few days later.

There is not much passion in Hart's reflections on 13 June:

> *Spent a pleasant afternoon, and felt quiet & happy with Hessie*

[as he always called her] *beside me; I don't feel the chain when she is at hand; it is only when away from her that I am sensible of...loss of freedom. But she is an intelligent, lively, unaffected, & <u>wide-awake</u> young lassie...able to hold her own against most comers...I shall do all I can to make her happy and comfortable, and — if the past could only be blotted out — I could almost feel certain of unalloyed happiness for the future. 0 the past! the past! with its ghosts of dead sins, & its living results of manhood's first errors. 'Let the dead past bury its dead:'[20] — that is easy enough: what is not so easy is to keep the future free from intrusiveness...of the products of the past. Does complete confidence mean 'to have no secrets for the future', or 'to reveal all that has been done in the past'?*

He evidently decided on the former interpretation, with which he thought Hester agreed. In the letter written a week before his wedding, in which he told her about his failed engagement in 1856 and a period of dissipation afterwards, he quoted himself as having previously said: *'Remember, Hessie, you are marrying me <u>for the future.</u>'* There is no mention of Ayaou.

His forebodings about the products of the past proved fully justified, but meanwhile his affection for Hester was growing. She charmed his family when she visited on 15 June, leading him to write *'She is a darling girl, and I love her with all my heart.'* His feelings had elements of paternal protectiveness for a young girl who had just lost her father. She was *'my little girl'* in an August letter to her. He had himself just made a mental farewell to his Chinese companion and his daughter by her. Each found something they needed in the other.

Nevertheless, in the long entry of Sunday 15 July in which he had explained why the previous entries had been short, his main reflections are not about his coming marriage, but on whether it would not have been wiser to spend more time in London and the continent in May and June, accompanying the official Chinese party, and making the contacts that might put him in the way of a CB (Companion of the Bath) or other honour. He decided that you could not have everything you wanted; had he done this, he could not have spent so much time with old friends in Ireland. Honours were important to a man of his background, to gain visible social equality with his diplomatic peers

— but even more so were life-long friends. Despite the shortness of his leave, he found time in July for a three-day visit to his old Queen's friend, James Brazier, now Professor of Chemistry in Aberdeen. He called at Rugby on his way back to London to fulfil a promise to his former boss and friend, Meadows, to look up his daughters, who were now being educated with relatives in England. As they were on a visit to Penge, south of London, he pursued them there. He found they *'have forgotten their Chinese, but speak English well: sent their "love & kisses to Papa, Mamma, & little sister'*. This may have made him hope, though he did not put this in the diary, that his own young children would adapt equally well. He then went to Paris to recruit some French staff, and to make his farewells to the Chinese party. His diary entries stop on 7 August 1866; the next volume begins on 1 January 1867.

Hester and he were married on 22 August, in Dublin. They had a short honeymoon in Killarney and in September they left for Peking. James Campbell, who had been promoted to become Hart's Chief Secretary and Auditor, returned with them, and their friendship deepened. Campbell was given a mission in Europe in June 1868. Illness prevented his return. He subsequently took charge of the London office of the Customs, where he received Hart's official requests and, in a separate series of letters, his confidential comments and requests. In a letter of 6 May 1869 Hart told him *'I have not had a really confidential chat with anyone since you went away!'* Hart could not have a confidential friendship with most of his subordinates in China, or with diplomats whose loyalty was to their own governments. He could make exceptions of family, so having his brother Jem[21] and later, his brother-in-law, Robert Bredon, with him in China, was important to him.

He also needed women friends who could understand some of the feelings he was not able to display to men, in the days when they were expected to keep a 'stiff upper lip'. The right wife could have done this if, as he hoped, she was able to share his devotion to his career and to China. With Hester, the marriage started happily, and on their first anniversary he wrote: *'No-one could have a better wife than I have got & so far, we have got on well. At the same time, matrimony does interfere with a man's work at times.'* Already this gives a hint of trouble to come, although both at first tried to find common interests. The 1868 diary crows: *'21st June. Hessie is 21 years of age today & has just finished the first book of the Aeneid.'* On 16 November 1870, when he was learning the violin, he asked Campbell to get some piano and violin music they could play together. There is no doubt he became fond of her. He admired the courage with which she survived four days of labour and the immediate death of their son, in 1867, an event which must have reminded the nervous husband of the horrid outcome of a confinement in Ningbo. Their daughter, Evey, arrived safely on 31 December 1869, and a son, Bruce, followed in July 1873. But on 19 July 1874, the diary has this reflection: *'Business...is my first consideration. I let nothing take me from it; I give up everything for it.'*[22]

For a man for whom work comes first, marriage can only be fully successful if the wife accepts his career as her own. As we shall see, this kind of companionship did not materialise. However, both his own loyal nature and the ethos of the times would make him regard marriage as a commitment 'till death do us part'.

CHAPTER THREE

THEO SAMPSON AND EMMA

Sampson's Early Life

The only photograph of Theophilus Sampson, Emma's third husband (often known as Theo) was taken in 1874 (Figure 3.1). He came from a more prosperous background than Hart. In his will Sampson left to his sister 'the likeness of my father and mother painted on ivory and in ivory frames' and various books belonging to his father. This suggests a comfortably-off, bookish family. Joseph Holden Sampson was a merchant and broker in Hull, a busy seaport for the trade with northern Europe. He and his wife, Martha Shipton, had nine children. Theo was the second youngest, born in 1831 in Sculcoates, a village that had become a Hull suburb. In the 1841 census Theo was listed there, with several brothers, the three eldest of them clerks. Their parents are recorded at Skelton Rectory, also in Yorkshire, where they and a daughter were visiting Martha's mother, so Theo's maternal grandfather was probably a Church of England cleric. One of Theo's brothers, John, became a clergyman, implying a university education. Another brother, Arthur, listed in the 1851 census as a twenty-one-year-old BA, joined the prestigious Indian Civil Service. Theo, judging by the quality of his later writing, his linguistic ability and the way he could absorb, apply and develop what he read in a great variety of fields, must have had a sound education in English grammar and logic, Latin and mathematics, which were standard fare in a grammar-school type of education at the time, but he did not have the university education of his brothers.

Dr Emil Bretschneider, for many years the physician at the Russian embassy in Peking, an expert in Chinese who reviewed Chinese botanical knowledge as shown in their historical documents, asked Sampson to provide him with some biographical data. He was surprised that (by European standards):

> ...not much care had been bestowed upon his primary education, for, at the early age of fourteen years he had already gone to sea as an apprentice in the merchant service, and followed that occupation for eight years, when he found himself at Whampoa, without employ, and without a dollar in his pocket, and was offered and accepted the humble and subordinate situation of constable to the British Vice-Consulate at Whampoa.

> ...From Sampson's interesting articles and notes relating to Chinese botany and other matters, which appeared about thirty years ago in the pages of Notes and Queries on China and Japan, we always had the impression that the intelligent author of these papers, then not personally known to us, must be a man, not only of a thorough general education, but also well acquainted with the Chinese written language, and an able botanist. We may therefore conclude that he has the merit of being one of those self-taught scholars, who acquire learning and scientific attainments by their own exertion, without having been regularly trained in universities.[1]

Vice-consul Alex Bird gave him this testimonial, dated 31 January 1857:

> *Since December 1853 when you became assistant in the British Vice-Consul's establishment at Whampoa, to this date, during which you have served under me, with the exception of eight months and a half in 1854, when I had leave of absence, I have found you very useful, intelligent and steady. I consider you well qualified for a much better appointment, and trust you will enjoy prosperity and happiness.*

An incident that occurred while Charles Winchester was Vice-Consul gives an idea of Sampson's dangerous duties. He had to deal with four men, armed with knives, whose gang-leader, Suicar, had already killed an American. Suicar's men had boarded a British ship to enable the gunner to desert. Despite Suicar's reputation, and the knives of his men, Sampson went to the lodging house Suicar owned and arrested the gunner. His duties included being boarding officer for shipping and dogsbody in the office. Though consuls and vice-consuls relied heavily on their constable, the pay was miserable, and P D Coates describes the constables as in many cases poor types addicted to drink.[2] They rated very low in the expatriate social hierarchy.

Sampson's luck turned in 1856–7, when he worked with Harry Parkes and Henry Hance. In January 1857 Parkes had an office in Hong Kong, while still nominally Consul in Canton. Hance was his Assistant. Their initial task was to compile a list of the losses incurred by British subjects in Canton. These included claims totalling £840.1.10 ½d from Winchester and Hance, and a mere $17 from Sampson, for a hairbrush, a clothes brush, and a few clothes. Parkes wrote to HE hoping he could authorise immediate payment of this small sum to 'the constable at Whampoa — who then and since has been most active and zealous in his services'.

In September, Sampson appealed to Parkes for a rise:

> Sir, Owing to the present high price of provisions, and other circumstances incidental to my residing in Hongkong, my ordinary expenses, notwithstanding every regard to economy, fully double the rate at which I formerly supported my wants at Whampoa, and I beg therefore respectfully to request that my monthly pay be so increased as to enable me to meet this increased expenditure, during the current quarter, and so long as existing circumstances may continue.
>
> I trust that my endeavours to render myself useful to you since the commencement of the troubles at Canton will have enabled you to form an opinion of my character.

Parkes recommended his pay be raised from $50 per month to $85, as Hance had been seconded to the Hong Kong Secretariat and Sampson was now the only person doing Assistant's duties.[3]

Sampson and Hance had been sharing a desk in the small office. Dr Henry Fletcher Hance, after some years in the Hong Kong civil service, and a leave in England in 1851–2 where he acquired a musical wife, transferred to the consular service in 1854. He had been educated in London and Belgium, and spoke and wrote Latin, Greek, French and German. He taught himself botany, and as a result of his many learned botanical papers, received an honorary PhD from the University of Giessen. He was Assistant in the consular office in the factories at Canton till they were burnt down. His claim for compensation covered a sparse amount of furniture, many serious books (in English, French, Latin and Greek), and his wife's two pianos and music.[4] He had already built up a communications network with other collectors and botanists working in China and abroad[5] and his correspondents included Charles Darwin, successive directors of Kew Gardens and their equivalents in other European countries. When Canton reopened in 1858, Hance returned to the consulate there, but chose to be Vice-Consul at Whampoa in 1861, because the *Alligator* offered accommodation for his growing family. There he remained for most of his career, as he refused to learn Chinese, which the Foreign Office had come to regard as essential for promotion to Consul. Sampson told Thisleton Dyer, Director of Kew, that it was Hance who revived his boyhood enthusiasm for botany while they were in Hong Kong.[6]

Parkes' elevation to be one of the Allied Commissioners in Canton enabled him to appoint Sampson to be its Chief Clerk and Cashier. Sampson told Bretschneider that it was Parkes who gave him the appointment *'which gave him entrance to the society of the European settlement at Canton'*. Sampson had had the society of the Chinese and British sailors and miscreants at Whampoa, but he now gained not only the salary that enabled him to marry Emma, but also the status to enter 'society' — those who regarded themselves as 'gentlemen', addressed on envelopes as Esquire. His wife, Emma, could join the British General in command of the Allied forces when he took the 'ladies' into Canton city.

The Coolie Trade

The Allied Commission was temporary, but at the end of 1859 Sampson acquired the post of Sub-Emigration Agent at Canton for the British West Indies, under J G Austin, whom he succeeded in 1862.[7] A description of his work not only provides a background to Emma's husband but also throws light on an area of the lives of Chinese women at the time.

Officially, the Imperial government had forbidden emigration, but as with the ban on opium, this was not enforced. The result was that in the 1840s and 1850s, the recruitment of Chinese workers for the plantations of Asia, Latin America and the Caribbean, or for mining work and construction elsewhere, was entirely unregulated and subject to many abuses. Chinese 'crimpers' persuaded, tricked or kidnapped Chinese labourers left destitute by natural disasters or the civil war and sold them on to traders who carried them to countries with a demand for their labour. The labourers may or may not have understood the contracts which they signed for several years of indentured labour in return for their passage money. While those going to the Californian and Australian goldfields could do well for themselves, the conditions of the unfortunates destined for Peru and Cuba were soon raising an uproar from the Anti-Slavery Society, which still powerfully influenced public opinion in Britain. Many British consuls deplored the trade, but their legal powers were uncertain.

In 1855 the British Government passed the Chinese Passengers Act, which required all British ships in the trade to be inspected, to ensure that the emigrants were leaving voluntarily, and that the ships were properly equipped and ventilated. This had the effect of moving the centre of the trade from Hong Kong to Macao. In 1859 there were six boats at Whampoa, three from the United States, one each from Germany, Holland and Peru, ferrying men to the receiving barracks in Macao. Austin had been Immigration Agent in Guyana, and came to Hong Kong as Emigration Agent to see if labour could be secured under a more humane system. His objective was to do away with the 'crimpers' and their abuses by substituting receiving houses in appropriate ports, jointly supervised by the Chinese and British authorities, to which would-be emigrants to the West Indies had to come in person. The Governor of Canton co-operated, for the rough methods of the Chinese crimpers had whipped up general anti-foreign feeling which was threatening all trade. He issued a proclamation in 1859 permitting those 'who, being poor and without the means of obtaining a livelihood themselves, desire to go abroad to seek the means of subsistence' to go to the Emigration House in Canton, where they could negotiate their contract and destination. As Sub-Agent, Sampson put up Austin's posters in the villages and obtained the support of Chinese local authorities and gentry, and of missionaries who encouraged their converts to go. Amongst these latter was the Rev. Wilhelm Lobscheid who may have helped Hart with his children. In 1861 Lobscheid travelled out with one boatload of emigrants to Demerera, to gain personal experience of the conditions at sea and on the plantations.[8]

Parkes reported to Sir Frederick Bruce on 15 November 1859 that:

Directly that the establishment was declared to be open, applicants begin to offer themselves at the Emigration House, and Mr. Sampson, the local Agent, has stated to me to-day that he is now almost incommoded by the number of Chinese who flock into the premises, and that although numbers of these come from idle or inquisitive motives only, and many others are not encouraged, because seen to be unsuitable for the purpose for which they are required, he has already registered fifty-one men as labourers, whom he thinks will be approved by Mr. Austin.

Many emigrants were Hakka people, who had supported the Taiping rebellion, and who suffered by its final defeat. The French also supported this local 'Canton system'. The Imperial authorities were forced to recognise the regulated trade in additional ports in 1860 after the Allies entered Peking. The reports of the British Emigration Agent were submitted annually to the Colonial Office, which also had reports from the Governors of the receiving islands on the condition of the immigrants on arrival, and their progress thereafter, both being made available to the public.

A special effort was made to secure female migrants as well as males, as the West Indies wanted permanent settlers. Austin's posters offered $20 to each wife and adult daughter, and $5 for each child. (The Governor of Guyana complained they also gave a misleading idea of the level of wages there, possibly due to the difference between the US and the Mexican dollar.) This led to some emigrants acquiring cheap 'wives' — some of whom were elderly, or otherwise unfit for manual labour, or prostitutes. Sampson acknowledged in a letter of 29 October 1866 that most of the women sent had been obtained by the Chinese usage of purchase — but always, he said, with the woman's consent. They were often the destitute widows of men who had disappeared in 'the long protracted clan fights of the interior'. He went on to explain that during the most recent season the Chinese had put a stop to the whole practice of buying wives, in society generally as well as for emigration specifically, and that therefore his last shipment contained only women who were the *bona fide* wives or mothers of the male emigrants.

I have, of course, always been alive to the fact that the persons

who brought [the purchased] *class of women did so for*
pecuniary gain, and that I was thus permitting an influence to
enter female emigration which I deprecated when applied to
males...I have watched the operations with a caution amounting
to dread, and taken every pain to ensure the women knew and
approved of the step they were about to take.

The colonies objected to paying passage money for women with feet deformed by binding and complained when a high proportion of those shipped from Amoy were too crippled to work in the fields. Sampson had delegated recruitment in Amoy to a commercial firm. However, even before Governor Hincks of Guyana requested that he should make other arrangements, Sampson had decided to halt recruitment there as he was unable to recruit the desired proportion of females.

Correspondence between him and the Vice-Consul in Canton, W F Mayers, shows that although Chinese wives did not customarily follow migrating husbands, some women amongst the Hakka clan (who did not bind feet) were desirous of doing so. Mayers had received a letter from a Chinese official, the Grain Intendant of the province, reporting that seven thousand Hakkas had put themselves under his protection during his efforts to suppress the long feud between the Hakka and Punti clans, and that he would gladly send any willing to emigrate to Sampson. Mayers hoped that Sampson could agree to what would be 'a humane and satisfactory solution'. (In the back of his mind he must have had the Chinese record of wholesale executions.)

Sampson replied the same day, 27 October 1866, stating that he had not yet heard from the Governments of British Guyana and Trinidad that they agreed to the detailed regulations of a Convention of March 1866. This elaborated the principles agreed on the coolie trade in the Convention of Peking in 1860, amongst other things by guaranteeing that the emigrant would receive his return fare or an equivalent amount as a bonus if he stayed. The rules imposed, and the uncertainties they created, meant that emigration to the West Indies declined. Sampson thought it likely that the West Indian colonies would give up Chinese immigration. However, 'in view of the urgency of the case', he was willing to take personal responsibility for engaging up to 2,500 people, if their contract included clauses guaranteeing them the same wages as other workers on the plantations, but from which $1 per month should be deducted to cover repatriation if desired, or returned if they stayed the contracted five years. The emigrant should also be permitted to free himself of his contract by paying $15 for each unexpired year. (These clauses would limit his personal obligation as agent to supply funds if the colonial government did not provide return passage money.) On 29 October Mayers replied that the monthly deduction of $1 was not sanctioned by the Convention, and therefore Sampson's plan could not be agreed.[9] In 1872 an agreement was finally reached which allowed a resumption of legal emigration to the West Indies and Sampson resumed recruitment till the closure of the Emigration post in 1874. The last known shipment he organised was in December 1873, when the *Corona* departed with 314 Hakka men, 40 women, 26 boys, 5 girls and 3 infants, recruited with the help of a returning emigrant. Sampson explained his difficulty in recruiting more women: 'in plain language, the feuds which rendered large numbers of women destitute widows are at an end'.

As emigration dried up, Sampson at some stage took on additional work as Naval Accountant to the Viceroy in Canton, who was responsible for the southern portion of the modernised Chinese navy.

The Botanist

The decline of emigration meant that Sampson had more leisure for botanical collection in the areas he had visited when recruiting emigrants, and for writing short articles on plants and other topics in *Notes and Queries*. Titles of thirty-one articles written between 1867 and 1870, on such diverse topics as plants, geology, architecture, and the meaning of Chinese words, are listed in the notes collated on him in 1984, and there are later articles in *The China Review*. He gave Bretschneider details of his plant collecting. There were many visits to the Pakwan or White Cloud Hills, about five miles north of Canton, where there was a monastery overlooking the city. Sampson first visited these hills with Parkes in 1859, and in 1863 with Hance. There were 'a few hundred rambles within a circuit of ten miles of the city'.[10] I imagine that Emma and her children accompanied him on at least some of these outings, for her grand-daughter Kath remembered her saying she had helped him with his collection.[11] One of the pleasures for Emma after life in Whampoa must have been the evening walks, which, once the security situation was improved, could be taken across the river, where the banks separating the rice fields were shaded by fruit trees, or on top of the wide city wall, which a young missionary woman described as covered with 'ferns, flowers and beautiful shrubs'.[12]

Sampson also made long trips up the rivers feeding into the Pearl River Delta, the West River frequently, the North River three times (once with Hance), and the East River with the Hong Kong scholar, Dr Ernst J Eitel.[13] As guests of George B Glover, then Commissioner of the Customs in Canton, Sampson and Hance visited Hainan in 1866, and Sampson went there again with Edward Bowra who became Acting Commissioner when Glover went on home leave in 1870. Bowra, an excellent Chinese scholar, and a botanical enthusiast, described him as one of his and his wife's greatest Canton friends. Bowra's wife Thirza described Canton on her arrival in 1866 as a dull bachelor community with only a half dozen European ladies, but by the time they returned there in 1870 there were many more ladies, and it had become a very sociable place with picnics, tiffins, dances and croquet. Bowra kept a photograph of the formal farewell picnic for the consul, D B Robertson, in which his son was able to pick out Sampson and Archdeacon Gray. When Bowra left in 1874 Sampson bought some of his books and gave a leaving present to his wife Thirza, who was only a few years older than Emma Carrall, his wife's daughter by her first husband.[14] The Carrall friendship with the Bowras continued into the 1900s.

Hance paid Sampson this tribute:

> Before other collectors, to whom I owe and here pay the greatest possible thanks, it is a joy to praise Theophilus Sampson, an indefatigable man, who, stirred by my advice, applied himself to the study of botany, and from the journeys which he made through various districts of the province of Canton, brought back very many new or extremely rare plants, with specimens of almost all of which he liberally enriched my herbarium.[15]

Sampson himself was humble, calling himself *'more…of a collector and presenter than of a scientific nomenclaturist and botanical systematist'.*[16] He therefore sent duplicates of all his new plants to Hance for the latter to name and send on to the great herbaria of Europe. It was not till 6 February 1880 that Sampson himself wrote to the Director of Kew:

'*My esteemed friend Dr. Hance having suggested I should make up a parcel of grasses and Crypanacone for Baron Mueller, it occurred to me that a similar parcel might be acceptable to you.*' [Annotated at Kew: *Rc'd. 23.iv.80. Very good.*][17]

It was just as well he did so, for in 1883 he lost 1,800 plants 'all mounted, carefully preserved and poisoned' when his house, together with those of other foreigners on Shamien, was burnt down during a riot, and they had to take refuge aboard ships. (Figure 3.2 gives an idea of the work involved.) According to *The Times*, the immediate cause was that a group of Portuguese had killed a Chinese man, but both its reporter and Hart related it to the anti-foreign feeling provoked by the French, who were seeking to extend their colony of Indo-China. Sampson's friend, Hance, was Acting Consul there at the time.[18] The French activities were later to affect his stepson.

Canton Society

Jim Carrall, Sampson's stepson, described Shamien as 'one of the most picturesque foreign settlements in China'. After the occupation of Canton this mud flat had been selected as the foreign residential quarter. At British and French government expense, it was provided with a granite embankment and filled in. The larger British portion was divided into eighty-two lots, not all occupied in 1873, while most of the unused French part had become a cricket pitch. The principal buildings were the German and British consulates, the Anglican church (Figure 3.3), next door to which was the imposing house built for the Commissioner of Customs, the Club and Public Hall, and 'thirteen Merchant Hongs' (as Carrall called the buildings belonging to commercial firms).

The Reverend John Henry Gray lived in a large Italian-style two-storey house. He had come out as a young priest in February 1852, and Emma had met him over the christening of her daughter in 1855. His book, *China, A History of the Laws, Manners and Customs of the People* was first published in 1878. Sampson was involved with the church and he and Gray probably shared observations on Chinese customs. Gray was known for his interdenominationalism and for his Chinese friends who invited him into their homes. He married only on his first leave in 1875 so Emma, who left that year to go on leave, would not have known his wife. Mrs Gray published a book on her short stay there, which was abbreviated by illness.

D B Robertson was back in Canton as Consul, remaining there till 1870, but he lived across the river in the centre of the city, in what had been Ye Mingchen's Yamen, surrounded by a large park. Though he was cut off at nightfall from Shamien when the city gates closed, he probably set a tone of friendliness to Chinese officials which would have influenced others in the small British community. Because of his known tact and effectiveness he was even consulted by the French Roman Catholic bishop. He had appointed, as the medical doctor to the community, one of the few Chinese who had obtained a degree from Edinburgh, who still kept his hair in a queue.[19] Thirza Bowra was hesitant about having him attend her first confinement, preferring a Mission doctor. The most distinguished of these was Dr Andrew P Happer, an American Presbyterian missionary and doctor, pastor of the first Presbyterian church in Canton. Happer founded several schools and colleges, one of which became Lingnan University. Hart knew the family well from his time in Canton. His diary shows that in January 1865 he promised Dr Happer $500 a year for four years to pay for his son's education. His daughters Lucy and Lillie worked him a pair of slippers in return. Hart thought Lucy's accompanying letter very poor for a girl of fourteen. We shall see that he revised his opinion of her later.

The majority of those living on Shamien, in the commercial houses, were young men, probably more interested in cricket, riding and shooting than in Chinese culture. Their superiors preferred to live in Hong Kong, exercising supervision through the daily steamer service. However, the older social group to which Sampson and Emma belonged was more interested than most expatriates in Chinese culture and language. It crossed national and professional boundaries and many also had scientific interests. They were in touch with the great debates going on in Europe. Hance wrote from Whampoa in 1867 to Hooker, the Director of Kew Gardens, who had enquired about his attitude to Darwin. Hance referred to his earlier studies of Strauss and other Tübingen theologians on the way the Bible should be interpreted — those whose theories had appalled Hart's missionary friends in Ningpo in 1853 — and added: *'Darwinism, in conclusion, seems to me almost unassailable if it is kept within certain limits; and with this proviso I am an adherent, certainly in no wise prepared to go to the length proposed by the author in his last book.'* Hance's proviso relates to the human soul. He acknowledged all that we have in common with other animals, and then added: *'Against this analogous argument I can only plead the almost universal intuition or instinct, amongst all men and in all times, that we have an immortal soul, and what this may be worth, I do not pretend to say.'*[20]

It was in this social and intellectual atmosphere that Emma's clever daughter, Emma Carrall, grew up, after her brother had left for secondary schooling in England. There was no school, and Emma educated her children, probably with the help of friends like Mrs Hance and the Happers. The Hances were in Canton till 1861, and even after they moved to Whampoa, they were within visiting distance. The chaplain could get there and back in a day. Gray may have helped with scripture and Latin lessons, for, as his wife was later to remark, he only had a small number of Anglicans in his pastoral care.[21] Sampson passed on to the young Jim Carrall an enthusiasm for plants, geology and the microscope. It seems likely the young Emma learnt German from the German consul's family or from missionaries like Lobscheid, and she would have picked up Chinese from her Amah, and maybe more from her stepfather. British and American missionary wives and daughters were learning Chinese so as to be able to teach in it. Emma and her children were probably introduced to the few Chinese families in Canton that were willing to invite Europeans (as Mrs Gray was by her husband). Emma senior wrote to Hart in 1900 after the Boxer rebellion that *'I try to convince them* [English friends] *that the Chinese people are not all cruel'* and it is likely she could cite examples from personal knowledge.

Emma senior's happiness would have increased when her son, Jim Carrall, having been given the promised job in the Customs, was posted to Canton in the early 1870s, serving under their friend Edward Bowra. However, by 1875 Emma's marriage was under strain. She was forty-six, and Sampson would have lost hope of having children with her. His stepson, Jim Carrall, was now self-supporting, but providing for his stepdaughter, in some style, was expensive. By 1875 Emma Carrall was accomplished and elegantly dressed. Sampson could apparently afford a horse and riding habits for her. She was then twenty-three and he might reasonably have expected her to be married and off his hands.

Sampson and the two Emmas went home in July 1875 for his first leave. They travelled more rapidly than on Emma's journey out, for steamers could now use the Suez Canal. He returned alone. Emma senior stayed in London to help her daughter find a husband or a job. She and Sampson lived apart till 1889.

The Teacher

In 1870 Hart had appointed Sampson Teacher of English in the Tongwen Guan in Canton. This was one of the three colleges for Chinese wishing to study Western languages and sciences which the Customs supported. (The most important one was in Beijing, where it was under Hart's personal supervision.) It was a surprising appointment, given Sampson's lack of formal qualifications, but fully justified by its results. Sampson may have feared that he owed this post not to his own merits but to his wife's friendship with Hart, which he came to resent. In 1900 Emma wrote to Hart: *'Do you remember many years ago I asked you not to write to me? This was the reason: Mr. Sampson scolded me for presuming to write to his chief.'*

Sampson continued his writing, and described the exceptional whirlwind in Canton in 1878, which crossed the artificial island and moved north through a densely populated Chinese suburb where 'In a few minutes houses were unroofed or blown down, trees uprooted or twisted short off, thousands of persons killed'. (Expatriates in Shamien, in their stoutly built houses, were not killed.) He collected information on its course and reckoned it travelled at six to nine miles an hour, apologising that a more exact measurement was impossible due to the absence of church clocks to standardise time in Chinese localities, while 'our watches on Shamien, though every one of them is right (in the opinion of the owner), have a strong tendency to differ from one another'.[22] He collected more plants after his house was burnt in 1883, but only from the neighbourhood of Canton, for teaching was now absorbing him.

As a teacher he flourished. He developed his own textbooks. I have not been able to find an example of one in Britain, but on the back of notes found in Kew Gardens were sentences showing the difference between to hear and to listen, different ways of expressing the future etc. which probably became part of the text.[23] He became the expatriate Headmaster of the College. The tribute paid to him on his retirement, and his reply, were published in the *Hong Kong Daily Press*, 12 November 1888, which noted he was one of the oldest foreign residents in Canton, having lived there continuously, except for one year, since 1853. The letters show that he regarded his students as friends, and to some extent they may have compensated him for the lack of his own family. The students wrote:

Dear Sir,

On the eve of your departure from Canton on two years' leave of absence, we humbly beg your kind acceptance of an embroidered scroll, etc, as a mark of our esteem and respect. We are greatly indebted to you for the kindness with which you have treated us, and the instruction which we have received from you, for the past twenty years. You have not only taught us English literature and Western customs, but also moral and virtuous principles. We thank you most heartily for the great interest you have taken in the school and the extensive labour that you have spent in writing books for the sole purpose of instructing us. In short, so much are we indebted to you for your kindness, that we shall never forget it, but shall treasure it up in our hearts through our lives.

They go on to hope that he will return after his two years' leave, 'so that we may again have the benefit of your instruction and the pleasure of your society and friendship'. It was signed by fifty-nine of them.

Sampson replied in the same terms; thanking them for the gifts.

As long as I live I shall treasure them as a memento of my highly esteemed friends and pupils in the T'ung Wen Kwan in Canton, and in course of time I hope they will be preserved by future generations as a family heirloom. *[In his will he left them to his brother, Arthur Birks Sampson.]*

...You speak of my services in higher terms than they deserve. I have but endeavoured to do my duty to the best of my ability, and for that I am rewarded beyond my deserts by your appreciation of my exertions.

Some of you whom I am addressing have long ago ceased to be under my tuition, and some of you are still on the threshold of your education; to all of you I am deeply indebted for having, by your dutiful and respectful conduct, rendered the work of teaching a pleasant occupation…I shall always look back upon the many happy years I have spent in the T'ung Wen Kwan with feelings of the greatest pleasure.

After saying the time had come for settling down amongst his relations, he added:

I shall never cease to take a warm interest in your welfare, and one of the greatest joys of the future years of my life…will be to know of the happiness and prosperity of those in whose education I have had the privilege of taking a part.

He signs it 'Your affectionate friend Theo. Sampson'. An editorial note called him 'one of the oldest foreign residents in Canton, having lived there continuously, except for one year, since 1853'.

Retirement and a Difficult Readjustment

Sampson was in no particular hurry to return to England. On 7 December 1888 he was still in Canton, thanking the Director of Kew for Vols. 1-5 of the *Index of Chinese Plants*, and asking for future numbers to be sent to his brother, the Rev J E Sampson, at Barrow Vicarage, Hull, as he expected to leave China for Melbourne in January and to spend a month or so in Australia. This was presumably for its botanical interest, as there seems to be no family connection. By 3 September 1890, he was writing from 12 Madeira Road, Streatham, London SW, telling Kew to send future parts of the Index to his new address. He had rejoined Emma, and both were living there during the 1891 census. In his letter to Kew he added that *'I have not worked at my Chinese plants since the spring began, but have devoted my time to the collection of British plants; I hope to resume my visits to Kew during the winter, for the identification of some doubtful species.'*[24]

This is an activity that we can imagine Emma enjoyed sharing. One must hope that they recovered a good companionship for she had had to sacrifice her old friends when he returned. In the 1900 letter to Hart quoted earlier she continued: *'When he retired from China I had to give up all my friends because he very much disliked society. I do not regret doing this because it made him happier, & my friends are still kind to me.'* This was quite a sacrifice for a sociable woman, and shows that she still felt affection for him. Madeira Road in Streatham has quite large houses, with room for his books and botanical collections and workshop. The census of 1891 shows that a niece, Jane Sampson, aged twenty-one, who was a 'student of Mathematic', born in India, daughter of his brother, Arthur Birks Sampson, was living with them. Though his 1890 letter to Kew suggests a man of leisure, Sampson may have found that his income was not enough to support the style of life he wished to enjoy. When she reported his death, Emma described herself as the widow of an Inspector of Schools, suggesting that he preferred to find work rather than to live in the cramped houses to which Mrs Henry Gray noted that many exiles were obliged to return.

When he died on 29 December 1897 his estate was valued for probate at £10,568. A good half of his financial assets, as well as items of property (houses, the ivory paintings of his parents, and books) went to his brothers and sister, with smaller amounts for two nephews, three Chinese friends, and an English friend and executor. The residue was left to his 'dear wife'. This left Emma rather badly off. It probably did not much exceed £4,000, from which Emma would have been lucky to get £120 to £130 p.a. in interest. The will was made in April 1896, and provided that, if she predeceased him, £2,000 from the residue should go to his stepson, Jim Carrall, and the remainder to his siblings.

Sampson is a difficult man to characterise. He was clever, conscientious, and worked hard at whatever he undertook. He was loyal to the family he had left in his teens, and probably devoted to Emma from the time they first met. His failure to have children may have soured him, for being the father of sons was even more important in China than in Britain. Settling on his return with Emma suggests that affection for her was still present — though Kew Gardens was probably also a reason for living in London rather than near the two brothers still in Yorkshire. He won the respect and affection of his students, and of men like Hance. People liked him, though there were acerbic notes in his character, which spice some of his writings. His failure to take advantage of the type of education which his father could evidently afford for his brothers, and being instead left stranded in poverty in Whampoa, possibly gave him a feeling of inferiority. This could have made him prickly, and very desirous of achieving recognition and status by his own intelligence and hard work. Money does not seem to have been a great consideration to him, and his failure to leave Emma enough to live in reasonable comfort as his widow may have been due to over-optimism about the size of his final assets.

Hart's first letter to my aunt Kath in 1896 shows that Emma felt free to resume their correspondence when he was no longer her husband's boss. After Sampson's death she moved back to southwest London, where she was in 1881 census, to be nearer to her old friends. In 1900 she was writing to Hart from 'Thirlemere', a house in New Park Road, Norbiton. Her September 1900 letter following the siege of Peking shows both her long-lasting affection for Hart and the sociability she had sacrificed for Sampson:

> *I feel I must give myself the pleasure of writing to you. I congratulate you warmly on your narrow escape from cruel persons, it makes one look with emotions of gratitude to the God of all mercy for his infinite goodness towards you & to all those who were with you. When we heard that you were all safe our relief was intense. I shall never forget the thrill of joy it gave us. I say we because I see some of Jim's dear wife's sisters, nieces, uncle & nephews daily. Their home is about twelve minutes walk from me and Dr. & Mrs. Pritchard live nearly opposite to the Fawcus family, our chief topic of conversation is about China.... I like Dr. & Mrs. Pritchard very much, their kind sociable ways are delightful. He has been giving me his advice. I am now stronger than I have been for many years, for those who have lived in India or China it is best to go to a Dr. who has had experience of either of those places. [Dr Pritchard had worked in India.]*

The Fawcus family, to which Emma refers, was the Northumberland family into which her son, Jim Carrall, had married on his first leave from Hart's Customs Service in China.

CHAPTER FOUR

EMMA CARRALL AND HART'S MID-LIFE CRISIS

Hart liked two kinds of women. The first group were those who were highly intelligent and who shared his interest in China, with whom he could have deep friendships. The second group were those who were kind, uncomplaining, and amenable to their husbands' needs and the demands of a Customs career. In the years 1875–81 he faced the fact that Hester fell into neither group. Even musically he, a late starter on the violin, was outpacing her, and in these years there are no references to her accompanying him. However, separation from her would also mean loss of his adored daughter. He had already lost the children he had with Ayaou (Chapter Two) and seems to have put them out of his mind, but their problems brought them back, along with their mother, in 1875–8.

Loyalty was a key element of his character: loyalty to his work, his family, his friends, his country. Conflicts between these loyalties caused internal tension and depression, leading to a complete breakdown in 1878–9. Work came first, so marriage could only succeed if his wife could understand and share his goals. The crisis with Hester coincided with, was even in some way provoked by, the visit of my great-aunt, Emma Sampson's daughter, Emma Carrall, in 1875. Her photograph, taken at this time, appears as Figure 4.1. It also coincided with the first conflict of loyalties between his home country and the country he had undertaken to serve and also with poignant reminders of his children by Ayaou.

Emma Carrall's Visit, 1875

I discovered what Emma Carrall had meant to him when I read this letter from Hart to my Aunt Kath, written on 26 January 1902. He was explaining that her second visit to Peking must be delayed:

I am hoping to — or rather I <u>was</u> — hoping to have my first garden party on Wednesday, the last of April: but I do not feel inclined for it now. That day will be May Eve and is associated with one of my dearest friends, Mrs. Brazier,[1] who has just passed away, and I don't look forward to it now in the same way as before. The news of her death came to me on the 14th and I c'd not believe it at first, but a reply telegram confirmed it on the 18th. She died on the 12th — a quiet, conscious, painless death — and was buried on the 15th. The child, a girl, was alive and well, and she had just got my November letter assenting to be Godfather, & it pleased her before she died. I still see her graceful figure moving about & I can hear her talking, & I cannot still realize that she has left us & will be no more seen on earth. I am a bit case-hardened: I have known so many people that have died, & have had to part with so many friends that the fountain of tears is dry and death has also become a commonplace in a long life and does not hurt now as it once did. But I feel dear Mrs. Brazier's death sadly: we were excellent friends and I had the greatest respect & liking for her. Your papa's sister, Emily [sic] Carrall, was also a great friend of mine long ago and spent a month with me in 1875: she was a lovely girl then. I had some photographs of her, from seven years of age up to twenty-four: but those terrible Boxers deprived me of all my treasures...[2]

The last photograph he had is likely to have been Figure 4.2, taken in London in 1876 or 1877.

This entry made me search Hart's 1875 diary. In the first months it was mainly on business matters, with some personal meditations. It also refers to his seven-year-old daughter Evey, more frequently mentioned than either his two-year-old son, Bruce, or his wife. On a significant birthday he wrote:

20 February. Today I am 40. [A self-examination of his failings follows —*how inferior I am to others.*]

Evey was very sad this morning because she had no present for me. Yesterday she wrote a very good round-hand letter to her grandmother.

Dear Grandma Bredon, Please send me a letter soon. I send love. Evey.

One must ask, and maybe Hart wondered, why Hester had not prompted their daughter to make something for her father. A few days later Hester was again showing a certain lack of motherly skill:

Saturday 13 March. Hessie gave me a great fright yesterday. She came running and shouts out that Evey had cut her tongue. I thought she had said cut her throat. I ran myself and found Evey with her mouth full of blood. So we sent for the doctor. We then washed her mouth and found she had only bitten her lip! So we sent again to tell the doctor not to come. Hessie had given Evey a tap on the shoulder, and she, throwing herself on the floor, had hit her chin against the table. Hinc illae lachrymae. [From this the tears.]

On Saturday, 20 March he made various social calls, and *'Gossiped with Mdm. Butzow. Then home.'* There is no mention of Hester accompanying him. Later entries show that he found Mdm. Butzow good for a gossip — her husband, Eugène de Butzow, headed the Russian Legation. The gossip was probably in French or German, and Hester may not have learnt either as schoolgirl. Peking did not have the varied expatriate community of a port city, so Hester's main associates were her husband's staff and a few diplomatic families. Many of the latter had aristocratic lineages and a very different background from that of a provincial doctor's daughter. One of Hart's letters to Campbell suggests that the wives of successive Heads of Mission at the British Legation looked down on her. On 5 August 1877, when Hester was in London, he wrote to Campbell:

I was amused to hear how Ladies Wade and Alcock received Mrs. Hart. I consider it Mrs. H.'s duty to go and see the ladies she had known in Peking, and instead of regarding her as "snubbed" by them not returning the visit, etc., I merely think that the "credit balance" is in our favour, and that they have shown themselves ill-natured and ill-mannered.

(Calling and leaving cards was then a highly regulated social routine amongst the upper class, and the failure to return the call showed that they did not wish to continue the acquaintance.)

Hart at this stage was trying to lessen Hester's isolation and make her life in Peking more agreeable. On 26 April 1873 he told Campbell that he had appointed Robert Bredon (referred to as R.E.B.), Hester's eldest brother, as Assistant Secretary, so he was also in Peking. Appointing him at a senior rank caused talk, but, like Alcock, he was a former army surgeon, a man with three degrees from Trinity College, Dublin, and Hart considered him one of the smartest fellows he knew. On 13 March 1875 he emphasised to Campbell that the governess required for Evey must enrich her parents' domestic life: *'As we want to have an addition to our society in the Governess to be got for Evey, I wish her — apart from what she may have to do as a teacher — to be a thoroughly good musician, both playing and singing well...'*

The diary of 12 March shows that Miss Carrall was escorting up from Canton a German nursery maid and a lady's maid. This suggests that Emma spoke German, and that Hart was able to use this as an excuse for inviting the woman he had first noticed in 1858 as an attractive child to come and stay for a month before she left China permanently. *'Monday 22 March. Miss Carrall arrived with the two German girls. The lady's maid is a tidy looking little woman, but the nurse, a big blonde, is...captivating!'* The rest of the entry is work-related. The "big blonde" was called Frieda. His enthusiasm about her looks was perhaps intended to divert Hester from the pleasure he probably showed at the arrival of Emma.

Miss Carrall, as the Harts' house guest, would have attended their social events, though not at first specifically mentioned. Thus: *Wed. 23 March: 'Dined at Butzow's last night...Hessie wore her new white dress and looked well. Mr. Wade complimented me on my taste. After dinner a "hop", got home about 12'.* When the Harts held a dinner party on Friday 26 March the entry is mainly about a dispute with China. The British Legation's interpreter, Margary, had been murdered on a mission to explore a trading route to Burma via Yunnan (Kunming) on 21 February. Thomas Wade, now the head of the British Legation in Peking, was determined to use this to extort further trade concessions from China. He frequently visited Hart about this, at this stage on friendly terms.

Emma was specifically mentioned on Saturday 26 March:

Dined last night at de Rochechouart's — arrived 7 — found 7.30 to be the dinner hour — and spent ¾ hour in the cold salon. 24 sat down: I had Miss Carrall on my left and Mayers on my right. Hessie was between Butzow & Wade — who sat opposite de R…

Wednesday 31 March. Last night dined at Wade's meeting the Butzows and Von Brandt, with Miss Carrall, there were only eight. A note (Mayers) called Wade from the table…. . Coming away at 11 ½ his last words were "I have got the documents". So the German affair is not to lead to a breach yet awhile: just as well for many reasons, but how long will this kind of peace last?

The Comte de Rochechouart was the French Minister in Peking. Von Brandt was the German Minister, and Germany was also in dispute with China at this time. Wade, like Hart, found Miss Carrall someone who could grace a small party at the highest level of Peking's international society, and at a tricky diplomatic moment.

But Emma's Peking life was not all diplomatic dinners. She also played with Evey and kept company with Hester, who, at twenty-seven, was only four years older than her.

Friday 2 April. Last night I smoked in the dining room and Miss C played me the prank of retiring Evey via the Billiard room escorted by R.E.B., to give me a surprise on my return to the library in finding her gone. Today she & Hessie & the Misses Lane have gone on a picnic to the Wan Shaw Shan. Mr. Butzow cried off yesterday, & I too am at home & minding my business.

Saturday 3 April. Hessie's picnic was a success but Miss Carrall got something in her eye and is suffering a good deal.

Sunday 4 April. [After discussing business matters] Hot wind blowing today. Hessie and Miss Carrall gone to walk outside the Chien Men.

Tuesday 6 April. Rode out with Hessie, Miss Carrall & R.E.B. & called on Mrs. Schenswisky and Mrs. Pietinks. I don't like the rate at which they go through the streets. Miss C. likes to go fast.

He was away from Peking for some days in April. The next entries referring to Emma are in May.

Monday 3 May R.E.B. with Miss Carrall & Mrs. Florin have gone to the Quin Ming Quin today. They got back at two having been out from 7.30.

Sunday 9 May. Hessie says Miss C. has been telling R.E.B. that she might be K.'s w. but seems to think better of C'ton H.

This is one of the few entries reporting Hester's remarks. The abbreviations presumably refer to two of Emma's admirers.

Thursday, 13 May has an enigmatic entry.

Dined last night at the Russian Legation. Hessie went down in Gibb's cart, Mrs. G. and Miss C. having the chairs. Rindhoff, Brandt & Otie were the other outsiders there. It is very curious having Mrs. G. and Miss C. in the house together. Well: all things end, & this is their last day here — tomorrow they go. R.E.B. goes with them — he'll stay a fortnight at T'tsin to work in the office there...

Friday 14 May. Mrs. Glover & Miss Carrall left...this morning at 7 ½ & were at Chow at 11 am. It is doubtful which steamer they'll be able to go by for the Shingking leaves on Friday, instead of Sunday. Glover from S'hai writes [entry continues on business matters. The isolation of Peking is noticeable.]

The American George B Glover had been in the Customs since August 1859. In 1875 he was Commissioner at Shanghai. One of his interests was coinage, and Hart at this time was hoping that amongst the concessions Wade would gain from the dispute would be Chinese agreement to establish a mint and a national coinage to replace the mixture of various coins, often chipped, that had had to be weighed by Buckton's comprador to establish their value. Just before going on home leave from Canton in 1870, Glover, aged forty-nine, had made a runaway marriage with the nineteen-year-old Lucy Happer, daughter of the distinguished Presbyterian missionary whom Hart had known in Canton. According to Thirza Bowra, Lucy loved Glover *devotedly* and as her family had known Glover and welcomed him into their home on the most *intimate* terms, she was surprised at the parental opposition, which led the groom to hire a yacht, and to get the captain to marry them at sea. They later also married in church. Born and brought up in Canton, Lucy Glover is likely to have spoken Cantonese fluently.[3]

She and Emma, twenty-five and twenty-three respectively, are likely to have known each other well.

Over the next two years business matters brought Glover and his wife frequently to Hart in the north, or took Hart to stay with them in Shanghai. On this occasion only Glover's wife is mentioned. The discreet diary, written in the house of which Hester was mistress, does not say why it was curious having these two attractive young women together, and, apart from showing that Emma liked riding fast and playing practical jokes (incidentally ignoring the convention that the billiard room was for men only), it does not explain why Emma was remembered as a great friend in 1902. But a letter to Campbell in July tells more:

> *2 July 1875*
>
> *The Sampson family went home from Canton a month ago…Sampson married a Mrs. Carrall [sic]. Her son is J. W. Carrall, now a second class clerk in our Service. There is, besides, a daughter, Miss Emma W. Carrall — an exceedingly clever girl and a great ally of mine. There is some trouble in the family and Miss C, if she doesn't marry, will probably try to do something for her own support in England. One of her ideas was to become a Hospital Nurse (and do mother to medical students!), but I suggested that if she found she must work, she ought to look in the direction of Savings Banks, Post Offices, Telegraph work, etc. and it then occurred to me to tell her to go and see you — so I gave her your <u>office</u> address. Now it is possible that she may never go near you — but it is also possible she may: if she does go to see you, be quite practical with her — give her your best advice, and, if she wants to know how to go about it to get any such employment, try and assist her, please. I wish her brother — not a bad lad by any means — had her brains! (I fancy Samivel's father's advice was not taken: Hinc illae lachrymae.)[4]*

The diary told us nothing about the conversations in which she evidently told him that her stepfather, Sampson, was tired of supporting her, and her determination to find work by which she could support herself. The letter shows the very limited openings for an intelligent woman who wanted to earn her living in the England of 1875.

Tensions with Hester — and Two Sets of Children

The same letter of 2 July 1875 also tells Campbell that the musical governess and 'house-companion' required in March is no longer wanted:

> Mrs. Hart has positively declared that she will go home next
> spring: if she does it will be as well not to have sent anyone to us,
> and she seems very decided. Last year (as also in 1871 & 73) I
> wanted her to go back but she would not; my mother and father
> were then alive, and I sh'd have liked them to see Evey; but both
> are now dead...and home, and life are all changed for me, and, the
> fact of being an ancestor, and not a descendant being now
> uppermost, I'd rather keep Evey with me, — but if her Mama goes
> (and it will be good for her health, mentally and bodily, to do so)
> of course she'll go too.

Thus, at some time between March and July, Hester had determined to leave China — and Hart. Despite his attempted discretion, she must have noticed his affection for, and admiration of, the clever Miss Carrall, and as we shall see, of Mrs Glover. Hester, twenty-eight in August 1875, was decidedly not the accommodating, uncomplaining wife. The young lassie whom he had described in 1866 as *"able to hold her own against most comers"* could also oppose her husband. He also evidently felt Peking was making her neurotic.

His irritation with her ways shows in an entry on *Mon 7 June:*

> Signed my will...Hessie trips off for Tung Chow at 4 pm — ought
> to have started at noon. I thought they'd never get away [so
> unlike the punctual departure of Mrs G and Miss C]. Evey is
> sentimental over our last day together and is inclined to cry, so is
> Hessie too. Rain keeps off, but darkness is increasing.

Hester and the children were probably off to Chefoo, already regarded as a summer resort, where the IG had a bungalow reserved for him in the grounds of the Commissioner's house. She had spent some previous summers there, away from the heat and dust of Peking.

We can have sympathy for Hester. Besides resenting his admiration of Mrs G and Emma, she was probably bored with the small Peking society, tired of the social and language problem she had with some of her husband's associates, and fed up with the lack of amenities (where you travelled in a cart, not in a well sprung carriage). She was unfortunate in experiencing difficult births and may have found that the demands of motherhood exceeded its compensations. Hart probably had this in mind when he told Campbell on 1 September 1871:

> *Mrs. Wade has just presented H.B.M.'s representative with a third son…and only married three years and three months. For my part I think it's unfair to maltreat a woman thus…means so much positive suffering and so much slavery and drudgery for the gentler sex, that one ought to — but this is delicate ground and I'd better pull up!*

Even within marriage he evidently disciplined himself to avoid over-burdening his wife.

For his part, Hart had not only just turned forty, when many men review their life and whether they are achieving what they want from it, but, as the 2 July letter shows, he had also recently lost both his parents, whom he had so proudly supported as a young man. Now it was he who was the older generation, the head of the Hart family. Ulster was special to him while it was the home of his parents; it became less special after their death. While he had spent most of his 1866 leave there, in 1878–9 he paid it only a brief visit. He had lost not only his parents but also his attachment to a particular 'home'. China was now his real home.

At the very same time another part of his past was catching up with him. He had received an abrupt reminder of his amenable Chinese companion, Ayaou, and his three children by her. *'Thursday 3 June. Some mail…Mrs. D writes that her wards are growing up & what's to be done with them by & by?'*

They were in London, where Hester was so soon to reside. She must not meet them. He wrote on 5 June 1875 to Campbell, without imagining what the children might now be like:

> *In 1866 I sent home my three wards — (Anna, Herbert and Arthur Hart) and Smith Elder & Co. committed them to the charge of their book-keeper's wife, Mrs. Davidson, with whom they still remain. Time has slipped away so fast that I have put off longer than I ought the duty of arranging for the future of these youngsters, and as Anna is now sixteen, I must take the affair in hand without delay.*

As to the boys, no special difficulty presents itself. I want them sent at once to Clifton College [near Bristol]. Herbert is just thirteen and Arthur almost ten years old, and at these ages, the Junior school would, I suppose, be the right place for them, and when being placed at one of the boarding houses, I want it to be arranged that they should spend their 1875–76 vacations there. From the first I want it to be understood that they are to be trained for the Indian Civil Service, unless they either show no fitness for it, or develop a special talent in some other direction.

As regards Anna, I want her to be sent for three years to a Protestant Boarding school on the continent where she can devote herself to music, French and German, and where she will be comfortably lodged and well treated.

I know no-one to apply for aid in this affair except yourself.... . As soon as you find a girls' boarding school of the kind wanted, forward Anna to it, or take her yourself if you can spare the time.... . I want the child to have a comfortable home, carry on her general studies, acquire French and German, and to become as proficient a musician as nature will allow her to be.

His requirements for Anna's education shows the accomplishments he valued in a woman.

With Hester and the children away, he turned back to his music, but found he was struggling with his violin exercises. Then a new idea came into his head, and he jotted down a tune which rather pleased him.

Going to bed & feeling happy & well I did what I never did before: in my prayers I prayed that the time I spend on the violin may not be wasted but may be a good kind of recreation for myself &...my playing or my composing the source of innocent & diverting pleasure for others.

Well this morning I practised as usual & to my astonishment found myself able to play without the music one of the exercises I had been trying over...yesterday! I say nothing about the connection of the two things as cause & effect, but as simple <u>sequences</u> they are curious: bungling, prayer, success; of course the supernatural <u>can</u> be explained away, but I never prayed for a blessing on my music till last night, & this morning I played *through a difficult exercise <u>without the music</u>.* (He continues for some lines in the same vein.)

Hart, like many thinking men, would have been challenged by Darwin's *Origin of Species* which came out in 1859. He seems, like Meadows in Ningpo, and Hance in Whampoa, to have moved towards Strauss's interpretation of large parts of the Bible, including apparently supernatural interventions, as myths told with a purpose rather than as literal truths. The official church was doing little to help intellectuals resolve conflicts between old religious beliefs and new knowledge.

His diary does not mention family again till '*Friday 22 October. Fires in most of the rooms today, adding materially to the comfort of each. Evey & Bruce began to stay in the room with their former nurse Frieda last night.*' (Frieda had been promoted to governess.) Hart had been complaining in his diary that it was colder inside than out since the beginning of the month, evidently with no effect on Hester, who seems to have retained childhood notions that fires should not be lit till November. Warmth was very important to Hart. He put it even above food in listing basic necessities. After a particularly trying journey to Tientsin in November 1876, in a cart whose jolting over a stony road gave him a headache, the comfort of a sparsely furnished but warm room led him to this meditation. At the basic level '*you may define comfort as freedom from cold and hunger; as you rise in the scale other things come in, and, arrived at my standpoint, cleanliness, taste, fitness and repose come to be the chief attributes, always presupposing one has warmth and food*'.

The fires cheered him up, and he wrote poetry and enjoyed his children.

> *Sat 23 October. For the first time for months versified a little today. It's curious how the ability to write verse comes and goes…*

> *Thurs 28 October. Evey dined with us last night — she is to do so every Wednesday evening. This morning* [after reporting Evey's talk of dreams] *I said to Bruce "Well, young gentleman". He at once retorted. "You young gentleman! Me — Mr. Bruce!" Dear little children they both are. God bless them.*

> *Sunday 31 October. Hessie and Evey went with me to Church today…Bruce at breakfast "You too much — too much". Curious to watch intellect developing & language picked up!*

*Sunday 7 November. Very few people at church. Finished first part
of my report today.*

From this point on, the diary shows that on many Sundays and
holidays, which should have been days of leisure with the family, he
was working hard on a paper on the benefits of commerce for China,
which the Yamen had asked him to write in response to Wade's pressure
for more treaty ports.

The winter season began in November, with the Harts giving dinner
parties and dining out.

Friday 12 November. Last night had our first dinner party.

*Saturday 13 November. Last night Hessie & I read till eleven
W??'s paper on self-assistance. Shallow. He'll do better ten years
hence.*

This is the only example I have found in my scanning of the 1875–
6 diaries of him sharing an intellectual interest with Hester. As the next
entry and the one of 27 March 1875 shows, they did not always even
manage church together to discuss the sermon: '*Sunday 14 November....
Today Evey & I went to Church. Hessie did not go. Collins preached a good
sermon.*'

But his children fascinated him.

*Thursday 17 November. Evey anxious to say me a portion she had
learnt yesterday: 'God is the shepherd I don't want'. Dear little
child, what an innocent loving little darling she is! Bruce takes my
gloves to bed with him, he has a most extraordinary mania for
gloves...*

But, alas, the children he had had with Ayaou were still causing
problems. He would have received during the autumn Campbell's reports
on his arrangements for them. Campbell had visited Mrs Davidson in
August, and found that children treated her as their mother, and she
said she loved them as she did her own. Herbert was a strong healthy
lad, looking English except for his hair and eyes, Anna more Chinese,
and Arthur thoroughly so, and rather delicate. At this first interview
Campbell thought they looked happy, spoke nicely, and had good
manners, and Anna could play the piano, accurately but without showing
much musical feeling. However, when Campbell took the boys to Clifton,

they failed the entry examination, and the headmaster recommended they spend at least a year or two at a private school run by the Rev. Bird. Campbell, on better acquaintance, realised the boys might have social as well as educational problems at Clifton — they dropped their Hs — so he followed the headmaster's advice. Mr Bird only had about fourteen boys, whom he treated as family. Hart, on receiving his letters in November, told Campbell to pay Mrs Davidson anything that was fair as she had evidently treated them kindly. Campbell, meanwhile, was experiencing some trouble: Mrs D's friends were advising her not to give up the children without compensation. Her husband was annoyed with their sudden removal, and was refusing to give his wife money for their clothes. Campbell provided £20 for their outfits, as 'they only had a few home-made clothes'. In Victorian terms, the Davidsons were lower middle-class, respectable, but unskilled in the ways and language of the professional classes.[5]

Campbell also found a home for Anna with a Miss Peile, who had a school for about twelve girls in Vevey, Switzerland. He took her there himself and told Hart he thought she would be comfortable there. Poor Anna, separated not only from the woman she had come to regard as Mother, but also from her brothers, evidently felt homesick and lonely. On 10 December Campbell passed on to Hart notes from both Anna and Herbert, commenting that he had written to Anna telling her to cheer up, and sending her twenty francs for Christmas. He had also advised Miss Peile to improve her knowledge of English and the elementary subjects where she was deficient, and to let her tackle only one foreign language at a time, leaving German aside until she had some mastery of French. During their journey to Vevey he had evidently come to feel a personal interest in her well-being. His letters made Hart realise that his expectations for his children might have to be reduced.

23 November 1875

...I am disappointed in the youngsters' educational achievements, but it can't be helped. Ask Mr. Bird to watch them carefully, and advise as to what they are likely to be best fitted for. Above all things I'd like to get them into the Indian Civil Service, but I don't want to push them for anything they are not likely to accomplish. What an ugly little beggar Arthur is! Anna is very like what her mother was when I first saw her in 1857, only her mother was not

pock-marked. I want Anna to stay at school four years more, and I hope she will be a nice, presentable girl by that time. Her mother was one of the most amiable and sensible people imaginable. Her father thought he was a wise man once, but subsequently confessed in his heart of hearts, that he was a fool!

Amiable and sensible — ah, yes! Surely Ayaou would have let him have fires when he wanted them!

Meanwhile, Hester was back from Chefoo with their children, and the Peking winter season was in full swing. He had to forget his illicit children and get on with normal life.

Tues 25 November. Hessie rather seedy since Tuesday. Much against her will I sent for Bushell.

Friday 26 November. Guests to dinner. Hessie did not appear.

Sat 27 November. Hessie is much better. Her Japanese dressing gown is very becoming, & its softness, lightness, looseness & warmth disincline her to get out of it.

He still found her attractive, and there were parts of married life he was going to miss. Was this in his mind on Monday, 31 January, 1876: *'Last night lay long awake.'* He describes a struggle in his mind between duty and inclination *'despite my age'*. The *'duty'* may have been not to get her pregnant at this stage.

The time of Hester's return to England was drawing near, but is not directly discussed in the diary, even in the entry on Monday, 14 February. "Valentine's Day, 1876" – see Figure 4.4.

Oh! The days for Valentines are gone — forever gone! There's nothing half so sweet in life. As Love's young dreams — and its concomitants.

People go on and grow into old fogies — & love —

O you young rascal, where do you go to?

By this time he would have received from Campbell Anna's sad little letter. Love's young dreams with Ayaou had led to the "concomitant" of the little daughter, who had entranced him at first sight. I think this note is about Ayaou, for he was not an emotional young man when he courted Hester. The diary in February is otherwise mainly concerned with his frequent discussions with Wade on the still unsolved dispute with China.

By March the house must have been in full packing mode and the signs of departure everywhere. On 16 March he told Campbell of Hester's travel arrangements and asked him to open an account for her at his London bank. He showed his feelings in his diary.

> The day of their departure is so near, and the parting is such a considerable one, that I can hardly settle to anything today: at times I realise the separation suddenly and then feel as if I were just about to "walk the plank" or be hung! I can hardly believe that ten years have actually gone by since our party sailed eastward in the Alphée, what changes!

Hester's departure would not have caused much gossip in Peking. It followed one pattern of expatriate life, in which a wife resided at least part of the time in the home country to oversee the education of the children.[6] But Hart was uncertain whether they would meet again.

> Sat 18 March. Evey dined with us last night and would have it that I was packed up & going home. "I know you are, I know it, I know you are." Poor dear pet, I fear she'll feel for me once she's off.

> Sun 19 March...10 a.m. Hessie, Evey & Bruce, with Frieda and Dorothea...left a quarter of an hour ago. Bruce was joyous going on a journey, Evey crying to me to an extent that made her almost shrink from me & Hessie tearful enough in all conscience... . So I am alone and my dear ones are gone. When will we meet again? China? At home? Here or hereafter? God alone knows. His will be done. If not on earth may we with all we have loved...be with each other in a better life...

> Mon 20 March. Breakfast & dinner & after dinner yesterday & early breakfast this morning were very lonely times for me. How I miss them — Hessie, & Evey & Bruce!

The diary then continues much as usual, with occasional notes on Hester's progress.

Thurs 17 April. Hessie wrote from H.K. 3rd & 6th . All well so far.

Sat 29 April. Hessie's party ought to be getting away from Aden today. How far they are away from me!…

30 April. Up at 7½ for the first time in the last six weeks! Had my usual hour at the violin before tea & again after twelve — have lost power considerably, both in bowing & fingering, since my fingers bring me up, but I think I shall soon regain what I had, & move on a little…

Mon 1 May. [A holiday, but though the entry was longer than usual, covering 2 pages, there was scant reference to Hester.] *It is not yet nine o'clock, & yet I have fiddled an hour & half & some 120 lines of Virgil.* [Half page on a dream about Evey being ill.] *Felt uncomfortable ever since… . French mail in. Letters from Hessie and Jem from Saigon.*

His only comment on Hester's letter is an item about Bruce losing a finger nail. He passed rapidly on to a letter about a forthcoming new arrival at the Russian Legation, and his visit there in consequence.]

At least, his other children seem to have settled down. On 21 April 1876 Campbell enclosed a letter addressed to Hart from Anna, and the reports on the boys. These must have been good, for Campbell wrote that he was glad they were all happy. The children seem to have been able to capture the hearts of the people to whom they were entrusted.

A Crisis of Political Loyalties, 1876

Meanwhile, Wade's exploitation of the Margary murder was building up into a major crisis between Britain and China:

Friday 12 May 1876. Wade in again. [Argumentative discussion, not altogether friendly, amongst other things over special rules for ports on the Yangzi.] *He then had a big glass of sherry & went…*

Saturday 13 May. A coast mail in last night. R.E.B. writes Sampson is dangerously ill & not likely to come out again!

Bredon was now Commissioner of Customs in Canton. Sampson was on leave in England with his wife and stepdaughter. The entry continues with several business matters, but the news of Sampson reminded him of the significance of Emma Carrall's visit the year before. The diary shows depression setting in — the next entries are melancholic and introspective:

Sunday 14 May. Yesterday year Mrs. Glover & Miss Carrall left. Today, wrote a long letter to Andreas Hippe, a chit to Mrs. Glover & a letter to Katie.... French mail in: no letter from Hessie! From Teresa [his sister] *I have the news of her husband's death; she thinks he died a Christian's death.... What a relief! Twenty years tied to an old man (married at 44, died at 65) whom she c'd not love, — away from friends, — suffering, deceived, ill-treated. Poor girl! Perhaps she was God's gift to him; but what a treasure someone else has lost in her! And now, what to do with her? She has four daughters, a widow, & has not a penny.* [Teresa was the sister whose marriage he had heard of without approval on Christmas Day 1854 in Ningpo. Now she was another relative needing help. It is a reminder of the perils of widowhood for Victorian women.]

Monday 15 May. Had horrible dream last night. [He was condemned to death — legal dodges help him escape.] *This morning, "it is borne in on me", as the saying is, that life is but very short, & especially that what we scheme for, gain or win here, we must leave here, & we cannot take with us.... Thus there's that two years' gratuity...£16,000, how many will envy me it, & what a value I myself have put on it — how fearful I might miss it — how anxious to arrange to get it! And now that I am on the point of touching it, I declare I almost shrink, afraid that it will crumble — or that I will disappear — the moment it is in my hands. Even suppose I live a few years to enjoy all this wealth that has come to me so surprisingly, in a few years I must go away & leave it all — I must go "naked" like others, or I must come near the new life not a whit better — perhaps all the worse — for it, than others!...God help me! Give me grace & goodness!*

He is referring to the additional year's salary after each seven years of service, which he had negotiated with the Chinese for Customs staff, in lieu of a pension. In his case, paid £8,000 a year, it amounted to a considerable sum — not so for my grandfather, then a second-class-clerk, likely to have earned less than £400 but much better off than humble tide-waiters. Salary differences were large in those days.

Hart's depression was not only due to the absence of family and the contrast revived in his mind between his wife and his ideal woman, but also to worries as to whether his services to China would be worth the sacrifices he was making:

> *Sunday 4 June...How lazy I feel! How tired of Peking life — of this horrible isolation!*
>
> *The Yamen has not sent to consult me about Wade's affairs for an age: is it considerateness, or suspicious?...I feel half inclined at times to go and say "Wd you like me to resign? I'm ready to do so" Then I think: no, my happiness does not wait in talking to no purpose at the Yamen, I have held on till now for a purpose, & I am gradually — nay, quickly nearing it. Shall I not hold on a year or two more till it is won? O life, O life! O life! What does your worth consist of for me who begins to query my value? Is this habit of introspection a good one? It grows gloom & doubt & dread: it fixes one's eyes on the perils of the bottom — shutting one's mind too much to the fact that between our ship & there the good God has placed many a fathom of unnavigable & keel-protecting water! The fact of it is one is constantly brought to say with 'the Preacher' "vanity of vanities, all is vanity". Let us hear the conclusion of the whole matter: "Fear God & keep his commandments — for this is the whole duty of man!" Yes, doubt as we may, wander as we please — sin as we choose — despair if we will — this is what we come to in the end. Away from Christ there is no true peace, for the Christian alone is there fixed & certain happiness. Let the eyes be single — let a man give himself unreservedly to God — and doubts & fears disappear & Satan sinks, abashed. As it is, with me, I feel I am full of sin, my mind is full of horrible blasphemies, and I find it harder to give up wicked thoughts than to refrain from outward sin! "God have mercy on me, a sinner!"*
>
> *Sunday 18 June. In the afternoon, read thro' Job at a sitting (1 ½ hours). What magnificent passages! Nothing has been written*

since to surpass some of them, and all the stories, all the speculations, all the discernment of the 30 centuries that have gone by, have not advanced the wisdom of the humble souls or changed the language of the scorner in respect of the Almighty! Who worships must use the language of this wonderful book to rise to the highest flights of devotion — who believes in nothing can do nothing to increase the force of the negation to be found therein ready for him.

On 21 June he remembered that it was Hester's twenty-ninth birthday, but did not find time to write the intended letter. He sent her his thirteenth letter on 23 June, when he also told Campbell that his twenty-third summer in China and another month of "agony" over the Margary case were taking toll. Isolation from Wade was an agony, for Wade had been his senior in the consular service, and the chief of the first foreign-run Customs service in Shanghai. He was a noted Chinese scholar. Hart had been able to work happily with previous British Ministers towards an outcome he could feel was good for both sides, but Wade also was suffering from his long years in China, and was no longer at his best.[7]

Hart knew that China's leadership was fragile and weak. The young Emperor, the son of the Dowager Empress Cixi, had died in 1874, and Cixi was still struggling to appoint another Emperor who would also be under her tutelage. Wade's aggressive stance aggravated the tension that Hart felt between his position as a servant of the Chinese government, whom he should protect as far as he could in these circumstances and his feelings as a British citizen and former British diplomat, in a situation which could lead to another Sino-British war. The opening of more ports to trade was, Hart thought, in China's interest, as his paper for the Tsungli Yamen on commercial development showed, and he hoped to gain other beneficial reforms, such as a national coinage and a national postal service. (The Customs used its own courier service for its internal mail, and there were foreign post offices for dispatching foreign mail from the Treaty Ports. China had a good horse post system for internal Government mail, but its private citizens had to use whatever commercial operators functioned in the nearest town). But Hart thought Wade was going too far in demanding that the Governor of Yunnan (Kunming) be brought to trial in Peking (despite being cleared of direct involvement in Margary's murder by a British diplomat sent to investigate). He wrote to Campbell on 27 June 1876:

> Nothing else he could ask would be more thoroughly distasteful to the Govt. of China...because nothing else would force it...before all China...[to] say that the foreigner is a personage to be respected... . As an <u>Englishman</u> I don't think he could devise a better demand...but as <u>I.G. of Customs</u>, I know that China would rather do anything else, and that the Dynasty will go to pot rather than consent to this without war...[He thought the person most desirous of peace on the Chinese side was] the fighting fellow, the friend of Vavasseur and Krupp, <u>Li Hung Chang</u> himself! He knows what a thrashing he would get...' [and that defeat would strip him of his honours and wealth].

Meanwhile, inward struggles to maintain the duty he felt to his absent wife continue. Saturday 1 July had a long entry on the stages of progress from a fiery youth plunging into excess to later struggles and relapses:

> till at last he shakes off the flesh... . I have been watching this progress in myself, sexuality is my great temptation. I find I have omitted one step...when one ceases to sin outwardly, one is very likely to go through the same sins in the imagination, thus making a harem of one's mind.

Who was inhabiting that harem? Emma was now far away in London, but Mrs Glover was frequently present to remind him of what an intelligent woman, interested in her husband's career, could bring to a marriage.

By July 1876 the political crisis was coming to a head, and Glover (and his wife) had come up from Shanghai to assist in the forthcoming negotiations, as had Gustav Detring, the influential German Commissioner of Customs at Tientsin who had a close relationship with Li Hongzhang.[8] Hester's letter telling him of her arrival back at Portadown and her pleasure in meeting her people merited only a brief aside in his diary on 16 July, while about Mrs G the next day he wrote:

> Mon 17 July. Busy all morning, many callers in the afternoon — Wade in then... . Told Mrs. Glover of my Stars & Stripes [an

ode he had written on the centenary of American independence, 4 July 1776] *& gossiped long after breakfast — she's intelligent & thinks much…what's the matter with Glover these last few days — has he any trouble?* [Had Glover noticed the attention being paid to his wife?]

By mid-August Hart had managed to arrange meetings between Wade and Li Hongzhang, whom the Chinese had appointed as their negotiator with plenary powers. These took place in Chefoo, and the outcome was the Chefoo Convention, signed on 12 September 1876. It was ratified by China four days later and by Britain only in July 1885. Hart and his senior Commissioners were in Chefoo during the negotiations.

> *'Mon 21 August. Band from Veneto came to the veranda at 8 a.m. & serenaded Mrs. Detring beginning with an Austrian hymn & ending with the Watch on the Rhine. Mrs. Glover in pink morning gown, looking very pretty.'*

Hart's taste was evidently not for the stiff elaborate ladies' fashions of the time but for looser gowns — Hester in her Japanese dressing gown and Mrs Glover in an informal morning dress both winning his approval. On Sunday 3 September he was *'Up at 5. Work till 8. Gossiped with Mrs. Glover to 9.'* He also talks of dips — there was time for sea-bathing.

Mostly, however, he was working hard and single-mindedly, for he had by now resolved the conflict of loyalties between Britain, as represented by his old chief, Wade, and China, in favour of China. He told Campbell on 24 August 1876

> *…I have been in nothing so like real work during my whole previous career and my hands are now so free that I feel easy and cheerful to an extent I never knew before. By my advice the great Li has been sent here with "large powers" to treat with Wade, and we'll do all we* [i.e. himself and Li] *can to settle things here.* [He gives some details of the points in dispute.] *Wade's attitude threatens war…we cannot stand this, for we want peace, and accordingly…first of all we'll try to bring him to terms — personally I'd like him to have the settling of it… . Unfortunately for many things, the relations between Wade and myself are no longer what they were: he has taken offence and we are merely on bowing terms now: I regret this… . But in the present crisis…no*

longer a go-between, dodging between both fires, I am plainly on one side and am able to work boldly and with energy.

The American Commissioner, Andrew Drew, of whom more later, wrote 'History, I think, will give to him a share of the credit for preventing war with Britain in 1876, after the Margary murder, at the very last moment — when hostilities seemed inevitable.' Hart was pleased the agreement led to the expansion of trade through the establishment of new Treaty Ports along the Yangzi and in the south, but very disappointed that China was not pressed to establish a national mint and post office. He had hoped these would be part of his legacy of careful modernisation in China. The postal service was delayed to the late 1890s, the coinage reform even longer.

Hart accompanied Mrs Glover on the way down to Shanghai, overcoming his own sea sickness to look after her. On Saturday, 23 September they were in Shanghai, and Hart was able to do what was impossible in Peking — visit the dentist and order a warm suit. That evening he had a surprisingly intimate conversation with Mrs Glover, on the occasion of her younger sister's eighteenth birthday.

> *Mrs. Glover & I dined alone, G. being out, so we had champagne & drank Mary's health: the toast was "Mary's health! May her future be as bright as her face is beautiful, & may she always be assured of friends who love her as dearly as those who now drink her health!" To which Mrs. Glover's response is "Thank you! Mary!"* [He then summarises their conversation] *Liking is not loving. She discovered it was liking & not loving very soon. Years passed & the heart & duty began to fight: the heart to rebel against the isolation & duty to urge to more wifely devotion. Then comes a burst of the old love, & she grew young again in thought & exterior. They come together, as husband & wife. Query: are not the odds in favour of a child? I think they are. If so, the old will disappear, & clinging to duty, the oak, a new ivy, love, will grow up. The road? in 1877.*

Victorian conventions had been relaxed by the champagne. Making such intimate confessions shows, I think, her trust in him as a friend: the entry does not read as if he was planning to seduce her. In the very next entry on Sunday, he quotes Glover with some admiration on a sermon they had just listened to: *'"The worst of it is," says Glover, "you can't feel sure he believes a word he says!" What a shepherd to follow!'*

Meanwhile, he did not know where his family was, and had to ask Campbell to send his letters on. (On 7 October Campbell telegraphed that they were in Scarborough.) His first children were adding their share to his family costs. On 17 November 1876 he sent Campbell £900 for Mrs Hart's account, and another £600 to meet bills as: *'Those "wards" are frightfully expensive, poor children!'* Anna had evidently hoped she might be able to go to England in the summer holidays, but Campbell told Hart that Miss Peile, on a visit to London, recommended she should not go, as it would interfere with her studies, term times being different in the two countries. Anna then asked if she could go home for Christmas, so Campbell had to tell her that her guardian wanted her to spend her holidays abroad so he could not arrange this. Hart must have been affected by these pleas from his first daughter, who so much reminded him of her mother, Ayaou, but he could not risk an evidently intelligent seventeen-year-old trying to contact his legal family if she were in England.

The multiple tensions of the year were telling on Hart, and the handwriting in his diary at the end of 1876 showed it, being larger and more irregular than usual.

> *Sunday 31 Dec 1876. Here we have the last day of the Year and the last page of this volume of my journal. Tomorrow begins 1877: and a new volume: — will tomorrow begin a new chapter in my life? How much I have to be thankful for, & yet how discontented & ungrateful I am! God forgive me!*
>
> *Today is also Evey's birthday. She is eight years old. God help the child...*
>
> *Heard thunder at 12 ¼, and more at 4. The snow is falling fairly fast.*

In fact, 1877 saw him more cheerful. He was often on tour, visiting the various Customs posts, new and old, meeting his staff, inspecting new houses and offices, and generally overseeing the expansion of Customs work along the Yangzi and in the south. This involved many transits through Shanghai, where he stayed with the Glovers. He did not forget his wife, thinking ahead the necessary two months to ask Campbell to buy her a very nice writing case for her birthday on 21

June — he could go up to £100 — and he forwarded some expensive jewellery for their eleventh wedding anniversary on 22 August.

> *Pray excuse all the private trouble I am giving you — remember I am keeping the public interest safe by sticking to my post here. That's the only excuse I can offer to asking you to attend to so many private commissions.*

The private dealings included more delicate work in regard to Anna. On 4 February 1877 Campbell enclosed a letter from Miss Peile, suggesting that Anna should have a clothes allowance. Campbell thought this a good idea, as a way of teaching her the value of money, and purchased her a watch for £8. He also forwarded Hart three letters from Anna. The last one, he said, was very awkward. Anna had evidently been enquiring about her mother. Remembering that Hart had referred to her in the past tense in his letter of November 1875, he told her that she was dead.[10] He warned that the boys might begin asking questions soon, but thought it would be easier to deal with them. Hart was indeed lucky to have such a friend in London. In June 1877 Campbell sent him two photographs and a note from Mr Bird giving a progress report on the boys. Herbert was a pleasing boy, and particular over his clothes. He enclosed a letter from Anna in which she had evidently asked if her brothers could visit her. He told her the boys were too young to travel alone, and he could not make this request to Hart by telegram, as she suggested, since that was too expensive.

Hart's recovered cheerfulness also derived from at least partial success in what he conceived as his mission in China, and the end of the conflict of loyalties. Several letters instructed Campbell to support and if possible guide the first Chinese envoy to Europe, to stick up for China's rights (in this instance the right of the Customs harbourmasters to order a ship hulk to be moved, against the *'enormous pretensions of the English Legation'*).

On 30 August he sent Campbell another £900 for Hester, apologising if it was late and delaying her plans to go somewhere on the Continent. His constant travels were making it difficult to keep up with his own accounts. He added: *'P.S. Mrs. Hart is always telling me how kind you are and how many things you do so willingly for her: a thousand thanks.'*

Hart's Last Leave in Europe

By the middle of September 1877 Hart was on holiday in Chefoo — with the Glovers — before returning to Peking in mid-October. By then one of his preoccupations was the preparation of Chinese exhibits for the International Exhibition to be held in Paris in May 1878. These international fairs, following on from the success of the Crystal Palace exhibition in 1851 in London, had become prestigious and popular events, showing off the latest technologies and arts of various countries. Detring was in charge of collecting exhibits from northern China, and Bredon, in Canton, those from the south. Hart was wondering whether to go to it. His letter to Campbell of 9 November says: *'I want a change, and yet I dread the Paris life. I have not enough "go" in me for such a busy time or so gay a place.'*

The letter also follows up a telegram he sent about a birthday present for Evey.

> *I suggested a handsome work box, as I suppose with doll's clothing to look after, and sewing of her own to attend to, she will find such a thing useful and be proud to have one of her own all to herself.*

A needlework box would be a sign she was growing up, for caring for the household's clothes and linen was an important part of a woman's role at this time.

His 30 November 1877 letter to Campbell shows some doubt that the Exhibition would bring about a reunion with Hester. *'I have written to Mrs. Hart to take it for granted that I am going and to make whatever arrangements she likes or thinks called for...'*

On 7 December he stressed again he needed *'rest and — fun'*, but despite his tiredness, he was ending 1877 less stressed than in 1876. His handwriting had reverted to normal and introspection seems to have ceased. He noted, but did not analyse, a queer dream:

> *Monday 31 December. Queer dream last night. Glover tapping Mrs. G. on the shoulder & her hair swung round her face. I awoke this morning at 6: she was close to me & had just kissed (!) me, & I was saying "L— dear". How odd dreams are.*
>
> *Evey's ninth birthday. Wrote her a birthday letter: dear child, God help her!*

By 12 January 1878 he evidently knew Hester and the children would join him and sent Campbell instructions on the kind of house they would need:

I should like it to have a bit of garden for the children to go into, and it must have at least two or three "sitting" rooms and five or six bedrooms [for not more than £2,000]…There is no Govt. appropriation for the expenses of the Commission at Paris, we simply get our full pay… . If I go, I intend to spend my time in Paris. I shall not gad about, and therefore I want a house for myself, which shall be at once comfortable and as showy as the Service would like to see its chief in on such an occasion. I suppose four men and four maids will suffice in the way of servants, and I shall hire two carriages from some first class establishment for the period…

On 9 February he received letters from Campbell with Arthur and Herbert's reports, and enclosing a letter from Arthur, with, as he noted, a strange signature. It was a first sign of trouble to come. Hart replied:

How the deuce did Arthur come to style himself as he did? [He refers to Elizabeth Barrett Browning's poem 'Aurora Leigh' and its comments on the lasting effect of sin.] *It is another way of saying "what you sow that you'll reap". But youngsters don't think of these things!*

Hart left Peking on Friday 1 March 1878. Perhaps again suffering the same sense of confusion as he had suffered in 1866, he did not keep the diary while at sea. The Glovers travelled by the same ship. The diary resumes as they arrived in Marseilles on 21 April. He made a brief visit to London by rail, perhaps to see his lawyer, then took the train back to Paris. On *Wednesday 24 April: 'Arrived Paris 5.45. Met by Hessie & children at the station. Bruce a fine boy. Evey delicate-looking with a bleeding lip, Hessie looking much as before.'*

Most of the Paris entries are similarly brief. They note formal attendances at the Exhibition — on 14 May the Prince of Wales visited and *'bowed to Hessie and me'*. (He shook hands with them at a reception at the German Embassy a few days later.) He also records outings with the children, going to the opera, the theatre, dinners with friends (his brother was in Paris for part of the time), and a visit by a relative (Maggie and her mother). A few longer entries are on personnel matters, such as the suicide of a valued staff member.

One entry is on his health — and that of Evey. After a week in which he had had a troublesome cough:

> *Sunday 26 May. Examined by Dr. Macrae… . He says my lungs, heart, kidneys & liver are all right, but my condition is languid — my system below par etc; will give me a bottle for my cold, an atomiser to spray into my throat, a dose of* [left blank] *for ??? if I ever am back in London; & some Fromkstahl* [?] *water for biliousness.*
>
> *Drove to the church of St. Denis & saw the tombs of the kings of France.*

He refers to an unimportant encounter the day before, and then, on a new line: '*Dr. M also examined Evey today, & says she ought not to go back to China*'. Is it significant that he leaves this till last — was he reluctant to face the probable renewed separation from an evidently much loved daughter?

Brief entries continue till Sunday 9 June, after which a few pencil entries, possibly added later, gives his movements between London, Dublin (for a stay of less than two weeks in Ireland) and Paris, to which he returned on 25 July. Figure 4.5 shows the family at Bad Ischl, Austria, one of the two spas recommended by Dr Macrae. At least his illness enabled him to have a spell of country life and time with the children before he returned to Peking.

His First Children during a Second Attempt at Married Life

There are no more entries until 1 June 1879:

> *Peking. I got back to this place on 2 May. Since my last entry my history has been, in a few words, as follows. I remained in Paris till the end of July, and spent August in Ischl — spent September in Baden Baden — was at Brighton from October to February — went to London for a fortnight & a few days in Paris, left…from Marseilles on Sunday 23rd March. After passing Singapore, I had fever — nausea & diarrhoea, and am still more or less ailing.*
>
> *From Singapore to Hong Kong, by the S.S. President of the US.*

General Grant was a fellow passenger. The gov. of Saigon asked us to dinner, but I was not well enough to go. At Hong Kong we dined with Prof ?? staying with the Jacksons. At Shanghai we stayed ten days with Jem, called on the Tartar Lim,[11] but did not accept any invitations out; came up north...called on Li Chung Tang [Hart's other way of naming Li Hongzhang] *& Tartar Cheng at T'sin, where I remained two days.*

I went to the Yamen on the 28 and was fairly well received. On the 29 I called on the German and French legations and the Italian Minister. On the 30 I called at the Prussian, Russian and English legations. On the 30th...I called on the President of the College, Dr. Martin. [This was the Tongwen Guan in Peking.] *My head aches on slight provocation & currently I must nurse myself.*

One would not know from this bare account that Hester and little Bruce came back with him, or that he had left his darling Evey at school in Bournemouth. In Europe he had continued to send the occasional letter and brief instructions to Campbell, though admitting that while he could enjoy physical activity and country walks in Bad Ischl, mental work brought on an incapacitating headache.

Some of these letters concerned his first family. It seems that the dual burden of their expenses and the expenses of himself and his legal family while on leave on half pay were beginning to tell. Later events show that by 1900 Hester knew about these children, and I think that he told her about them at this time, to explain why he was hard pressed financially. Campbell, in a letter of 20 June 1879, was evidently responding to a request to reduce their cost, for he said that Hutchins (Hart's lawyer) had not found it easy to find a family willing to take charge of them at lesser expense. He recommended letting them stay another year with Mr Bird. The older boy was worth helping but was too young to be articled, and the younger one was small and weak and would not be fit for work for some years. He suggested that perhaps they could be placed in one family where Anna could assist in house-keeping or tuition while looking after her brothers, perhaps in London, but she would have less comfort than she had become accustomed to. Anna, now twenty, had her own views. *'She expresses regret at leaving Miss Peile's and hopes that she'll be given a present, as Mr. D. got £200.'*

Hart responded quickly on 24 August 1879, obviously already aware that Hester's stay in Peking was temporary. He apologised for giving Campbell and Hutchins so much trouble but: *'What a worry this affair is to myself — it is always coming up in some heart-breaking manner...I think...anywhere rather than London, and any people rather than the Davidsons.'* The tone of the rest of the letter is harsher than his sympathetic attitude to the children earlier. My feeling is that Hester, now fully aware of their expense, was insisting on a reduction of their costs. Hart told Campbell to make a druggist of one, a draper of the other; to get them any apprenticeship by which they could earn a living, as *'I fear they have been to too high-class schools hitherto'*.

Fortunately, those who had met them remained keen to do their best for them. On 7 November 1879 Campbell reported that he and Hutchins had met Mr Bird and the boys in London. Bird was giving up his school and taking a post at a new grammar school in Bristol. He would take the boys with him as his family, for £200 p.a., including Arthur's school fees, as he was confident they would give no trouble. The boys seemed ready to cry for joy at this news. Herbert was well grown, quiet and intelligent. Arthur looked younger than his age. Bird thought Herbert would succeed as an artist, if not an architect, and that the younger would make a sharp business boy. Herbert would be apprenticed to an architect as soon as possible (there had already been comments on his skill at drawing) and after a year's schooling, Arthur would be apprenticed in a commercial office. Annie would remain at Miss Peile's for £60 p.a. all found, as she was beginning to make herself useful and would soon earn something herself there. Campbell would try to keep total expenses within the £300 Hart was allowing. He and Hutchins were both very impressed with Mr Bird, who seems indeed to have treated the 'orphans' with a love that was returned.

Hart was evidently satisfied by what they had done. In a letter of 15 May 1881, he approved some additional payments, including the fee for Herbert's articles of apprenticeship, and resumed his former kindly tone: *'Have you seen or heard of these young people lately? I hope they are doing well.'* On 30 June 1882 Campbell was able to tell Hart that Arthur had been apprenticed to an accountant, and that Herbert, now articled, was doing fairly well. He also reported that Miss Peile said Anna required a change on account of her health, and that it was proposed to let her go on a paying visit to Mr Bird. (This was handled by Hutchins, so there are no more details.)

By this time Hart had recovered physically. At Peking he had made an effort to delegate more, at first only working four hours a day, extending this to six by November, and later to his usual regime of hard work. His diary entries also return to the norm of a few lines to a half page each day. However, neither he nor Hester found living together again an experience they wanted to continue. He had needed her care while sick, while for her part, she probably had enough affection left not to leave him till he had fully recovered. They had another daughter — Mabel, nicknamed Nollie — born on 1 November 1879. Hart told Campbell on 21 December: *'Her mother is very well pleased with her, but to me she seems a peculiarly ugly child. She is thriving and her mother is quite well.'* It seems as if from the start he was distancing himself from this daughter, in anticipation of future separation. Generally, the letters to Campbell say little of Hester, or of Nollie, but mention Bruce more frequently. Two months later, on 6 February 1881, he was telling Campbell that Hester and the children would go home in spring 1882. He could give as one reason the uncertain state of China at the time, with anti-foreign riots in places. They would be in the way if there was a crisis in Peking. He told Campbell on 25 April 1881:

> *I don't like rows* [riots from the context] *but I would much rather go through one on my own account, with the women and children ten thousand miles off, than have them here at hand to witness one's devotion and — cripple every effort!*

On 2 September he told Campbell in the middle of a paragraph about this and that: *'before next summer comes round Mrs. Hart and the children will be in Europe again "for good".'*

Hester had learnt that she was happiest being her own mistress, controlling the allowance Hart gave her to live well and to travel frequently. Gertrude Bell, meeting her in London, thought "she enjoyed living alone".[12] Hart had evidently come to the same conclusion. His family's departure caused no emotional upheaval, no moans to Campbell about loneliness. His letter from Shanghai on 8 April 1882 discusses a problem he had had with his bank, and continues:

> *I said good bye to Mrs. Hart and the children in the midst of this money alarm, and, since then, your telegram of the 6th saying*

that K.C.M.G. notification is coming, has arrived to brighten my
surroundings.

Hart had resigned himself to solving the conflict between family life and work by ditching the former. He was glad his work was being recognised by Britain, this time with a Knighthood (KCMG). (He had been aggrieved at only getting a CMG after the Chefoo Convention.) With family life he also ditched sex — he had learnt that a Chinese concubine and family also led to problems — and no scandal ever attached to his name. He carried on a friendly relationship with Hester by correspondence, and he continued to miss Evey.

By this stage Hart's primary need was for women as friends — friends, young and old, who understood his passion for his work and his enthrallment with China, and the second half of this book illustrates this in relation to several female Carralls. To the younger ones he offered kindly avuncular affection. In this he was unusual by the standards of our sex-fixated times, but not unique. The journalist Mary Sieghart felt that the older Bill Deedes had a similar need, taking young female journalists under his wing when his wife had no interest in his work. She wrote, "I adored him, but in an utterly chaste way." I am sure my great-aunt Emma Carrall and my aunt Kathleen Carrall, would have said exactly the same about their relationship with Hart.[13]

Emma Carrall – the Sequel

Meanwhile, what happened to Emma Carrall?

It is likely that she pursued her intention to become a nurse. Her mother was a surgeon's daughter, and may have encouraged her in this path. Figure 4.2 shows her wearing a large cross, and at this time there were several women's religious orders or associations which undertook nursing. There is also a photograph of her mother's sister, Catherine, wearing a similar cross, so her aunt may have been a mission nurse in Antigua. Alternatively, the cross and the unusual neck-piece may signify that she became a deaconess, and the photograph could have been sent to show her insignia to Hart. By this time, caring work, like teaching and nursing, particularly if motivated by religion, was seen as an appropriate and respectable outlet for middle-class spinsters. The new career of deaconess in the church had opened to women in the 1860s, and one of their tasks was nursing the poor or helping them after they had left hospital.[14] When Emma Carrall eventually married, on 2 June 1880, it was to Edward Almack, described on the marriage certificate and in the 1881 census as Secretary, Kings College Hospital. If she was a nurse or visiting deaconess there, it could explain how they met. In 1881 they were living at 27 Carey Street, St Clement Danes, London, convenient for the hospital, but probably not too healthy. She died on 20 August 1885, two days after the death of her ten-day-old daughter, christened Mildred Hart Almack. The immediate cause was puerperal infection, and the doctor also mentions a kidney problem for four years. Her mother, Emma Spry Sampson, present at the death, undertook the task of reporting this on behalf of the distressed husband. By this time the Almacks were living in Streatham, and Edward Almack was Secretary of the Conservative Association.

I wonder if Hart met her during that long, undiarised stay in Brighton — or when he was in London. He kept in touch with her, sending Campbell letters to forward to 'Almack', two in 1881, one in 1884, and two in 1885. The one written in July 1885 was presumably to consent to be godfather of the forthcoming baby, who was given his name, and the one in September to give his sympathy to the grieving husband. The diary entry of Friday 21 August records: 'Telegram from Almack: yesterday's date: it says "I have lost my wife & child". Poor dear Emma Carrall! Heaven rest your soul!' The next volume of the diary has the Death notice from *The Times* inserted at the beginning:

> August 18th at Fawley, Streatham, Mildred Hart, aged 10 days, daughter of Edward and Emma Almack, and on 20th August, at the same place, Emma, the wife of Edward Almack. China papers, please copy.

At this time Hart's diary is full of his reflections on whether to stay with China as IG Customs, or to accept the invitation from the British Government to become its Minister in Peking, which would also bring the hereditary title of Baronet. Once again his final decision was for China. He wanted to maintain the good work and reputation which meant China would keep the service on which his staff depended for their living, though he knew his wife would disapprove. The entry of 7 September ironically unites Hester and Emma:

> ...but Hessie & the Baronetcy — she will be furious and it will be lost.

> *Letter from now dead Emma Carrall. She wants one of Gordon's*
> *letters for her husband.[15]*
>   *Very warm day: I feel quite limp and done up — whatever's the*
> *reason.*

The brief entries on Emma do not reflect the grief that is shown by the way he coupled her with the loss of Mrs Brazier in his letter to Kath in 1902, but his diary that month shows a resumption of melancholy and headaches. The conflict of political loyalties had again unhappily coincided with personal losses and worries. Besides receiving news of Emma's death, he heard that his daughter Evey had tonsillitis. The mixture of anxieties is shown in his entry of 29 September, after he had telegraphed Campbell for news of Evey.

> *I am really quite uneasy about her, <u>dear pet</u>! It is really very hard*
> *and very trying to be separated thus from one's children — and*
> *more especially when one's own, and one's wife's views differ:*
> *Hessie is all for the town and society — I am for the country and*
> *quiet. O dear me — how facts, like a rough brush, deprive*
> *beautiful life of its brilliant colours! And how bitter the days that*
> *ever sneak past in one's cup: my life has been made miserable by*
> *the offer of the Legation for instance. If I take it, I can't go home*
> *and the service may go to ruin. If I don't take it, I lose its ease &*
> *rewards and irritate others & in the end fail to put off for ever the*
> *changes that threaten to harm the Customs. So, henceforth, take it*
> *or don't take it, it will be always a worry! I wish I c'd cease to*
> *think about it, & I do try, but I am daily getting to think I did*
> *wrong not to go to the Legation.*

Glover also died that year, in Shanghai, just as he was about to take his retirement leave. He had been unwell since 1884, and resigned in 1885. Mrs Glover left China; she did not remarry. Hart recovered his emotional stability, and moved on to achieve more services of modernisation for China. One of his pleasures at this time came from a note from Brandt, the German Minister, who was glad Hart was staying to continue the great service he was giving through the Customs, operating so much better than those in India and other colonial territories. And the Baronetcy arrived in 1893.

Edward Almack also moved on. Hart's final letter to him, sent via

Campbell in 1891, was presumably to congratulate him on his remarriage in that year. The fact that Almack felt the need to explain his decision to remarry implies that he knew all about his first wife's close relationship with Hart, and felt no discomfort about it. This confirms me in my belief that Hart's relationship with the young Emma was not sexual. It seems likely that from childhood she had regarded Hart as a kind substitute uncle. For his part, he may have felt in 1875 tweaks of physical attraction towards this young woman, but they were probably suppressed by consciousness of his duty towards his wife, and his respect for his old friend, Emma Sampson, who had happily entrusted her daughter to his hospitality and care. What he could acknowledge and enjoy, as his letter to Campbell showed, was her intelligence and her friendship.

Emma Carrall is only one example of the enduring nature of his friendships. Another was her mother, Emma Sampson, and yet another was Mrs Nevius. And Campbell evidently knew he was always interested in news of Mrs Glover, for on 14 August 1903 he wrote to Hart: *"Mrs. Glover dined with us the other night. She looked fairly well."*[16]

As for Emma Spry Sampson, she too never forgot her daughter. On the back of a framed photograph (Figure 4.6) she wrote:

> *At Fawley, Mount Nod Road, Streatham, Emma, the wife of Edward Almack passed away, August 20th 1885*

> *Grant her eternal rest O Lord, and let light perpetual shine upon her.*

> *Transmigravera.*

> *They have passed over.*

She then added details of her burial place in Norwood cemetery. Years later, in 1900, in a letter to Sir Robert, she wrote: *'I still have the lovely comfort in feeling that my darling Emma is always near me.'*

Faith in an afterlife sustained many in an age when the death of a loved one might come at any time. It helped my mother in 1902. And Sir Robert Hart continued the 1902 letter to Aunt Kath quoted at the beginning of the chapter with these words:

> *I wonder where all the dead are: are they asleep, waiting for the "last trump"? I do not think so: but, if they are alive & moving*

about, I wonder too what interests them most, what their old friends on earth are doing, or the novelties of another life & other acquaintances? "Eyes hath not seen & ear hath not heard" — so we must wait till our own turn comes, & then we shall know!

Aunt Kath and her sisters, daughters of Emma's brother Jim Carrall, first came into Hart's life in 1882–3, soon after his second separation from Hester and their children.

CHAPTER FIVE

JIM CARRALL FINDS A WIFE, AND ALMOST CRASHES HIS CAREER

It was fortunate there was no psychology for Emma Sampson's son, Jim Carrall, to read, or he might have thought himself condemned to failure. This was a boy with no permanent male role model, whose mother had three husbands, who grew up eclipsed by his sister. While lacking the latter's sparkle, he managed, after some reverses, to have a successful career and a durable marriage, and to rear nine children who, though they sometimes laughed at his foibles, respected him, and who, certainly in my mother's case, loved him dearly. I still have his walking stick which she must have requested as a memento of him.

School and School Friends

Jim needed at least a grammar school education to take up Hart's promise of a post in the Customs. As a stepfather, Theo Sampson seems to have regarded this as chiefly Emma's responsibility to arrange, though he gave some help. He provided an introduction to his clerical brother, then at St Thomas, York, who baptised Jim in January 1864 as James Willcox [sic] Carrall of London. This probably indicates his first Christmas break, so he had presumably arrived to start school in September 1863. Learning Chinese had been another of Hart's stipulations, and, according to Aunt Kath, Sampson taught him Chinese when he returned to Canton (presumably the written form, as he would have spoken Cantonese as a child). On 2 July 1868 Hart wrote in his diary *'Have given an appoint. to Jimmie Carrall (Sampson)'*. This was at the lowest Indoor rank of fourth class clerk. For his twenty-first birthday he sent a photo to his mother and father, Emma and Theo Sampson (Figure 5.1).

Emma must have found someone to take him back to England in 1863, possibly her relative Master Mariner Osman Edwards, a cousin born a few years before her in the same South Hams village, Chillington. He and his wife were the witnesses at the wedding of Emma's niece, Lavinia Zinzan, to George Harris, a Master Mariner in Shanghai in 1862. Lavinia's first son was born in Shanghai, in 1864. Emma, cut off from relatives for so long, would certainly have made great efforts to see them, using the fast steamers by then connecting Hong Kong and Shanghai. Two things suggest she and Theo knew them well. Lavinia's sixth child was named Theophilus, and Jim called the son born in 1889 Osmond Eric. The first name was never used, but it suggests that Jim had good memories of a man called Osman but may not have known the unusual spelling.

Jim had a wealthy grandfather in JCW2, but only limited help could be expected from him — money perhaps, but not a comforting presence for a boy in a strange land. JCW2 probably paid the fees for him to attend St James's Grammar School in Streatham, London, for he was known as Wilcocks there, according to Aunt Kath. (This would not be unusual: Hart was also willing to pay school fees for an illicit grandson.) The holidays were a problem, for JCW2's current partner, Celia Larcombe, would not have wanted him in Exeter. His grandfather must have allowed him to visit his legitimate son, JCW3, living near Plymouth, since Jim knew the latter's children, JCW4 and his sister Grace.

Jim's grandmother, Anna Sess Carrall, was living quite near, at 1 Falcon Road, Battersea, with her widower son-in-law and his six children. There may not have been room for him in that crowded house, particularly in the holidays. However, two boys from the north of England, Jack and Arthur Fawcus, became his life-long friends and invited him to their home. Their father, Robert Fawcus, was a well-to-do merchant from Hartlepool. About 1865 Robert Fawcus had leased Over Dinsdale Hall, in beautiful surroundings west of Darlington, which all his children remembered as idyllic. His wife, Anna Maria, came from the Quaker Speciall family. They had ten sons and four daughters, so Jim also met their younger sister Frances, who was of an age to hero-worship an exotic older boy (Figure 5.2).

Anna Maria Fawcus's letters to her husband while he was on a business trip to the Baltic in 1856 illustrate her mischievous sense of humour, her independent spirit (she was not 'a pipe-filling wife!'), and the intellectual companionship she and her husband had over books (the latest Dickens and Macaulay) and the development of his business. They also exhibit the strong religious beliefs that Anna had retained from her Quaker upbringing, and which were shared by the Anglican Robert. Robert led family prayers every morning, the boys reading the lessons. Jack Fawcus could read the psalms from the age of five. Jim probably acquired some Quaker values while staying with them, plus a model of a large and happy family life (Figure 5.3).

Starting Work

Jim Carrall began work in Tianjin on 1 August 1868. About 1869 he was sent for language study in Peking for eighteen months, a step to better things. Hart had followed the Foreign Office example of centring language training in Peking, though, typically, he made his students work much harder. He kept a close eye on his young hopefuls, who were of many nationalities, and invited them to his dinner parties. Each had an individual teacher, but there was a very competitive spirit, for it was known that future Commissioners must have good Chinese.[1]

Carrall's next appointment was in Canton under Edward Bowra. Here he wrote *The Tourist Guide for the City of Canton, Compiled from Various Sources,* Imperial Maritime Customs, Canton. He dated it on one page as '1 September 1873', though it was published in Macao only in 1877. It starts with a list of places worth seeing, with their names in Chinese characters as well as in English, grouped geographically. It includes craft shops, restaurants (including the Dog & Cat Restaurant where the animals could be eaten, not fed), temples and other ancient monuments, the Roman Catholic Cathedral, a Protestant hospital, and the White Cloud Mountains. There is then a section with notes and descriptions of the ancient monuments and the best time to visit them, followed by a 'Short History of Canton', which includes its economy and current features. It is useful but rather wooden, but his affection for the place shows through.

Hart encouraged his young men to do such things in their leisure-time, and to have scientific hobbies. While he was on leave in 1876–78 Carrall applied successfully to become a Fellow of the Geological Society of London, and he gave a short paper, read after his return, on 3

November, 1880: *Notes on the Locality of some Fossils found in the Carboniferous Rocks at T'ang Shan, China, about 120 miles N.N.E of Tientsin.* This was evidently written after his leave, for he says a Chinese company had been formed in 1878 to work the coal deposits there with European techniques.

Leave and Marriage

Indoor Customs officers were entitled to two years leave on half pay after seven years (and thereafter, every ten years). Carrall probably waited till his salary improved. From Canton he had been sent back to Tianjin. He had risen to Second Assistant B in 1876 when he accompanied the first Chinese Minister to London, Guo Songtao, on his journey to Britain.[2] Marriage would be an important objective, and, like Hart, he needed the help of friends and relatives to find a well-educated and attractive wife. He wasted little time. In the second of two letters written on 17 November 1876, Hart authorised Campbell to summon two of the three young officers on leave to give interpreting assistance if needed to Guo Songtao. Campbell replied, on 5 January 1877, that he had not asked Carrall as he was going to be married. This surprised me, for Jim Carrall had not married Frances Fawcus till March 1878.

Carrall's first choice must have been Grace Wilcocks, daughter of JCW3 in the legal Wilcocks line. She sent him her photograph, signing it with the date 1876 on the back . A girl could send a photograph to a fiancé, but not to a casual friend. Carrall had his photo taken on 10 November 1876, in Hamburg, where his friend Arthur Fawcus was working, to send her in exchange (Figures 5.4 a and b). But there was no marriage. Grace was not mentioned in the 1881 and 1891 censuses, but in 1901, aged forty-six, single, she was in a lunatic asylum. Non-fulfilment of an engagement was a serious social crime. We know that in this case her brother did not take offence, for JCW4 sent Carrall a photo which he initialled and dated 1878. This was probably to wish Carrall well on his marriage that year to Frances Fawcus. Declining mental health, or hysteria at the prospect, probably made it obvious that Grace could not go to China. As another Customs' colleague, Charles Brewitt-Taylor, was to find, China was a hard place for mentally frail wives.[3]

Once Carrall had recovered from this disappointment, Jack Fawcus, now living in London, must have re-introduced him to his younger sister Frances. She had grown taller than him, which Carrall may have found off-putting at first, but he must have seen that behind her gentle nature there was the courage and calmness a girl needed to face life in China.

Frances's mother, Anna Maria Speciall, had died at Over Dinsdale in 1871, while Frances was a boarder at her aunt's Quaker school in Lewes, Sussex. A fellow pupil has described:

> Miss Rachel Speciall, a very clever woman, who mostly taught the two upper classes...enjoyed teaching the clever and advanced girls. She schooled herself to be very patient with the naturally stupid ones, but to those of middling abilities her sharp tongue was a terror — she could never believe we were doing our best.

Frances probably fell into the middle group, for Rachel Speciall wrote on the back of her photo, taken in 1872, *'I'm disappointed in her.'* Frances was not academically clever, but she had good sense.

Rachel Speciall ran the school with her friends, the two Trusted sisters. They had about twenty-five pupils, of whom about fifteen boarded. There was a German woman assistant to teach that language, and they enjoyed singing German hymns with Rachel herself on Sunday evenings. There were regular visits from good masters from Brighton, to teach French and drawing, and they had occasional visiting lecturers for science. Rachel taught English and other subjects with enthusiasm and thoroughness. There were no games, but the girls did drill and practised good deportment in the playroom, which also had a jumping board and a swing. At weekends there were walks in the surrounding hills, and twice on Sundays and Wednesdays they went to the Friends' Meeting House. Almost every Sunday they were invited into a beautiful garden owned by one of the wealthier Quakers. It was an unusually good education for girls of the time, but only a few pupils learnt music as an extra, from a master across the road.[4] Frances and her teacher are shown in Figure 5.5, a and b, and she appears aged twenty in Figure 5.6, very like myself at the same age.

Although her father must have had doubts about letting Frances depart for China, he gave his consent and he and Emma Sampson were the two witnesses to her marriage to Carrall in Dinsdale Church, Durham, on 19 March 1878. Soon after, they left for China. Her father endowed her with some capital which provided a small income. As she, rather than her husband, controlled this, it may have been done during their 1887–9 leave after the Married Women's Property Act of 1882 made this possible.

Frances herself must have had some sadness to overcome. My aunt remembered how her mother always kept the photo shown in Figure 5.3 on her mantelpiece in China. 'They were such a united family that it had been a heartbreak for Mother to leave them.... When I was ten, I remember my shock in first seeing my mother in tears. She had just received a cable announcing the death of her father.'[5] Separation from family and old friends was one of the costs of expatriate life.

Frances Carrall Meets Hart

Carrall was posted back to Tianjin. Their daughters Kathleen and Maude met people who remembered them fondly when they visited Tianjin in 1900. Frances certainly needed friends, for four children were born between 17 September 1878 and 13 February 1882. The first, Edward, was premature, and died soon after birth. Both parents grieved, but it was a particular disaster for Carrall, who shared Chinese notions about the importance of sons. Their next children were girls, Emily, Muriel and Maude.

Carrall's appointment as Hart's Private Secretary in November 1883 seems accidental. Hart had intended to send him to Shanghai, but illnesses often made sudden adjustments in postings necessary. Hart's diary records: '*Sat 4 Nov...Carralls arrived at 2 p.m. Usual dinner party and music after. Mon 6 Nov.... Walked with Mrs. Carrall in the garden last night and talked again about their movements today*'. Hart told Campbell on 7 January 1883 that he had a musical dinner every Saturday with four colleagues playing various instruments and himself the cello and violin. This was not an activity the Carralls were able to share. They took care later to ensure that their children had the good musical education which they lacked.

They were expected, however, to join in socially, and Frances seems to have had some responsibilities for helping at the round of dinners and dances that Hart gave during the Christmas and Chinese New Year season. Some of these events got mentioned in his diary.

7 November 1882. I gave a dance last night, 9 ½ to 2 ½ , and had
supper for 72 of which 20 were dancing ladies. It went off well,
and is the third big dance Peking has already had this winter. So
you see, we are gay, after a fashion.

26 December 1882. I had a Christmas tree & Christmas dinner
dance on 22nd. On 29th I give a dance to which I expect some 60
people. Peking is gone mad on the subject of dancing.

Christmas trees bore a present for each guest, and Frances probably
helped in choosing and wrapping them. She may not have been amongst
the dancing ladies as she was expecting again, but her daughter Kathleen's
1900 diary shows that she certainly learnt how to organise festivities.
In 1882–3, however, she sometimes found Peking's dinners a strain. Hart
noted in his diary on 15 February 1883:

Mrs. Carrall left the table early — crying I think. She had been
talking of last night's menu, & seemed to get confused with the
number of courses on it, and as I put some questions laughingly,
she got confused more & then came a fit of tears — well it did not
get the length of tears. Carrall said "she came home very tired last
night, hardly able to stand."

Carrall was not meeting Hart's expectations.

Wed 31 January…At work today…I begin to feel puzzled what to
do with Carrall. I wish he had been able to go to S' hai in
November last.

Fri 7 Feb. Tried Carrall with an Edict yesterday, but he c'd make
neither head nor tail of it.

The Edict seems to have been about the misdoings of some long-
dead mandarin, his concubine and Imperial punishment. Carrall's
Chinese was probably more workaday.

Wed 22 March…Tried Carrall last night with a single letter — he
failed.

Hart recorded the arrival of my Aunt Kath.

Fri 20 April. Mrs. Carrall had another daughter — the fourth in
succession at 5.30 this morning: she dined with us last night, and

was chatting with me till 10 o'clock & then retired thinking it might not come for a fortnight yet — altho' always alluded to it arriving on the morning of the 21st. Carrall looked very lugubrious over it. Dudgeon and Limmer were there, and then Mrs. Pisnett came along.

17 May. Monday. The little Carrall christened in the dining room. Brereton and myself godfathers and godmothers Mrs. Glover & Mrs. C's youngest sister: named Kathleen Fawcus, afterwards we sat down 16 to breakfast. I took in Mrs. Carrall and...Mrs. ? looked very sorry over it!

Hart was obviously ignoring the protocol by which he should have given his arm to the socially most senior lady — according to her husband's rank. Jim Carrall had probably known Mrs Glover since their childhood in Canton as they were about the same age. He probably also knew that choosing her would please Hart.

A group of May entries includes Carrall's next posting and Hart's opinion of him.

21 May. Told Mrs. Carrall they will go to Foochow [Fuzhou]... . Appointed Carrall Asst Deputy Commissioner at Foochow... . He thanked me for "promotion": I said "It's not promotion; it's only an early appointment with the same salary you have now. Mc?? thinks he's a goose; in some ways he is... . With Mrs. Carrall called on the doctor and inspected the new house and furniture.

22 May. Had a dinner party last night: after it played Jool Ecarté.[6]...I beat Scherzer, then beat Carrall, then Mrs. Grosvenor, then asked Tittbach to play for the pool, and my luck against his skills, and beat him too. My luck was really wonderful:...Very pleasant evening.

26th May, Saturday...Muriel [Carrall] rather feverish these last two days. I hope the dear wee pet is not going to be ill. Dudgeon rushed in & rushed out: very inattentive indeed!

Tuesday, 5th June. This day 17 years ago, I asked Hessie to come to China.

This morning the Carralls, after being here since the 4th November, left en route for Foochow. He is a prim, selfish, thick-

headed prig; she is soft, unaffected, good natured and not
exacting; the children are charming — Emily bright, Muriel
loving, Maude brave & Kathleen a mystery of the future… . It's
delightful to have the house & one's time all to one's own self
again!

The delight was temporary. The disastrous impression Jim Carrall left on his boss was partly because Hart was missing his own family. He complained to Campbell on 17 June 1883:

I want to be with the wife and children and to have repose for
cultivating myself internally in a way I can't do here with so much
work to do and so many calls on my time and my brains!

The Carralls had arrived just six months after he had said farewell to his wife and children. The selfish epithet on Carrall — given his remark on Wade — probably referred to his inflicting so many children on Frances, and prim and prig to some Quaker principles he may have acquired. Though he had disliked her husband, Hart had been enchanted by Frances and the children, who brought home to him what he was missing. In his first letter to Kathleen in 1896 he told her:

I fancy Emily & Muriel have quite forgotten me, but they were
great pals of mine ten or twelve years ago, for they lived in my
house from October to June and Muriel always went round the
garden on my shoulder & called me "<u>Mr. Sir Robert!</u>"

Though the diary mentions an evening walk with Frances only on 6 November, his third letter to Kathleen in December 1896 enquires '*Does your Mama remember walking with me in the winter of 1882, I wonder?*' which suggests she often shared his evening constitutionals round and round the garden. This letter adds an interesting touch about the christening:

It was I that selected your name for you (and I hope you like it!),
but I wanted it to be Kathleen <u>Mavourian</u>. And it was your dear
Mama who cancelled the second and accepted the first.

Frances wrote regularly to Hart thereafter, on his birthday and at Christmas, and as we will see, she regarded him as a father figure to whom she could always turn for advice. As for him, his characterisation of her shows that she fell into the second category of women he liked — those who were kind, unselfish and uncomplaining — though, as the christening illustrates, she could be firm on matters important to her. Mavourian was an Irish name: Kathleen's second name was Fawcus, included in the names of all her children.

Foochow (Fuzhou) and Carrall Shows His Mettle

Assistant Deputy Commissioner sounds as if Carrall was two steps away from being in charge of what was then the second port of China in terms of British trade but he found himself Acting Commissioner in 1884 when Foochow became the centre of a Chinese conflict with the French.[7] Figure 5.7 shows a typical aspect of a Chinese port with the sanpans that housed many of its population on the water.

Carrall's posting did not begin well. Though the family left Peking on 5 June, he became ill on the journey south, and could report for duty only on 27 July. The next day he was again granted sick leave, returning to duty on 12 August. He reported sick again the following day and finally began work only on 23 August. The type of illness was not mentioned, but it could have been malaria, very prevalent in the humid summer season. It may have been the source of the chronic fevers from which he was to suffer later. At this time the virtues of cinchona bark, from which quinine is extracted, as a cure for malaria, were known to some old China hands, but not to all doctors, and if Carrall caught the sickness while travelling, he might not have been able to obtain it. In any case, the amount of the bitter 'bark mixture' taken was often insufficient to kill all the malarial parasites in the blood, which could regroup and multiply. When people were run down the malaria could reappear with symptoms similar to influenza. Frances, in addition to caring for four small girls under five, had also to nurse a sick husband.

Fortunately, Foochow had many mission doctors, some of whom were American women. A US naval surgeon, G W Woods, visiting in January-February 1885 gives a good picture of expatriate life, and describes these women:

> Mrs. Dr. Cowles is rigid and forbidding.... Mrs. Carey is sweet, winning, and most refined. Mrs. Coffin is bright, pretty, young, and full of life, all these female doctors are well posted, honest in

their purposes, have had large experience, and are doing a good work here. Mrs. Coffin is now devoting herself to her husband and the domestic office having given up general practice...[Mrs Dr Cowles, aged over forty, had just married.] *Mr. Cowles a meek retiring book worm, a noted scholar in Chinese and oriental literature. <u>She</u> provides the house and it suggests itself to everyone that the usual relations of the sexes have been reversed in this alliance...*

Some of the expatriate houses belonging to the tea firms were by the river, but

Many of the foreign houses are...little oases in the midst of the Chinese suburbs of narrow tortuous streets, sloppy pavements, filthy stones, and smoking joss-houses, which cover the lower hills: but passing beyond these, on reaching their summit, the city has ended.... . Here are some of the finest residences, beautiful country houses including those occupied by our own [American] and the Russian consul, the Missionary Hospital, and the Club-House.... . From the balconies of the Club-House furnished with easy chairs and tea tables, while comfortably imbibing beer or a cup of tea, one can look down upon the river.... . The old stone bridge seems to be compact with a <u>blue</u> crowd hurrying in both directions, and the river seems to be floored over with the city of boats...

The Carralls' house was in this high area, known as Nantai. As Acting Deputy Commissioner Carrall would have gone to the Club, and Frances also at the times when it was open to ladies. However, Mrs Dr Coffin could not, because her husband's firm sold '*<u>retail</u>*', and '*...the members of that firm do not belong to the club, or the race organisations, and the ladies of the wholesale firms will not call on Mrs. Coffin...*'. Mr Coffin's shop must have been useful to the community, providing them with almost everything required for a European or American life-style. Woods noted the hospitality that ranged from '*tea and chocolate milk...brought to us in bed*' to dinners with fine wines.[8]

Coffin's firm, Hedge & Co, also did much of the freighting in barges and steam launches between Foochow and the Pagoda anchorage, which was nine miles downstream. Here the larger steam ships halted. At or near Pagoda Island there was a small expatriate community consisting of French and British teachers from the Naval school and others who were attached to the Foochow Naval shipyard (these, with the Arsenal, were upstream of the anchorage), a Customs harbourmaster and tidewaiters, a doctor, and a British vice-consul with his constable.

Woods noted that Hedge & Co operated a pigeon post to Pagoda Island. The birds took only eight minutes, while against the tide the journey took a steam launch two hours. Mail came in fortnightly by steamer from other ports and from abroad. For urgent messages, telegraph services were beginning to link the Treaty Ports to each other and to the outside world. The telegraph, operated by a British company, had not quite reached Foochow, but runners carried messages to the nearest station at Sharp Peak, and messages could normally get to Peking by the next day. It was used by the Viceroy at Foochow to communicate with Peking, the Customs officials to reach Hart, and the consuls of various nations to reach their mission heads, as well as by traders and missionaries. Brevity was essential: every word above twelve added to the cost.

Jim Carrall, once he had begun work, made a good impression — even in his knowledge of Chinese which Hart had deplored. Commissioner Hannen reported to Hart on 3 July 1884:

> *I have made use of his services, in every way, both written and spoken, at any time since my assuming charge in November last, and the result of that test of his capabilities as a Chinese Secretary in regard to both the Colloquial and Documentary is that I pronounce him as thoroughly efficient.*

Background to the French Attack on Fuzhou, August 1884

In a disastrous war with Germany in 1871, France had seen Paris occupied and their Emperor Napoleon III overthrown. The victorious Prussians proclaimed in the Palace of Versailles the final unification of the states which still form modern Germany. After a period of confusion, the Third Republic was proclaimed in France in 1875 with a President and a *Premier Ministre* dependent on a shifting coalition of votes in the Assembly. Jules Ferry was Premier during 1880–1 and again from February 1883 to March 1885. He was determined to restore French prestige and to expand its empire. In Asia this meant enlarging the colony of Cochin-China northwards to include the kingdom of Vietnam, whose northern province, Tonkin, was adjacent to the Chinese province of Yunnan.[9] As early as 1874 the Vietnamese king had recognised the French possession of Cochin-China, and accepted French protection, but he also still sent tribute from time to time to China, and the Chinese Imperial authorities continued to regard him as their tributary. Meanwhile most of Tonkin was falling under the control of a Chinese exile from the Taiping rebellion, who commanded irregular soldiers known as the Black Flag. The French sent a small expeditionary force into Tonkin, whose naval commander, Rivière, exceeded his orders by capturing Hanoi in March 1882. The town was soon surrounded by Black Flag forces who made alliance with the Vietnamese in opposing the French advance.

It would be tedious to follow the French and Chinese battles and negotiations in detail. On both sides there were some political forces in favour of a peaceful settlement, and some in favour of aggressive action in support of their claims. For both, 'face', that is, honour and prestige, was as important as reality. Misunderstandings were plentiful, due not only to different languages, but also to different political concepts and styles of government. The French had difficulty with 'tributary' and with the slow decision-making of Imperial China with its dispersed centres of power. In December 1882 the French Minister at Peking, Albert Bourée, and Li Hongzhang agreed that China would withdraw its troops from Tonkin, the French would make no conquests there, and China would allow French cross-border trade into Yunnan. This was accepted with some delay and doubt by Li's superiors in Peking, but was rejected by Ferry, when he became Premier again in February 1883, as he thought it still gave China an excuse to interfere in Vietnam. He removed Bourée. The rejection increased Chinese suspicion and distrust, and Chinese troops moved into Tonkin in support of the Black Flag irregulars. On 10 May 1883 Rivière, making a sally out of Hanoi, was defeated and killed, provoking anger in France. Prestige being at stake, Jules Ferry sent reinforcements. In August 1883 the French took the Vietnamese capital and by a new treaty reduced Vietnam to the status of a French protectorate. Initially they had limited success against the Black Flag in Tonkin, but for their own reasons did not follow up their later victories. The Chinese, who had warned France and the other powers that they would regard conflict between official Chinese and French troops as being the start of war, did not follow this up after some clashes.

From April 1883 Hart was regularly confiding his worries over the situation to Campbell in London, and the Carralls must have been aware of his fears of a widespread conflagration. Korea, another Chinese tributary, was also in an unstable condition, with Japan seeking to extend its influence there, and Russia might take a slice of northern China if opportunity offered. Hart also realised that France, if bogged down in a land war in Indo-China, might try exercising direct pressure on China by a march on Peking or a naval blockade of its ports. His fears were well justified. The French acting consul at Fuzhou, Ernest Frandon, had by October 1883 collected such detailed information on the forts and guns along the river that Nicole Tixier gives him much credit for the French success there a year later.[10] Within China there were divisions of opinion between Li Hongzhang and the Tsungli Yamen, and between the Yamen and other strong forces in the Court. The Tsungli Yamen was not a Foreign Office in a European sense, but a Council advising the Emperor on foreign matters. The Chinese Minister to Paris was another important player with his own connections to the Dowager Empress. As Hart told Campbell in June 1883, it was difficult to know with whom to tackle the question.

In March 1884 the French again defeated Chinese forces in Tonkin, and Hart's long-time ally in the Tsungli Yamen, Prince Kung, was dismissed, together with his supporters, to be replaced by advisers whom the Dowager Empress thought would be more aggressive in resisting the French. Open war now seemed likely. Detring, still Commissioner of Customs in Tianjin and a friend of Li Hongzhang, returned from leave to find himself posted to Canton. On his way there he met the French naval Captain François-Ernest Fournier, who was a personal friend of Jules Ferry, and as a result Hart was asked to recall Detring to Tianjin in April 1884 to help negotiate a settlement. Fournier steamed slowly up the China coast, accompanied by his Admiral and other French naval forces, and arrived in Tianjin on 11 May. By the Li-Fournier agreement then negotiated, Chinese troops were to be withdrawn from Tonkin immediately, French claims there were basically recognised, and France withdrew its demand for an indemnity. The French Minister in Peking was not involved and there were ambiguities. Li Hongzhang may have increased these by glossing over the withdrawal, which he knew would enrage strong forces at court, as he thought the French would not move in the rainy season. Li knew China's weakness, and wanted to avoid war, but he also feared for his own position. Hart thought the agreement ambiguous, but hoped, as did most people in May 1884, that it would lead to peace.

Unfortunately, despite the rains, the French did advance and, after local misunderstandings, there was a skirmish with Chinese troops on 23 June, in which twenty-two French soldiers were killed. France immediately demanded a large indemnity for this act of 'bad faith', which China refused. The French issued an ultimatum, threatening reprisals if not paid by 19 July, later extended to 31 July. The Chinese agreed to withdraw their troops from Tonkin, but not to pay an indemnity, offering instead some compassionate compensation for the killed. They tried to get another power to mediate, but on 7 August the French refused the US offer to do so. The French bombarded Chinese forts on Taiwan, but failed in an attempted landing. On 14 August a French fleet under Admiral Courbet steamed up to the Pagoda anchorage below Foochow. It was not fired on by the Chinese forts protecting the entrance to the river, who were not sure that they were at war, and it was assisted by pilots licensed by the Chinese Customs, two British, two German, one Italian, at very high rates of pay. This brought Jim Carrall into the picture.

The Battle

In a despatch of 11 July 1884, Hannen reported to Hart:

Re French ships using pilots illegally
...H. E. Tartar General, Hu Lu Shan, came alongside the Customs jetty...yesterday, and asked to see the Commissioner of Customs. As I was not at the office...Mr. Act. Dep. Commr. Carrall went on board the boat and had an interview with H.E. who wished to know whether the pilots could be prosecuted for piloting French Men-of-War into the port. Mr. Carrall explained that such a proceeding would be in violation of the Treaties so long as war had not been declared — of which H.E. seemed to be aware — but still signified his desire that the pilots should not bring such ships into the port. H.E. seemed disposed to engage the services of all the pilots, at so much per week or month — but made no definite proposal of the sort. Before leaving H.E. said that he would be glad if the Commissioner on his arrival at the office would send him his opinion in writing on the point. This I did not

do…preferring to send Mr. Act. Dep. Commr. Carrall to give my
views which were set forth on a rough Memo…

After the office closed Mr. Carrall went in and saw the Tartar
General and what passed at the interview is set forth in the same
Memorandum as that conveying my views on the subject…my
absence from the office and my sending the Dep. Commr. to see the
Tartar General…were owing to pressure of business, private and
official, connected with arrangements for my departure on leave
on urgent private affairs…

With Hannen's departure, Carrall was left holding the baby until
October 1884. Judging by the way events unfolded, Hannen's advice
was that the pilots would be acting illegally only if the French activities
became warlike.

The British consul at the time was Charles Sinclair. He had mouldered
in Foochow for twenty-five years and has been described as 'incompetent,
stupid, and spiteful',[11] while the French officials were young and active.
The British vice-consul at Pagoda Island, Warren, referring to Chinese
soldiers having fired at English steam launches after the battle, thought
it was because

steamboats carrying our ensigns have been in the hire of the
French fleet, carrying dispatches & the French Vice Consul up &
down the river [who was] living on board of an English tea ship
alongside of our Men-of-war.

Sir Harry Parkes, after eighteen years as Ambassador to Japan, had
recently replaced Wade as British Minister in Peking. Sinclair sent him
a coded telegram on 21 July reporting: *'Courbet is here threatening Foochow.*
Anxious about making peace or declaration of war, wish to know'. On 22
July Parkes telegraphed: *'Report by telegram in what manner the Admiral*
in command of the French fleet has threatened Foochow. French Minister is
negotiating at Shanghai. What are French ships doing?' Sinclair replied on
26 July: *'French ships guard river preventing Chinese blockade. Port not*
obstructed. French c in c at anchorage ready for action. Sinclair.' On 25 July
he had sent a longer, clearer despatch by steamer. The city was full of
fear because the original ultimatum from Courbet had been due to expire
on 20 July, but this was then extended to 1 August. The Chinese believed
that the French intended to take Foochow as a pledge for the observance

of any agreement, but he had learnt the French would confine their actions to the Pagoda Anchorage. On 5 August he reported: '*All the ladies but three or four of the community have left with their children*'. He blamed this on Carrall, who had circulated a notice that the Customs Harbour Master at Pagoda Island had received from Admiral Courbet, telling him to get the merchant ships there to move out of range of fire of the guns, as he was expecting instructions to commence hostilities '*d'un moment à l'autre*'. Sinclair thought this a false alarm. The British Vice-Admiral Sir William Dowell had two ships, one at Foochow by the factories and one at the anchorage, and according to Sinclair, Dowell also thought there would be a settlement.

Sinclair's reports show that the local Chinese authorities were trying to ensure that other nations did not become involved, issuing proclamations asking citizens to do all they could to protect merchants of every nation so that there was no cause for any other dispute. The Viceroy cancelled a planned military and naval review at Pagoda anchorage to avoid provoking the French. On 5 August he had stopped the runners going to the telegraph station at Sharp Peak, because they were carrying messages from the French Admiral, but on 11 August he alleviated this inconvenience by telling the Commissioner of Customs to issue passes to the runners so they should not be stopped by the soldiers. Parkes telegraphed Sinclair on 6 August: '*Yamen states Viceroy telegraphs that naval authorities propose to land men in opposition to his wishes & that you decline to intervene. Send explanation by telegraph in this case & report by telegraph on state of affairs.*' (The captain of the British naval ship at Foochow had landed a force to demonstrate ability to protect foreigners, but this had aroused anti-foreign feeling. He now agreed that his men should be kept in readiness on board.) On 7 August Sinclair protested to the local authorities about the granite blocks placed in the river between the city and Pagoda anchorage. He reported on 16 August that the reply was that these were precautionary measures due to the question of peace or war being undecided, and that '*It is emphatically not in our view to occasion any unpleasantness to your country*'. The partial blockage would be undone when peace negotiations had been successfully concluded. The French contributed to the uncertainty about war with '*everything positioned for immediate fighting — and yet on the Emperor's birthday* [16th] *French ships hoisted flags in honour of the day...incomprehensible*'.

The Chinese authorities in Foochow were not getting much help from divided councils in Peking. The Chinese navy had been partially modernised, but in the decentralised Chinese system, there was no person or institution in charge of the navy as a whole. The fleet based in Foochow was comparatively weak. In his report sent to Hart on the battle on 30 September Carrall said:

> the French had 11 vessels: 4 cruisers, 1 corvette, 3 gun-vessels and 2 torpedo vessels, 77 guns in total. The Chinese forces under Captain Chang Ch'eng...had 11 boats and 45 guns. Most were lightly constructed, intended for the suppression of piracy and policing work rather than conflict.

Sinclair, in his despatch of 11 August, said only three could be called war vessels: the corvette *Yang Wu*, and two gunboats with one powerful gun each. The most powerful part of the Chinese navy was in the north, under Li Hongzhang, who was concerned by events in Korea, and neither he nor the commander of the fleet at Shanghai sent any ships to the aid of Foochow.

The French Vice-Consul at Pagoda Island gave notice to Warren on 22 August that warlike operations would start the next day in reprisal for the battle in Tonkin. The weather was so bad that Warren could not get the message to the Customs people on the other side of the river till midnight. The other residents were told to get on board the neutral ships anchored below Pagoda Island.

Carrall's report says that at 1: 56 p.m. on 23 August, the ships had swung to the ebb tide. Then:

> As the red flag was hoisted on the "Volta" the "Lynx" opened fire, followed by the rest of the French fleet, some of which got under weigh [sic]. The "Chen Hang" and "Yung Pao" sank in a few seconds. The "I Hsin" and "Fu Po" escaped up river and took the ground at Lin p'u. The "Fu Shing" and "Chun Sheng", their bows pointing up stream, were unable to bring their 18 ton guns to bear, and were soon adrift and in a sinking condition. The "Yang Wu" replied to the first broadside of the "Volta" with her stern-chaser and with good effect. Her first shell exploded on the "Volta's" bridge, killing the pilot (Thomas of Shanghai) and 6 men. Admiral Courbet had a narrow escape, as he was standing close to

the pilot when the shell burst. The "Yang Wu" only succeeded in firing one broadside when a torpedo vessel from under the Volta's quarter was sent at her. The torpedo struck her under the starboard quarter and she was blown up within 27 seconds of the commencement of the fight. The "Hu Hsing", "Chi An" and "Fei Yun" were disabled almost at first fire, and the gallant little "Chen Wei", exposed to the broadsides of the "Villars" and "D'Estaing" and riddled by a terrific discharge from the heavy guns of the "Triomphante" as she passed, fought to the last. In flames fore and aft, drifting helplessly down the stream, and sinking, she plied her guns again and again, till one of the French torpedo vessels, dashing in through the smoke, completed the work of destruction, but even as she sank, the last shot from the brave little craft struck her destroyer and seriously wounded her commander and two of his men.

Though in seven minutes from the firing of the first shot, every Chinese vessel was practically disabled, the French continued to pour in shot, shell and Hotchkiss fire, regardless of the wounded and helpless men in the crippled ships. It could not be called a battle; it was a butchery...

The Chinese had received orders from the Imperial Commissioner Chang Pei Lun [in charge of coastal defence] *not to fire the first shot and to remain where they were anchored. Admiral Courbet was thus able to choose his own time...when...the ships having swung to the ebb, seven of the Chinese vessels were unable to bring any but their stern guns to bear. Had the* [two ships] *with their 18 ton guns been moored stern and stern, the cost of this day's work, to the French, would have been far heavier.*

Warren's report agrees with Carrall's account.

The heavy guns of the French shattered the weak transports and toy gunboats in a way sickening to see and amongst all those looking the only feeling was one of intense pity and disgust.

The exception to this appears to be the US naval officers who glorified the departing French ships. For the *Triomphante*: 'Plough on brave ship, thy way to fresh glory and new honeur; may the Gods of war be seated ever on thy prow.' And for the *D'Estaing* 'Fresh honeur awaits thee! The "Chinois" shall feel thy fangs yet again.' The writers do agree, however, that however bravely the Chinese had fought, they had no hope against the superior weight, guns and armour of the French ships. The largest French ship, the *Triomphante,* was of 4,127 tons against the biggest Chinese ship, the *Yang Wu,* 1,400 tons. The French had machine guns, canons capable of constant fire, and the latest kind of torpedo; the Chinese did not.[12] Warren had reported earlier, on 10 August, that the Chinese tactics would be to concentrate on sinking the *Volta,* and having got its range, they might have succeeded, had the torpedo not put an end to the *Yang Wu's* efforts. Hart, who had by 31 August received reports of the affair, told Campbell: '*As for the French doings...I cannot call them anything else than a series of wilful, unnecessary because unfair, and wicked murders...'.*

Carrall's report continues with the events of 24 August, when '*Shortly after 10 a.m. the "Volta", "Aspic" and "Lynx" steamed up to abreast of the Arsenal and opened on it with their heavy guns and the Hotchkiss shells'.* Carrall heard five heavy explosions, and from his house above Foochow saw a huge cloud of fire and smoke ascending at 3 p.m. The large shipyard, built with French aid, was demolished. The French then attempted a landing, but the appearance of a large Chinese force on the hills above sent them back to their ships, from which they trained their guns on the Chinese, causing them to disperse. On the 25th, the French began going down river, bombarding the Chinese forts guarding the river. These were unable to reply as their guns were constructed to command the river against incoming ships, not those approaching from their rear. However, *La Gallissonnière*

> the most powerful Ironclad of the French fleet in these waters, steamed into the entrance of the river... . At a distance of two and a half miles she presented her broadside to the forts and the challenge was quickly accepted. The first of these shots did not strike the vessel and she returned a heavy fire, her shells bursting all over the face of the batteries. Soon, however, the forts began to get her range, and two shots struck her in rapid succession... . Others followed, and finding her situation unpleasantly warm, the "La Gallissonnière" turned back...she has since been sent to Hongkong to be docked and repaired.

Carrall then describes further French actions in destroying forts up to 29 August, when the fleet steamed out of the river. He noted that the Imperial Commissioner for Coastal Defence and the Imperial Commissioner for the Arsenal had left their posts at the first shot. He concluded his report with this assessment of the legal issues:

> The action of Admiral Courbet in committing hostile acts whilst in the port of a Power against whom war had not been declared, and which he had entered with the "implied consent" of the sovereign of that Power, is surely a breach of the Law of Nations, as laid down by Wheaton, page 140 §104: [He quotes the text].

Carrall said the French had lost one officer and fourteen men killed, and forty men wounded. Estimates of Chinese losses were of up to 3,000 men. The wrath of the Chinese population against all foreigners is understandable. In Hong Kong, Chinese workmen refused to work on La Gallissonnière.

Carrall now felt able to proceed against the pilots who had helped the French. On 23 August he had asked the British and American consuls (the latter being responsible for the Germans and Italians, whose own consuls were in Amoy (Xiamen) to warn the pilots for whom they were responsible not to take part in hostilities. Both apparently did so, but the Harbour Master told Carrall on 26 August that they were all still in French ships. Carrall told him to suspend their licences. He also asked the Tartar General and Governor to write to the appropriate consuls asking them to apprehend the pilots 'for a most improper breach of international law', copying this to the British and American consuls. The Chinese authorities did so on 30 September. Sinclair replied that he could not apprehend the British pilots, as they were still with the French ships, but that he would do so if they returned. However, he warned that the Shanghai Supreme Court might feel that their guilt depended on whether war had been declared or not. On 9 September he reported that the high authorities had notified him that by Imperial Edict of 27 August China had reluctantly declared war on the French. Sinclair wrote that he thought the situation was such that war was obviously in existence, but he had told the high authorities that he would need to know that a declaration had also been made through recognised channels if they wished to obtain the advantages of the neutrality of other nations. Parkes told Sinclair on 7 October that he was not aware that a Chinese declaration of war had been conveyed either to the foreign representatives at Peking or via the Chinese Minister in Europe.[13]

The only pilot apprehended was one of the Germans, who alleged that he had served on the *Triomphante* under compulsion. Carrall thought this contradicted the statement the man had made to him, but the pilot was supported by the German consul in Amoy. Carrall took steps to replace all five pilots, with the backing of the Chamber of Commerce. The consuls did not object, but it is not clear that any pilot was ever brought to court.

On 9 September Admiral Dowell told Sinclair that H.M.S. *Zephyr* had been fired on by one of the river forts on 6 September and that an officer had been seriously wounded. Such an incident could have caused a British retaliation if not handled carefully. Sinclair informed the Viceroy, who immediately sent two high officials to convey his regret and apologies to Admiral Dowell, with Sinclair and his interpreter Hurst in attendance. It was agreed that the Chinese officer responsible should make a full and public personal apology and that the question of compensation would be referred by the British Admiral to his home authorities. Reading between the lines it is clear that Admiral Dowell was anxious to settle matters peaceably, and that he referred the compensation question home to avoid involving Sinclair.

Carrall made a partial report to Hart on 19 September on Chinese remedial action. The *Zephyr* had been mistaken for a French war vessel. The High Provincial Authorities, at the suggestion of Dowell, had sent a Deputy and two students from the Arsenal to a point on the river where they would supply each incoming vessel (not being French) with a large flag which would bear in black shirting a character denoting its nationality. Carrall was sending a Tidewaiter, Schmidt, to help with this.

He had in fact been involved earlier as a mediator. He delayed reporting this till 11 October when he knew that he had been successful, for it was a task he had undertaken reluctantly.

Zephyr case

Viceroy and the Foreign Board called on Sir W. Dowell to apologise.

> On the 9th September, Liu Sui Chi, Grain Intendant and
> Senior member of the Foreign Board, called on me on behalf of
> H.E. the Viceroy, and asked me to give my assistance in fixing the
> amount of compensation to be paid to such of the crew of H.M.S.
> "Zephyr" who had been injured owing to the firing. I replied that I
> thought H.B.M.'s Consul was the proper person to apply to, on
> which Liu Taotai told me that he had already been to see Mr.
> Sinclair, but that he declined to have anything to do with the
> question, saying that as the Admiral had telegraphed direct to
> H.B.M.'s Minister, the affair would be settled between the Foreign
> Minister and the Tsungli Yamen. I then agreed to try what I could
> do, but said that not only was it an affair which did not altogether
> belong to my department, but that it was one which required such
> careful handling that I might only burn my own fingers in having
> anything to do with it without profiting them (the Local
> Authorities).
>
> The Taotai replied that the times were urgent and that in a
> case like the present he did not think I could be accused with
> meddling outside of my own province, and he further added the
> Viceroy would look upon it as a great favour if I would exert
> myself in this instance.
>
> I was exceedingly loathe to have anything to do with the case,
> not only as I did not feel sure of my ground and did not wish to
> stand the chance of failure, but because besides I might incur a
> reprimand from you for having taken upon myself to interfere in
> the question — however, being pressed for my assistance I finally
> promised to do my best to bring this unfortunate affair to a
> satisfactory ending.

As the wounded officer had died, Carrall suggested that £3,000 compensation be paid to his widowed mother, and £500 be shared by the more lightly wounded seamen. Capt. Powell forwarded this to the British Government. The amount was accepted, and it was paid through Carrall. Sinclair reported to Parkes that he had had no hand in the negotiations, which he thought treated the Chinese too leniently, but Parkes told him that he and the navy were entirely satisfied with the apology and settlement.

When the decree on the 'reluctant' declaration of war was issued on 26 August, the Tsungli Yamen in Peking had called in the British and German ministers and asked them to deny coaling and repair facilities to the French in accordance with international law.[14] However, the British Foreign Office lawyers remained uncertain whether a legal state of war existed. It was not till late November that the Foreign Office in London decided that a state of war did exist, and that such a ban could be made. Meanwhile, on 6 September the Chinese authorities informed Carrall that they had heard from Shanghai that a British ship, the *Sir Garnet Wolsey* had left that port with coal, and asked him to find out her destination. On 9 September he told them that she was supplying coal to the French fleet outside the river at Matsoo (Matsu Tao island), and that he had obtained witness statements. The Chinese authorities replied that they would convey the information to the British consul. Carrall then sent copies of the affidavits to the Commissioners of the Customs at other ports to enable them to proceed against the *Sir Garnet* for infringement of Article 47 of the British treaty, should she visit their ports. Buck-passing then ensued, with the Commissioner at Amoy saying that he needed the Chinese authorities at Foochow to instruct those at Amoy to tell him to apprehend the ship. The authorities at Foochow delayed, then complained about Sinclair's notes to them that it was up to the Chinese authorities to send a Revenue Cruiser to apprehend the *Sir Garnet* (regardless of the destruction of their ships in the French attack).

On 28 November 1884 Hart thanked Carrall for his actions, but followed it up with a despatch to Commissioner Hannen, who was back at post:

> *Mr. Carrall appears to me to have handled this matter both carefully and judiciously; but, now that it can be more calmly looked at, and away from the local excitement of the moment, it is not quite clear to me that a British Court will authorize a sentence of confiscation, or the British Authorities consent to so severe a penalty as forbidding the vessel to take any more at Chinese ports. In any case, if China decides to push the affair further, it will be necessary to pay special attention to the following points:*

He then summarised what lawyers might make of the case, including that 'the depositions of the Chinese pilots might be handled in court as to prove nothing'. He would put the question before the Yamen, and let

Hannen know the outcome, but he wished to prepare him for the possible breakdown of the charge if the Customs seized the vessel.

A third issue was equally unsuccessfully resolved from the Chinese point of view. On 17 September Sinclair reported to Parkes that the Viceroy had written, at the instance of the Acting Commissioner of Customs, that the British-owned Eastern Telegraph office at Sharp Peak was sending messages daily to the French Fleet and that this was extremely improper. *'He begs me to at once to communicate with you to have the practice put a stop to.'* Sinclair said that Admiral Sir William Dowell also thought that the Chinese had a case, and he seems to have written to the company to this effect. Five runners in the employ of the Customs were arrested by the Chinese authorities and all their messages seized, leading to protests from foreign traders. They seem later to have been released. On 23 September Parkes reprimanded Sinclair for writing to the telegraph company. *'The Company is bound to receive messages from both sides till one or other assumes responsibility for preventing them'*, in the absence of a proper declaration of war.

It must have been a relief to Carrall when Hannen returned to take responsibility for all these cases. Much later he recalled these stressful days when expressing sympathy to Bredon on the situation in Peking:

> *19 June 1900…You must be having an anxious time. I am the*
> *better able to realise what it means, having gone through a*
> *somewhat similar experience at Foochow in 1884. Sleepless nights*
> *for weeks with hard work during the day…*[15]

The cases illustrate the difficulties of Customs officers. They were employees of the Chinese government, and while they worked locally with a Chinese Superintendent who, till 1911, received and forwarded the Customs revenue, and who theoretically dealt with political business, they were not directly responsible to the local Chinese Viceroy or to the local magistrate of the port, the Taotai, who dealt with the Consuls, but there were occasions when each needed the other. They were responsible to Hart, who was responsible to the Tsungli Yamen, which itself could not give orders to the Viceroys and Governors of the Provinces. It also illustrates the extreme difficulty the Chinese local authorities had in getting effective action taken against foreign citizens who broke their laws or who acted against Chinese interests in international disputes — difficulties arising in part from the strength of the foreigners, but also from the very decentralised nature of the Chinese system of administration. Commissioners had to tread a fine line between respecting the Superintendent's position and damaging foreign prestige in the Customs by yielding entirely to Chinese authority.[16]

The line between the Consul and the Commissioner could be equally difficult to tread. There were times when Hart felt that Carrall overstepped the mark and he received a reproof. At other times action was implicitly recognised as necessary. In this case, Carrall had, in Hart's eyes, redeemed himself. The legal uncertainties and potential international repercussions meant Hart needed to find 'careful and judicious' Commissioners, able to exercise common sense diplomatically in emergency, even though most Customs work was so routine that only the ability 'to read, write and count' was required. In January 1885, Carrall received his promotion to First Assistant A (Acting Deputy Commissioner) and his salary was increased to taels 300 per month. (Customs salaries were paid in the Chinese silver tael, whose variable value against the gold £ sterling was to give trouble later, but at the time his salary was equivalent to £1000 per annum.[17]) On 4 July 1885 he was further promoted to Deputy Commissioner, and was told he would be sent to Shanghai on 31 July. From that point on he made steady progress in his career.

Thanks from the Chinese

During 1885 Hart was facing crucial decisions. Parkes had died suddenly. At his funeral on 30 March Hart was offered the post of British Minister, a post that would have been the peak of his expectations as a young man joining the consular service, and which would bring with it a baronetcy and high status in British society. He dithered, telegraphed his wife, who wanted him to accept, but finally turned it down in the summer. He then spent the next few months wondering whether he had done right.

Meanwhile he was also pursuing, with the Tsungli Yamen's approval, a settlement with the French. Campbell was sent to Paris to see Jules Ferry personally on a minor Customs grievance, and received encouragement that led to negotiations. The agreement reached survived both the fall of Jules Ferry in France (which followed a Chinese defeat of French forces in a land battle in Tonkin) and the hesitations of the Yamen in China. On 4 April 1885 a protocol was signed in Paris, which led to France sending a new Minister to China to arrange the details. The final treaty was signed on 9 June at Tianjin by Li Hongzhang and Jules Patenôtre on the basis of the former Li-Fournier agreement.[18]

Chinese gratitude was rapidly expressed. On 5 July 1885 Hart told Campbell that the Emperor had awarded him the order of the Double Dragon, 1st Class of the 2nd Division, equivalent to that given to ambassadors, and that Campbell would receive the 2nd Class of the 2nd Division. Carrall was awarded the 1st Class of the 3rd Division, for people of the rank of consul and colonel. The order, in the manner of European orders at the time, was strictly graded by class and occupation. Division 1 was for sovereigns. In the Customs list consulted by Aunt Kath, both the award of the order and the promotion to Deputy Commissioner were dated 3 September 1885, which suggests that one of Hart's motives in promoting him was to qualify him for the 1st Class of 3rd Division. Another Englishman, Charles Brewitt-Taylor, was awarded the 2nd Class in the 3rd Division, equivalent to Vice-Consul, at the recommendation of the Commander of the naval arsenal at Foochow for his five years of meritorious service as professor of Navigation at the Naval School, but as with Carrall, Hart and Campbell, Brewitt-Taylor's behaviour during the events of 1884 may also have been in Chinese minds.[19] Our family records do not say who recommended Carrall, but it may have been the local Viceroy. His insignia are still in the hands of a great-grandson (Figure C). Probably at the same time Carrall received a robe and mandarin's hat (Figures A and B). The robe shows signs of having been much worn, and was probably used by my grandfather on suitable occasions, such as when he entertained the chief Chinese merchants of the port in which he served.

Frances of course did not receive open recognition. But Hart recorded in his diary: '*Saturday 15 August* [1885]. *Li is in with news of Mrs. Carrall's pluck in staying at Foochow last year.*' She did not flee as did most of the foreign women, despite the anxieties she must have had for her own safety and that of her four little girls. Sinclair, in his long report to Parkes of 11 August spoke of the fear that had gripped the city around 19 July 1884, with wealthy Chinese heading out of the city with their families and goods, a scarcity of rice developing, and robbery abounding.

On 14 October 1884 Frances had given birth to their fifth daughter,

Figure 5.7. The Bridge of Ten Thousand Ages, Fuzhou, c. 1907, taken by G W Swire. The scene would have been little different in 1884 (courtesy of John Swire & Sons Ltd).

Figure 6.1. (a). Chefoo, from Temple Hill, looking towards Settlement Hill and the harbour, taken by Mr Kirschtein (Ca01-64). The cemetery was below, in the pine wood, and is now a primary school. The western wall of Yantai is visible (centre left).

Figure 6.1b. Enlargement of the harbour side of Settlement Hill. 'Hillside' with its large white chimneys can be identified by the two flights of steps leading down from the long terrace in front of the house. The gardens stretched from its front gate near the hill top to its south gate on the lower road which ran between it and the Japanese consulate (large many-windowed house left of centre).

Figure 6.2. Hillside in 1900, from the orchard (Ca02-12). There was a lawn and a tennis court immediately below the walled terrace in front of the house. A second flight of steps (right) led down to the lower tennis court, below which there was the orchard. (There was also a kitchen garden and fish pond.)

Figure 6.3. The girls' school, 1899. Nobody is named. The teacher at the centre rear is wearing the Chinese attire used by some missionaries (Ca01-048). She is probably the then Principal, Emily Burton. The building is now part of a Chinese Naval Academy.

Figure 6.4. The younger children on the terrace at the impressive Commissioner's house in Canton. Baby Phyllis is on her mother's lap. The young Frances is evidently convalescing. My mother, Gwen, is sitting rather inelegantly on the stool, next to Eric. In the background is a bird's cage (Ca01-023).

Figure 6.5. This photo was taken in Amoy in 1895 (Ca-s02). Emily is standing at the top. My mother Gwen is on her mother's lap, and Eric, the only boy, is beside his mother.

Figure 6.6. The school Christmas Play: Beauty and the Beast, *1899 (Ca1-033). A master was imported for one male part, but the prince was a girl adorned with a moustache. The players are not named, but the girl second from the right looks like Emily.*

Figure 6.7. A half page of the larger album, Ca1, showing the fifth form in June 1898, featuring Maude and Kathleen Carrall (back row, left and centre).

Epiphany. Old Xmas Day. Twelfth Day.   **6 ~~THURSDAY~~** [6–359] *Saturday.*   [XII Moon, 14th Day]

四拜禮日六初月正英   日四十月二十華

In morning Eue & Frances & I practised our pieces at the Club. We all eight with Father went to an Xmas party given by Mrs Molyneux. He had a Christmas tree, & I was given a dainty pair of China vases. Everyone was there, including V.R.E. who is all right again. The tree caught fire at the end, & all the children were sent out of the room, but the fire was quickly extinguished. In the evening we of course went to the "Grand Evening Concert" got up by Mrs Griffith in aid of the widows & orphans of our killed & wounded British soldiers. Em & I opened it with an overture duett, & I played my solo — Liszt's "Rhapsodie Hongroise" was terribly nervous, but Father was satisfied, & was congratulated by several people V.R.E. declaring it to be the best, but of course that is his Germanism. Mr McLaren recited beautifully, & his recitations with Mr Burne's songs were the best items on the programme.

Partial Eclipse of the Moon [*see p.* 2].   **7 ~~FRIDAY~~** [7–358] *Sunday.*   [XII Moon, 15th Day]
Accession of Abbas Pacha, Khedive of Egypt, 1892.

五拜禮日七初月正英   日五十月二十華

Rose later in consequence of concert. Special prayers said for sufferers from war, & for friends & relatives of murdered Rev. Brooks. Mr Burne preached. Went round the hill with Vroyan who said Ada & Lilly disliked idea of coming out here. Vyr. came to tiffin as usual. Afterwards Mu, Frances, Maude & I with Vyr. went for a long walk towards & round the foot of the pinnacle Rather cold but exhilarating many people skating. Vyr. briefly regaled us with Florence Marryat's "Three Fates" (?) which he had read while in bed. Gwen gave us a very original Xmas tree after tea. Consisting of my violin stand ornamented with bits of straw, & herself, in an old rug, Baby's white cap, & a red doll's dress in her mouth for a beard represented Santa Claus: Father lying down, having caught a chill.

○ Full Moon, 8.30 a.m.   **8 ~~SATURDAY~~** [8–357] *Monday.*   [XII Moon, 16th Day]

六拜禮日八初月正英   日六十月二十華

Father much better. Subscriptions concert, offertories, self-denial for Patriotic Fund collected in Chefoo amount now to about $1760. In morning & evening finished sewing for children's party. Went for a walk down to the rink & back. Vyr. called in evening to see how Father was & is to take us skating tomorrow. Lady from Shanghai is to take Miss Burton's place.

First Sunday after Epiphany.   Release for H.M.S. "Phoebe" probably not coming out for 3 months, so more chance of C. being able
Accession of King of Italy, 1878.   to stay out on   **9 ~~SUNDAY~~** [9–356] *Tuesday.* China [XII Moon, 17th Day] stati

拜禮日九初月正英   日七十月二十華

Practised piano & violin, & ticketed presents for children in the morning. Poster Molly. called, & as usual urged us to go out & not stay in so much. He refused to allow Maude to skate. Vyr came up to tea, & after it, Mrs Frances, Eue, I & he went down to Singtai's pond. The ice was excellent & quite a number of people came to skate. Vyr & Mr Maltchenko each gave me a lesson, & I enjoyed it immensely. Mr Emery & Mr Ennolent also whirled me up & down. We came back by moonlight, & decided to have the acting after all

Figure 6.8. Kathleen's diary, 6–8 January 1900.

Figure 6.9. Taken in December 1901, looking down the garden, and north-east over the harbour to the hills beyond (Ca2-050). The house below is the Japanese consulate — 9 on the Chefoo map on page 147. It still seemed visible at the end of the peninsula in 2002 (Figure D). (The white spots are acid damage.)

also called Frances. We must hope that Carrall was more philosophical than he had been at the birth of the fourth.

Family Matters and Leave in England, 1887–9

Jim Carrall must have been affected by the death of his sister on 20 August 1885, and worried by its effect on his mother, alone in England. However, the second home leave only became due ten years after the first, and he took it 1887–9. My aunt Kath wrote:

> For us children it was our first experience of English life and ways. I remember that Christmas especially because of Grandfather's kindness. Round the billiard table we each found a place set with parcels. How proud I was to get my first doll's pram!

Robert Fawcus, Frances' father, had by then moved from the north to Kingston-on-Thames, to be nearer to several of his sons working in London or nearby. He called his house there *Over Dinsdale,* in memory of the happy family home. This leave was the last time that Frances saw her father, who died in 1894. For Emily Spry Sampson the 1887–9 leave was the first time she met her granddaughters, and became better acquainted with the woman who had married her son.

By the time of the leave, the five daughters were aged from ten to four years old. Frances would have taught them to read, write and do arithmetic, and introduced them to the Bible, history and geography. We can imagine her multi-tasking like her mother before her, who wrote in 1856 to her husband in Germany:

> Willie sitting facing me, doing his lesson, he just observed in his peculiar way to Anna Maria "I would not be a dunce." Anna Maria was greatly delighted with your letter and it is not her fault that it is not answered, but I really cannot get quietly sat down with them. I am now writing with baby on my lap.

Contrary to the common perception of expatriate wives in China, Frances did not lead an idle life. She ran the household, entertained as befitted her husband's status, and nursed her family during their inevitable illnesses. She mended their clothes and probably made or altered them, for money was not plentiful. She had the help of a Chinese

Amah as nursemaid and babysitter, and other servants would take care of the laundry, cooking, cleaning, etc. under her direction. (She would have missed this while on leave.) As the older ones took up more of her time as teacher the younger ones picked up Chinese and pigeon English from the Amah and other house servants. The consular records show they returned from leave with a companion-governess, Miss Sarah Ives, to help out in their next posting, Amoy (Xiamen). Here the long-desired son, Eric, was born on 16 May 1889. In September 1890 Jim Carrall was posted to Chefoo as Acting Commissioner. He was to spend the rest of his career there, except for short spells in Amoy and Canton.

I do not think my grandmother would have agreed with Hart that many children were '*so much slavery and drudgery for the gentler sex*'. She was happy in the role of wife and mother, which, as she told Hart in a later letter, she thought the most satisfying one for women. Her letters to him show her pride in her daughters, and she loved babies. In a letter to Hart in February 1902 Aunt Kath wrote:

> We are quite a household, having an extra baby to look after while his parents are away for a holiday. He and our baby are a little jealous of each other and always demand the same attention, but I believe Mother likes it because she says it's like having twins!

She was not so happy in the role of teacher. Miss Ives does not seem to have lasted long. In 1892 the five older girls entered the girls' school in Chefoo, and she put my mother's early education firmly in the hands of her older daughters.

Frances was, like her mother, a good letter-writer. Aunt Kath wrote that the greatest pleasure of her grandmother in later life was to receive her daughter-in-law's chatty letters. She kept them in an album, which, when Kath wrote, was still 'in the family' (unfortunately now untraceable). The strong family network Frances maintained was to prove invaluable later. Carrall taught his daughters to be methodical about letter-writing, and at the end of the out-of-date official Customs diary in which Kath kept her 1900 diary, she had also filled up the last pages, the REGISTER OF CORRESPONDENCE, with its columns headed Date, From whom received, Reply sent, To whom written, Reply received. The list of Kath's correspondents in 1900 included friends, numerous relatives, and both her godmothers, her Aunt Lucy and Mrs Glover.

She also of course recorded the letters sent to or received from her godfather, Sir Robert Hart. Their correspondence started in 1896, when she was thirteen, at school in Chefoo. It will be an important part of the next chapters, which illustrate expatriate family life in China at the time and Hart's intimate relationship with the families of his staff.

CHAPTER SIX

THE CHEFOO SCHOOLGIRLS AND SIR ROBERT HART

Chefoo was the China my aunts and my mother always remembered. It had the schools of the China Inland Mission (CIM), set up to cater for the children of missionaries, but open also to other families who wished to avoid the expense and the emotional pain of the long separation involved in sending children to board in their home country. Local schooling was a necessity for Jim Carrall with his large family, and the diary Aunt Kath kept in 1900 shows it enabled him to play an active role as father.

Chefoo and Shantung Province

On 24 July 1890 Hart told Campbell that: *'Fellows have to serve a long time now for each step: the men who are now coming to the front count from 1863–8, and even so only acting'*. Carrall, in the 1868 intake as a fourth-class clerk, was doing well to become Acting Commissioner in charge of Chefoo on 1 September 1890. He was to remain there till his death in 1902, except for three years in Amoy and Canton. Although Chefoo was not a plum post in salary terms, it was desirable because it was thought to be healthier than most places in China. The cold winters and hot summers enabled a range of sports, which were known to be good for health. Kath's diary shows how she appreciated its mountain scenery and sea views. Figure 6.4 shows a convalescent young Frances in Canton, but even in Chefoo, family life was punctuated by dangerous illnesses. The high death rate was common to both Chinese and European members of the Customs staff: it was due to genuinely unhealthy conditions, rather than European unfitness for tropical climates.[1]

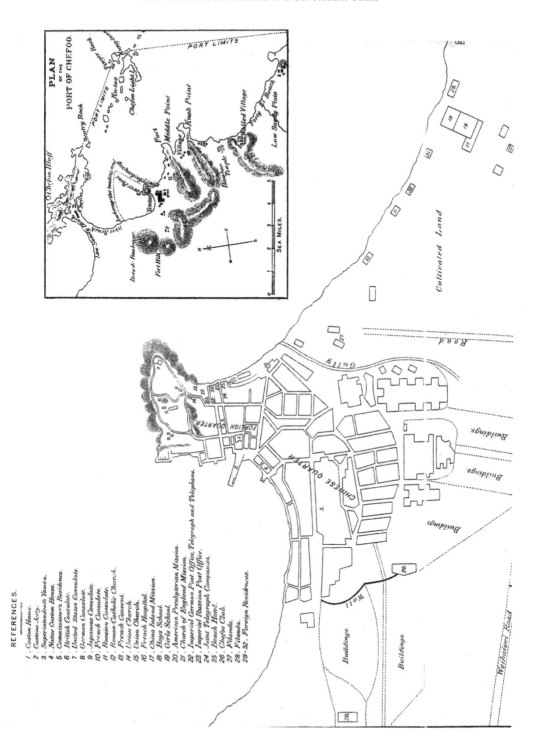

REFERENCES.

1. Custom House.
2. Customs Jetty.
3. Superintendent's Yamén.
4. Native Custom House.
5. Commissioner's Residence.
6. British Consulate.
7. United States Consulate.
8. German Consulate.
9. Japanese Consulate.
10. French Consulate.
11. Russian Consulate.
12. Roman Catholic Church.
13. French Convent.
14. Union Church.
15. Union Church.
16. French Hospital.
17. China Inland Mission.
18. Boys School.
19. Girls School.
20. American Presbyterian Mission.
21. Church of England Mission.
22. Imperial German Post Office, Telegraph and Telephone.
23. Imperial Russian Post Office.
24. Joint Telegraph Companies.
25. Beach Hotel.
26. Chefoo Club.
27. Filanda.
28. Filanda.
29–32. Foreign Residences.

Chefoo port area and 'Yentai'
as depicted by J W Carrall, 'Chefoo' Decennial Reports, 1905.

Hart had instituted decennial reports on each port. Carrall's report for 1892–1901 includes the maps shown on page 147. The name Chefoo referred to the whole port area. Carrall shows Yentai (Yantai) as its main town. There was no formal foreign settlement (though one was mooted in 1899), but the most prestigious expatriate homes were on what was called locally Settlement Hill, a promontory projecting out into the bay. To its west was the main commercial area, adjacent to the harbour (2), and the Customs office (1). On the east, a sandy beach extended down the coast to the CIM head office and schools (17–19). Apart from the missionaries, most expatriates lived either on the Hill or at the Hill end of the eastern beach. This was also the location of the Club (26).

An excellent photo of Chefoo in 1900 was taken from Temple Hill by a friend of the Carralls, Mr Kirschtein, who seems to have been a semi-professional photographer (Figure 6.1a). The quality of the photo is such that an enlargement of a small section shows the dominating position of the Commissioner of Customs' house, Hillside, on the harbour side of Settlement Hill (Figure 6.1b). The white balustrades of the steps leading down on either side of a central round point immediately in front of the house can be clearly seen. Figure 6.2 shows these steps and the house from the view point of the orchard, which was two levels below it. There was a cottage for the use of the Inspector-General, which the Carralls used for additional summer accommodation.

Immediately southwest of the harbour and Settlement Hill was Yantai, the Chinese town, of which Carrall wrote:

No efforts have been made [since 1891] to improve the sanitary condition of the people...and the example set by the Foreign quarter [which had an unofficial General Purposes Committee] is treated with indifference. Chefoo, in and round about, in the Western meaning of the word, is without roads and without drains, and, to make matters worse, some of the streets in the city have manure dumped along the sides, while in other places human excrement is kept in heaps for sale to farmers. This disregard of health is the cause of sickness amongst Foreigners and Natives alike, as, in the spring, the dry particles of filth in the form of dust are carried in the air by the hot dry winds from the south, thus causing fevers and eye and throat troubles.[2]

The crowded houses of the Chinese town are visible in Figure 6.1a. Kath's diary describes a visit to a friend at a mission station, when:

we had to go right through the heart of the Chinese city which...naturally was in a filthy dirty squalid condition. After an hour or so we came out the other side (able to breath once more a little fresh air) to open country...passing through the tumbled down archway of the great wall of the city.

The stench of Chinese cities where people picked their way along narrow streets was one of the first things to strike late nineteenth-century Europeans. Their expectations of public health measures had changed very much since Carrall's mother, Emma Spry Edwards, had lived in 1840s London. Yantai has happily also changed considerably since 1900. Figure D shows my photo from a similar standpoint on Temple Hill to that of Mr Kirschtein.

The Customs House (1) was not far from Hillside, near the Customs' jetty, though Carrall's dignity required that he go there in a sedan chair. In 2002 the old building was still in use, though only for training courses, and was approached by its former back door on the main street leading up to Settlement Hill. Its more elaborate facade on the harbour side was in 2002 half hidden by encroaching buildings.

Carrall reckoned that the Chinese population of Yantai nearly doubled between 1891 and 1901, reaching about 57,000. He noted that the inhabitants were constantly changing: thousands left the port each year for Port Arthur (Lushun), Vladivostok and Manchuria [Manchow] to work on the railways or to collect seaweed. The coolie trade was still thriving, for parts of Shantung's farm land were subject to floods from the Yellow River (Huang He), while at other times it suffered drought. It was also an active mission field, with three Roman Catholic bishoprics and several Protestant churches. Poverty and hostility to the missions, which many Chinese felt were undermining their culture, made it a fertile breeding ground for what became known as the Boxer movement in the late 1890s.

The foreign population of the district had risen from 270 to 655 in the same period but, of these, only 293 lived in Chefoo. The rest were inland. These were mainly missionaries, but they included a few people who had bought or leased land for vineyards or other agricultural enterprises. In 1901 the town had twenty-six foreign firms, of which ten were Japanese and seven British. The town also held a French Roman Catholic bishopric, convent and hospital. There was an American Presbyterian Mission on the west side of the town (20) with the imposing church visible in Figure 6.1 (a).

The adult foreigners in Chefoo must have been aware of China's growing weakness, which was not only due to internal discontent. The modernised Japan was the rising power, on the look-out for expansion. In 1894 the Korean king asked for Chinese help to crush a rebellion. China agreed, but the Japanese sent in a larger force, took Seoul, and replaced the ruler with one favouring them. China declared war but was defeated on land and at sea. Japan gained Formosa (Taiwan) and parts of Manchuria, the right to enter the Treaty Port system and to build factories, and an indemnity which helped throw Chinese finances into chaos.[3] One result, as Carrall noted, was a great increase in Japanese and Korean trade through Chefoo.

Alarmed by its growing power, Russia and France put pressure on Japan to renounce its claim to Port Arthur (Lushun), the ice-free port directly north across the sea from Chefoo, in return for an increased indemnity. The final peace treaty brought Korea effectively within the Japanese sphere of influence. Russia extended its sphere in Manchuria, building railways (hence the coolie trade) and took control of Port Arthur. Germany took the murder of a missionary as the opportunity to lease Qingdao (Kiaochow) in southern Shantung in 1897, treating it like a colony.[4] They constructed a railway into the interior, which diverted a lot of Shantung's exports away from Chefoo. In 1900 they opened a German post office, telephone and telegraph office in Chefoo, at a time when the Customs had taken responsibility for running the Chinese post on modern lines. Britain gained an agreement that no other power would be allowed control of the Yangzi River and leases of new territories adjacent to Kowloon, opposite Hong Kong, in 1898, and of Wei-Hai-Wei, east of Chefoo. (The Japanese had taken this Chinese naval station, but had agreed to withdraw.) In 1898 the sickly Emperor of China, now a young man, tried to inaugurate bold reforms to modernise China following the example of Japan, but he was soon put firmly once more under the tutelage of the canny, conservative Dowager Empress.

Within Chefoo, the US opened a consulate in 1896, as did the French and Germans in 1898. Carrall also shows the Japanese (9) and Russian

(11) consulates on his map. The British consulate (8) was much older. Relations with the German and Russian consuls gave Carrall considerable trouble, but his daughters enjoyed the variety of the small foreign population. Kathleen told Hart in a 1902 letter:

> *Emily and I have German and French lessons every week with the Consuls' wives; this is a very cosmopolitan place, one hears all languages spoken, which is an advantage to us girls.*

French and Russian hostility to Britain was expressed by lobbying against a pay rise for the Customs, because it was led by the Britisher Hart. This had a direct effect on Carrall's ability to save for his next leave and his retirement in Europe. The silver tael in which they were paid was steadily falling in value against gold, a fact which was worrying Hart from 1891. (Most European currencies were based on gold, including Britain's £ sterling.) Hart was aware of the discontent amongst his staff but the Sino-Japanese war was not the time to ask for remedial action. Salaries were finally doubled on 1 July 1898.

Hart Contacts the Carrall School Girls

The CIM had three schools in Chefoo, a senior boys' school, a prep school for younger boys, and a girls' school (Figure 6.3). The older Carrall girls entered in 1892. It was not large by modern standards, but it offered a better education for girls than most British schools of that time:

> *Chefoo Aug 14 1890...English girls' school. I cannot speak too highly of the standard of education: it is well equal and in many ways supersedes a first-class English school with masters. Girls are not crammed, but are taught to think, and to a large extent to learn independence and self-help.[5]*

These characteristics were not necessarily assets in the marriage market of the time, as the girls were to find on their return to Britain. A further disadvantage of even a good local school was that it did not provide a network of school friends in the home country, useful to supplement family networks in finding employment and spouses. In class-ridden Britain a school in China did not add to their social status in the way that having attended the 'right' school in Britain did.[6]

On 8 February 1893 Hart told Campbell:

We'll be in the agony of Spring movements presently…[Returns from leave] will upset and oust all the present acting appointments…I shall probably send Drew to Canton and either Hippisley or Carrall (who is turning out a very good man indeed) for chief secretary. I don't see much of the C's and I doubt if they are specially friendly to me, but he is an excellent workman at his post, and she is one of the sweetest, kindest & best of women!

But at the end of March 1893, Carrall was taken seriously ill. He was on sick leave till 5 June 1893, when he was transferred to Amoy.[7] My mother was born in Chefoo on 11 April 1893, but there was no time to christen her while Frances coped with a sick husband and the planning necessary for a move. Her younger sister and great companion, Phyllis, was born in Amoy in September 1895. Here Carrall evidently joined in the local expatriate sport of shooting tigers, for Maude's album has a photo of a dead one on his lawn.[8] From Amoy Carrall was transferred to Canton, Hart commenting to Campbell on 19 July 1896 *'Carrall is also a good man at C'ton'.*

The girls had entered the school as day pupils, but during this time they were boarders. Hart's first letter to Aunt Kath, when she was thirteen, refers to the rough sea trips this necessitated. The letter was prompted by his old friend, Emma Sampson. It is playful in tone, but he adapted his style as he got to know her better and as she grew up. She was not the only girl he wrote to, nor his only godchild. There are stacks of letters in the Hart archive at QUB from women friends, some of whom had known him when they were young girls in Peking attending his Christmas parties. He continued to correspond with those whom he particularly liked long after they grew up and married, as we have seen with Mrs Brazier and Emma Carrall. As becomes evident, he provided presents as well as letters.

In Hart's apparently inconsequential letters to a young girl, he reveals much about his life at the time:

Peking

26 Oct 1896

Now guess! Shut your eyes and before you read more, guess who the writer is: who is it? Give it up? Well, my dear Miss Kathleen, it is myself! But who am I? Your godfather! And having introduced myself thus lest I should frighten you by styling you Dearest Kathleen right off, I may now proceed. [He tells her about her christening, already quoted.] *As I have a nice bit of news to give you I seize the opportunity of writing a letter to you in the hope of extracting one from you. In fact I have one of your letters in my possession, for your Grandmama Mrs. Sampson — who is very fond & very proud of you – sent me in her last letter the note you wrote for her birthday, dated 18th July. I am very glad to have it, for it is written by you — very nice writing and very well expressed! But dear me, where is my bit of news gone off to? O yes — Mr. Bredon is going home: so I have moved your Papa from Canton & made him the Commissioner at Chefoo! Do you like that? You and Minnie and Maude & Eric & Fanny will all be up at Chefoo and living in the house on the hill — the Commissioner's house — in a fortnight, and instead of having to steam down to Canton for Xmas and back again to school, you will have your holidays at Chefoo and no sea sickness in the storms — no pitching and tossing — and perhaps no more change till you can go home once more to England. I wish the river did not freeze in winter, for then you could come up & pay me a visit in Peking during the holidays, but it does freeze and there's no railway from Chefoo — and so you can't come to me. Perhaps next summer, if I am here & if you are tired of ozone & salt spray & would like dust & Peking dry air instead, you might manage a visit: or shall I run down & see you?*

[He remembers Muriel and Emily in his garden.] *What big girls you must all be by now: it w'd puzzle me to walk off with one of you as I did when you were little people — and very nice little people you all were!*

Give my love to Emily & Muriel: keep a big lump for yourself: and write me a nice letter when you have time. The only address you need put on it is this

Sir Robert Hart,

Peking.

(*Peking* was also the only word he put above the date of his letters.) Jim Carrall had presumably already been informed that he was now a full Commissioner. At last he earned enough to make investments aimed at providing a retirement income, though he could only make real savings after the salary rise of 1898. Attractive high returns are balanced by high risks, as he was to learn.

Hart soon got a reply, lost like all his letters received before June 1900, but we can guess at some of what Kath wrote. He wrote back immediately:

4th December 1896

Dearest Kathleen,

When the mail came in yesterday I at once picked out one letter to read, partly because I did not recognise the handwriting but chiefly because the address was so neat, so well written, and so brief: it was yours. [He emphasises the sufficiency of *Sir Robert Hart, Peking*]...

I was so sorry to hear that your Mama & sisters had to remain at Shanghai on Maude's account: I fear they'll have a terribly cold voyage up. [Maude had been taken ill; the two older sisters evidently stayed to help in nursing her, while the younger children went on to Chefoo with their father and Amah.] *The last week has been desperately cold, with a fierce northerly wind blowing all the time and water freezing in every direction: the ink still holds out, but it is not far from the fire. How is it at Chefoo? Have you dry cutting wind, or is the place all under snow? I like the hot months best, when one can wear lighter clothing & need take no trouble to keep warm: the days are so short that I want all the daylight for office work, and so I get my exercise in the garden after dark: five times round makes a good mile, and between seven & eight o'clock I generally manage to do three or four miles, and then I can keep warm all the evening after, sitting by the fire & reading up to eleven or twelve o'c.*

How did you come off in the Examination? How many firsts did you take & how many prizes did you win? What study do you like best, and what kind of play gives you most pleasure? Who is your greatest friend among the girls, & what is she like? I suppose you are quite tall by this time — you'll be fourteen next birthday, will you not? Is your hair dark or fair? Better send me a lock, tied up with ribbon of the colour you like best!

Now that we have broken the "ice" of silence, I hope the "water" of correspondence will continue to flow & that I shall hear often from you. If I am not discharging the duties & fulfilling the responsibilities of godfather very well, blame business & not inclination: if you were here, you w'd find me quite alive to all the privileges of the position, especially at the mistletoe season!

I enclose a Christmas gift for you five girls to divide (Emily, Muriel, Maude, Kathleen & Fanny) — one fifth for each. Give my love to the others and accept a special kiss from me for yourself — and so, goodbye! A very merry Christmas & a happy new year!

Lovingly yours

Robert Hart

PS I send you a photo of <u>Sir R's Band</u>: that's myself behind the big drum.

He soon had to write again

17 December 1896

Thousand thanks, Darling Kathleen, for your lovely letter and card, but O what a goose I was to send you Gracie's cheque instead of your own! And I took special pains, too, to be right, for I took out the cheques to be quite sure each was in its proper cover, and then, Irishman as I am, I went & put them in the wrong ones: wasn't it a stupid thing to do? [He tells her about an incident when he received two letters each containing the wrong photo — showing they had been opened en route to him.] *What a row there w'd have been had I been choosing a wife by photo — and what a disappointment if the Cornish girl had come to me when expecting the Highland lassie! And so you are five feet six! Goodness me, that upsets my ideas completely; not only are you too big to go round the garden on my shoulder, but I w'd have to sit on a very high chair if you wanted to crawl up on my knee, and as for a kiss — why I'd have to get a ladder to reach up to your lips!* [Like Kathleen's father, Hart was short.] *What a tyrant is time — all my cherished god-paternal dreams destroyed by its passage & your growth! But, as for that <u>lock of hair</u> yes, I*

<u>do</u> want it: so, be sure you send it & tie it up, nicely plaited, in your favourite "blue" ribbon!

You are quite right to like Botany & Astronomy: they are both so interesting! I, too, was very fond of the latter, and, when spring comes, I'll send you one of my stellar atlases. Here's a nice poem which I met once in an American magazine: it was styled Ab Astris" — Latin for "From the stars" — it runs thus:

I saw the stars sweep through ethereal space
Stars, suns and systems, in infinity
Our earth an atom in the shoreless sea
Where each had its appointed path and place
And I was lost in my own nothingness.
But then I said, Dost thou not know that He
Who guides these orbs through the trackless space, guides thee?
No longer, grovelling thus, thyself abase,
For in the vast, harmonious, perfect whole,
In infinite progression moving on,
Thou hast thy place, immortal human soul,
Thy place and past, not less than star or sun.
Then with the grand procession fall in line,
The mystic march led on by power divine![9]

Is not that beautiful? I repeat it aloud almost every evening when I take my "constitutional" alone round & round the garden, with nobody near and all those lovely, countless, wonderful stars overhead. I walk from 7 to 8 generally & at that hour it is so dark that even heaven has to light all its lamps, and I get the benefit of them under the trees. Does your Mama remember walking with me in the winter of 1882, I wonder?…I wish you c'd step in & 'step out' with me — for I do feel awfully lonely at times. There is no one here in the house with me: Lady Hart & the children went home more than a year before you were born, and, except for two short visits Evey paid me in 1892 and Bruce in 1895, I have been always alone. Nollie, my youngest girl, went home when two years of age — she is now in her 18th year & I have never seen her since! If that is the way the Fates make me play the part of father, how can you be astonished if I did not "wake up" sooner to the duties of god-father?

All right — bring Emily and Muriel with you, by all means: I have lots of room — six vacant bedrooms — & shall be delighted to have all of you!

Write as often as you feel inclined: I see you can write a very good letter, & I shall always welcome your neat covers. Let yourself out & write quite freely to me as if you knew me well & we were old friends — as in fact we are!...

With love to you all, and a kiss and a hug for yourself,

Lovingly yours,

Robert Hart

P.S. I hope dear Maudie's news is good.

Hart's letter shows the costs to him of losing his family. Evey may have grown up healthier in England, but she and Bruce disappointed him when they met again in the 1890s, and in this letter Hart is reducing the time that they stayed. Maude's illness had long after-effects. A note on her report for the winter term of 1899 shows her progress in music being interrupted by illness and the Customs doctor, Molyneux, forbade her to go skating in the winter of 1900.

Kath next wrote about the delayed christening in Chefoo of her two baby sisters, Gwen and Phyllis. My mother, aged four, had evidently misbehaved.

3 April 1897

Dearest Kathleen

Out of the mail bag there tumbled yesterday one of the neatest of neat letters which I at once knew to be <u>yours</u> and was very glad to get. What you tell me about Gwen was very amusing, but of course such things will occur if baptism is deferred: <u>you</u> did not do so! [He remembers a similar incident when a child misbehaved in Ulster.]

As to my violins — I had several, but Bruce took away all the good ones. I had some old Italian instruments, but none made by the classical makers. I have one good one here but I have not played on it since before the Japanese war; and as for my 'cello, I have not touched it since February last year. I have been so awfully busy with office work etc I c'd not spare the time for practice, I regret to say. I am very fond of music and that & riding used to be my chief relaxations: I now do neither. I have, you know, a Brass Band with fifteen or sixteen Chinese band boys in it: they play remarkably well & their dance music, though a little loud, is excellent. They play with spirit & expression and keep delightful time. In the winter they play in the garden from 11 to 12 every Wednesday & Saturday forenoon, and in the summer from 5–7 on the same days. After dinner they play in a room off the hall whenever we want music either to hear or to dance to. The enclosed programme is what they played this morning. I was talking business all the time with a Mandarin in my Chinese Reception room!

I am glad to hear dear Maude is able to move about now, and I trust she will grow stronger and by & by be freed from this suffering. What prizes did she win with her painting? I congratulate her on her success! I am amused to hear you are studying "domestic economy": does that include how to make rice pudding & sweet omelettes, and how to live well on next to nothing a year? Mix your studies & your play properly: girls & boys require both! I must not forget to thank you for the lock of hair: it is pleasant for one's eyes to dwell on such colour & for one's fingers to stroke such silken softness!

[He refers to a visitor who may have passed through Chefoo, and ends *'with love to all of you and a special kiss for yourself'*]

Lovingly yours

Robert Hart

Domestic economy cannot have been my aunt's favourite subject. When I first visited her in the late 1940s, I was struck by her low standards of housekeeping and cooking compared to my own mother! Her next letter to him was for Christmas, and he replied:

1 Jan'y 1898

Dearest Kathleen

It blew hard, but no, the "ink" did not freeze: it went in other directions, and I doubt if the spray pleased all the faces it blackened & smutted; so, thank heaven it kept out of your way a while! Your welcome Xmas letter & card came just at the right time, & also a very nice one from your Papa & Mama, & I thank all of you for remembering me so kindly at this season. It does not feel a bit like other Xmas & New Year to me, so busy am I & so preoccupied: but the two office holidays being on Saturdays have felt like additional Sunday time, and the day after the 28th December was neither "fish, flesh nor fowl" — I suppose tomorrow will be a similar puzzle.

I wish I c'd be at Chefoo to help you in your season's doings & see all the youngsters of that locality — including dear Mrs. Nevius, who was a great friend of mine at Ningpo in 1854. I sh'd also hang up my "sock" — I don't possess stockings — but I'd be half afraid of finding somebody else's "foot" in it, and not a souvenir of Santa Claus's visit. I have no time this year — there are some fifty children to provide for & almost as many grown people: so I decided to stand aside for once, especially as there were trees at five or six other houses. [Trees carried presents addressed to each child.] We had a big Xmas dinner & danced afterwards and now we have a kind of fancy dress ball at the English Legation and theatricals at the French. I find I shall not get to either, as my old enemy <u>Lumbago</u> made a sudden inroad on me two days ago & I am anything but gay — I can't sit down or rise without a frown, and if I chance to sneeze injudiciously — O my, don't I catch it? Just as if I were torn in two! But I must not cry out for on the whole I have had far better health than falls to the lot of most others — I think I hear you say "Then why don't you write a better hand?" and I reply "You are quite right, my dear: it is abominable! — but isn't it 'sweetness long drawn out' for, while other letters can be read in a jiffy & then thrown in the fire, don't mine last a week & puzzle people far longer?

With love to all & special kiss for yourself, affectionately yours,

Robert Hart

Hart usually received many letters for his birthday on 20 February, including ones from Kath and her mother. Measles was giving a lot of trouble that year. Families with victims were isolated — in quarantine — in the effort to prevent it spreading.

26 May 1898

Dearest Kathleen,

I am sadly in everybody's debt in regards correspondence and I can't help it: my hands are altogether too full of work and I see no prospect of respite; so I find I must throw myself on the good nature of all concerned and hope that they may be able to see that in my case, at least, although there's a "will", there is not a "way"!

I am sorry to hear the measles epidemic has walled you in and so kept you from sharing the doings of Chefoo, but you are not alone in your sufferings, here at Peking the Squiers & Canghak families are in the same condition! We have not had rains for an age, and the heat & dry air and floating germs of all kinds are finding out weak spots in most of us. Our great festival — ten days of it — has been connected with the visit of Prince Henry, a fine-looking man and a charming prince. H.R.H. won the hearts by his unaffected manner and unfailing affability, but ten days is quite long enough for a fête to last & we are all glad to be quiet again. The Prince brought his band with him and it was quite a treat to have their violins & mandolins. I was at six evening fixtures and six midday outings & I felt I had done enough in that way for a year. I am not as young as I used to be and the late hours knock me up. I did not go to the Races, but remained in my office as usual & got through some important work. Now the excitement is over a tennis tournament — Tientsin comes up today to play Peking and then T'sienites hope to have their revenge for a cricket beating they rec'd from the King-ites last month. Mrs. Rogers is our great tennis lady & it is wonderful to see the grace, agility and dexterity on display: Mr. W? is our strong man & hard to beat. Do you play tennis? It certainly is a capital game when played well!

[He tells of a call from the Squiers, and repeats that they are in quarantine.]

*My own movements are as uncertain as ever. I hoped when Mr.
Bredon was made Deputy IG etc I could get away, but those new
<u>Likin</u> arrangements came along & that has to be my "war" for
another year: in fact I think you are just as likely to see England
first yourself! People blame me for being such a "recluse", but, in
point of fact, I can't budge.* [The 'Likin' referred to a new
Customs responsibility — the standardisation and collection
of local internal taxes on foreign products once they had left
the port areas.]

    *Ask your mama to forgive me my letter debts please. With love
to you all and a kiss for yourself,*

Affectionately yours,

Robert Hart

The prince was Queen Victoria's grandson, Prince Henry of Prussia,
son of the Kaiser. Carrall and the Chefoo consuls had dinner with him
on 29 May 1899 on board the German navy's ship *Deutschland* when
he asked Carrall to remember him to Hart.[10]

Kath evidently next wrote to him after she had taken her first public
examinations.

Peking, 7 July 1898

Dearest Kathleen

*Thanks for your nice letter telling me abut the fearful ordeal you went
through at the Examinations. I hope you are all recovered from the
trial and that decomposition has not followed so many hours of
exposition followed perhaps in some cases by mortification!*

    I am just off for a holiday to <u>Peitaiho</u> [Beidaihe — a summer
resort on the coast for the Peking crowd.] *I am staying a week
or a month or even longer, according to weather & taste. Already I
feel how difficult it is to be without work, for, having just got my
boxes and everything off, I must wait doing nothing here then
when I start for the "country sticks" in a chair. Fancy, since I
came here in 1886 I have not been away from Peking: I have not
yet even seen the railway — and I feel quite like a 'fish out of
water' now that I have up-anchor'd and decided to clear out of
port.*

I hope the summer is passing pleasantly for you all in good weather, good health and daily enjoyment. Get lots of fun & make up for the hard work of school time! I am glad Muriel got her prize... . I know how she writes for one letter of hers was sent all the way from ——————— I won't tell you where — for myself to read: & I thought it great fun — although it did abound in dashes and notes of exclamation! I was very glad to get the photo of the Carrall staircase some time ago. Emily is quite a young lady — no longer a girl, and the rest of you look like so many young — well, swans, about to spread your wings or take a dive on your own account: I suppose you'll all soon be doing that!

With love to all & a god-fatherly kiss for yourself, my dear, affectionately yours,

Robert Hart

Peitaiho

The letter was probably from Granny Sampson, and may have enclosed the photograph shown in Figure 6.5.

Soon after writing this Hart invited Emily and Muriel to Peking. Their mother probably suggested it would be appropriate to invite the two elder sisters first. They appear in his diary, but without comment.

Sat 17 Nov. Worked in office quietly and without interruption all day...[In the evening] Em and Mu Carrall and nine students [listed], singing, playing banjo, and ??? Very jolly, but the cold!

Tues 22 Nov. Dined last night at ? with the Secks & their guests & the Carrall girls — took Emily into dinner.

Hart was then preoccupied with the illness of the reforming Emperor, the Empress's return, the snapping of the powers at bits of China, postal matters and participation in another exhibition in France, so the visit probably did not come at a very good time. The presence of the nine students illustrates how he kept up with promising young men entering the service. The next letter, which is mainly about another stay at Peitaiho, shows that the visit had important consequences for Emily:

Peitaiho

9 July 1899

Dearest Kathleen,

Many thanks for your nice letter of the 4th. I am glad you had that run in the "Whiting", but if the pace had been 30 instead of 15 miles an hour, you'd have been even more astonished &
delighted. [H.M.S. *Whiting,* – a fast torpedo boat of which more later. The navy sometimes invited a party of schoolgirls aboard their ships. There is a photo in Maude's album of a visit to H.M.S. *Aeolus* in 1895.] *We saw the lunar eclipse in Peking, and the view of the sky when the silvery moon had emerged from its fiery, brown bag about a quarter & cut its shape in two disks — the sky was just as ?ing as fury c'd paint! I read Steevens' book last month & enjoyed it: the chapter in which he describes Kitchener & the other about Gordon's Special Force are specially good.*[11] *I have quite a lot of books here for summer reading, but they are all of the very lightest kind — novels etc that I never tried before. I enjoy the kind of mental dissipation very thoroughly, but I am afterwards sorry that I wasted my time on it instead of studying something solid. But, of course, one must have a ?? occasionally!*

I came here on the 2nd...and I cannot say I enjoy the place quite as much as last year. Last year I was really very tired, & the rest was delicious; but this year I don't seem to require the holiday, and I'd as soon be in the office in Peking. There are plenty of people at all their places — [he describes how they are scattered along the coast]...*I find many an excuse for not going away from my own end: one day the sun is too hot, — another day the rain is too threatening, etc. The great drawback here is the want of shade: the moment we quit the house we are in the sun, &, although the sea air is invigorating, the glare is a constant worry.* [Sunglasses were not invented till 1929.] *There is no amusement beyond the fun of splashing in the water in company — and we can't keep it up all the 24 hours of the day! I did not bring ponies this year: the flies troubled them so much last year that they were miserable & my riding was without enjoyment.*

It was curious that Emily's departure from Peking last fall should bring her in the way of the "Phoenix": in fact the way people meet & get married is a constant wonder to me! On this point I have some nice lines in my hand which I'll copy out for you: the writer is unknown & I found them in a Californian 'paper wrapped round a parcel of chocolate.

With love to you all & a special kiss for yourself

Lovingly yours

Robert Hart

P.S. *Thank your papa, please, for the first basket of apples: came in excellent condition! RH.*

(The copied poem is *Fate* by Susan Marr Spalding.)

During her return journey to Chefoo Emily had met Charles Forbes, a young Lieutenant on the sloop H.M.S. *Phoenix*, and a year later they were engaged. A Lieutenant's pay was not enough to set up house, so marriage had to wait. A second result of the visit seems to have been that Hart realised that Emily was musically talented, but that the family had no piano, only an organ of some kind that was probably inherited with the house. He sent the Carralls the splendid gift of a good piano, as we learn from two of Mrs Sampson's letters to him. The second of these, on 16 January 1901, says

Letters from Chefoo lately have given me much pleasure, & it is all about your kind gift, the Piano. Gwendoline now learns music. Emily teaches her & says she is very clever with her fingers & delights in her music lessons. It gives me great satisfaction knowing your valuable gift is appreciated and not wasted.

Schooldays Remembered

Emily and Muriel left school in May 1899, Maude in December 1899. None of them took examinations, which were considered stressful for girls, and unnecessary for their future lives as wives and mothers. Emily probably had the ability to do well, judging by the competence and intelligence with which she impressed me after I first met her in 1946, but her determination as the eldest was to marry early so as not to hold back her sisters. (There was still some feeling that the eldest should marry first.) Kath was the only one who undertook the *'fearful ordeal'* of taking the lowest level of the College of Preceptors exams, termed Class 3, in which she gained the highest grade, Division 1. In 1900 she began keeping a diary, and this shows that, despite this earlier success, she was very unsure of her results in the Class 1 exams which she took in November 1899, so challenging were they thought to be for women. In economical Carrall fashion the diary was an 1898 office one which her father had not used much (Figure 6.8).

These examinations had been instituted in the 1850s to provide a qualification for teachers, and achieving its Class 1 had also been used to demonstrate ability to go on to university. However, by 1900 Oxford and Cambridge were demanding that candidates had the Higher level of their own local examinations, which required study for a further year. In Britain the new high schools were preparing bright girls, including the Carrall girls' cousin, Mabel Fawcus in Newcastle, for university — though only a few of the private girls' boarding schools patronised by the upper classes did so. Kath persuaded her father to let her stay on in the Upper Sixth at least till the summer. Her teachers took care to tell her of former students pursuing qualifications. Thus, on 16 January 1900, when she and Maude went over to the boarding school to see their school friend Elsie Rendell, they had tea with Mrs Beer, their form mistress, and Kath noted in her diary that she *'showed us a photo and a letter of Mabel Cassidy, who is being qualified for a doctor'*. When Kath returned to school in February, she and Elsie Rendell were the only girls staying on at this level, studying German, French, History, Literature and Physiology, and Kath in addition the violin and piano. She and Elsie drew up some rules for themselves, *'& mean to stick to them & get on'*.

Frances senior sent the girls' reports to Grandmother Sampson, and proud Granny forwarded them to Hart. The 1899 ones for Maude, Kath and young Frances appear in his post-1900 letter collection. They show the small size of the forms, usually six to eight girls, and their ranking in each subject. (Figure 6.7 shows the Fifth form in 1898.) They possibly joined the boys for science, where the number in the form was seventeen. Kath was comparatively weak in arithmetic and algebra and did not take Euclid (geometry) — but she usually took first place on the arts side. She may not have realised that Euclid, supposedly demonstrating ability to think logically, was at that time an essential qualification if she wanted to follow Cousin Mabel to Cambridge.

Kath later did an affectionate broadcast about their schooldays. Her typescript shows:

As early as six o'clock of a morning, Amah, our Chinese maid, would be standing at my bedside, with her gentle summons "Bath ready, Su-Kuniang". In the adjoining bathroom, shared by my sisters, hot water steamed in large pudding-shaped earthenware tubs, glazed green, with a cork in the lower side by which they were emptied later by the bath-coolie, who had filled them from long buckets hung from a pole on his shoulders. [I remember these from my visit to Chefoo with my mother in 1939. In Hong Kong, where we were living at the time, we had normal baths with taps.] Before seating myself up to the neck in mine, I would carefully look to see if any insect floated there, for centipedes or scorpions had been found enjoying the cool interior when the bath was empty.... Our sponges were covered with mosquito-netting, to keep insects from creeping into the cool holes.

After breakfast of boiled rice and stewed fruit, bread and butter, which came to us in tins from Denmark, we were ready for school. Seated comfortably in the stern of the rowing boat, we would hastily go over our lessons while the men plied their oars. Many a line of Milton, many a passage of Shakespeare comes back to me now, associated with the bright sunshine on the sparkling waves, and the lap of water against the boat...

In the winter the five of us formed quite a small procession on pony-back or in sedan chairs along the highroad.[12] Here would come a string of gaily trapped mules, their neck bells jingling, and their red forehead tassels swinging to and fro, to ward off the flies. That mule litter with closed curtains might contain some Chinese lady and child, and we would pity the occupants if the mules failed to keep step. A Mandarin's official chair would force us to squeeze to the side of the roads, for he would be surrounded by his guard...

By nine sharp we were in our desks in the large assembly hall for the daily recital of a verse of the Bible which preceded the prayers. Many a time I've felt grateful for this habit, which made me learn large portions of the scriptures by heart. Lessons followed till dinner at one o'clock. Then came a general siesta on beds, supervised by a teacher to preserve complete silence. Afterwards, preparation for us day-girls, who might then return home, while the boarders went for a walk, along the cliffs or down a country road, stared at but unmolested by small boys, for learning is respected in China. When they came back, they had to do their preparation till evening prayers, then supper and play till bedtime.[13] [The school also gave them an interest in drama, and photographs of productions appear in their albums (Figure 6.6).]

Winter Festivities, 1900

Christmas and the European New Year gave the men days off from work, as did the Chinese New Year, which started on January 31 that year. Winter was a time of dinners and dances, theatrical performances and concerts, and children's parties. The last required particular preparation, to get ready presents, decorations and games. (Servants attended to the cooking.)

The sixteen-year-old Kath opened her 1900 diary thus:

Today began another year and another century! We opened it with Family Prayers. Mother — who stumbled while going round the hill two days ago and hurt her eye and mouth badly and was much shaken — was up on the sofa but we five had to receive all visitors, of which there were any number (Drs. Moly. [Molyneux] & Gulowsen, Messrs Anz, Maltchenko, Eckford, M. Smith, Kenal etc. etc.) In the afternoon we had a rehearsal of our acting, which is to be on January 4th but only Messrs Maltchenko & Eckford came. Vyvyan's people started from home today: what fun it will be to see them again! In the evening, we had a large Customs' dinner of 16 in all — the Innocents, Dawsons, Allens, Messrs Maltchenko, Kindblad, Williams & Dr. Molyneux. After dinner we played games — the owl game, dumb crambo etc — & ended at 12.30 p.m. [sic].

Kath does not mention that her mother was pregnant. Frances seems to have had a difficult time during her tenth pregnancy at the age of forty-three, and retired to bed the next day. The acting was postponed.

The names mentioned recur frequently. The Customs dinner shows the Indoor Customs staff, and the two Customs doctors. Vyvyan Eckford, Vyv, V or V.R.E., two years older than Emily, was the son of Charles Jennings, who had been Harbour Master at Chefoo, 1877–1884, but died by suicide after being bitten by a rabid dog. His mother subsequently married Andrew Eckford, a partner in one of Chefoo's biggest firms, and a wealthy man. Vyvyan and his twin sisters took his name. In 1900 Vyvyan was working in his stepfather's office. The senior Eckfords were in Europe, collecting his twin sisters, Ada and Lilla, from their finishing school in Germany. During their absence Vyv had Sunday tiffin regularly with the Carralls. He appears in the diary four or five times a week in January and February. As the use of his first name shows, he was treated as an older brother rather than as a potential spouse. Their parents trusted him to escort the girls home on many early evening occasions. He frequently dropped in to join them in skating, walks, dancing, acting, etc.[14]

Mail days were important, keeping them in touch with relatives and friends. On 4 January:

> Went for a walk in the afternoon, returned to find mail in &
> heard from Grandmother… . Heard news of brutal murder of Mr.
> Brooks (Mrs. Brown's brother) by Chinese sect… . Cousin
> Crichton fighting against Boers… . Uncle Jack sending me some
> music…

Sidney Brooks was a missionary killed by the Boxers on 31 December 1899 when returning to his post by wheelbarrow after spending Christmas with his sister.[15] But for the moment the community was preoccupied by news of the Boer War. The Rev. Griffith of Bishop Scott's Mission was organising a concert in aid of the widows and orphans of the British soldiers. On 5 January Kath

> spent the morning at the club trying my piece for the concert. The
> piano is Mrs. Anderson's and not a very good one. [They had a
> better one, thanks to Hart's gift.] Went round the hill
> afterwards with Em & Frances. In the afternoon practised piano
> & violin…spent the rest of the day in making baskets etc. for our

children's party. Mr. & Mrs. Burne came in for Mr. Burne to try
his songs over with Emily who accompanies him.

Mr Burne was Minister at their church. As the entry for the next day in Figure 6.7 shows, next day, Saturday, there was not only a children's party given by Dr Molyneux, at which the tree, with its real candles, caught fire, but the concert in the evening. Emily, young Frances and Kath were performing. It was successful and Kath could record that her father was proud of his girls.

The next few days they were intermittently occupied with preparations for their own children's party. This took place on Monday 15 January, for fifty-four children and nine non-family adults who came as helpers. It went off well, but her mother was *'over-fatigued'*. Next day, at Father's wish, the girls cancelled their theatricals. Frances senior recovered and gave another dinner party on 25 January, diplomatically including the Russian Consul. Young Frances and Kath did not sit down to the dinner, as that would have made thirteen, but they joined in the games afterwards — singing proverbs and acting the titles of books. Another dinner for sixteen on 5 February was followed by musical performances and games. People made their own music at social events so musical ability was a valued feminine accomplishment.

The mail of 11 January had brought a letter to their mother from Hart, inviting Maude and Kath to visit for a week or two in the spring. This meant that they needed to know the steps for ballroom and popular country dances. The girls helped out at children's dancing classes, but during the winter there were dancing classes at their house for those slightly older. After the last dancing class of the season on Saturday 3 February Kath was confident she could manage.

> *Every-one came and we had very good dancing. I waltzed with Mr.*
> *Emery, Mr. Maltchenko and Mr. Russell, & feel now that I really*
> *know how to! We also got on splendidly with the Caledonians,*
> *going through them & the Saratoga without a hitch. We ended up*
> *with the Swedish Dance which I danced with Mr. Russell. V. got*
> *up "three cheers for Mrs. Carrall" & all said they had had most*
> *enjoyable afternoons and would miss them.*

She was delighted that Hart had also said they would not be transferred till spring 1901. *'That will just suit us all well. How good God is to us!'* Carrall went off later for the '2nd Grand Smoking Concert' — presumably male-only affairs. He had a headache the next day.

The Chinese New Year began on Monday 31 January:

> *All Father's house & office servants came up to the house &*
> *'salaamed' to him. The streets were full of Chinese in their best*
> *holiday attire, & also of disreputable old & young beggars.*

There were twenty-four house servants. Some, like Amah and the cook, were their personal servants, but gardeners, gate-keepers and others were on the Customs payroll. Westerners did not participate in any festivities going on in Yantai town, but the holiday meant Kath could take a long walk along the beach with her father while her sisters helped at the children's dancing class. Next day Mrs Donnelly had a large children's fancy dress party at which they all helped.

> *There was a large model of a ship, illuminated and decorated with*
> *a cargo of presents, & afterwards, dancing & games. Messrs*
> *Parkhill & Anz begged Mother to let us go with them & Mrs. Burne*
> *& Vyvyan to see the Xmas tree which ten of the Chefoo bachelors had*
> *given the CIM children in compensation for the one they gave up for*
> *the Patriotic Fund* [for Boer War victims]… . *We had great fun*
> *going & coming. Vyvyan brought us back & dined with us.*

That winter the main outdoor pastime was skating. Kath skated for the first time on Tuesday 8 January when Vyv came up to tea and then took her, Mu, Frances and Eric to a pond. *'Vyv and Mr. Maltchenko each gave me a lesson, & I enjoyed it immensely. Mr. Emery and Mr. Innocent also whirled me up and down. We came back by moonlight.'* Next day they skated twice at the rink just prepared at the Club, in the morning and again at 4: 30 p.m., when most of the men had stopped work. — *'very good, especially skating with a partner round the rink'.* Skating continued several times a week till 10 February, when the ice deteriorated. Spring seemed on its way, but 1 March:

> *A heavy fall of snow had taken place in the night, &…had*
> *covered every tree, plant & shrub with soft flaky puffs of snow.*
> *Each twig bore about 3 inches of snow…the garden…looked like*
> *fairy land…*

One snow scene is shown in Figure 6.9.

Carrall seems to have preferred to interact with his daughters one at a time. Kath often met him when the office closed, as on 6 February:

I went to fetch him at 4 p.m., & we then turned into the Chinese city & discovered a clean little Japanese shop which we entered & explored. We then went down the road, and came back by the beach. The evening was lovely and calm and the sun set amidst a haze of soft light pink & blue clouds which were reflected in the still silvery sea.

On another occasion, when a walk with her father was thwarted by fog, he '*instructed Maude for some hours in the mysteries of the microscope, which she is going to study*'. Knowing of Hart's aversion to being bored, Carrall was preparing Maude to show an intelligent interest in scientific matters during her visit. An important objective of educating girls was to enable them to make interesting conversation when they came 'out', attended adult functions and started dining with their parents in the evenings instead of having a children's supper. Emily and Muriel were 'out', and as a sign, wore their hair up. Maude, whose eighteenth birthday was on 13 February, was about to make this important transition. As term began again after the end of the Chinese New Year festivities and as Saturday was a working day, Kathleen's and young Frances' participation in adult social life was normally restricted to Sundays.

Meanwhile, Emily had her own preoccupations. On 14 January Kath noted '*Mrs. Lavers* [another Customs family] *has asked Em to go to Shanghai to meet Charlie if he can get leave & go up from Hong Kong*'. The mail of 17 January

…brought a parcel for us from Aunt Annie which contained a very pretty dress for Em & ties for us… . Em heard from Admiral Seymour who said…he had sent home Charlie's application for a re-commission on the China station, but he did not think he would get it…

The girls normally wore simple dark skirts, ringing the changes with their blouses and ties. The same skirts were used for tennis. Dresses were special. The family were evidently on friendly terms with Admiral Sir Edward Seymour, Commander of the British fleet on the China

Station. He was soon to lead an unsuccessful international attempt to rescue the foreigners besieged in Peking by the Boxers.

On 26 January *'Em heard from Uncle Harry who said he was going to see old Capt. Forbes on the latter's invitation'*. Emily's fiancé's father was investigating her background, as was to be expected then. Henry (Harry) Fawcus was the eldest of Frances Carrall's brothers, so the Forbes regarded him as the head of the Fawcus family. Captain Forbes would not be impressed by his Newcastle accent.[16] Late on 28 January there was a telegram from Charlie to say that he had thirty-five days leave, and had left Hong Kong for Shanghai. Emily hesitated whether to go, or to hope he might come on to Chefoo. She decided he might find that difficult because of the Chinese New Year, so she left by steamer on 29 January. Even though she was staying with family friends, it was quite liberal of her parents to allow the visit. Subsequently there are references in the diary to happy letters from her. On 27 February Kath notes *'Today Charlie leaves Emily, and goes back to Hong Kong — how forlorn she will be'*. Poor Emily: his application for a re-commission in China failed. He was transferred to the *Talbot* in April for Northern duties based in Britain, leaving them indefinitely separated.[17]

Photographs had become important in social life. The Carralls had one of the portable box cameras which became available in the mid-1890s, in which the negative was formed by inserting a small glass plate. This was developed at home in a dark room. It was possibly Hart's gift to Muriel. On 8 February Kath and Mu went to tea with Mrs Etterick, Mrs Corbett and Dr Cooper (a woman) and while Kath played them pieces on the piano, *'Mu discussed photography & collecting butterflies with Mr. Etterick'*. If it was Mu who took the 1899–1900 photos in the surviving albums, her experiments with different chemicals, colours and techniques are clearly evident. Some photos were black and white, others sepia or blue cyanotype.

Though the senior Carralls had greeted the Eckford family when they returned on 27 February, the girls first met Ada and Lilla (Vyvyan's nineteen-year-old twin sisters) at church on Sunday 4 March. Afterwards,

> *...just before tiffin all the family called & asked us to go for a walk with them. We went down to meet them at 3 p.m. & took a walk to the cemetery... . We then went up to the Temple on the top of the hill which we explored. Coming home we went to tea at the*

Eckfords in their very pretty drawing room...Mu & Maude dined
there in the evening.

From this point on Ada and Lilla became an important part of the girls' social set. Thus, on Sunday 18 March:

Mu, Eric & I went down for a walk to the schools & back with
[the Eckfords]. *Then they all came back to tea here – Mr. and*
Mrs. Eckford with Father & Mother in the drawing room, Ada &
Lilla & Vyvyan with us five [Emily was back] *in the dining*
room, & Edith, Eric & Arthur & the little ones in the Little
Dining room.

Hillside could cope with three simultaneous tea parties, though the drawing room was the heart of the house (Figures 6.10 and 11).

The visit to Hart was now approaching, and started family discussions on whether Kath should be regarded as 'out'. A half-way stage was decided on. On 26 March '*Mrs. Eckford came up in the evening to give the tailor some hints about our new frocks, & afterwards she did up my hair into a plat* [sic] *behind, tied with a huge bow*'. Fresh from Europe, her fashion tips were welcome. On Sunday 1 April: '*Church as usual at 11 a.m. Frances & I went for the first time with our hair half-up! Monday. School as usual. Elsie admired my coiffure...*'

Tuesday 3 April was

A day to be indeed remembered with thankfulness & praise. At 8
p.m. Miss Churcher's note was received by Mother & contained
the news of the College results. Frances had passed in College of
Preceptors, Class II, Division 1. and I, Class I Division 1 with
distinctions in Scripture & Physiology.

Miss Churcher had succeeded Miss Burton as headmistress. (When I was at a convent school in India 1942–5 we studied Hygiene and Physiology. Our textbook made no mention of the reproductive system. I imagine there was the same omission in the College of Preceptors course on Physiology. Girls were kept entirely innocent of anything to do with sex. My mother was introduced to the 'facts of life' by her husband after the ring was safely on her finger.)

4 April. On arriving at School we found it was to be a holiday in
honour of [the exam results]...*the next three days I am to pack,*

173

*and shall not be back at school till next term. In the evening as Mu
could not go, I with Father, Em & Maude went to dinner at the
Eckfords. It was the twins' birthday-party. We played a trio
together, Ada & I on our violins, Lilla on her 'cello & Mrs. E.
accompanied us on the piano. Then we played games & had great
fun. Mr. Wood took me in to dinner. We returned at 12.30!*

She was getting more practice for the Peking visit, an occasion she
never forgot. Sir Robert proved a wonderful host to his girl visitors and
the students whom he roped in to escort them, just a month before
the Boxer rebellion brought shocking events in its train.

Figure 6.10. A corner of the large crowded drawing room at Hillside, (the fireplace and mirror were at the centre of the back wall). (Photo from Mr William Forbes-Newton, Emily's grandson.)

Figure 6.11. Left: The other end of the sitting room (Ca01-085). Taken in 1902 it shows young Frances with her hair up, holding baby Jim, still in skirts.

Figure 7.1. Kathleen (a) (below left) and Maude (b) (below right) taken professionally in Chefoo, August 1900 (Ca01-067).

Figure 7.2. Left: At Tientsin. (a) The Drews' carriage — this improvement on the sedan chair and the Peking cart needed the smooth roads of an official Western settlement (Ca01-076).

Figure 7.2 Below: (b) At the races (Ca-01-075).

Figure 7.3. Left: At the Observatory. Maude looks insecure on her perch, and Kath has her foot out beside her. Mrs Hansard looks an agreeable chaperone between Mr de Luca and Mr Wintour in the back row, while young Effie Ragsdale perches on high (Ca02-016).

Figure 7.4. Above: Sir Robert's Garden Party (Ca02-100 — cut out of a magazine).

Figure 7.5. Right: On the boat, focussing on Effie, in short skirts! Maude and Kath are out of focus to the side (Ca02-013).

Figure 7.6. At the Princess Tomb. Kath is the unnamed tall girl centre back next to Mr. Brewitt-Taylor and Maude, who identified the other people on this page in her album, is below her. (Ca01-p29). Mr. Sandercock is sitting very close to Effie in the front row.

Figure 7.7. HMS Taku, the captured Chinese ship (Ca01-095), with Lt Mackenzie and Lt Moreton, leaning, left centre.

Figure 7.8. The scrolls presented to Jim Carrall by the Chinese merchants of Chefoo.

Figure 8.1. Above: The Ladies' Driving Race — the ladies still in their long skirts (Ca02-022).

Figure 8.2. Right: Muriel, aged twenty, in August 1900. Kath noted in her diary that Muriel had changed into her best green silk blouse (Ca2-09).

Figure 8.3. Below: Hugh's visit. The young Frances sits taller than Hugh on the bench. The shorter girls, Maude and Emily, behind the bench, are dwarfed by Kath standing left (Ca02-23).

CHAPTER SEVEN

GIRLS GROWING UP: THE BOXER REBELLION

The Tientsin and Peking visits

On 25 February 1900, Hart hints at girlish innocence when he teased Kath about her disappointment that Charles had not come to see Emily in Chefoo. The pleasure both he and the girls derived from the Peking visit is clear from both their accounts, while the depth of the sadness which was hidden under his determination to help put China together again after the devastating but unforeseen events of the summer is seen in his post siege letter. The Chefoo community held steady thanks partly to the social leadership of Jim and Frances Carrall.

> *Dearest Kathleen,*
>
> *Thanks for your kind letter & good wishes for my birthday! It has now slipped away with the past, &, after being waited for sixty- five years, it has not the kindness to stay a bit longer or be a bit more amusing than any of the sixty-four that preceded! I fancy my first birthday must have been the jolliest, for doubtless at little expense to myself I gave lots of trouble to other people — and that's about the best way to occupy them improvingly, isn't it?*
>
> *I'm sorry you missed the fun of teasing Emily & her sweetheart: when your turn will come — wait a bit! And I wonder how you'll like teasing yourself! For see there are occasions, when, as the saying is, 'Two's company: three's none!' and surely billing & cooing is just the very best & most charming of such occasions!*

However, that's a closed book to you yet, but — but— but —just wait and see!

Peking has been very gay this winter: theatricals, dinners, rinking, paper hunts & other doings: I have sent my band to make music for them everywhere, but I have not been out much since before Christmas: I caught cold & kept the house, there I have excellent fires, good light, splendid books, and my time has just been so fully occupied, I never [fret?] long! The frost is now disappearing & so I think I shall begin to go out again for a change: but I don't like to be bored: I like less to bore — and I am sure where so many young people are larking about, an old fogey like myself is not missed — in fact better away!

I want you & Maude to come at Easter: can you arrange to come here about the 14th April? I don't want you to arrive later, but if others require it, five days earlier does not matter. And I want you to stay a fortnight . Will that do?

Love to you all & a kiss for yourself! Affectionately yours,

Robert Hart

Figure 7.1 shows the portraits of Kath and Maude, aged seventeen and eighteen, just after their memorable visit. Easter was on April 15 and Hart sent detailed instructions on 2 April. He started with sending a note to Mr Drew by the previous steamer, covered each step of the journey, and ended:

6th As for luggage, you may have as many large boxes as you like, but I advise you to avoid having many small parcels or loose articles. They are easily lost & troublesome to look after. I also expect Winnie Stewart & Effie Ragsdale, two nice young girls. [They were to find that Effie, about fifteen, was still in short skirts, but mature in other ways.]

On Saturday, 31 March, '*Mother had a letter from Elsa Drew to say she also had been invited by Sir Robert to go to Peking, & to ask us to spend a few days with them in Tientsin either going or coming.*' Elsa's father, Edward Bangs Drew, was the American Commissioner of Customs in Tientsin. She took the place of Winnie Stewart who did not visit Hart that year.

By Monday, 9 April the girls were packed and ready to go, but there was no steamer. About 8 p.m. on Tuesday Father heard the SS *Dorado* was going in two hours. All the cabins were taken, but the Captain lent them his. (Chefoo did not have regularly scheduled liners, but having a father in the Customs helped.) The sea was very rough the next day and the sea-sick girls had to endure the ship being heaved to for five hours. At 2 a.m. on Thursday morning they awoke to find they had reached the bar and were about five miles from Taku (Dagu). She and Maude

> *dressed rapidly, packed our boxes, & went on deck to find some other passengers there and the sea comparatively calm. About 10–30 Mr. Strangman (tide surveyor) came out in a steam launch for us & took us off.* [They steamed up the Taku river between mud flats till they reached Tongku (Tanggu) and noticed the apparently strong Chinese forts guarding it.] *Here we telephoned Mr. Drew* [probably the first time they had used this instrument] *& then Mr. S. put us in a coupé on the train.*

At Tientsin Mr Drew and Elsa met them, and took them in their carriage first to their home, then on a drive to the race-course with Elsa's sister (another Kathleen), and Mrs Drew, and then to the tennis courts. The carriage merited a photograph, as the roads of Chefoo were too rough for such vehicles (Figure 7.2a). It had been a long day, but they did not get a lie-in next morning. Elsa called them to dress at 6 a.m., and they went off to see the pony-training for the races — such was the importance of these social occasions (Figure 7.2b).

Later that Friday there was a message from Sir Robert asking them to stay a few days in Tientsin, as he was seedy, so on Saturday they unpacked. Then they went to the cemetery. *'We saw Edward's grave, a plain cross, with Edward Fawcus Carrall cut into the stone.'* Their parents had presumably asked them to look for this memorial to their first-born son. In the afternoon, they drove with Mrs Drew to the race-course, the Drew girls and their son Lionel being on bikes or ponies. After tea in the Grandstand they went with Elsa and Lucy Drew to a meeting of the Choral Club. They walked home, and Kath played the violin with Lucy after dinner.

On Easter Sunday a Miss Marten collected Maude and Kath for early Communion. They also went with the Drews to the 11 a.m. service at the English Church, but found it was already full. Three of them got seats, the rest of the party taking rickshaws to the Union Chapel. (Rickshaws were another novelty which had not yet arrived in Chefoo.) Afterwards they went round to see the Gipperichs,[1] and paid another visit to the cemetery.

Other days were occupied with visits to the dentist for a temporary filling, watching cricket, playing tennis, shopping, visiting the Gordon Library, learning to cycle and to play whist, socialising, and writing letters home. Friday 20 April was Kath's seventeenth birthday. The Drews had laid out a small table with her presents:

> an ivory paper knife from Mr. Drew, a silver spoon from his wife, a white tie from Elsa, an address book from Lucy, a photo hanger from Kathleen & a stamp box from Lionel. [Kath collected stamps.] M. presented me with Moore's poems from the girls & herself, & a pair of kid gloves from the little ones.

Kath became violently ill later from eating shrimps and had to retire to bed early. She skipped the morning visit to the race-course, but made the trip to Peking as planned. This no longer took two or three days. Mrs Drew took her and Elsa to the station at 11 a.m. and

> put us in a car [carriage] which we shared with Mrs. Hansard (our chaperone), Effie Ragsdale, Messrs Bellingham, Jamieson & Bristow[2]…[At 2: 30 p.m. they arrived at the railway station, which Hart had told them was three miles from the city.] Messrs Bethell & Wintour (Customs students) met us & put us in the electric tram which took us in seven minutes to the Yung-ting Gate. Here, green sedan chairs borne by four coolies with two runners & outriders conveyed us to Sir R.'s house, & my birthplace. Sir R. was waiting to receive us in the hall & kissed us. After tea we went into the lovely & large garden & heard the band. In the evening Elsa sang, accompanied by me, & I played the violin accompanied by Maude. Misses Brazier & Annie Myers[3] came to dinner & talked of old Amoy times.

Sixty years later Kath added that the impressive sedan chairs had caused a Chinese onlooker to remark: 'There goes the Taotai with his four wives.' She also described Hart as a slim man aged sixty-five of medium height, with discerning eyes and a kind welcoming smile.[4] Kissing a non-relative was a sufficiently unusual greeting to get noted.

The next day, being Sunday, was relatively quiet. After a 9: 30 a.m. breakfast, Sir Robert took them over the house and *'into his "den" which was littered with papers'*. He did not accompany them to the Legation church at 11 a.m., where Kath noted a very small congregation. After tiffin with Sir R, Mr Bredon escorted Maude, Kath and Mrs Hansard for a walk on the wall. The roofs and temples of the Imperial Palace could be seen from it. Kath noticed that though it was fifty feet broad, it was covered with thorns and brambles and in many places broken down. It was to provide the Boxers with vantage points during the siege of the Legations a few weeks later. After dinner, his guests again entertained Sir Robert with music.

Monday 24 April was more typically busy.

> *Wrote letters in the morning. After tiffin M & I & Effie went to play tennis with Mrs. van Rostern⁵ & Elspeth Gipperich at the Austrian Legation, thence to the tennis club where Mrs. H. & Elsa were playing. Sir R. gave a dance in the evening. Mr. & Mrs. Brazier, Miss Bredon, & Customs & Legation students came. It was lovely, his stringed band played, & we danced till 12 with an interval for music. (Sir R. gave me the menus to write!) We met old friends in Mr. Wagner & Harry Bristow.*

Figure G shows Hart's specially printed dance programme, with Maude's partners written in.

Next morning, 24 April, Kath rose late, and Harry Bristow came round with his pony to teach her to ride. In the afternoon they went in carts to the Wintours for tea, joined by Messrs Bethell, de Luca, Ferguson and Strauch,⁶ and then went to the Observatory (Figure 7.3) and the Examination Hall, returning to Hart's house via the wall. Letters from home told them of the arrival in the family of a baby <u>Boy</u>! A boy merited underlining in her diary, but not, for the economical Carralls, a telegram.

On 25 April, after shopping, they called on Mrs Ker⁷ at the British Legation, who drove them back in her mule cart. Sir Robert gave a garden party, at which some very clever Chinese jugglers and a ventriloquist performed.

> *The brass band played, & when it became chilly we strolled about in couples & ended up with the lancers on the lawn, which was*

*great fun. Mrs. Hansard & Elsa dined out, so we three had an
evening with Sir R., who entertained us with recitations &
showed us photos.*

On 26 April, Harry Bristow took Maude and Kath to the Coal Hill.
'*We rode in the cart back & were severely bumped about. Had tea in his rooms
with Mrs. Ker as chaperone, & Messrs Drury & Bower.*' That evening, Sir
Robert gave a dinner dance. '*Enjoyed myself muchly*' wrote Kath. On 27
April it was Mrs Ker who gave a garden party to which Effie, Maude
and Kath went, with about thirty Customs and legation students. Kath
won two sets of tennis. They had a quiet evening with Sir Robert and
the Hansards. Mr Hansard had come to fetch his wife home, leaving
them, as Kath noted, '*chaperoneless!*' On Saturday, after the office closed,
Messrs de Luca and Bethell took them to tea at 5 p.m. with Mr Von
Rautenfeld (Customs).[8] They enjoyed looking at his menagerie, and
having their photos taken by the young men, followed by a jolly ride
home in rickshaws. Sir Robert came out of his office and they joined
him in a second tea. The three girls dined at the Braziers that evening,
and '*played absurd games*'. These seem as much a feature of evening
entertainment in aristocratic Peking as in the more bourgeois Chefoo.
On Sunday 29 April a day-long expedition led to many photographs.

*At 10.30 a.m. Messrs Wagner, Sandercock, de Luca & Bethell
came to escort us all to a picnic at the "Princess" Tomb, a lovely
green spot. We rode in carts to the Canal, & then had two rickety
Chinese barges to take us, the Bredons, Braziers & Customs'
students (25 in all), up the canal. The boats were towed by boys &
we played games, & made Effie recite on the way.* [Figure 7.5
shows she was the centre of attention in her short skirt.]
*The banks were green, & white ducks swam about on all sides.
Arrived there we tiffened in a joss-house with big pieces of plaster
hanging from the walls & ceiling. Afterwards played running
games & the men had a shooting competition, each drew for a
lady. M's man won the 2nd prize for her. Came on to be dusty &
rain so we went to the Temple & had photos taken* [Figure 7.6]
*& then tea & went home by boats. Sir R. came & talked to us
before our usual 2nd tea, & we had an evening alone with him.*

On Monday there was more tennis, a call on the Braziers and in the

evening, Sir Robert's third dinner dance. *'We danced till past 12 &
promenaded between dances in the cool garden.'* On Tuesday 1 May, they
called on Mrs Scott, wife of the Bishop of North China. *'Juliet Bredon
came round & talked to us till lunch.'* Mr Drury came at 2 p.m. to take
them on an eighteen mile excursion, in a cart, but on a good road, to
the Ten Thousand Ages Temple. They were late back, and found Sir
R. and Elsa had feared that the city gates might close before they reached
them.

Next day, Juliet was round again *'to chat'*, and at 4: 30 p.m. some
young Customs men escorted them to tennis. That evening Hart got
out his poetry and read *'various charming pieces. At our request he then
commenced an ode on Effie & Mr. Sandercock.'* The latter was one of his
Customs students.

On Thursday 3 May

> *At 4 p.m. we went calling! We called on Mrs. Brazier, Mrs. v.
> Rostern, Mrs. Focky & Mrs. Homström.* [As a result of this
> grown-up activity (calling and leaving a card) she improved
> in spelling some but not all of the names.] *Messrs de Luca &
> Bethell came at 5 p.m. to escort us to Mr. v. Rautenfeld's who was
> giving a large garden party.... . Chinese girls performed, singing
> songs to accompaniments of fiddles, wooden clackers etc. We were
> shown Mr. R's rooms, they were splendidly arranged with Chinese
> & Japanese curios & furniture. Messrs de Luca, Bethell,
> Sandercock, Ferguson & Richardson escorted us back & came
> into our little sitting room to write their names in our autograph
> books. Sir R. gave a lovely dance in the evening. While M & I were
> dressing he passed us in each two pieces of jewellery — mine were
> a silver watch & chain & a lovely necklet with diamond pendant.
> He took me in to dinner & I sat on his right, with Mr. Rose on my
> right. Danced every dance, & enjoyed it heartily.*

On Friday 4 May they set off in chairs at 10.15 for the races. Kath
records nothing about the horses, but noted some very showy dresses
on display, the fun they had with the young men at tiffin, and that *'Capt.
Strouts begged to take me to tea so I let him do so, & asked why he had not
come near us in Tientsin. Said he had paid a dinner call the day before we
came!'* Captain Strouts of the Marines was later to distinguish himself
in organising the defence of the Legations. Back home they met Sir

R. and Juliet Bredon in the garden. Sir R. and Kath practised their violins together *'in fine style'* for three-quarters of an hour. After dinner the band played in the garden and there was a display of fireworks. They ended by dancing The Lancers. Saturday was similar — a day at the races, including *'a very jolly tiffin. Mr. de Luca said I was the only one of the party who did not need a chaperone!'* Kath seems to have taken this as a compliment, but it may be the same reluctance to allow physical contact that Sir Robert noticed with his later references to her 'shy cheek'. *'Capt. Strouts came up again to talk to us & claimed us as marriage connections.... In the evening I played the Rhapsodie and Serenade to Sir R. who said he did not know I could play so well.'* They played their violins together for an hour, while the others went to the Braziers.

By Sunday 6 May Kath was feeling very tired! Mr Bredon took them to church at 11 a.m. and they walked on the wall with Mr de Luca and Mr Sandercock, till driven back by a dust storm. *'After dinner Sir R. showed us his decorations, about 23 in all.'* Monday 7 May was wet, and *'Juliet came in twice to chat'*. Chat is a word only used for Juliet, and suggests that they found her a bit tiresome.[9] Sir Robert arranged for them to stay till Saturday, despite Mrs Drew having written that she wanted Elsa home the next day.

On Wednesday 9 May they had tennis in the morning with Mrs Von Rosthorn and tea at the British Legation with Harry Bristow.

> *Messrs Dru Drury & Barr were there & Mrs. Cockburn acted as chaperone.* [Her husband was Chinese Secretary at the British Legation.] *After a regular bachelor's tea — butter in tin, Swiss milk, hard toast, etc — we saw the magic-lantern pictures, chiefly views of Bedford, Peking & Tientsin & also "Beauty & the Beast". It was very jolly.... We had a quiet evening with Sir R. I played four piano pieces & Elsa's accompaniments. We also practised waltzing & curtseying to Sir R.'s amusement who taught us!*

On Thursday Sir Robert gave his final dinner-dance. In the morning Kath wrote out the menus. At 4 p.m. Mrs Brewitt-Taylor called, then some students collected them for tennis. At the dinner-dance

> *Lord Suendale & Miss Blake & all the Customs Hsin-yu-an Mess & some Nan-yu-an,* [the Customs students, more numerous

than in Bowra's time, were divided into two messes] *&*
Messrs Giles, Townsend, Rose, Bristow & Porter of the
[Legation] students came. There were 7 dances & an interval
during which Mr. Lauru played the violin; I played Schubert's
"Serenade" on the piano. I enjoyed myself very much indeed,
dancing with nearly everybody & promenading in the garden after
each dance. (15 Bachelors versus 3 non-Bachelors! Note of
admiration!) Mr. Richardson took me into dinner.

Friday 11 May was:

Our last day!! Rose early despite last night, & walked round the
garden with Elsa. Sir R. spent nearly the whole morning with us,
sitting on the window sill, talking about everything; about 11.30
Juliet found us all & stayed to chat. After tiffin, packed. At 4.30
Messrs Wintour, Bethell, de Luca & Sandercock came to take us to
see the cloisonné shops... . We saw the whole process, & then each
of us was presented by the men with little souvenirs. Mine from
Mr. de Luca was a lovely ink-pot. We then all went to tea at the
Hsin-yu-an Mess, & had the most splendid time. First we tea'd in
Mr. Sandercock's room & then inspected the others' rooms, which
were all done up with photos & embroideries [probably Chinese
embroidered pictures]. *We then had an impromptu dance in the*
mess room... . We had the greatest fun & found Sir R. in the
garden, having overheard our 'peals, torrents & ripples of musical
laughter' as he said. Went over to say goodbye to Mrs. Rostern &
Focke. The Braziers, Bredons & Homströms called on us. A perfect
evening with Sir R. & at the end — farewell.

Actually, not quite. There was still time after breakfast on Saturday
to walk round the garden many times

with Sir R, talking of our return in the autumn, of the lovely time
we had had, etc. Then Miss Myers came over, & Messrs Bethell &
Sandercock, & about 10.15 we got into our chairs. Then round the
corner appeared all the Customs men, about 30 of them, the Hsin
Yuan, the Nan Yuan, the Braziers, Mr. Bredon...& they all shook
hands with us in our chairs and waved their handkerchiefs at the
gate to us. Messrs B. & S. escorted us to the station in rickshaws
and half way Messrs Dru Drury & Bristow joined us, riding.

They were met at Tientsin by Mr Drew. *'We had lovely gifts & photos to show them, and talked all the afternoon of our visit.'* (They had no cameras at this stage; the photos were gifts from the people they had met.)

Kath drew upon memories of this wonderful visit for the rest of her life. For Sir Robert too it had been a memorable break from his normal isolation, and he replied immediately to the letters of thanks which they wrote in Tientsin on Sunday 13 May.

15th May 1900

Dear Kathleen,

I was very busy all Saturday, but when I sat down to dinner the room felt very empty — I missed the cheerful chatter, and when I went into the other room & lit my cigarette loneliness settled down on me like an extinguisher on a candle — and I felt very desolate; but by Sunday I had gone back to myself again & I found company in my ordinary occupations. It is hard now to realize that your visit has been paid and is a thing of the past! However, it has left pleasant memories with me: I am so glad you have grown up such a nice loving & sensible girl, with such nice ways & ideas & tastes, and it has been a great pleasure to me to make your acquaintance. Dear Maude, too — what a bright sunny nature hers is: I thought you quite a delightful pair — you with your seriousness & simplicity, & she with her playfulness and vivacity! Our party was quite a success — the mock rule of Queen Elsa, and the pretty ways of 'baby' Effie completed the guest table for the happy host.

We had wind & dust & cold all Saturday afternoon: and again we had wind & dust & mist — like the south of France — on Sunday: yesterday was a delightful day, & today is so-so — sultry & overcast. I went out calling Sunday & Monday & intended to do so today, but I am giving myself a whisky, and among other things, writing this little note to you. Your letters came alright reporting your safe arrival: but so far, nothing from Effie — I hope she is not sickly: perhaps after the fun & excitement of Peking, she may be a bit 'under the weather' at Tientsin, but I hope it is my anxiety & not her condition that is to blame. The admiral is to arrive today & I am to dine at the Legation tomorrow — and also on the 24th. I must give a couple of Legation dinners myself & also start my Wednesday garden parties: what a pity you are all so far away — I sh'd love to have you all at hand to take part in all that goes on here & to grace my entertainments!

With love to Miss Maude and a final kiss for your own shy cheek

Lovingly yours,
Robert Hart

PS I hope your dentistry experiences were not too trying!

He is referring to Admiral Seymour, who had sent Captain Strouts of the Marines to discuss the reinforcement of the Legation guard. Some anxiety was already being felt in Peking about the political situation, though this is not apparent in Kath's diary. It is only in a later memoir that she mentions that 'one evening, Sir Robert, who usually discounted alarmist rumours, appeared disquieted and regretfully arranged for our departure'.

His remarks on the girls show Sir Robert's usual good judgement of character. *'Seriousness and simplicity'* captures exactly what I remember of my Aunt Kath when I knew her in the late 1940s and 1950s. She was intelligently interested and serious about many matters, but there was also a simplicity about her, partly, I think, that she never liked to think ill of people, and partly that she found her pleasures in the world of the mind, so was quite unconcerned about her restricted domestic surroundings. I spent a week with my Aunt Maude and her husband a year or so before she died of cancer in 1949, and I remember well her *'bright sunny nature'*, her contentedness with her lot, and her well-managed house.

Kath and Maude stayed in Tientsin till Monday 21 May, partly because both needed several visits to the dentist, who only visited Chefoo infrequently. They enjoyed the usual social round, the races, and tennis. Thus on 15 May:

Went to the dentist's at 9 a.m. At 11.30 drove out to the races with Elsa. A great number of people were there, but the meeting as a whole was slow, & it was awfully hot. We all had tiffin with the Detrings. They have a lovely house, & an excellent lunch. Mr. v. Hanneken &

> *Mr. Kettles sat on my right & left. The former talked of the times when he knew Father & Mother…[10] Mr. & Mrs. van Aalst[11] called & we went to see the ruins of last night's fire which at the time was very exciting to us who watched it from the garden at 1 a.m.*

It was only later that she realised that the huge fire was arson by the Boxers and a sign of worse to come.

On Sunday 20 May, it was very windy, so instead of morning church

> *read instead some very interesting articles which Mrs. Drew pointed out in magazines, on Woman's Work, critiques, etc. After tea went to Church…Capt. Strouts called on M. & me. Messrs Adams, Eames & he came to dinner in the evening. Mr. Drew took me in, & I sat between him & Mr. Eames. Played "Serenade" & a song for Elsa. Then we talked… . Discovered that Capt. Strouts is also one of nine, & a married man with a child!!*

I guess that Mrs Drew engineered this discovery, fearing that Kath was becoming too interested in the dashing Captain. She was encouraging her to think of university. *'Mrs. Drew has told me a lot about College life in America & showed me Dora's papers & some very interesting pamphlets & magazines.'* Dora was the eldest Drew girl.

They heard on Monday 21 May that a steamer was going to Chefoo the next day. Captain Strouts wrote to say goodbye. Mr Drew took them to the train and put them in the charge of a married couple whom Kath described as *'typical rich American globe-trotters, & rather nice'*. They arrived in Chefoo at 6: 30 a.m. on 23 May.

> *We rushed up to the house, found mother and the baby fast asleep, but both woke up, & we talked to Mother for an hour without ceasing, & exhibited our presents & photos to the admiring girls & Father. Unpacked all morning. Went for a walk with Father, Mu & Maude down to the Boys' school, & met the Eckford tribe at the top of our hill who greeted us with surprise. Had dinner with Father & Mother.*

She was obviously considered grown-up after her Peking stay!

Chefoo in the Shadow of the Boxer Rebellion, Summer 1900

Kath immediately resumed school, but after her 'coming out' in Peking she participated more in adult social life. Indeed, on her first day back at school, on 24 May, *'Vyvyan, Ada and Lilla gave a "surprise" dance to their parents, to which we all went & everybody in Chefoo. It was held in the garden, dinner under the trees & dancing on the lawn. Very windy, but fun all the same.'* She tried a waltz with Dennis Donnelly, a seventeen-year-old who had begun to join adult company, but gave it up as he had evidently not participated in the winter's dancing classes! However, young Dennis became a frequent visitor that summer, showing a talent for singing comic songs. The friendship with the Eckfords continued: on Sunday 27 May, the Carralls, Fowlers and Eckfords went in three boats across to West Beach and from there up to the vineyards owned by Baron von Babo.[12] *'We had tea in his little house, & returned on the boats, we had a race across the water with the Eckford boat, and of course, we won!'*

On 25 May, Kath received photos of Peking from Dru Drury and Harry Bristow, by the soon to be interrupted mail service. On 31 May:

> *In the evening Father had news for us — The "Boxers"*
> *have…risen in reality in armed numbers! They have murdered*
> *Messrs Norman & Robinson (two Church of England*
> *missionaries) & have burnt down Fengtai, the railway-station 15*
> *minutes from Peking. We have much to be thankful for that Maude*
> *& I are back safely before these disturbances, which threaten to be*
> *serious.* [13]

The burning of Fengtai and the attack on Belgian railway engineers prompted the diplomats to send for troops on 28 May to protect their legations. On Friday, Kath took the news to school, causing *'much perturbation'*. H.M.S. *Centurion*, *Whiting* and *Endymion* left Weihai for Taku. They heard that the Chartered Bank in Tientsin had been burnt down. For the rest of the summer the diary is a strange mixture of gruesome news, the usual social jollities of Chefoo, and Kath's own studies and music.

On Whit Sunday, 3 June, the new baby was christened. Young Frances and Kath went down to the church to decorate the font before and found it already being done by the Eckfords, so they helped them finish. All the children of the Customs staff came to it and had tea afterwards under a tent on the Hillside lawn. In the evening the Eckfords joined their Sunday evening hymns and music. In the summer, the family sat on the terrace for these, the girls taking it in turns to go inside to play the music as each chose their favourites.

Next day, at school, the news was that 'every house in the Settlement was armed, as thousands of Boxers were in the city. A volunteer corps was got up impromptu, & patrols go round the settlement from 10–30 to 4 a.m. every night! Some Tientsin people are here.' On 5 June she gives details of movements of men and ships at Taku and Tientsin, and that, far away, 'the British entered Pretoria!'

> 8 June Friday. Lessons as usual. Pao-ting-fu is in flames, & Tung-Chow[14] has been burnt. The missionaries are safe. 5000 Russians have landed at Tientsin. Great excitement here. We expect the Drews...[In pencil, obviously added later] Siege of Peking commenced.

On 9 June she records that Sir Claude Macdonald had telegraphed Shanghai that the position was serious, and that eight hundred troops under Admiral Seymour and an American commander were forcing their way up to Peking. While the foreign warships were at Taku, Chinese warships had come into Chefoo, but this caused no alarm:

> 10 June Sunday. Church as usual at 11a.m. The Eckfords came up to the house after service to ask if we might go out with them in boats & have tea on the water. At 4.30 we started. Em, Maude, Count d' Anjou[15] & I & Mr. Russell in one boat, & Vyvyan, Mr. Emery, the twins, Mu & Frances in the other. We pulled down to Fuller's (about ½ mile) & then anchored close to each other, & had tea. We then returned, landed Em to go to Church, [where she played the organ] & rowed out again, round a Chinese man-o'-war — Mr. d'Anjou's spirits rose unaccountably, & he dived out of the boat, fully dressed, but was valiantly rescued & sent ashore for his misdemeanour! Vyvyan & Mr. Russell brought us home. Five Chinese men-o'-war are in harbour! A patrol of 8 gentlemen go round the settlement every night.

> 11 June. The telegraph to Peking has ceased working.... The Taotai here has graciously allowed us a troop of Chinese soldiers to protect us, and four or five meander up each road, armed with staves!!

12 June. The column had an encounter with the Boxers & shot 50. All telegraph poles have been cut down. The grandstand at Peking burnt on Saturday. Here all seems safe, though an attack is expected on the night of the 14th inst. H.M.S. Phoenix has come into harbour, & the German & Austrian consuls have telegraphed for warships here.

13 June. The Chinese soldiers are in a most discontented state, as they have not been paid wages for long, & it is suspected most of them are "Boxers" & sympathise with them. A nice state of things for us.

One of the volunteers pointed out to Carrall that the guns of the forts at the entrance to the harbour had the settlement in their sights. Carrall went to the Taotai, and with him saw to the removal of the breech blocks, rendering them useless. The guns were left in place, to avoid the suspicion of Boxer adherents. Nothing happened on 14 June. On 17 June Em and Mu moved back from the bungalow into the house, where they had a dozen rifles and a box of cartridges. Kath wondered later who could use them.[16]

Carrall began making copies of all reports coming into his office by runner or by ship.[17] He discussed these at home, so the events are in Kath's diary but she also got news elsewhere.

18 June Monday. On going to my violin lesson I learnt from Mr. McOwan that the Taku forts have been taken by the Powers. The Chinese were given 24 hrs to evacuate them, but chose to fire before the time on the ships. The torpedo-destroyers "Flame" & "Whiting" & "Algerine" came up quite close, opened fire on two of them, utterly breaking them down. The Japs took the other. Thus they were taken by the small ships, the big men-o'-war not being able to get near.

She summarised the allied casualties which are detailed in her father's report, noting 'the Chinese suffered too'. Carrall copied into his record Lt. Moreton's letter to his wife, written when H.M.S. *Whiting* was briefly at Chefoo.

H.M.S. Whiting, June 20th

Dear Mrs. Carrall,

We are just off to Nagasaki & are sorry to say cannot stay here a minute as we have to proceed there with all despatch.

Will you tell Miss Maudie that I have to apologise for the taking of the Taku forts. She, I think, said we should never do it. [She had remembered their appearance on her way to Peking.] *The "Whiting" forced the passage of them before we took them, & the Chinese attempted to block us up with a mine, but it did for a junk instead. We have been hit by four or five shells & are off to Nagasaki to have new plates in the side, & repair a boiler a shell went through. The "Fame" & ourselves had the pleasure of capturing the four Chinese destroyers by boarding. They did not offer much resistance. There was no news from Peking but the C. in C. should be there with a strong force of seamen & Tientsin is holding out all-right* [sic].

Sincerely yours

(Signed) J. A. Moreton

Miss Maudie kept his photo in her album (Figure 7.7).

An attack on the Europeans in Chefoo was rumoured for 20 June. Several ladies and the boarders at school packed their necessities in bundles, ready to flee. Nothing happened. The peculiarities of a 'war' with China were in evidence again the next day, with some Chinese ships being captured and others safeguarded. On 21 June Kath noted:

The Chinese soldiers on guard have been doubled here. The Russians wished to take the 3 Chinese men-o'-war in harbour here, but they received warning & slipped out to Wei-hai-wei, where they are safe in British territory. News of fighting in Tientsin, but none from Peking, and much anxiety felt about both places.

Today was our usual "At home", & many people turned up. [During the summer they had a regular tennis at home on Thursdays.] *Three Japanese, one German, one American & H.M.S. "Orlando" are in harbour. There are also 23 steamers with*

refugees in, simply crowded, 14 in a cabin, & not allowed to land,
as the Br. Consul will take no more responsibility!

Kath may have asked her father whether there was a war, for next day she writes of an 'Ultimatum' by the Powers that they were only at war with the Boxers. *'Nevertheless numbers of Chinese are leaving here for the south for fear of the Foreigners. Our cook has left, & amah wishes to return to Canton!'* (Amah changed her mind and stayed.)

On Saturday 23 June they heard that the Customs' Mess in Peking had been burnt down. In Tientsin, the bravery of the Russians had saved other troops from being cut to pieces, but H.M.S. *Orlando* brought news that most of the city was in ruins. On Sunday afternoon the five Carrall girls and the Eckford twins went for a row round the warships, which saluted them. The Austrian band entertained at the Club. *'More refugees came down & General Dorwood with 950 of the Weihaiwei Chinese regiment*[18] *passed up. In the evening hymns & music after dinner.'*

They learned that, though Tientsin had been relieved, Admiral Seymour's force was still in desperate straits. (They heard of his relief on 28 June.) On 25 June Kath noted that more girls were leaving the school to return to their families. *'as the consuls can guarantee the large number of children (about 200) no protection here if anything happened'.* There was a rumour that 1,500 Boxers were nearby. On 28 June:

> *Much alarm is being felt by more than half of the settlement at the report that the "Boxers" are at Pingdu (4 days from here). The Eckfords have now packed their necessities in bundles for flight, except Vyvyan who stoutly refuses to do so, his mother has therefore secretly taken a shirt & a pair of socks in her bundle for him!!!*

The naval forces added a new element to social life in Chefoo. On Friday 29 June,

> *the girls had met a lot of the "Terrible's" officers* [Kath being at school] *& Mother and Father dined at the Eckfords to meet Capt. Scott, who is a very interesting personage as having been the man to mount the naval guns on wheels at Ladysmith.*

(Naval guns were also used in the final relief of Peking.) The same day the number of missionaries arriving from the interior so worried the British Consul that *'Mr. Tratman issued a degree [sic] that they must* move on south as they endanger the lives of the other residents whose flight would be impeded by such numbers'. This 'degree' was disregarded: on 4 July Kath noted that 'room is being made for them at our school'.

It was an anxious time. On 2 July forty-two missionaries from Tung-Chow arrived. Kath learnt that the Germans had burnt the Tsungli-Yâmen (inaccurate) and that Chinese had mounted guns on the city walls pointing into the British and other Legations (accurate). '*There seems hardly any help for them. Pray God they maybe saved.*'

The Worst Day in Chefoo

The rumours of local Boxer activity were not without foundation. Kath gave a limited account of the events of Saturday 30 June as Carrall evidently made light of the danger to his daughters.

> *School in the morning. Mother took Em, Mu & Maude & the Eckford twins to tiffin on board the H.M.S. "Terrible" with Capt. Scott. They...went all over the ship, saw silver models of the guns used at Ladysmith, & the Queen's chocolate boxes, even tasted the chocolate in them, & also saw Boer shells. When they returned, they went to Mr. & Mrs. Krier's wedding reception. About 5.30 p.m. Frances & I being alone in the house, Gwen & Phyllis came home with news of a riot in the street. Mother came up to reassure us & it appears a report got among some 150 Chinese who were to go up to Vladivostok as mining coolies that they were really to be sent to be made into soldiers & maltreated, thereupon they refused to board their steamer & a riot ensued. A large mob of Chinese who stoned some foreigners & broke windows were dispersed by the gallant volunteers who rushed out with rifles & fired blank cartridges among them. At length quiet was restored.*

Carrall's semi-official report, written on 5 July, gives a very different account:

> *On the 30th at about 4 p.m. a panic occurred amongst a lot of coolies bound for Vladivostok per S.S. "Seiko Maru", Agents — Anz & Co. A mob collected and broke the windows of L. H. Smith & Co's offices owing to a report circulated by some coal coolies that the emigrant coolies were being sent to Vladivostok to serve in*

the army and would have their queues cut off. Persons in the crowd stated that some of the emigrant coolies had already had their queues cut by the Japanese on board the S.S. "Seiko Maru" and they together with the 500 emigrant coolies were locked up in Messrs. L. H. Smith & Co.'s godown. I was on the spot [In her later memoir Kath says he heard of the riot at the wedding reception — which had merited his top hat and frock coat] *and at once sent for and obtained Mr. L. H. Smith's permission to search his premises. I then told the Subdistrict Deputy Magistrate and the Headman to select three men from the crowd who declared that there were Chinese locked up...to go with me to search the premises. This was done and a diligent scrutiny made every where for the 500 men and for any Chinese minus his queue. But only the employees on the premises were there. Consequently, in order to make a proper report to the Taotai of the result of the investigation, the three men from the crowd were invited by the Subdistrict Deputy Magistrate to go to the Taotai's Yamen and there make and sign their statement together with another man who was declared to be one of the ringleaders of the disturbance. By the time this had been accomplished the Taotai arrived. I told him what had been done and the result...and he then directed that the crowd should be cleared. Afterwards I went on board the S.S. "Seiko Maru" accompanied by the Steamer Agent's Assistant and the Subdistrict Deputy Magistrate, to count the coolies on board, but when we got there it was found that they had left. On returning to shore and the Magistrate informing the small crowd that still remained that there was no-one on board the ship, they left and the Bund was clear again by about 7.30 p.m. Thus ended what might have been a very serious disturbance.*[19]

He makes no mention of the *'gallant volunteers'* who would have been a handicap rather than otherwise during negotiations with the hostile crowd. They probably appeared later to disperse the *'small crowd that still remained'*. In a personal letter to Hart on 21 December Carrall referred to these events again.

The Bund and principal street were crammed with Chinese so compactly that it was with very great difficulty I could move along...I was afterwards congratulated by Capt. Rodgers of the

U.S.S. "Nashville" upon the way in which I managed the crowd. It certainly required some nerve to go unarmed and alone among so many, but as no one owed me a grudge I did not receive a dig from a knife.[20]

Kath later recalled her father saying that he never wished for more critical moments than while he watched the men searching the warehouse. He returned to the house about 8 p.m., where his wife was anxiously pacing up and down the tennis court.

The Chinese merchants of Chefoo were in no doubt that Carrall's actions had saved the town from the fate of the Chinese city of Tientsin (where Kath reported on 6 July *'a large part of the native city has been burnt'*). Had the crowd attacked foreigners, the foreign warships in the harbour might well have retaliated with their cannon and put men ashore, which could, as in Tientsin, have been followed by looting. On 4 July Kath wrote

> *The native merchants here have arranged to organise a native guard to keep order & protect Foreign property. Some Chinese were much alarmed on hearing the saluting to the "Nashville", thinking it was directed against them, so they brought presents of figs, dainties etc & begged to be spared!!*

On 10 July Kath reported:

> *Position of affairs at Taku improving. Japs doing very well. 1,600 Americans have arrived at S'hai en route for Taku. French troops "frightened", Austrians "fond of cover", Japs, "plucky — but perfect little brutes". They & the Russians kill every Chinaman irrespective of age or sex they meet. "Loot, loot, loot is the order of the day at Tientsin."*

In addition to organising a guard the merchants decided to make a magnificent gift to the man whom they credited with saving their city. This took time to organise, and it was only on 1 January 1901 that Carrall reported to Bredon:

> *Re Acceptance of silk scrolls*
>
> *On the 31st Dec. I entertained the foreign merchants to a New Year's eve dinner and today I gave a tiffin to the chief Chinese*

merchants of the place. The Chefoo Guild sent me at my house on
the 31st inst. some silk scarves and a piece of plate inscribed with
my name and their thanks in commemoration of my action at the
riot on the 30th June last. I have accepted the scrolls and piece of
plate, having first ascertained that the Taotai would be more
pleased than otherwise at my acceptance.

At noon today, I rec'd. from the Governor Yuan Shih K'ai a
telegram wishing me New Year felicitations.

The red silk scrolls were inscribed in gold by a fine calligrapher, whose
work would have been costly (Figures 7.8 and in colour, Figure H). Four
scrolls are known to survive. Parts of scrolls two and four (from right
to left, translated for me by Xu Zhang) read:

The rebels destroyed railways, punished agencies and assembled
mobs. Chefoo was under the control of rebels. Rumours about
revolution echoed. Then thousands of people, from all walks of
life, all cut their long hair, left their families, and in desperation
risked danger and took part in the Rebellion, led by robbers and
brigands.

You always played a very important part in the local
administration and development. Your merits here in the coastal
region of the Eastern Sea were so significant that we cannot
praise you enough. Future historians will certainly notice and
extol your achievements…. Who could save our nation and calm
these rebels down? Only you! Only you could head off the danger.
Your contribution to the event was known to everybody in this
area. Being engaged in a magnificent cause, you always kept calm
and were never corrupted. Especially in the recent fight against the
Boxer rebels, nothing less than one of the most significant events
in Chinese history, you still kept your head and never showed any
bewilderment.

The sixth scroll came to me from my mother and is signed off:

All members of Chefoo Merchants Association, kneeling down and
kow-towing, present this tribute to His Honour James Wilcocks
Carrall, Commissioner of the Chefoo Customs.

As in Foochow, Carrall worked closely with the local authorities, and in this case, with local merchants as well. He supported their efforts to raise money and obtain technical advice to get the harbour bund extended westward (an early suggestion of his), but in the aftermath of the Boxer rebellion, felt that he and they received little backing from Bredon. Bredon, as Deputy IG, had moved with most of the headquarters staff to Shanghai while Hart remained in Peking to help the Chinese in their negotiations with the victorious powers.

Summer Holidays and the End of the Siege

Returning to the summer, Kath's diary shows the young people making plans for a regatta. '*Maude is going to cox for Mr. Russell and Dennis, Frances for Messrs Anz & Parkhill, and Em & Mu are to row in the ladies' doubles with Mr. Parkhill as Cox!*' On 8 July they heard a rumour that the Boxers had entered the Legations. '*What would we not give to know the truth?*' but on 17 July '*our governor, Yuan Shihkai…states that the British Legation was safe up to the 9th inst*'. On 20 July the regatta was postponed on account of serious rumours. Instead Dennis organised a water picnic, for which the Eckfords and Carralls supplied provisions. On 23 July: '*A deputation of Christian natives told Mr. Tratman that the Boxers have destroyed some mission houses a few miles from here, and were expected to come to Chefoo.*' The alarms were not over, but the new task was to help with the wounded who were being taken to the British naval station at Wei Hai Wei.

> *27 July Friday. Today we ended school for the holidays. Miss Churcher very kindly gave me some nice words of advice on leaving school as I am probably not going back next term.*
>
> *In the afternoon three lady nurses — Misses Mills, Unwin & Cameron — from Corea for Wei-Hai arrived… . They had dinner with us… . Mother has instituted a rule that we shall each roll <u>six</u> bandages of 6 yds length every day! for the wounded at Wei-hai.*

The news from the north was grim. On 31 July there was a

> *Long telegram from Dr. Morrison,[21] Sir R. and Sir Claude. 62 killed including Capt. Strouts, Mr. Wagner and Mr. Oliphant. 128 wounded. The rest are contentedly waiting relief, living on rice and horseflesh. How terrible this is. I took baby round to see Miss*

> *Downing and arranged a literary society with Lotty, Elsie &*
> *Eunice.*

The news evidently took time to sink in; it was the next day, 1 August, that she felt *'very depressed at the news of the deaths at Peking. I can't realise we ever went there at all, & I trust & pray that dear Sir Robert may be saved & all the others.'*

She had not forgotten the ambitions awoken by Mrs Drew and that afternoon, during *'a long walk with Father down the beach...he has promised to let me continue school next term'*. The only reason for doing this would be to work for Higher School Certificate exams in December as a qualification for university. On 16 August the school said that Mrs Beer could teach her. Father, with five children younger than her to educate, a widowed mother to help, and who, at fifty, needed to save for retirement, must have been worried about the cost. The diary shows she kept up her studies, taking up an offer from Mr Anz to give her German lessons three times a week throughout the holidays. She also continued reading the classics of English literature. Em and Maude joined her in a Literary Society, which decided to study Tennyson's life and works.

This did not stop her from participating in the round of tennis 'at homes', or in the frequent summer activity of *'pulling about on the water'* — i.e. rowing. Bandage rolling continued, sometimes in parties at which the men also helped, and with the accompaniment of Dennis Donnelly's comic songs. On Saturday 28 July they *'bathed in the morning for the first time. It was lovely. We all went out in our boat with Ada and Lilla & dived from it.'* There had been several previous references to the weather being very hot. During August they bathed two or three times a week. On 16 August they heard that *'The vanguard of the relief force starts tomorrow. May it reach Peking quickly!'*

Emily had to make an important decision on 11 August. She must have discussed it with her parents, but not her sisters, for Kath only mentions it briefly, after describing a children's party given as a goodbye to the Innocents in the afternoon, a *'mad row in the moonlight'* and a session of bandage-winding. Then *'Emily received a telegram from Charlie telling her to "come as soon as possible". She has answered that if marriage is to be on arrival she will go — not unless. I wonder what it means.'* Charlie was in Britain and evidently could not promise immediate marriage. He appears no more in the diary, except on 23

September, his birthday, when *'Father made a speech & we drank his health!'*

By this time they were getting almost daily news of the Allies' advance on Peking. On 17 August

> *we five went in our dinghy for a long pull — 1 ½ miles — round the Jap. man o'war. Returning we met Vyvy & Lilla in theirs, & the Gipperichs in their dinghy, so we all moored close to the Zenta & waited while the Baron v. Babo, & the Zenta commander came rowing up.... Going round the hill afterwards we were told by the Gipperichs the news just received which make this a red letter day indeed —* Peking was relieved on the night of the 15th [underlined in red].

Father immediately sent a telegram to James Campbell in London. It arrived late at night, but Campbell got it round to the *Morning Post*, which had a scoop next morning, first with the news.[22]

The extraordinary normality of the summer was partly due to the social leadership of the senior Carralls. Kath's mother told Hart in her second letter to him after the relief of Peking:

> *...we never gave up all hope of you though there were some days we felt bad. We tried to keep things going as usual & turned up regularly at each other's tennis days — Mondays Fergussons, Ewings, Tuesdays & ourselves Thursdays & Fridays the harbour master's. Once, fixed for the end of July, we even proposed holding a regatta — expecting before the actual day arrived to have heard of your relief but as the day came & still the strange silence it seemed too ghastly and we postponed it sine die; however it served its purpose & kept the young people going, practising, pulling & arranging about colours. We have not let the bathing drop either, in spite of having no visitors, as far as possible we tried to act as if all were as it should be — the community seems to have managed to keep on quite fairly friendly terms all through — it is a little difficult & requires a good deal of diplomacy now we have Mrs. Eckford back, her energy is greater than her tact! But she is thoroughly kind-hearted at the bottom I believe and it is as well not to stagnate!*

Kath wrote later that when Tientsin was attacked, Father had wanted

Mother to take the children to Japan. But, as in Foochow, Frances senior thought they should continue their usual routine, so as not to betray nervousness to the community and the Chinese.

After the Siege

On 22 August they heard that the mail was open to Peking again. They had gone in the morning to be photographed (Figure 7.1), and afterwards Mother, Kath and Maude wrote short letters to Sir Robert, expressing their delight, Father also writing from the office. Frances senior wrote:

> ...I must write to tell you how thankful we were to at last hear of the relief of Peking. You have all been much in our thoughts and for that matter are still for we shall be unable to settle down to everyday thought till we know just how you are and have some particulars of your late terrible experiences. I am so glad for you that, with the exception of poor Mr. Wagner, all your staff are safe through it.
>
> There! I am not going to say a word more about it: four sheets even would not convey what we feel and you do not want sheets with the heaps & heaps of congratulatory telegrams and letters which you must be receiving, why from this house alone four of us feel that it is our special privilege to write and that if we did not you would miss our letters & so it will be over the world...

A normal letter was one sheet of foolscap, folded to make four pages. Four sheets would have been a very long letter of sixteen pages. Anything less than four sides of a sheet was a 'note' or a 'chit' (for which Sir Robert had special paper).

At 6 p.m. Kath and Emily went down to the church for choir practice, and afterwards went rowing with Maude and Frances junior. It was fairly rough — 'we had a wild time with our rudder'. Next day 'we all went for a glorious bathe with Ada & Lilla, the waves were very high & we all enjoyed it'. This suggests that they were bathing off the beach, where Father and several others had bathing huts against the wall of the French convent which was next to the Chefoo Club. (The next year there was an upset in the community, when the nuns requested that the huts be moved. Father complied, and the nuns dismantled some that were not moved. This led to unpleasant retaliatory action by others. There are no photos to show their bathing costumes, but they probably had shorter skirts than those they used for tennis and hockey, which may have offended the nuns.)[23] On 24 August they heard at Mrs May's 'At home' of the death of five children in the siege, including Mrs Brazier's youngest, and of disputes between the allies. (Mr May was Chief Tide Surveyor and Harbour Master, who collaborated with Carrall in collecting information for his record of Chefoo events.) Any hope of seeing Sir Robert in Chefoo was dashed by a letter from Mrs Drew on 26 August saying that he had decided to stay in Peking with a skeleton staff of eight unmarried men.

The diary became intermittent when Kath and young Frances started school again on 3 September. There are just a few entries on social occasions, such as the joint birthday of Emily, twenty-one, and Phyllis, five, on Sunday 16 September. They and the Eckfords went on board S.M.S *Geier*, and the German officers showed them their pets, including an alligator, parroquet, and opossum from South America. That month also saw the return of Dr Molyneux, who had been with the Relief Force, and the first of the Customs students — Mr Wintour (on crutches) and Mr Smyth — passing through on their way to home leave. Chefoo enjoyed two new activities that autumn, whist and hockey, a fashionable women's sport at the time. The Hockey committee met on 26 September to arrange two teams who would play on Saturdays. '*We girls are to make our own blouses & caps!*'

Saturday 29 September was Father's fifty-first birthday, which the family celebrated more by their activities than by masses of presents.

> *At 7 a.m. his family assembled in Mother's bed-room to wish him "Many Happy Returns", Em & Maude gave him a dozen handkerchiefs embroidered with his monogram, & Mu an oil-painting, Mother presented him with a check from all of us for a gold signet-ring. Mr. Moreton came up in the morning to ask us to the Cricket match, but as we had arranged a Family concert, we could not go. (Em, Mu & Maude were in the midst of making Father's cake!) At 4 p.m. we all had tea, & commenced the concert directly after till 6 p.m. when E. & Maude went to Choir practice, & the rest for a walk, or practising archery. Capt. Mackensie [sic] & Mr. Moreton ("Whiting") came to dinner to which Eric... stayed up, & after we finished the concert & Mr. Mackensie sang while we played whist, "Old Maid" & then all joined in the latter*

*game (Mr. Moreton's fate was to be old bachelor), which was
followed by "Fortunes", screaming fun! (We were to have gone on
board S.M.S. "Geier" to a dance but she had sudden orders to
leave. Mr. Moreton asked us on board "Whiting" to see the
unexploded shell which she had in her boiler but the Concert put
off all.) Chaffed "Whiting" officers on their photos in "Black &
White"!* [Figure 7.9.]

Chefoo was still full of naval ships. They could barely get into their
little church for the Harvest Festival on 30 September, because it was
full with 20 ratings each from two ships, but, as Kath slyly remarked,
'*a doz. obliging sailors turned out to make room for us four!*'. Mr Smyth of
Customs, Peking, came to dinner and reported

> *everyone was very well — nearly all the Customs have three
> months sick leave — all the students but six have also gone — Sir
> R. most considerate & bravest man & Frau v. Rosthorn bravest
> lady — Bredon family selfish & cowardly!*[24] *Misses Myers &
> Brazier kept house with Lady MacDonald. All Customs lost nearly
> everything. Sir Robert only has the suit of clothes he was wearing.*

Meanwhile, Kath's personal plans had gone awry. On 18 September:
'*Went to school & heard that Mrs. Beer was going to England, so that ends
Elsie's & my schooling for the present, as they are "too shorthanded to give
us the individual teaching we require" — Miss Churcher told me so with many
regrets*'. Next day, as Elsie was returning to England with Mrs Beer, she
made herself a timetable to keep up her studies on her own. She
continued her music lessons with Miss Norris, who was seriously
overloaded with work as another teacher was absent through illness.
Her mother, perhaps foreseeing that Kath might need a career,
encouraged her to offer help, which was accepted.

Frances senior told Hart about this in her second post-siege letter
on 26 September:

My dear Sir Robert

*When I wrote to congratulate you last month we were then hoping
daily to see you but as apparently even the late troubles have not
been sufficient to tear you away from your beloved Peking. I am
going to endeavour to send you a more chatty letter than I did*

before in case others like myself still feel you are somewhere away from us up in the clouds beyond us in fact and perhaps personally you are tired of being thus deified and wish to hear now and again something of ordinary port life by way of a change…I have seen no one as yet who has been with you through the troubles but everyone who has come down & who has had an opportunity of talking over things with others has congratulated us on having such a chief, and as it had to be I cannot help being glad of this chance of seeing you in your true light, so often concealed by your I.G.ship. Your next obituary (years hence I trust) will come nearer the mark in describing your character! There! you are not to think it cheek on my part writing like this but after that winter we spent with you I so well understand the thoughtfulness and unselfishness which appear to have so impressed all who were shut up with you and I cannot help being jubilant for I know how well you deserve the praise they all concur in giving you — I could never say these things to you being slow of speech as of yore but I think them & you must please not scold me for writing them this once.

She continues with the comments on the summer in Chefoo already quoted, and adds her hopes of seeing her eldest brother's son:

…he is attached to B. Battery R.H.A. …— the Indian transports only call in at Wei-hai-wei going north so we saw nothing of him which was most disappointing: my first & only relation who has been out to China & it is provoking knowing he is so near as Tientsin & yet not being able to see him. We are going to make him a birthday cake for his 25th birthday & send it up!…We have been disappointed about Kathleen — she was to have continued her studies under a special teacher & it was all nicely arranged & working well when the lady in question was telegraphed for to go home. [She tells him about Kath helping with music lessons.] *I am glad, for the school has done well by us with regard to the girls & they were very good that time Maude was ill so that it is nice to be able to make a little return & they have acted very well in keeping the school open & working during the late scare — many of the children there are orphaned through these massacres. Here is the end of my paper. I will not alarm you by commencing a new sheet…. With kindest regards dear Sir Robert…*

Two new teachers arrived on 12 October, and Father told Miss Churcher that Kath should resume her studies. The diary has few items, so they evidently kept her busy. There was an entry for 23 November: *'Mother's birthday! We girls gave her some embroidery & a thimble.'* Despite the sessions with the dentist at Tientsin toothache prevented her from joining in the evening party. She also marked 29 November:

> *Last day of school, & quite the last school day for me! Spent the morning collecting books & finishing up generally. Have arranged to continue reading "Maria Stuart" & "Les Fourberries de Scapin" to keep up my German & my French, & to spend one morning a week with Miss Norris over my music.*

She did not go to Shanghai to take her Higher School Certificate examinations in December, as young Frances did the following year. Kath lacked confidence in her abilities, and probably felt unready to attempt them after her interrupted studies. Events later made this a costly omission. The better girls' schools were now expecting their teachers to have a degree and the College of Preceptors' certificate had become a less regarded qualification.[25] Kath did not complain in her letters to Hart, but she confided in her grandmother, who told him in January 1901 that *'She was in grief because she was leaving school that term, she is the one who delights in her studies'*.

Sir Robert's Account of the Siege, and Letters Flow

Sir Robert replied to their letters on 12 November. His letter is much creased, evidence that it was read, reread, and passed around, making his handwriting even more difficult to interpret than usual.

> *Dearest Kathleen*

> *How lucky I did not induce you girls to stay another month! How c'd I possibly have matronised and ciceroned you during those eight weeks of horse-flesh diet and the music of shells and bullets? I went through it all right, came out of it all right, and have been all right ever since! I got to work at once as soon as the "relief force" came, and have ever since been trying to put "Humpty Dumpty" up on the wall again but I have not yet succeeded: however, we will do it yet! Of course China deserves any amount*

of thrashing, and the Princes and Ministers punished for these cruel doings and cruel attempts to do worse, but the question of vengeance is small — what we have to arrange is the future, and so I am calmly facing that problem and pegging away at it. Of course I ought to be off for a holiday, but I am feeling "fit" and [two Chinese characters] *never to abandon the "ship" now she is on her "beam ends"; we must right her first, in her own interest and everybody else's. I succeeded in renting rooms behind Kierulff's stores, and it seems as if the house has just been finished for my occupation.* [He was unlucky; the onset of frosts stopped work till spring.]

I am far from comfortable but I am better off than most others and so far I am standing the cold far better than I expected. Another place I took is the temple near the Ha-ta-mû - Kao-tsing-miao, which was pointed out to me in 1861 as a place I might take if the British Legation c'd not put me up! I have with me Pinz, Granzella, Van Strauch, Kurhowyoff, Ferguson, and Encarmano. All the others have gone to Shanghai with the Deputy I.G., or on leave. Poor Mr. Wagner was killed and Mr. de Courcy has since died, our people looked? ??? and it was interesting to see how manly and courageous those youths Bethell & Sandercock were: Bismarck & Willie Dupré ??? ???? most nights on the rifles — they killed any number of Boxers! I had a letter from Elsa Drew the other day, longing to be back in Tientsin, but I have not heard from Effie since May. I look back with immense pleasure to the visit you all paid me, but it seems ages & ages ago: in fact I have been through an eternity since then, for I thought those Legation weeks w'd never end.

I went round the old place the other day, and came back with my hands full of roses, my eyes full of tears and my heart as sore as heart could be! You never saw such destruction! I lost all I had, and I can never replace what the flames destroyed. I managed to get a message off on the 4th August with a telegram to London asking them to send some clothes: for I had only the light summer suits: my man got through, & on 23rd August the mail steamer started with some nice things for me. They arrived here and were opened on 19th instant, when I was still in summer attire, and on 20th it snowed & the thermometer went down some 20 degrees:

*how lucky I was to have something warm to put on! The French
Legation got a terrible battering: how the people held on there, I
can't imagine! I think they and the Japs and Col. Shiba carried off
the honours of the siege. Poor Capt. Strouts' death so near the end
was very sad: he was up and about day & night, with his pipe
always in his mouth, keeping his own counsel and seeing to
everything. We had some nasty half-hours and the fires close to
our walls were terrible to see and fight and fortunately they never
got over our walls. The Customs folk were in the [the Legation
students' building],[26] opposite the chapel and some forty of
us ate, eight at a time, at the common table. We were well
looked after & catered for by Mrs Mears, assisted by Mrs.
Russell and Miss Dudgeon: indeed I don't know what we should
have done without the first — she was truly invaluable! Two of
my boys went through it with me: Afong, who has been with me
since 1859, and Wen Chi who has been with me twelve years or so:
they behaved splendidly. You w'd not know our lane now — not a
house in it standing! And, as for the people, they are all gone! I am
myself sorry that my Band came to grief — but perhaps its motto
sh'd be "Resurgam!" If I hold on another year — as I am hoping
to do, & there are all you young people in a flourishing condition
— I shall very likely start it again: but the house will never be the
same!*

*With love to you all and a special kiss for yourself — if you'll
not turn away your mouth!*

Lovingly yours

Robert Hart

*P.S. Excuse me to your Mama and Maude: no time to write to
them yet!*

There is an interesting social point in this letter. Hart could be quite
prickly about his own social position, but he disregarded it in others.
He put Mrs Mears, the wife of Christopher B. Mears, Customs
handyman and gas engineer from 1880, in charge of the catering.
Another observer, Dr Coltman, praised Mrs Russell and Mrs Mears
*'for their constant, untiring efforts to render palatable the daily ration of horse-
meat and rice'.*[27] For Dr Coltman, Mrs Russell came first, reflecting her

husband's senior social position as a Professor who post-siege became Commissioner in Fuzhou.

Kath had already had some of this news, for on 3 October Bertie Simpson, their first visitor direct from Peking, came to tiffin. He *'gave us interesting details of the siege, but some very sad — Mr. de Courcy died on Sunday, Mr. Sandercock is off his head & may go quite mad, and Mr. Dru Drury is reported to be dying.'* This shows how gruelling the necessity to fight and kill had been for young men who never expected to have to do so. Leslie Sandercock had entered the Customs in 1898, and after his recovery from what we would now call post-traumatic stress disorder he went on to become a Commissioner. The courage Hart mentions came at a cost; in a letter to Campbell of 9 November 1902 he said that Anthony Bethell had not been himself since the siege, and the accident he had just had when a train ran over both feet, necessitating their amputation, might have been attempted suicide. Bethell also recovered and retired as Commissioner in 1929.

Kath replied immediately:

November 12th 1900

My dear Godfather

I was most pleased to find your well-known envelope waiting for me on the mantel-piece when I came home from school the other day…— you have answered all the questions I would have asked…and it was most kind of you to write to me, when you must have such a great deal to think about & do just now. Indeed it must be an appalling task to put "Humpty-Dumpty" up on the wall again.

I am very glad you are feeling well & "fit" and I hope you will soon become more settled and comfortable — what a curious coincidence about the Kao-tsing-miao! I was extremely sorry to hear of the destruction of your dear old house. I can't realize that it doesn't exist any more, for I always connect it with the very happy times we had there and whenever I recall Peking that house and garden — where we had such delightful strolls listening to the band, and watching the fire-works — always come first to my mind. Its loss, with everything you had collected and valued so much, oh it must indeed be very hard to bear. It was cheering to

*hear that at least two of your boys did not desert you, I should
like to pat them on their backs! though it is no more than what
they owed to all your goodness to them. I remember Afang very
well. He was my favourite, while Elsa liked the fatter one, whose
mouth worked so curiously! Yes, it does seem ages ago — after all
that has happened since — that we four were up there with you
having such fun. Mr. Symth and Mr. Wintour also gave us some
interesting details of the siege. Mr. Wintour's knee is getting much
better, Mr. Symth has been a great help to him. Today Miss
Brazier & Mr. Barr were here for a few hours.*

*We have started the winter very energetically. We have
organised a Ladies' Hockey Club, and the members meet every
Saturday for a game. We have also got up a little violin orchestra
in which Emily is the accompanist & I one of the performers. It is
quite informal and very enjoyable.*

*There are still three weeks of school before Frances' and my
holidays begin. I am studying quite alone now, the girls of my
class having left, one by one, to put up their hair & become
"grown up", which fate will soon be mine too I expect! It is quite
cold walking down to school every morning. Yesterday there was
snow on distant hills, and a little ice in the ponds.*

*Baby (do you remember the excitement when we heard of his
arrival?) is flourishing very well. He gets much spoiling but
doesn't mind it at all! & demands a great deal of attention.*

*I do hope you will be able to start your band again. It played so
well, and was such an entertainment, perhaps as things get
quieter, the bandsmen will gradually return to you.*

Emma Sampson also wrote a second letter after the siege, for she
too took pride in the praise being heaped on her old friend:

*I know a Mr. Fowler & his wife & daughters here they live but a
short distance from me; he is a friend of Sir Claude Macdonald,
& naturally takes great interest in Peking affairs & spoke of you
saying how brave & unselfish you were, how hard you worked —
and Mrs. Pritchard has a friend from China & she tells me the
same. I hope the terrible strain will not injure your health. I hope
you do not feel very lonely & that you will soon be able to leave
China, & a rest in dear old England.*

*I am deeply grateful to you for all your great kindness to my
grandchildren which adds very much to my happiness.*

With kindest regards

Always yours sincerely, Emma S. Sampson

She wrote again on 29 November, to tell him of a letter from her
nephew (half-brother William's son) to say that the Chinese in Port
Elizabeth, South Africa, had raised £145 for *'the comfort of our soldiers'*.

Naturally, the Carralls wrote to Sir Robert for Christmas and Kath
and Maude sent him gifts. Maude sent him a pair of mittens '— *you
must excuse their funny shape but Mother remembered you preferred holes to
thumb-pieces, as the former was better for writing purposes'*. She told him
about new winter entertainments, in the shape of noisy progressive
whist parties, the first being at Mrs Eckford's house. The hockey matches
were ending because of the cold and windy weather. Instead, *'there is
some talk of having ladies' bowling days at the Club once a week. How muscular
we will all get!'*.

Kath's letter told of Christmas preparations, but it was her mother's
letter that mentioned the gift she must have sent with it:

> *I hope Kathleen's cap will fit — she is not a great hand at working
> & has been very anxious over it. Her great idea was to have old
> gold or emerald blue such as you had. They said you used to come
> in your cap to tea & take it off & "stuff it in your pocket" & she
> was afraid of hers not being soft enough to do likewise.*

'Working' refers to needlework — women's work — and not to the
industriousness that Kath showed in other fields.

Kath's diary resumes on 23 December. On 24 December the sisters
helped decorate the church, and did the family tree in the afternoon.
On Christmas Day they all went to early Communion at 8 a.m. and
to morning service at 11, Kath also playing for the children's Carol service
at 3 p.m. They had a jolly dinner at Mrs Eckford's, with games afterwards.

On the last day of an eventful year Kath closed her diary with an
account of an ordinary day. She had continued to study, and after giving
a music lesson to her brother Eric she had Greek and Latin lessons with
Mr Burne. In the afternoon she helped prepare for her parents' New
Year's Eve dinner for the foreign merchants: *'six Eckfords, Donnellys, Messrs*

Wake, Tratman, Bryant, Guernier, Dicks & ourselves, & drank healths, & had speeches & good wishes. Tomorrow we shall for the first & last time see the opening of a new century!'

For the Carralls, as for others, that century was to hold tragic events which would disrupt both personal lives and Victorian society. More immediately, the harmonious family life and the friendship with the Eckfords which Kath depicted was about to be shattered by her older sisters. Break social conventions in a small treaty port and gossip spread like a deadly wild fire.

CHAPTER EIGHT

GIRLS GROWING UP: ROMANTIC UPHEAVALS, 1901–2

In the autumn of 1900, as we shall see, Hart's younger daughter, Nollie, wanted to marry a young Customs man whom Hester considered not good enough. Hart wrote her a letter that Nollie thought was sympathetic, but he also refused to give his approval and she gave the young man up in May 1901. This helps explain his intense interest in the travails of the Carrall family in July 1901. A letter from Hart set off an explosion in the Carrall family.

A Quiet Winter and Spring — but with Some Sport

1901 had started quietly. The mild January meant no skating parties. The death of Queen Victoria on 21 January caused some festivities to be postponed. Kath wrote on 10 February:

> *Was not it a shock about the Queen's death? We had not heard of her illness until the day of her death, and so the news came to us very suddenly. Our planned dissipations were of course put off, and we are in mourning for a month. There was a memorial service on Sunday to which the Consuls came in uniform, and Emily played the "Dead march in Saul". It seems strange to hear the King's name mentioned in the Services.*

A concert arranged to raise money for a school for Chinese deaf-mutes survived the mourning. Kath told Hart how pleased she was with the reception given to the new violin orchestra. Frances senior wrote her usual birthday letter about these events, and then she realised:

I expect Kathleen...will give you more details — she & Maude
will grumble if I give you any more news, like Frances (who had
to write home to thank for something) who said to me "they say it
is no use mentioning skating, school opening, concert, bowls or the
weather and then they expect me to write a letter" [of the
expected four sides].

Sixteen-year-old Frances was now coming more to the fore. She could
be quite frank not only to, but also about, her parents.

The innovation of ladies' bowling had led to ructions. After the
mourning was over the gentlemen challenged the ladies, making
chivalrous allowance of sixty points for women's low abilities and an
additional thirty for their nervous disposition. It was a misjudgement.
Maude broke the ladies' record with 138 points and the women averaged
95 points each against the nervous men's 101. With their allowances:

The ladies won by 448 points...we...challenged immediately, offering
to play them again on their own terms. (We have not been accepted
yet, it takes some time evidently for them to get over their defeat!)

On 20 and 21 April Frances senior and Kath wrote to Sir Robert again,
both delighted to hear that they were not to be moved out of Chefoo
that summer. By then spring picnics and dances were in full swing, often
involving the Eckfords. Frances senior told Hart:

All the seven girls & Eric are at a party at the Eckfords — their
(Eckfords) third dance this week! Before they went Baby had his
birthday tea & when fixing his 1st candle to a little glass plate
(which I kept as a souvenir of a very happy birthday I spent in
Peking ages ago) I could not but think of you...then Mr. Hobson
being again Shanghai Commissioner. If I were not so very stay-at-
home in my old age [forty-four!] I should feel inclined to write &
ask him if there was not a room at the "Dragon" for me to come
& do the family shopping!

She was to see Mr Hobson sooner than expected. She also reported
that Emily's fiancé was re-appointed to the China station and that
Kathleen continued as studious as ever, despite having left school.

Kath told him about the 'sports' day which again demonstrated the
general attitude to female athletic abilities:

211

It is just a year since our lovely visit to you, and yet it seems ever so long ago, such a lot has happened since!...It is jolly to think that we may have another summer here.... We have lately spent several fine days out on the hills and next week we are going to take tea to the "Blossoms", a lovely fruit-garden just in flower at the foot of the Pinnacle.

We had some very good athletic sports last week, the ladies took quite as much interest in them as the men, and they joined in three of the races, and practised for them beforehand! We all five went in for them vigorously. You never saw anything so absurd as those ladies' races.... The first was the usual egg-and-spoon race, & it turned out quite a family affair, for Muriel won the first prize, Maude, the second & Emily, the third, and I came in fourth! The second race was a "ladies' driving race", each lady's pony was a gentleman blindfolded whom she had to drive to the winning-post by pulling the reins (tied to his arms) right or left. It was really awfully difficult to steer safely over a course crowded with fifteen blindfolded men, & their fifteen partners, & it was most funny to see some ponies rushing headlong to destruction, or the reins giving way, galloping as hard as they could away from their poor stranded ladies! But the most laughable race was the third which consisted in the lady adding up an arithmetic sum, and her partner eating a ten-day-old bun, the prize being given to the lady whose sum was correct, and whose partner finished the bun first. Comte d'Anjou was my champion bun-eater, and as I managed the sum all right, we carried off the first prize, Maudie and her partner winning the third prize.

A Mr Schroeder was in the second race. His athletic form, in shorts, made a hit with one of the girls (Figure 8.1).

In his reply Sir Robert prophetically advised her to enjoy the good times while they lasted.

25 Ap. 1901

Dearest Kathleen

I am so glad to read in yours of 21st Mar. today that you were all well & having a good time. The sun shines — so, make hay! I am always busy, but I have very little to show for it: like riding on a "hobby-horse" — plenty of work, and not getting "forrader". I have done lots of reading, and Shakespeare has given a thousand enjoyments: what a man — what an Englishman he was! I was out today at the American Legation: Mrs. Squiers was "at home". The American 9th Regiment band was playing in the courtyard and all sorts & conditions of men & women were there. It was very gay, and the weather pleasant.

I wish the old house was still standing & some of you coming up again, but I am homeless and I can do no entertaining now. I wish I c'd get away for a change and perhaps may do so: while at present it is impossible — I might be away just when wanted, and it is therefore better to hold on. Now the boy says "Fan-teh-ho" (dinner ready) so I must stop, & finish the sheet later on.

It is eight o'clock, I suppose you were at dinner too — Bon appétit! Spring Soup, stewed chicken, boiled tongue, Cabinet pudding, oranges, dates, walnuts, cigarettes: that's what Mr. Pinz and myself have been doing justice to, now we have said good night — he's in his room & I am in mine.

I never heard from Effie since the siege: what a dear child she was! As for Mr. Sandercock, rumour says he has grown very fit & is engaged to somebody else at home & he's not twenty yet! I suppose you know that Mr. Bismarck is marrying a Miss Bishop in Japan: a lovely girl, judging by her photo. Mr. Kiernhoff is still here and also Ferguson & Von Strauch, but the Mess is scattered. The Boxer affair upset all our plans, changed all our lives, and I feel very sad & sore over it all. I very seldom go out: it is painful to see such a horrible scene of destruction all round! Thank your Mama for her letter of the 20th: I'll write by and by.

Rumours Abound and Reputations are at Risk

Sir Robert found Kath's next letter, in July, disappointing. He knew the family was in trouble, but she gave no indication of it.

15th July 1901

My dear Godfather

I hope you are having as pleasant a summer as we are. How different everything is from this time last year! We are worried with no rumours etc., everything is very quiet here. I wonder if it is so with you.

Mr. H. H. Bristow (the son) passed through some time ago, on his way down, and reminded us of the splendid time we had in Peking. I kept a diary of our stay — and find it very interesting to read over. I hope you are keeping very well & that you will be able to get away for the change you wanted. I wish you could come down here for a bit of the summer! Lately we have been playing tennis, bathing & boating vigorously. Last month the British men-o'-war came up from Wei-Hai-Wei for a week, and gave us a very gay time. The band played every day, and Capt. Percy Scott of H.M.S. "Terrible" gave a dance on board, which was lovely, plenty of "sitting out" places!!

Emily's fiancé has arrived at Shanghai in H.M.S. "Talbot". Em is longing to see him…it is a year & a half since he left China, and we all want to see him again, and continue his training.

We had a cousin from Shanhaikuan (in the R.H.A.), to stay with us for ten days, and he did give us a time of it! He was the first relation we've seen for 13 years, and the first we've had in China. So his coming was quite an event for us. He was a terrible tease, but he found us quite up to returning some of his chaff, & we had a very good time with him. [Hugh Fawcus, an officer in the Royal Horse Artillery, son of Frances senior's eldest brother, Henry, had finally been able to visit.]

Do you remember Maude's mania for reading fortunes from the hand? She still keeps it up, and loves to tell people when they are to be married — how many children they will have, etc. We are all well, except Father, who has been poorly lately, but is getting better.

I hope you aren't very busy, because then I may get a letter!

All the girls, and Kath especially, seemed to feel that young men needed 'training' to respect intelligent young women, but Hart had heard rumours of broken engagements, a serious matter then. He wrote to Frances senior what she referred to later as '*your kind questioning letter of sympathy*'. His letter revealed to an appalled father the depth of a crisis involving his most attractive daughter, Muriel (Figure 8.3), causing Carrall to have it out with his family on July 18 and to add the following to an official memo to Hart on 19 July:

'Personal'. Emily's marriage with Lieut. Forbes has not yet taken place because I will not give her an allowance. Muriel, who was engaged for 3 weeks to a man called Schroeder, Act. Supt. [Acting Superintendent] *at Chefoo of the Joint Telegraph Companies, has broken off the engagement because she found she did not love him, and my mother has written out by the last mail that she must take part of her Principal to buy an annuity.* [Sampson's will had not left Emma enough to live, but if she bought an annuity that would reduce what Carrall could expect on her death.] *Things have got sadly mixed lately by Muriel doing things without my knowledge, and saying things which were not true. I place the trouble partly at the door of the Rev. and Mrs. Burne of Bishop Serte's Mission, and he has never apologised to me in writing for his meddlesome action, and partly to my wife not following my suggestion and abstaining from inviting objectionable young men to the house. She has lately been trying to run too much on her own judgment and keeping me in the dark — the result, disaster — and I have ultimately to know all and to bear all, and I am not sure I do know all.*

Carrall's deep anger at being kept in the dark shows in his criticism of his wife, whom he knew Sir Robert regarded as a friend. The next letter from Frances senior shows that he had laid down the law on what was to be done. She for her part was probably trying not to trouble him while he was 'poorly'. My mother said that her sisters were afraid of his temper — though as a small child she felt assured of his love[1] — and his temper on this occasion was indeed in evidence.

Frances senior's letter was dated the day before, the emotion pouring through the black ink which comes through both sides of the paper, making it difficult to read:

Chefoo

July 18th 1901

My dear Sir Robert

Your letter had just been put into my hand [this seems to imply that Carrall had read it first — all their letters went to the office] *and I sit down at once to reply though I have not time, only inclination, to do so fully. It is so good to find one has friends, real friends, and thank you so much for writing. Emily, Muriel & I are packing up to go down to Shanghai. I wrote to Mr. Hobson & told him I had to come there & was in trouble with the girls' love affairs.... This is all with my husband's knowledge & consent.... Emily's fiancé has turned Roman Catholic & he has just returned to the China Station & so far his ship the "Talbot" has been at Wusung so I am taking Emily to see him. Muriel has got into a great deal of trouble over her love affairs and could never be happy now in the East as things are, so I am taking her down to Shanghai to find a suitable chaperone to send her to England & she will live with Mrs. Sampson till her affairs get straightened out. If we can put this through quietly & without any new cause for scandal I do trust things will come smooth again. We are keeping our plans very secret because Mrs. Eckford is up in arms! & I do not want to give her a handle for publishing our private affairs broadcast but I will write to you more fully & come to you for advice & help if need be. Today is our tennis afternoon & we are having it as usual, hence I am so rushed in writing to you & I am trusting if Mr. Hobson sends me a telegram (that the Talbot is still at Wusung) to leave here tomorrow. Emily's affairs are no hurry about but Muriel's are pretty urgent.... We should hate to break up our home here and I think we can live down the scandal by staying on here and not regarding any gossip that may be or rather I may say is flying round. We are all in accord in the action I am taking and have all agreed that we will, if I may put it very vulgarly, "wash our dirty linen at home". Dear Sir Robert, thank you awfully for writing. I was nearly broken up but what is the good of being English if you cannot make up your mind to play the game when it comes to the point, & as ever I want to be a good wife, a good mother & a good woman & I am going to be in spite of everybody. I hardly know what I am writing but I will write again from Shanghai.*

Yours afftectely, Frances M Carrall

Thursday was their tennis 'At home' day. The poor woman was torn in different directions as a wife and mother. As one who took pride in these roles, which were indeed her career and her identity, she must have been shaken to the foundations by her husband's wrath. But being

English meant keeping a stiff upper lip and neither complaining nor howling like an emotional southerner. Her deep distress was shown in a letter she wrote the next year to Sir Robert, after her husband's death:

In trouble, one does get comfort from sympathy and often I have thought that mentally I have suffered less than this time last year, when we seemed to be thrown out of our stride and yet had to go on and act as if all was right whereas this time I had a right to grieve and the girls are showing so much love and sympathy. This sorrow has drawn us yet nearer together instead of threatening to upset us like the last.

Back in Peking, Sir Robert replied to Kath's letter. He followed her example, and did not refer to Muriel, instead chaffing her about Cousin Hugh's visit.

19th July 1901

Dearest Kathleen,

You see what telepathy does! I was longing for a letter from you or Maude on the 18th and on that very day, after cycles of silence, you wrote, and I had your letter last night! I wrote to your Mama to ask for Hillside news and to tell you girls to go on putting me in your debt. Of course I can't give you letter for letter, but I dearly love to see how many nice things you can coax out of the English alphabet, and it is always a delight to hear from you! Yours of the 15th is, however, a bit stiff: you were not quite in the humour of yourself to write, and so spontaneity was absent and I can fancy you in a fix what to say next at the end of each sentence. Don't do that, please, but be natural and let the sweetness of your young heart overflow, and so temper the acidity of the inkbottle!

I'm glad to hear the fiancé is again within hail, and I hope dear Em's happiness goes on waxing. The visit of the Shanhaikuan cousin must have been a trial — a trial for him I mean, with half a dozen such nice girls to be cousinly with, but poor girls! How did he "go round"?...[His quotes from an unknown doggerel are indecipherable.]

Do you remember that last Sunday evening when with you and

Maude on either side, we had such a good chat before saying good night? I often recall it, & wish you were to come again: but alas & lackaday! Time goes on & on, and although each coming minute has its own value in fun or boredom, it is only the unsatisfying mirror of memory that deals with what's done & gone for ever! By the way, I had a nice chit from Effie last week: she says she returns to Tientsin with her mother in September. Unfortunately I have no quarters to invite people to, and no way of entertaining: so I fear I can't assemble another house party for either autumn, winter or spring; how gladly I'd bring you all back again! I am just now restarting the Band, but as they have not touched an instrument for over a year and a month, I don't expect much from them before Christmas: and, even then, it will be in other people's houses & not in my own that I'll hear them — more's the pity! O those Boxers — those Boxers! What a fix they've made for all of us! But one thing I thank heaven for, and that is that I got all you dear girls safe down to Tientsin before the trouble began; what luck!

I am always occupied — not that I have much to do, however, and I am even now more or less a prisoner for I fear to absent myself lest I sh'd be away just when wanted. My health keeps good, and being of the "Never say die" temperament, I am generally free from worry and in good spirits —

> *Poor little life that toddles half an hour*
> *Crown'd with a flower or two, and there an end —*[1]

Thank heaven for the "flower or two" but, to speak truly, garlands have been my happy lot!

With love to you all, and a special kiss for yourself, Mavourian (which, however, as you don't care for kisses, you can share with the deliciously appreciative Maude!)

Hart had not forgotten the Irish name that Frances had rejected when Kath was christened! His remark about the cousin's 'ordeal' shows his usual discernment. The Carrall girls, usually in a phalanx of three tall and two shorter sisters, could have been intimidating for some young men. Usually, their photos were posed to minimise the height differences, but one taken by Muriel emphasises them (Figure 8.3).

Maude also replied discreetly:

July 20th

My dear Sir Robert

Thank you very much for your message by Mother...Emily goes, as she wishes to meet Mr. Forbes again after not having seen him for nearly a year & a half, & she got news that the Talbot would remain in Shanghai for about another 2 or 3 weeks, so she thought that she might as well take this opportunity of going down, as Mr. Forbes cannot get leave to come here.

...Poor Mu has not found Chefoo one of the nicest of places for this last month or so, & I am sure she was glad for some reasons to get out of it!...They are going to stay with Mr. Hobson...as really in a place like Chefoo no one has, or seems to have, anything to do but talk about other people's affairs.

Kathleen & I have now...to look after the household in Mother's absence. I hope we will succeed well...but...the four youngest members of the family need a great deal of looking after.... The Baby, though only a year old, is the largest handful of the lot. He is an awfully sturdy little chap & very bouncy.... I must close now because I have to see where the children have got to, & amongst other things, interview the cook!

Muriel had realised that Chefoo had become too hot to hold her, and she was anxious to try pastures new, even at the cost of separation from her family. It was also at a cost to the family finances which Carrall could ill afford.

Frances senior revealed more in her next letter.

Shanghai, Monday July 22nd 1901

My dear Sir Robert

I am afraid I wrote you a very rushed letter the other day.... We left Friday for here & arrived yesterday (Emily, Muriel & myself). Mr. Hobson met us and we are staying with him till I can find a suitable chaperone for Muriel. Emily's fiancé was in Wusung [down river of Shanghai]...& he came out and spent the afternoon & dined & returned to Wusung, promising to get leave & come back today. I must then tackle him about his change of faith & ask him if he took the step with the view of throwing

Emily over. I really do not think he did as he is a very quiet undemonstrative fellow & has written to her regularly ever since he left this station for England whence he has returned three weeks ago on a new commission… . That is as far as I am in regard to Emily. I thought after 18 months or so of separation they should meet & talk over things, & were their engagement to be broken off there would be less scandal than if he were to come up & leave suddenly. I am afraid Muriel's story is not so creditable to her. I can only think she got tired of the monotony of home life & come what would must get a change, & believing that, I think we are doing the best thing for her in sending her to stay with Mrs. Sampson till she finds her balance once more. I do not think she thought how much mischief & trouble she would cause. She is a girl who very easily attracts men, and has thought it all rather a joke and would not see what amused her was not so amusing to others.

Some month or two back a Dane proposed to her & though she had been warned about it & told not to allow him to propose it ended in her accepting him & then coming to me the next day to ask me to let her break it off. I refused to as I thought if she broke it off then she would want it in a day or two, & so then she enlisted Vyvyan Eckford into her service. He is very much in love with her though she says she has often told him he has no chance. Her story to him was that I had insisted on her accepting this Mr. Schroder though she hated him & wanted to marry Mr. Allen. They visited Mr. Burne (in Bishop Scott's mission) to telegraph to Mr. Allen who is at home that Muriel Carrall was forced to marry a Dane etc. Unfortunately Muriel put all this in writing & Mrs. Eckford has got hold of copies of Muriel's various letters & is very vexed at her son Vyvyan having been brought in as a cat's paw. Muriel has done her best to clear up everything before we left Chefoo & we have given her permission to correspond with Mr. Allen. [Mr Allen appears no more on the scene.] *I do trust things will eventually come right. There are so many ramifications to the story that it is no use my writing more about it…the Chefoo community…have all sorts of variations… . Mrs. Eckford is not discreet and cannot leave her neighbour's affairs alone at any time, & now she has the additional grievance that her son's name has* been well mixed up. Our girls are really favourites with the community & I am sure they will not do anything to increase the ill feeling with the Eckford family that this has caused.

July 23rd. I did not finish this yesterday & reading it over it seems stupid worrying you to read it but I promised to tell you everything so I send it. I spoke to Charlie Forbes yesterday. He assured me he meant to play the game by Emily & promised to write to my husband & tell him so (in other words, of course, mine is simply so expressed for brevity). Emily does not wish to break off the engagement, as she says she had rather that he had something definite in the way of religion than that he was utterly callous to it, as before. He has leave till Friday & I do hope she is all right. There is no talk of their marriage until he has a promotion & that so far is in the future, but from first to last Emily has not had a word to say to another man, and has only thought of her Charlie! They have already been engaged two years short of three months. I cannot so far find any-one going home just now...[to chaperone Muriel on the journey]...Maude is A1, she is so sensible and straightforward. Kath is a very good second. Frances (the next) is working hard for a winter exam, then holidays come in August. She is also built on a large scale & bids fair to be the best looking of the lot, having very nice eyes. She is all right and has not yet come to think of love affairs but with 5 big girls at home we must expect this sort of thing, if only they will give us their confidence it will be all right. I think they will too for they all see that if Muriel had but spoken out this trouble would never have happened & they are all awfully fond of each other and just as anxious as can be that Muriel's name shall not suffer & that her affairs shall come out all right. Now I am going to answer the questions in your letter & then close for here is the end of a second sheet & this one will be smudged & besides what has so deeply interested us cannot be of such moment to you. It seems rather silly pouring this all out but you have always been so good to us that I do not want you to think by being reserved that I have forgotten it. You ask what number our family now is — 9 children — the five I have mentioned & then comes Eric, 12 years old, goes to the boys' school. Gwen, 8 and Phyllis 5, taught either by Emily or Muriel, & lastly, baby, 15 months, that completes the *list. Baby is a veritable Benjamin, and I think my husband having two boys is quite satisfied.* [She tells him of her good reports of the girls in Chefoo.] *Now goodbye, forgive spelling, grammar, composition & everything else & thank you most heartily for evincing so much interest in us. Your letter heartened me up so wonderfully. I did not so much mind for myself but to have the two girls down in their luck did rather bowl me over.*

Believe me, dear Sir Robert

Yours very sincerely

Frances M. Carrall

I cannot arrange to leave Muriel in Shanghai provided no chaperone turns up as the late fiancé went down to Shanghai just the steamer before ours! We all but travelled with him!! Not knowing his plans & he not knowing ours. Yesterday, Muriel & I driving to St. John's met him full face in another carriage!!!!

Her letter is dramatic evidence of the binding nature of a proposal and its acceptance in 1900. If a man broke an engagement off, he risked being sued for breach of promise, and such ungentlemanly behaviour would have compelled an officer's resignation from the service. If a girl broke it off she was labelled an unfeeling flirt and a jilt — unless she had good cause. A change of religious faith by him provided a justifiable reason for the girl to change her mind, so the family feared that Charles wanted to give Emily an excuse to end it. Aged twenty-two, she could marry without parental consent. It was her decision — and not an easy one. The next letter from Maude shows what the Carralls thought of Roman Catholics.

The other factor at play was class. Charles Forbes came from a proud Scottish landed family in Berwick, with many distinguished naval officers in his ancestry, and may have been aware of parental disapproval. The Fawcuses, being in trade, would be regarded as a distinct social step below the Forbes. This could be overlooked if Emily brought money with her, but Carrall could not promise an allowance to his eldest daughter, as it would create a precedent for her six younger sisters. Charles' father would certainly have investigated Carrall's ancestry and would have been less than pleased to find illegitimacy. Some rumours must have got around amongst the servants: Emily's grandson William remembers that his nanny, an ancient Forbes family retainer, disapproved of Emily and called Emma Sampson, with her three husbands and life in China, an adventuress. Charles himself visited Emma Sampson; who told Hart in September 1900 that: *'Mr. Forbes, Emily's fiancé, has been to spend a day with me. I asked Mrs. Fawcus to meet him also, her girls saw him after lunch. We all like him.'* One hopes the liking was mutual, but the Fawcus girls in question had been brought up in Germany and spoke English with a German accent, which emphasised that their background was in 'trade'. Social snobbery was very real.

Kath's next letter to Hart concentrates on her new household responsibilities. He had evidently passed on some tips as to how to amuse small girls.

1st August 1901

My dearest Godfather,

Thank you very much indeed for your letter of 19th July to me… . It is so nice to feel that you are always interested and sympathetic in what we do…[She thanks him for a book, interesting but cynical.]

I am sorry my letter was "a bit stiff", I felt it so when I sent it off, but I am not good at letter-writing. I never can say what I really feel! I remember that last Sunday evening's chat well, and how we enjoyed it, what a good time we would have if we could all meet like that again. Effie must be glad to be coming back to Tientsin. Elsa seems to find it somewhat flat at home [in the United States] *after gay China doings, we often hear from her. I was interested to hear about your band. I hope it will pick up again all right.*

Maude and I seem to be always busy — though three are away there are eight at home, & I am afraid Mother will find them a bit spoilt when she returns! I give them lessons every morning while Maude looks after the house. It is rather fun doing hostess "pidgin"…we had our tennis "at home" on Thursday just the same, but I must say I had no idea what a work it was looking after people, and giving them a good time!…never thought so much before of this side of the question & you will see, what with keeping the children happy & occupied — we found yours was a

*good idea about the paper dolls — and keeping Baby in good
health, we are getting new experiences in every way, & we shall be
turning into most proper German "Hausfraus"! Imagine it! The
doctor thinks it is very good for us, he was amused at our method
of nursing Baby through a cold, and particularly struck with our
knowledge — or rather lack of it — of what Babies of a year old
ought to eat! He asked Frances what Baby had in his milk, and F.
could only think of replying "Oh the amah warms it a little I
think" — I could at any rate have told him "Mellin's Food"!*[3]

After referring to the Shanghai events, she ends: 'With much love &
Maudie and I haven't found out how to share kisses yet and again thanking
you very much for your kind letter and the book.'

The girls evidently joked together about Hart's kisses. He had also
written to Maude, who gave him a little more information on Muriel
in her letter the next day:

*As to the "Hillside worries", I hope that they are nearly over
now…for myself I assure you I could never have been quite reconciled
to having a foreigner as a brother-in-law, & neither I believe could any
of the others. What possessed Mu to accept him in the first place
will never be satisfactorily known. Dear old Mu! I hope she will
get on all right in England where she will see fresh faces & scenes.*

*People are very kind here in asking us out to tennis etc. & their
offers of help have come in from all quarters, but we have not yet
had to draw upon anybody. We are very energetic now, getting up
at 6 for tennis & then bathing from 7.0 till 8.0. The water is
simply perfect & one could stay in the whole day & be none the
worse for it.*

*…Yes, from all accounts Emily is enjoying herself in Charlie
Forbes's society. I wonder when they will get married. Everything
is so unsettled nowadays, but I suppose it is as you say, we must
each take our own share of rain. Notwithstanding that, Chefoo
seems to have been entirely left out of this year's floods & rain!
There has not been any for some time & everything is frightfully
parched & burnt up including the Indian corn of which there will
be absolutely none. So perhaps it is just as well to have a little
occasionally, but not sufficient for a flood which it seems to me we
have had latterly with regard to what has happened.*

In the isolation of the 'settlement' she seems unaware of what suffering this must have caused to local farmers. After telling him that Gwen and Phyllis had taken up his suggestion of making paper dolls with enthusiasm she continues:

> *Mrs. Rémusat has just lost her baby girl, you will be sorry to hear, she died very suddenly from convulsions yesterday. The funeral took place this morning at the R. C Church. Frances & I went to the service, the coffin looked so small, & we wondered what was the use of that little life, barely six months old I believe. Of course the service was fully Roman Catholic, & they had the incense and holy water etc., it seemed such a farce, but I suppose every man for his own religion now-a-days.*

Rémusat, French, was Carrall's deputy. Maude does seem to have grasped that as her sister was marrying a Roman Catholic she would have to get used to strange papist rites! Unwittingly, she shows that the family thought of themselves not only as very English — no Dane for a brother-in-law, thank you — despite their very limited experience of England, but also very Protestant.

Her mother explained the chaperoneless arrangements for Muriel.

> *Chefoo*
>
> *August 11th 1901*
>
> My dear Sir Robert,
>
> *I am sure you have had a dose of the Carrall family letters of late, but I must send you a line to tell you that Mr. Hobson was awfully good to us and after much enquiry we finally hit on the P&O S.S. Malacca. It is one of the cargo boats and as it goes via Marseilles Muriel will only reach the London docks about Oct. 1st.* [Cargo boats were slow but cheaper than the regular passenger liners which made fewer stops.] *We put her under the captain's charge, he seemed very pleasant, a married man, who promised to look well after her…. The stewardess seemed kindly & a lady passenger with whom Muriel & I had already become acquainted in Shanghai promised to do all she could to help her. There was a good library on board & the ship looked very comfortable, so I do hope she will be all right. I feel quite in heart that it is the best*

*thing for her. We are giving her a chance of looking round her & I
know my relations will be ready to help her in any possible way &
Mrs. Sampson will be overjoyed to at last have one granddaughter
at home & will make much of her & it now rests with Muriel to
make the most of things. She is really a taking girl & people get
very fond of her, so I hope really for the best & do not intend to
worry till there is need.*

*We all three did get great benefit from the entire change &
Emily is very happy to again have her young man on the China
coast. I really think he seems square & that he is a good sensible
fellow. Why I never wrote to announce Muriel's engagement to you
was because I felt all along something was wrong & that there
were breakers ahead, but if she will be sensible & steady now &
start afresh, I trust all will be right in the long run for her too!*

*...Maude keeps teasing Frances (who is writing to you & who
is a much bigger girl than Maude) & telling her "Sir Robert sent
you the "Sketch", for you to cut up too, being one of our little
ones" — they are great on chaffing each other...*

Young Frances was delighted by an invitation from Sir Robert to
join her sisters on their next visit to him in 1902. They had just had a
regatta.

*It was a great success, but that was mainly due I suppose to
Maudie & I winning the Ladies dinghy race, & the boat Kathleen
was coxing coming in first in another race. You usually do find
things in which you are successful enjoyable don't you!! The band
from the German flagship was lent for the occasion. It was a very
good one & even after it grew dark continued playing without
music. The bachelors of Chefoo are trying to get it for a dance they
want to give some time next week.*

The frequency with which Sir Robert wrote to the young Frances
suggests that he had discerned her intelligence, a trait which always
attracted him.

An Autumn Wedding

A month later Frances senior wrote with important news.

Sept 30th 1901

…Thank you so much for your last kind letter & for your invitation to the three girls — they are awfully pleased about it. I sent you two photos of Frances & my husband with the boys meaning to write but…we have had a visit from Emily's fiancé and have arranged that Emily & he shall be at once married, it being so good an opportunity now the "Talbot" is at Wei-Hai-Wei. Emily is to live on with us as usual but by being Mrs. Forbes instead of only Miss Carrall, any time when his ship is likely to be some while in a place she can go to see him without needing a chaperone.

He only left us on Friday & on Saturday he wired "Talbot leaves Wei-Hai 27th can get leave 18th to 25th is time sufficient?" so you see to have her married in the English church the bans [sic] had to be published yesterday for the first time. We telegraphed that the 19th would suit for the wedding day but it is very short work especially as the girls will all be bridesmaids & Emily says she wants a pucker [sic] wedding dress for the occasion! [She got one - Figure 8.4]. They are to be married at the R. C. Church to please Charlie Forbes, at the Protestant Church to please Emily & at the English Consulate to satisfy my husband. If they are not then married, they never will be!…

I am now going to ask you a favour, the Dessinos have left today & if the new assistant is not coming just yet may Emily & Charlie have their honeymoon in the Hannen bungalow from 19th to 25th Oct?…The girls would get it ready for them — of course if it is not convenient we always have the "I.G.'s bungalow". Only Emily & Maude live there now, & it does not seem quite so nice as their being able to be a little more private than it is possible with our small fry always running riot in the garden.

…Kathleen & Eric went round the lights [lighthouses for which the Customs was responsible] *with their father in the "Ping Ching" & brought my nephew back from Shan-Hai-Kwan with them. We have just seen him off again northward today.*

Forgive an untidy letter & thank you very much for all your kindness. We get very cheerful letters from Muriel. She is evidently enjoying the voyage.

Hugh Fawcus had braved his cousins a second time. The photographs she mentioned caused trouble, as young Frances told Sir Robert.

Oct 2nd 1901

Father is very much worried that Mother sent off to you, with my photo, a very indifferent one of himself with the two boys, as he is sure you will notice he is not wearing his Sunday-go-to-meeting trousers!!! Indeed, it was only taken to send to Grandmother, to show her how very economical he was in wearing off his old bags!!...

By the time the month is over I expect everybody will know the marriage service off by heart, as there are to be two weddings before hers, Miss May's on the 12th, & Lilla Eckford's on the 16th.

I am sorry to say singing is not among my accomplishments. I have even stopped it at school now, in order to give the time up to study. Father however, still sings — when he is feeling not "too majestic", that is to say.

Father had a reputation for caring about his appearance, which the Fawcus brothers had noticed even when he was at school. He probably wanted to show his mother that he was not leading an extravagant life in China, and could only send her £50 a year to help her out.

Kath followed with an account of the wedding preparations.

My dear Godfather

I have such heaps to tell you! The first wedding in the family comes off in less than three weeks.... A whole trousseau to get ready & what we three think most important, bridesmaids' frocks!...Maude, principal bridesmaid, walks first with the best man (one of Charlie's fellow officers), then Frances and I, and Gwen & Phyllis last. [She mentions the two other marriages.] It takes quite a time to hear the three banns published one after the other. I took the organ for Em last Sunday when they were read for the first time.

As Charlie's ship goes to Hong Kong for the winter, Emily will

*probably go down there too. We three are simply delighted at the
idea of coming to you then, it will be lovely. We know we are in
for a good time and we are looking forward to it all!*

*How is the building of the house getting on? I hope the band
progresses well.*

[She tells him about the trip in the *Ping Ching* and their
cousin's second visit.] *It was very jolly having him, but it's
hard work keeping him in order, he is such a tease! His Battery
leaves for India on Oct. 16th, but we are hoping the orders may
be countermanded, so that he can come down for the wedding.
You may be sure the bridesmaids are going to have a good time
then!...*

Her mother also wrote to thank him for agreeing the use of the
Hannen bungalow, and to explain a change:

*Emily has had one disappointment. The R. C. Bishop here will not
allow two church ceremonies & so we are going to leave out the
service at St. Andrews' Church. Her fiancé is ready to drop his
wish, if Emily insists, but I feel that their married life ought to
commence as it is to go on & that it would not be a happy omen
for Emily to oppose her husband's wishes; as if married people do
not pull together, there cannot be much happiness. I hope I am
advising her rightly — it is dreadful when you have to come to
think for other people as well as for yourself, for you never know
how their consciences are & whether they see things that you do. I
am always wishing the children did not have to grow up. Excuse
this wording, the "you" means "me". When I get a pen in my
hand I want to talk!*

Emily thanked him for his wedding gift which '*nearly took my breath
away!*' (He usually sent a cheque on such occasions.)

*I wish that I could have had the pleasure of introducing my fiancé
to you...*[referring to the cancellation of the wedding at St
Andrew's Church] *I was much disappointed that it could not be
arranged, but perhaps it is best so, & you will probably agree with
me, for it gives me one interval less during which I might want to
change my mind, & if that happened how matters would be
complicated!...*

Kath sent Sir Robert a full account of the day.

Oct 21st 1901

Dear Sir Robert,

The eventful 19th is over!...Charlie, his best man, and six of the officers of the "Talbot" came up from Wei Hai Wei on the 18th, the latter seemed to enjoy it, and were very useful!

We spent the day before decorating the R. C. Church and the house with bamboo, grasses, and white flowers. On the morning of the day they went up quietly to the Consulate for the Civil ceremony, and then at 2–30 p.m. came the service at the Roman Catholic Church performed by the French Bishop, who however arranged that the questions and answers should be the same as in our English Service. Coming out the bride and bridegroom, followed by all of us bridesmaids, passed under an arch of crossed swords formed by the officers. We had a photo taken and must send you a copy if it turns out good. [It evidently did not.] *The reception seemed to go off all right, the Bride cut the cake in the true naval fashion with the sword! One poor little Middy was very nervous making his speech in reply to the toast for the bridesmaids! Of course the "happy couple" left amid showers of rice and old shoes for the "Honeymoon Cottage" as we've dubbed the Hannen Bungalow. They are very comfortable there, and it's nice having them near, we think. Maude and I went round and had tea with them today, and it was fun! It's a great pity Charlie's stay is so short, but it can't be helped, and he seems to be making the most of it.*

The new *Emily F Forbes* wrote with more thanks and described the brief visit Maude and she had made to Wei-Hei-Wei before the *Talbot* had sudden orders to go to Taku: *'I doubt if they enjoy that cheerful place. However, we have the remembrance of our pleasant honeymoon in the Hannen bungalow to fall back upon...I thank you again very much for lending it to us.'*

In her letter of 15 November Maude told Hart that the couple had had another short spell together. The girls could be as mocking about the men's abilities as the men were about female 'sports', though Maude's remarks were perhaps ill-timed in view of the bravery amateur young men had shown in Peking.

> *The Chefoo people having nothing to do are getting up a Volunteer Corps, composed of a mounted division and a "foot"…there will be about 15 men in each division! The Cavalry will be the nicest to watch, as very few of the men can ride properly, some only having got ponies very recently. Imagine them firing rifles from the backs of their respective steeds when they can barely hold on as it is, & as for riding in lines, that I expect will be out of the question altogether!*

Romance in Shanghai?

Their parents did not let their anxieties over Muriel's conduct redound on the other girls. Indeed, it was not her mother, but Maude, not quite twenty, who accompanied the seventeen-year-old Frances there in December. (Once back in England, my mother recollects not being allowed out alone in the evening even to post a letter at the end of the street.) Kath stayed in Chefoo to continue the younger girls' lessons and had a dull time as the men, preoccupied with their Volunteer Corps, had not organised a rink at the Club. Eric and she practised the violin together and with Emily she read the Iliad and Odyssey, in translation.

Meanwhile, Maude and young Frances had a very good time in Shanghai, after an unpleasantly stormy journey down. It was by far the biggest of the Treaty Ports, with a large expatriate population who had used their 'Settlement' status to provide modern urban services, including smooth roads, a police force, and leisure amenities.[4] Maude told Hart in her Christmas letter of 18 December 1901:

> *I find it such a change from Chefoo. We are staying with Mr. Hobson, & he is so good to us. We went to our first theatre on Saturday & enjoyed it very much. The house was crowded, as it was a popular play. I have never seen such a mixture of people before! Shanghai is so warm compared to Chefoo. We do not need furs really in the day time & in Chefoo it had been snowing hard when we left…*
>
> *On Saturday we are going to the Customs dance, with Mrs.*

*Acheson. Frances is going to put up her hair then & "come out". I
am with her acting as chaperone! Don't you think I'm good?*

<u>One</u> *of the attractions of Shanghai are [sic] the shops as
compared with "Sinatai & Singtai". They are lovely here & any
amount of things on view. I have chiefly spent the mornings going
round & undecided what to get.*

Back in Chefoo, Kath and her mother were writing their birthday
letters to Sir Robert. Neither seemed worried about Father being 'seedy',
it was not unusual for him in the winter. He could not accompany Kath
and her mother to a dance at the Beech Hotel, where Kath was the
only unmarried girl:

*The Cotillion especially was great fun. Some of the figures were
— the throwing of a huge dice box, the winner of course to dance
with the lady (it's the first time I have been tossed for in my life!)
— the gentlemen to present bouquets, the ladies to pin decorations
to the partners with whom they wished to dance. I found this and
a figure in which the ladies had to offer to pull crackers with
desired partners somewhat embarrassing — imagine having to
face two rows of gentlemen and to pick out your partner from
them! In one figure the gentlemen leapt through paper hoops; it
was absurd to see them.* [The eighteenth-century cotillion, a
square dance, was still much in favour, but had evolved lots
of variations, with prizes and forfeits, etc. She continues
with her sisters' doings in Shanghai.] *Emily and I spend most
of our time teaching Gwen and Phyllis, housekeeping in turn, and
studying together...*

Hart had evidently sent a New Year card with a joke of his own.
Frances senior responded, and recollected Hart's sympathy during the
summer crisis:

Chefoo, January 20th 1902

*...It is six months yesterday since our Muriel left Chefoo & then I
had been thinking very much of you & wishing to break a rather
long silence with a letter when your kind questioning letter of
sympathy came.... Our people are looking well after Muriel and
are very glad to have her — sometimes I feel from the tone of her*

*letters that she has never realized what it cost to part with her —
not that I want her to. Being her Mother I hope she never may and
that she will play her cards so that nothing but luck may come to
her, & that she will not make many (for it is only human nature
to make some) mistakes in her youthful confidence now that she
has been allowed a free hand — yet it is hard not to worry about
her — she seems since she obtained her way and cut herself loose
from her home to be dipping into everything & trying how many
new experiences she can put into her life. Well, well, successful or
not, she is ever my child. I did not mean to write all this for it is
but natural and just what the other two in Shanghai are doing,
but there is a difference, they are not trying to do without our help
but are keeping us au fait with all their concerns, telling us of
their dances & partners & their fun generally & sending regular
full scribbles of their different experiences so that we share their
life & feel they understand that their pleasure is ours.*

*...My husband nevertheless has been worried with an attack
of, I think, influenza. He has it every year and is quite depressed
while it lasts. Kathleen is being a very good little (or big rather)
Cinderella at home. A lady was telling her the other day that she
deserved to find "Prince Charming" here — as I write she is giving
the children a geography lesson. Emily too makes the best of
things. I was saying to her... "well I shall really have to send Gwen
& Phyllis to school after Easter, if you are all going — three to
Peking & you to Charlie," & she said so eagerly "Oh Mother, you
are only saying that to cheer me up. You know the Talbot won't be
here before summer." Of course for her sake I shall be only too glad
to have her go too, but still, when they ask, I can but counsel
prudence & probably they will all the more enjoy a summer
together in Wei-Hai for having had this exercise of patience now.*

Sir Robert replied to Kath a few days later, on 26 January 1902. This
is the letter already quoted in Chapter Four, on his grief over the death
of Mrs Brazier. After pondering what the dead were doing now, he
continued *'I'm old now, & mine may come any day: whereas you will be
writing 1952 later on & telling your grandchildren about your China and Chefoo
experiences...'* This was an accurate forecast. Fifty years later Aunt Kath
was telling me about China.

Meanwhile, in Shanghai, Maude and Frances had moved on to other friends, the Campbells, enjoying a round of dinners and dances, and the relaxed China attitude to chaperoning. Maude wrote to Sir Robert on 2 February.

> [The three Campbell girls] *have — as they say— to act as a "battery of chaperones" to _me! I who am the eldest of the whole five, and I may say the steadiest! We went to the theatre on the 1st to see "Lord & Lady Algy", it was awfully well got up & acted, but the play was of the "horsy" kind which I did not like so much. The concert given by the Misses von Möllendorffs was a great success, we went to hear it, the smallest girl — Dora — plays the violin beautifully, & she is only fourteen or fifteen I think. It must need some nerve to stand before a large audience & play music without reading it. She did it all by memory.*

Sir Robert would have been pleased to hear this. Amongst his letters from women friends in QUB was one dated 23 January 1902 from Mrs von Möllendorff, thanking him for a generous cheque which enabled her to continue her career as a music teacher and to have more lessons herself. She was the widow of P.G. von Möllendorff who had a complex relationship with Hart and was in and out of the Customs Service. He had died as Commissioner in Ningpo, in April 1901, leaving his widow and daughters struggling to earn a living.

Hart's generosity obliged Maude to write again the very next day:

> *Feb 3rd 1902*
>
> *My dear Sir Robert*
>
> *Thank you very much indeed for your lovely New Year Gift to Frances & myself. How could you possibly know that a girl's pocket money never seems enough? The fact was Frances & I had just settled to start economizing, having arrived at a fairly low situation when your letter put in an appearance!*
>
> *I have always longed for a Kodak, so that one can take photographs of things which would otherwise fade out of one's memory. When up in Peking I was able to get snapshots of places from one of the students and I often look over these & think of the lovely time we spent up there. Thank you so much for giving me the camera & it is such a nice one too!*

There is to be a fancy-dress dance on the 14th, we are therefore
going to stay over for it. Can you imagine me as a small girl of the
period of milk maids & sun bonnets? Frances is going as a
"grown up" milk maid! The dance at the Shanghai Country Club
was a great success & I enjoyed myself thoroughly, dancing every
dance through & there were sixteen! I never get tired now, & am
really the strongest of the family.

Young Frances' letter on the same topic shows that the gift they shared
was $200. She also decided to get a Kodak, and both got new dresses.
Maude told him that at the fancy-dress party *'Frances' & my dresses were*
much admired & we were able to get such pretty ones because of your generous
present to us.'

Maude and Frances also tried out cycling. Though slightly nervous
of roads so much more crowded than in Chefoo, they were soon doing
round trips of ten miles or so. The bicycle made a great difference to
a girl's social life, extending the range of the people she could visit.
Judging by the photo albums, their rides included trips out to the Jessfield
camp and acquaintance with British officers attached to Baluchi and
Sikh troops. Maude took many photos of them with her new camera,
not altogether successfully (Figure 8.6).

They would also have met the officers at dinners and dances. In her
usual birthday letter to Hart, Frances senior revealed that Maude had
had her first proposal. She did not tell him the name, since Maude had
not accepted. It could be that this was at the Fancy-Dress Ball for Maude
was still thinking of it three weeks after her return home, and from
her description of the arrangements, there would have been
opportunities for private conversations.

Chefoo

Hillside

March 23rd 1902

My dear Sir Robert,

Here we are back again at Chefoo. Frances & I returned about
three weeks ago…

A few days before we left we went to a fancy-dress dance… .
The ballroom looked quite "rusticated", it was decorated so as to

appear as much like a field as possible. The chairs, or rather seats,
were composed of stacks of hay & straw, and wheelbarrows &
logs of wood, & were placed about indiscriminately. In the centre
was a maypole. One of the chief points of interest was the out-
rooms, where one saw two little ponies & a small calf. The latter
looked so ridiculous, but blinked away seemingly content,
notwithstanding the lights & noise of the band in the next
compartment. Frances' & my dresses were much admired & we
were able to get such pretty ones because of your generous present
to us. All the ladies turned up and you will be amused to hear not
nearly all the men put in an appearance! The reason of this
seeming negligence was because of the horrible vanity of man.
Can you imagine it, but several of them had refused to go because
of the unbecomingness of their enforced costumes, i.e. "smocks" or
the ringers' garb for preference!

All good things come to an end & so did our visit… . After a
very rough passage from Shanghai, Chefoo welcomed us back with
a snow storm.

Kathleen never mentioned the proposal. Maude probably asked her mother not to tell her sisters, to avoid their teasing. She probably felt that she did not yet know the young man well enough. She knew from her sister's experience that love for a young officer had to be sufficiently secure to survive many separations. She told Hart on 23 March that Emily had *'received a telegram on the Friday & left on Monday. Evidently the "Talbot" is going to stay at Foochow for some time, & so the "happy couple" will be able to taste more fully of the joys of married life for as yet we may say they have only had two weeks of it.'*

It was fortunate that Charlie and Emily had a few short weeks together, for they were soon to be separated till August 1904. It was as well too, that the rains cleared up and they could enjoy spring picnics. The photo albums show Maude with her camera at the "Blossoms" on my mother's ninth birthday, April 11 (Figure 8.8). (Maude also photographed Chinese families picnicking and Chinese children watching some relaxed Europeans.) There was a children's party at Hillside on Easter Monday, and then, with Emily in Foochow, my mother Gwen was finally sent to school. There she caught scarlet fever. It was the end of play times with her dearest sister, Phyllis (Figure 8.9).

CHAPTER NINE

DEATH STRIKES

Jim Carrall in the Winter of 1902

In his July 1901 letter to Hart about his daughters, Jim Carrall had continued:

> If I were only £3000 richer than I am, I would apply for long leave and go to England. We have been out here since the Spring of 1889, now over twelve years ago, and I have had no short leave during that time; but "beggars cannot be choosers" and we must wait till the £3000 is collected. I hope however that before long something will turn up to put things a bit straight, especially as so many old Commissioners have lately resigned who had been receiving salaries larger than my own.

He optimistically hoped that his next posting would carry a higher salary. Taking leave was expensive because officers had to pay the travel costs of their families.

Meanwhile, like many staff, he was feeling overworked and under-supported. '*Office. I miss Innocent and Grevedon in the office very much.* [One replacement, now on long leave] *may be summed up as "an inferior, noisy American of no ability".*' Shipping was double what it had been ten years earlier, but he still had the same number of staff and in December 1901 he became responsible also for the *likin*, as the Customs took over this internal tax on trade in new ports. He told Hart on 27 December: '*All the information on the working of the native Customs I have gathered myself.... Now that I know the system of working, I shall send an Assistant to see how that system is carried out.*'

He was also unwell. He told Bredon on 11 February 1902:

> <u>Myself.</u> I am well again from my attack of influenza. However my sickness has led me to think that Gulowsen is not a man of much ability. For instance he did not know at first, what a "Bark mixture" was when I asked for one. He said that he had never heard of such a thing. He is not a man I'd employ if I were seriously ill…. . I have got better through insisting on having strong tonics.

Gulowsen, Norwegian, had been in Chefoo for at least a year but had not yet learnt from old China hands the virtues of chinchona bark against the chronic malarial fever from which Carrall probably suffered. He told Hart on 20 February 1902 that he still had daily fever at sunset but 'I do not want leave thank you as travelling is so expensive…'[1]

He had been below par for at least six weeks and was struggling to finish the Decennial Report on Chefoo. On 16 June 1905 his wife thanked Hart warmly for sending her a copy:

> I have often wished that I could see my husband's last report in print. He really worked hard at it & I well remember what a sigh of relief he gave when at last it was complete & ready for forwarding. He was very much out of health when he was busy with it & now re-reading it brings all that back to me. He may not have been the quickest or the cleverest commissioner in the service but I am sure that no one could have been more painstaking, more loyal to you or more anxious to please. He was ever faithful to your interests & a line of approbation from you was thoroughly appreciated by him & did him more good than anything else.

The letter shows that Frances knew her husband's strengths and weaknesses. They had the companionable marriage that Hart had lacked. Carrall took his work home, she read it (in 1905 it was re-read). Consequently, she felt part of the Customs service, despite the absence of provision for widows which by 1900 had become standard in the British civil service. Another letter shows she knew that her husband had always struggled to do his best for his wife and children.

Figure 8.4. Emily and Charlie in full rig. Emily's dress is a credit to the local dressmaker! (Ca02-042.)

Figure 8.5. A bicycle. This photo is included despite acid damage as it shows girls learnt to maintain as well as ride bikes. The kneeling girl behind the bike cannot be identified, but it dates from the visit to Shanghai (Ca02-98).

Figure 8.6. The albums contain several photographs of Sikh and Baluchi soldiers, but Maude was not very practised with her new camera.

Figure 8.7. "Picnic to the Blossoms, 11 April 1902. Taken by Mrs. Forsyth." Maude is holding her Kodak camera. (Most of the white spots on the fruit trees are the blossoms they had gone to admire, not acid penetration!) (Ca02-066.)

Figure 8.8. My mother, Gwen, with Phyllis up the tree, March 1902. Short skirts gave greater freedom! (Ca02-056.)

Figure 9.1. The Customs staff and building at Chefoo, date unknown. The photograph is in the Yantai Museum, Yantai Park.

Figure 9.2. Probably Jim Carrall's grave, but not labelled in the album (Ca01-127). It had flowers, but not yet an inscription.

Figure 9.3. Amah with Gwen, Phyllis and baby Jim, 25 September 1901 (Ca01-144). The girls are wearing pith helmets (topees) against the sun, like those I wore during my childhood in India.

Figure 9.4. Labelled "1 July 1902. The Start" (Ca2-088). Mother is watching while a coolie hoists up Kath (half hidden by the potted plant).

Figure 9.5. Above: Assembling on the beach by the Russian Consulate (Ca02-88). The convalescent Kath remains in the carrying chair, and a Mr Watson is attending to them. It can be seen why the merchants wanted the harbour bund extended! (Another photo shows bread being loaded on the small boats for delivery to a waiting ship.)

Figure 10.1. Left: Kath and her mother, taken in Kingston in the summer of 1903.

Figure 10.2. Below: Over Dinsdale, Kingston Hill, taken in 1926 (Emily's album).

Figure 10.3. Left: Uncle Jack, with Frances (centre), Maude, Kath, Eric with his rifle, and Jim, in 1905 (Emily's album).

Figure 10.4. Below left: Emily and Charlie on holiday at West Coates, Berwick, July 1904 (Emily's album).

Figure 10.5. Above right: Kath (left) and a friend in Winnipeg, winter 1911–12.

Figure 10.6. Above: A family reunion at Over Dinsdale in July 1925, in Emily's album. Back row: Jim, his French wife and model, and, possibly, Eric's wife, Irene. Middle row: Eric with his daughter on his lap, Maude, Mother, Muriel and Kath. Children on carpet, Muriel's daughter Betty, Kath's daughter Keeve, and Maude's daughter, Frances.

Figure 11.1. Right: Hart at seventy, in the photo he sent Kath in 1905. Copyright of Queen's University Belfast, Sir Robert Hart Collection, MS 15, originally in the Irons gift.

Scarlet Fever Kills

Scarlet fever, or scarlatina, caused by streptococcal bacteria typically attacking the mouth and throat, is now easily cured by antibiotics. Then, the high fever was often fatal and the patient who recovered felt weak and lethargic for many weeks. My mother sickened on 20 April. She would have been infectious a few days before the rash that gives the disease its name appeared. Thus she passed it on to her father and her playmate, Phyllis. Then Maude and young Frances caught it. Kath informed Hart on 4 May 1902:

> *My dear Sir Robert*
>
> *Father has asked me to write… . He is too ill to think and act for himself…*
>
> *He wishes to apply for six weeks "leave of absence", beginning from May 1st, as he and half the family have scarlet fever, we have all to be in quarantine for that time, and would like best to spend it quietly here at Chefoo…*
>
> *Father's fever is lower, but he is very weak indeed. I have been meaning to write to you for long, and now can only scribble this hurried note which I hope you will excuse. The last fortnight has been so full and busy. Frances has developed the fever too, so Mother and I are the only nurses now with five patients.*

Hart had already heard the news by telegram, and put the French chief assistant, J L Rémusat, in charge. Carrall died the next day. On 7 May Rémusat gave a full report to Hart saying that he had received a note that Carrall was sick on Monday 29 April, but it was not till Wednesday 1 May that this was identified as scarlet fever.

> *On that day in the evening Dr. Gulowsen…reported officially the gravity of the illness of Mr Carrall and his probable inability to attend to any business for a period of 4 to 6 weeks, which facts I the next day informed the Deputy Inspector G[l] by telegram. On Saturday 3rd he felt so much better that he gave orders for newspapers to be sent him. Sunday 4th the Doctor informed me in the afternoon that he was not so well & during the same night he sent for the Chinese Customs Writer twice, once at 10 and at 7 a.m. (Mrs Carrall countermanded the order.) Shortly before his*

death, Mrs Carrall and the Dr., thinking him somewhat easier, retired to rest; when the Dr., hearing him gasping for breath, only reached his bedside in time to see him die. It was then 4 a.m. I was informed of this on the morning of the 5th and at once wired to you the sad news, also informing the Consular Body by circular.

Having been asked by Mrs Carrall to take into my hands the preparations needful for the burial, I went to consult both the Doyen of the Consular Body and the British Consul, Mr Brady, as the former, Mr Fowler [the American consul was Doyen, being the longest in Chefoo] had kindly called officially in the morning to pay a visit of condolence and also to offer his services in regard to managing the funeral service etc. My reason for inviting the Consuls was because the deceased having died of a most contagious disease there was some talk amongst the Consuls as well as in the community, and objections raised to following a funeral cortege starting from his residence. In the meantime, the Taotai having sent me a message asking for particulars as to the ceremony, after due consideration I decided to reply that the Consuls had agreed to meet at the burying ground.

The Captain of the Chinese Cruiser "Haitien" having kindly volunteered to send a crew of 20 armed sailors, and a guard of 40 soldiers provided by the Taotai formed, together with the entire Customs staff and a good portion of the community, the cortege...passed from the Commissioner's residence through the native city to the cemetery (Temple Hill), where on arrival the remainder of the residents, including the Taotai, were congregated to pay their last respects to the late Commissioner of Customs, the coffin being carried from the gate to the grave by us, the Indoor staff, assisted by Lieut¹ Forbes.

You have doubtless heard of the illness of four of the daughters. Although the three elder are progressing favourably, I am more than sorry to say Phyllis the youngest is in a critical condition, and not expected to live. What has kept up Mrs Carrall during this terrible trial is the nursing of the child.

I trust I have not transgressed on your time by writing at such length, but thinking that you would like to be in possession of these sad details, I have taken the liberty of writing to you thus fully.

Carrall had probably known the Chinese Writer for a long time, whereas many of expatriate staff were recent appointments. Emily was the only one of Carrall's immediate family who could attend a funeral which testified to the affection and respect in which he was held by the Chinese and the expatriate community. The Customs staff who accompanied the Chinese sailors and soldiers were themselves quite numerous and the procession through the Chinese city to the cemetery above would have been impressive (Figure 9.1). It would doubtless have been joined by some of the Chinese merchants who had presented the scrolls. Figure 9.2 shows his grave, in the cemetery which had been a frequent destination for the girls' walks to Temple Hill.

Hart replied to Kathleen on 6 May, expressing his sympathy.

> *I am sorry, very sorry for you all, and I fear you are passing through a very trying time. Your poor father's death must have been a terrible shock: evidently you were very far from expecting anything of the sort when you wrote for him about six weeks' leave last Sunday! With the house full of sick ones your Mama & yourself will have more nursing to do than you are able for, and I trust the strain will not be too much for either of you, but I fear you will have to go on with it for weeks to come.*
>
> *You will probably have heard from Mr Rémusat that I anticipated the application for leave & sent it officially before your letter came here: little did I think I was sending it out to one who had already passed away! I remember your father as a nice little boy in 1858, a handsome young man in 1869, and our official relations have always been pleasant and I deeply regret that he has been taken away from his family & colleagues so soon.*
>
> *I am quite anxious about the state of the household and I hope letters from Chefoo will come in of a reassuring kind. I wrote a few lines of sympathy to your Mama a few days ago, and I assure you I feel for you very much.*

Kathleen wrote the same day in response to his earlier letter to her mother.

10 May 1902

My dear Sir Robert,

I was just about to sit down and write to you acknowledging your telegram and letter of 4th May, saying that Father was not to trouble about work (which arrived two days ago), when your letter of 6th May arrived. She, — and we all — thank you from our hearts for your kind sympathy & enquiries. She asks me to reply, as she cannot leave Phyllis. For the last three days Dr. Gulowsen has given us no hope about the little one, any moment the fever may go beyond control, any moment may be her last. You will understand then why Mother or any of us have not written you yet. Mother has not been able to attend to a thing outside Phyllis's bedroom, nor has she touched a pen to write even to Grandmother or Muriel, and Emily and I were until yesterday, when a nurse arrived – always either with her to help give the nourishment, call the doctor etc, or nursing Maude, Frances and Gwen, who are still in bed, but improving gradually.

We have attended – assisted by Charlie Forbes & the Rev. Mr Griffith (who are both living with us) – to all outside affairs for Mother, opened all letters, arranged everything. Charlie & Emily arrived on Tuesday (6th) from Wei Hai Wei just in time for the funeral at 4.30 p.m. Mr Griffith came to us on Monday morning and did everything about the funeral for Mother and me. I don't know what we should have done without him. Since Charlie arrived he has looked after all private affairs, opened Father's private papers, telegraphed to England, and done all that can be done so far…. Kind friends have all offered to be of use, but we have done without their help, excepting lately of a nurse who has taken the last two nights' nursing. As the disease is so infectious, we do not want in any way to be the means of spreading it. Mother thanks you very much for saying she "will not be disturbed or hurried in her arrangements", we have not yet been able – without discussing matters with her which is impossible at present – to make any plans for the future. The quarantine will be a long one, and it is very good of you to allow us to stay on so long here.

As regards the financial position Mother is perfectly sure that we have no outstanding debts, it has always been Father's great

struggle to keep out of debt. Until the last two years he could not
save anything, and what he has now is all invested out here. What
these investments are worth, we cannot as yet ascertain, but as
soon as we know, & Mother is able, she will write you on the
subject.

Mother is bearing up as well as possible. I shall not show her
this letter as she must not be disturbed.

I can write no more now. Please accept our thanks and
gratitude for your kind letter and sympathy with us all.

Charlie gave Sir Robert more information on the family's financial
position.

11th May 1902

Dear Sir Robert Hart

I hope you will excuse my writing to you, as we have never met,
but you know of me as Mrs Carrall's son-in-law. I am sure you
wish to hear how she is situated financially, and it must be a
considerable time before affairs can be wound up, owing to the
quarantine.

…Mr Carrall has left his papers in such excellent order, that
there is no difficulty in ascertaining the rough amount of his
personalty. Each year's accounts have been carefully kept down to
the minutest detail, and the receipts and expenditures shown. Mr
Carrall apparently saved very little until the increased rate of pay
came, two years ago. Of his retiring allowances — one was
expended in defraying the family expenses during the years 1887–
1889, when they were at home in England and another was lost
through some unfortunate speculations. He had insured for £2000
in 1889, but three years later he arranged to cease paying
premiums and receive £453 at the age of 55 or at death.

All his capital is invested in the East for the most part in
Shanghai Land Investment Co. Debentures. These are quoted at
6% and his income from this source should be about taels 3,400
which at present rates would be about £380 per ann. Out of
this, the sum of £50 is paid annually to his mother, Mrs
Sampson. Mrs Carrall herself has an income of about £160 per
ann. The total income would thus fall somewhat short of £500 per

ann., though if the present fall in silver continues of course it would be less.

It has been generally supposed that Mr Carrall was a wealthy man — this I have known for some time was to a great extent incorrect. Mrs Carrall is very sensitive on this point, knowing as she does that Mr Carrall died at his post in the attempt to make sufficient provision for his large family and she does not wish it to be generally known that the family means have been so reduced. Mrs Carrall bears up like the noble woman that she is, but I fear a bad collapse should Phyllis die. Poor little Phyllis has been fighting death for days and we still have hope. Mrs Carrall and her children are very grateful to you for your sympathy and for your kindness in allowing them to remain in the house for so long.

I hope I have explained affairs clearly in the absence of a man more versed in such matters.

Phyllis died on 14 May. It was only then that Frances senior had time for letters. and she wrote to Hart the next day.

My dear Sir Robert

Thank you very much indeed for your kind letter. I was not able to read it before. Today we buried little Phyllis in her Father's grave: she died too — yesterday about 7 p.m. and at 8 a.m. Emily, her husband, Eric & I took her to be with her father. Kathleen sickened yesterday morning. I am anxious about her for she has been nursing both her father & little Phyllis & knows all the symptoms which makes her nervous but as it is her second time for scarlatina, I trust she, like Maude & Frances, will make a good recovery & take their illness easily. Her commencing means a longer spell of quarantine. I cannot write to you now, for Kath's sake I must not think of the two who are gone but think of those I have to nurse. Eric & Jim still continue well. Emily has just come back, arriving with her husband an hour before the funeral, but she keeps well and Charlie Forbes could not have done more had he been my own son. He has sat up at night, nursed, attended to everything. I feel Emily <u>has</u> a good husband. Mrs Griffith, belonging to Bishop Scott's mission, came to see us as soon as she heard of my husband's death & is still with us for of course we

are in strict quarantine & see no one. I am writing this while
waiting for the doctor…I feel you will want to know how things
are. Charlie wrote in answer to your second letter but when I hear
from home from my brother who has Jim's will I shall then be
clearer about our affairs than I now am. He was always very
sanguine, but with our family we were obliged to spend a good
deal. I know this: he lost his life trying to get enough money
together for his family and that he never spent but he grudged
spending merely because he wanted to be independent & if we are
not so well off it is no blame to him but just want of luck & I am
glad that he died not knowing he was dying in China & leaving
the little ones. He counted that he had done his best for the elder
ones & always said that the younger ones should not suffer but
have equal advantages, that therefore he would not go home &
spend but wait here till he had saved for them. He did his best for
wife & children always & I feel has really died for us. The girls
are brave & strong – we have not talked things over yet, but we
will when the nursing is over & I will tell you what we decide.
Charlie Forbes and Mr Griffith probably leave us tomorrow, they
are arranging about it. Your letter to Kath has come & I have read
it to her.

Goodbye, dear Sir Robert. Yours very sincerely, F.M. Carrall.

She wrote again on 17 May, apologising if her last letter was
incoherent:

…you will understand I cannot be long absent from the sick rooms.
Kath today is much brighter & has regained her courage. I was so
afraid she was not going to struggle against her illness, however I
am quite hopeful again. All three (Maude, Kath & Frances) have
had this illness before, hence our surprise at their again taking it
& our hope that they will soon throw it off. We have a nurse from
the C.I.M. school taking night nursing now. It is a great boon, she
came a week ago I think – I am all out about the days. We are
already burning sulphur in the rooms where we nursed Phyllis &
are taking all precautions to keep Eric & Jim in health. Emily too
I hope may escape. Charlie Forbes goes to the hospital to
quarantine before returning to his ship. Mr Griffith also doing
quarantine. Your letter to Kath I have put away for her…she was

too ill to take it in. We do not write many letters, as only Emily &
I may do so & besides not having time, we do not know but that
people may be nervous to hear from us. I am going to wait till we
hear from home to see what they advise us to do, for till then we
cannot even pack as we must disinfect first…If you wish us to
move or anything before you hear from me please just write,
otherwise we shall go on living quietly here and we were saying
today at tiffin how much we had to be thankful for – these nice
grounds for us all to walk in & for Eric & Jim more especially as
of course they do not go out anywhere. Eric was 13 yesterday. I
was telling him my youngest brother lost his mother on his
birthday (the 15th May) just about his age & it was the first
really sad day I remembered in our family. I still feel glad Jim did
not know he died out here – he had set his heart on England for
ending his days, his mother will feel it keenly. I do hope this will
find you well – today at last it seems like summer. Maude asked
me to give you her love – I must go back to them now.

My mother wrote much later of how these deaths affected her:

These two died, and my grief and desolation was great. I was left
with no one to play with, no parent to call me, even when I was
naughty, 'the best of the bunch'. I wandered, like a lost soul, in
the garden, and cried at night in my solitude till Amah heard me.

She had described earlier how her amah had made a rebellious little
girl say her bed-time prayers, and when she had asked why Amah, not
being Christian, insisted, Amah had told her God was like a sun, with
many rays, and each should follow their mother's way to the same God.
Amah now told her:

Our mothers teach us there is no death. Don't cry, little one. Your
sister lives with your father on the other side. He would be lonely
without her. You loved him. Let him have one of his large family
for companionship in his new life. He lives, she lives. They can see,
hear, and understand our writing. Comfort yourself, little one. You
will go one day to join them. You ask your mother. It is the custom
of everyone who believes in a God, to know that God lives, and
has another world, and we too will live in it after this life, if we
do well.

> *Next morning I went to my mother's room, and made enquiries about this after-life, and found Amah's and my mother's custom was to believe in a God, in prayer, and in an after life. I took heart, and prayed to that God with all my might to give me faith, and knowledge that my sister was safe and happy with Him. I took Amah's advice, and wrote a letter to my sister, and posted it in a hole in the wall at the back of the kitchen. We had always used this as a letter box. Next day I went again, full of hope. There were two letters. One, mine to my sister, and underneath it, a letter in my small sister's writing. It had evidently been written to me while I was ill, and before my sister had fallen a victim to the infection. It spoke of her loneliness, and her hope that I would come out and play with her again. Some drawings and flowers ended the letter. I was overjoyed. Though I realised it had been written before death, it seemed an answer to my prayer, as I had not found it the day before. It now served a purpose, for it showed me God had heard the cry of a child. I ran to my mother and to Amah, crying with tears of joy: 'She is happy for she has written. She lives. There is indeed a God and an after-life.' My mother took the little letter and put it in her prayer-book.[2]*

The influence of that good woman still lives on, for my mother often spoke of her, and Amah's words helped form my own religious beliefs, and the advice I pass on to others. It illustrates how Chinese philosophies passed on to expatriate children in China, through the servants who cared for them. Amah meant a great deal to all the girls, and Figure 9.3 is one of three photos of her taken in 1901–2.

The Return to England

Frances senior considered staying in China, like Mrs von Möllendorff, but took Sir Robert's advice to return to her family. In the next few weeks she organised disinfection, packing, and sale of what they did not want while looking after her convalescent daughters. They left Chefoo on 1 July 1902. Figure 9.4 shows Kathleen being hoisted into a carrying chair on the terrace where they sung their Sunday hymns, as she still could not make the walk down to the beach from which small boats would carry the family to the ship taking them to

Wei-Hai (Figure 9.5). They had probably arranged to spend most of July in Wei-Hai to enable Emily and Charles to have time together. At the end of the month they went down to Shanghai. There Mr Hobson paid over the Retirement Allowance. This enabled Frances to negotiate, with his help, an economical passage home on a Japanese mail ship. Probate records show Frances kept her account in a Shanghai bank, with her investments carefully spread over a varied bunch of Chinese securities, to the end of her life. They left Shanghai on 4 August 1902.

Hart wrote to Kathleen before they left Shanghai.

Peking

16 July 1902

Dearest Kathleen,

I have only time for a hurried chit to catch you before you leave… . Letters from your Mama & Maude came yesterday & I infer that you are now also convalescent. What a time you have had & what sad experiences, but how happy it is that so many have been spared & pulled through! This is also such a capsizing of plans: on your side you little dreamt of quitting China so soon & under such circumstances, &, on mine, the visit I had been looking forward to is lost. I wonder when & where, if ever, we shall meet again? It is not likely to be in China, and is there any chance of my ever being free & revisiting England? If I do get home I shall surely try to see you all again: meantime I hope some of you will, in turns, write to me & let me know when & how you are, & what you are doing. I shall be anxious till I know how you are settled & I shall always take great interest in the doings of each. I am rejoiced to find how calmly and bravely your Mama faces the facts & I am sure all of you will be brave & do your best to help her & each other. Getting through life is very onerous & the way is different for each individual: I hope and pray you all may meet with more roses than thorns, but when you are in a difficulty, "grasp your nettle" & no sting will be felt.

I enclose something for you & your sisters: you girls will be all the better for some pocket money of your own on arrival in England & I wait my turn to go with you that far. In the future,

*& while I am to the fore, let me know if you are in any trouble, &
perhaps my sympathy may be of use.*

He also found time on 27 July to forewarn Campbell of their arrival,
praising the brave way they were behaving and asking him if possible
to see them on arrival, *'for they will feel very strange in England'*.

Frances only found time to write some days into the voyage. She
was still anguished by her failure to save her husband and Phyllis.

Bingo Maru, August 10th 1902

*…Thank you very much for wiring to Mr Hobson about the
Retiring allowance. He read me both your telegram and his reply
and I received and signed for the Retiring allowance. It seemed to
bring it all so much to me and to in a way close our long
connection with the service. Now we have left Hong Kong there
will be no more talks as of old of where so & so is etc, etc. You
have always been a good friend to us and my husband greatly
appreciated your friendship. It seemed hard that he could not know of
all the thought you showed for him as soon as you knew of his illness.
It is always so, though. We always wish we could have the
arranging of things & are full of useless regrets. If I only could
leave off worrying about Phyllis & him. It seems to me we ought
to have pulled them through…*[She makes the comparison with
her grief the previous year over Muriel, already quoted.]

Kath wrote the same day, while *'Passing Cochin China'*. They treated
the journey as a cruise, enjoying trips out at each port of call.

My dear Sir Robert

*Here we are, well on our voyage to England!…The Captain had
met Charlie Forbes…and he has already found amusements for us
— cricket, ping-pong and lessons in "Bridge"! The 1st officer and
1st and 2nd engineers are European, the doctor and others
Japanese. There are only a few First-Class passengers yet — two
married couples, both American, a Spanish priest & his friend, a
Chinese gentleman and a stodgy European (I don't know his
nationality!) — but at Singapore we ship a number of others,
who, it is to be hoped, will be more interesting and help us to make
up a good cricket team! The stewards are most attentive and the food*

*and serving very good, so that we could not be more comfortable
[Figure I]. The heat is very great at night or at ports, but during the
day there is usually a good breeze on deck, and electric fans working
in the saloon.*

*…We left Hong Kong at daylight on Coronation day, so we had
to celebrate on our own account. The saloon was decorated. At 9
p.m. all the passengers collected and drank the King's health, sang
the anthem to Emily's accompaniment and gave the customary
three cheers, so that whether the King's coronation has really come
off or not, we have done our share! We are due to arrive in London
about 25th September, we stop two days at ports, which makes a
long voyage.*

The King's coronation had been scheduled for 26 June, but he had
an attack of appendicitis two weeks beforehand. He was persuaded to
have an operation and the abscess was drained. This was thought safer
than excising the appendix. In the King's case, he recovered rapidly, and
the coronation took place on 9 August.

Though the energetic explorations of two-year-old Jim needed
constant oversight from an older sister, in place of much-missed Amah,
Frances senior found the journey easier than her return to China in
1888. She told Hart on 23 August from Colombo.

*…There is a good laundry which with our large party we find a great
boon. Really travelling nowadays is very easy. I wonder when you will
be making a trip home — do not leave it too long — perhaps like me,
you are wondering more what the end of the journey will be. After so
long of China life everything will be so strange. Courage, though,
seems to be the main thing & not to anticipate trouble which may
never come, or if it does, so different from what we expect.*

Reading this surprised me. I never knew my grandmother, but seem
to have inherited the same philosophy. I was also glad to read that: *'A
child came on board at Penang just Phyllis's age to the month. Gwen & she
are inseparable, before that she was rather dull.'* My mother's remaining
sisters were much older than her, and she did not get on well with her
brother Eric. As a boy, he was allowed to do things or have things which
she was refused as being 'only a girl' — a phrase which aroused her
bitter indignation. After Phyllis died, she often felt lonely.

Even the Red Sea was not trying. Young Frances wrote to Hart from Port Said:

> Some sports were arranged about a fortnight ago and they have helped to pass the days. I am the proud winner of two races, one for tying the best necktie in the shortest time, & the other for deck billiards. I am in the finals for two more. [She later won the ping pong tournament — I have her trophy still.] I am sorry we will not be able to stop longer at Port Said, as we only get there at midnight, & leave the next morning at six. We girls have "done" all the other places very well. It is so nice getting on "terra firma" again & exploring the different ports. It seems funny to think we will be in England in less than three weeks.

She was wrong about her own arrival time.

The holiday helped the girls to recover their spirits. as Frances senior described:

> ...Excuse this untidy letter. Gwen's friend upset my ink bottle & then Maude aimed an orange & upset a glass of water, and altogether there is not a Sunday calm around! I think we are all glad to be nearing Europe & to see land so close as we steam slowly along. The sea is a lovely colour & the weather perfect, a light breeze & the sun has not troubled us. There is a second deck overhead right along, which is a wonderful protection.... The better we get on the more I feel I want you to know of our good luck for you have shown us such sympathy in our trials.

Illness and Financial Worries at Marseille

Frances senior's eldest brother, Henry Fawcus, and his wife, Annie Shane, had arranged to meet them at Marseille to take Eric back by train to start school. On 14 September, Frances senior had also to disembark there as young Frances had 'peritonitis'.

> Grand Hôtel Noailles et Métropole, Marseille
>
> 24th Sep 1902
>
> My dear Sir Robert
>
> [She hoped he had heard the news from a letter she had sent

to Mr Hobson]. *Since Saturday Frances has progressed slowly but satisfactorily and this morning the doctor tells me he will for the future come but once a day which is the best possible sign seeing at first two doctors came twice daily. He thinks we must still reckon on being here 3 weeks longer. Frances is now allowed a little milk in weak tea, but nothing else. I had not much hope for her when we landed. You may guess how thankful I feel the illness did not develop earlier for I am sure the commencement was caused by violent sea sickness between Chefoo & Shanghai for since then Frances from time to time complained of sudden stabbing pains but they never lasted long & she did not make any fuss, only looking back I can trace it to then. My brother with his wife met us at Marseille & he remained with us till we were comfortably settled there, & then went on to Rome from whence he is now back. He returns to England Saturday night but my sister-in-law who has stayed with us all along will not hear of going home with him but insists on remaining to take care of us. She is a very gentle good nurse so in every way we could not be better off. I've had a telegram from home yesterday "all ashore well". It was hard to send them all home without me…happily now all danger is over, only great care is necessary.*

Till the day before reaching Marseille all had gone so well with us… . We are so anxious for all China news. Frances does not forget to ask me if there is anything new about China in the papers.

My brother strongly advises me to ask you for a nomination for Eric in the Customs Service. Of course it is early yet to mention it but if you would bear the boy in mind I would be very grateful…[the first of many appeals about Eric].

Her husband had left his estate to his trustees and executors, Arthur and John (Jack) Fawcus, her brothers and his friends, who were to use it on behalf of her and her children, an arrangement common at the time. Financial worries, in the midst of caring for young Frances, impelled another letter to Hart.

Marseille, October 15th 1902

…My brother now writes to me & suggests that I should ask you definitely whether the last retiring allowance which was paid to

*me in Shanghai, just before we left for England, belongs to me as
the widow or to the estate. Why is because, on its receipt, it was
paid into my S'hai current a/c & some of it at once used to settle
up & to pay our homeward passage money. In China we did not
include it in the estate, first because I had not received it, &
secondly, because I thought the widow was entitled to it, if it were
paid. Hence no probate was paid on it, whereas the insurance
money £433 (a cheque for which I took home with me) was
included & I have handed the latter over to my two brothers, who
are my husband's executors. If the last retiring allowance ought to
have been included I fear I have trenched very considerably on the
estate. My brothers naturally wish to do everything possible for
me, but they feel also bound to make sure exactly just what they
are doing. They mean, as executors, to realise the Chinese
investments very soon & to reinvest all the capital in such
securities as Trustees are entitled to hold* [trustees were limited
to British Government stock] — *of course such investments
will not yield anything like the interest that China investments do,
for Father left me nominally £6000 & it only now brings me in,
thus invested, £160 or thereabouts. On leaving here I had hoped at
once to settle down but if I ought to repay to the estate what I have
already spent of the last Retiring allowance I must just wait to try
to get the estate money clear first.*

*The above question has raised another question in my mind, so
I will put it to you. In Chefoo I received the last quarter's salary in
full, but part of it only (that up to May 5th) was included in the
estate (of course with Mr Brady's* [British consul at Chefoo]
*knowledge & sanction — the balance I used for our current
expenses. I feel* now *as if, unwittingly I had been dishonest, but, at
the time, it seemed the most obvious thing to do.*

This is a long-winded letter for only two questions:

*Did I do right in not including all the quarter's salary in the
estate?*

Does the last retiring allowance belong to me as the widow?

Next day she received another letter from her brothers and wrote
again.

You will see from it why I troubled you…it gives me the opportunity of telling you that Frances is now on the sofa & maybe the doctor will allow her to have a short drive in another 3 days. We read with great interest in The Times of six young ladies, guests of Sir Robert Hart, going to an audience at the Empress Dowager's & Frances heaved a long sigh to think how very nearly she had been one of the six. Kathleen has gone over to Hamburg till New Year with my brother Arthur and his wife, who live there. They had arranged their visit to England to meet me, however I could not leave here in time. I am very glad she has gone, for Maude & Frances had a most enjoyable time in Shanghai last winter and Kathleen had quite the brunt of anxiety & nursing, seeing she only sickened after the others were out of danger, so that quite a change from family cares will be a most excellent thing for her, & too, they have promised to help her on with her German.

We look in the paper regularly for any bits about China but except the little mention of you by name Frances complains they only give the "deaths of uninteresting Viceroys" (is that the proper plural?)

…The weather here is lovely, just the blue skies we have in China — indeed as a nation the French too remind me more of the Eastern character. I have not room to say why! Forgive another letter today. When I get to…England I shall be too busy to bombard any friends with lengthy epistles — Goodbye again dear Sir Robert from yours very sincerely, Frances M. Carrall

P.S. …Will you understand all that is not written & not think I think I have a right to be forever troubling you. F.M.C.

Another Death

Maude told Sir Robert on 5 November that 'Mother and Frances came over from Marseille about a week ago, both looking fairly well considering what they had gone through'. Frances senior wrote on 17 November to sympathise with Sir Robert on the death of his brother Jem, which she had just read in the paper:

...I know how keenly you will be feeling it, as your brother Jem was so great a favourite of yours. I am afraid you will look back on 1902 as a sad year for you, losing men in your service who had for long been so associated with it, and now, as the year closes, not only another but this time a brother for whom to mourn.

She then told him how the older girls were now preparing to work, something which would not have been on their mental horizon before.

I have decided to remain with my mother-in-law till our affairs are settled.... Mrs. Sampson has entirely lost her heart to the two boys, and I can fall in better with her hours than the girls. Maude is the only one with us, but she goes daily to town to Pitman's for shorthand & then to my brother's lady typists for type-writing and is away from 9 in the morning till 6 in the evening, except Saturday which is a holiday. There seems a good chance of her getting later employment in a solicitor's office; anyway, whether or no, my brother offered to stand all expenses if she cared about trying it & she accepted his offer, seeing there was no other likely opening for her. Kathleen in Hamburg is hoping to find a situation in a German family as a companion to some girl requiring English. Emily is at the Forbes of Berwick and seems very happy with them. Muriel and Frances are in Newcastle with my eldest brother [Henry]*, Frances to be taken care of as she is still far from strong, & Muriel full of plans — she is ambitious & does not easily make up her mind. Gwen is near us with my eldest sister & Eric a day scholar at Wimbledon, returning daily here & sleeping at one brother's house* [Jack]*. Jim II I take care of with Gwen's help. She comes across daily & is a good little soul. When the year turns, if all the girls are still absent, I must send her to a day school for she will be 10 next April & at present just does lessons at odd times.* [The education of girls was less urgent than that of boys.]

...It is anyway giving the girls a chance to try their wings and if they can fix on nothing I shall feel more justified in getting them to come back to me and helping me make both ends meet. I have told my mother-in-law that I will visit her as long as she likes but that she must have a home of her own and all her own things about her & that I must too. There can be but one mistress in a

house & I think she sees that too. The children of the present
generation are so much more independent than in old days and
chafe at much restriction. [It seems doubtful that this was
generally true of middle-class girls in England, but the
Carrall sisters had led a freer life than usual in China, and
had been to a school that encouraged girls to think of the
professions.] *Well, I did not mean to touch so much on our affairs*
but I thought doing so would perhaps divert your thoughts from
your own sorrow.

Poor Sir Robert, I am very sorry for you for I know how much
you feel such news and when alone troubles weigh on one so much.
At first sympathetic letters did not help me much, but now when I
feel lonely and at sea it comforts me much to look over the different
kind letters sent to me & for that reason I have ventured to express
my sympathy so openly to you.

PTO I know so well that my Jim, had he been alive, would have
been one of the first to write to you for he spoke so often of your
brother and always, when speaking of him, as if he had really
cared for him in their bachelor days. The last time we saw him
was when he brought his bride to Amoy on their way to visit the
Edgars. He seemed then so proud & happy but the time slips away
so fast that that is quite a while back now.

Now a much younger life neared its end. Uncle Henry and Aunt
Annie had hoped the brisk northern air would benefit young Frances,
but she became ill again. Her mother explained in a letter to Mr Hobson,
which she asked him to pass on to Sir Robert.

48 Osborne Road

Newcastle on Tyne

December 11th 1902

My dear Mr Hobson

[Explanations on the Shanghai bank pass books.] *We have*
been & are still in grave anxiety on Frances's account.... She was
quite bright here & wrote to me more than once that it was a
shame their being here & enjoying themselves & leaving me in
sole charge of Gwen & Baby Jim but quite suddenly a return of

her complaint came on & I was telegraphed for... . The doctor
here said an operation was inevitable. I arrived Saturday week ago
(Nov 29th) & Muriel went down south to replace me at her
grandmother's. Dec 2nd Frances was much worse & on the 9th the
doctors told me the risk of an operation was great but the risk in
delay was greater & so that morning we took her in an ambulance
to the doctor's private home. [Hospitals were still only for the
poor]. *I remained there with her till 6 p.m. & the operation was*
performed yesterday at 2 p.m. I have not been allowed to go again,
we have a telephone on & my brother goes to enquire as well. This
afternoon at 5-30 p.m. I may go to interview the nurse but may not
see Frances this week unless she is worse. [This would be to
avoid the danger of bringing in an infection.] *Her condition*
now is what they expected, very serious. Emily came from Berwick
yesterday... . My people have been everything, one and all & the
family generally (my children I mean) are severally all well looked
after. Muriel, Maude, Gwen & Jim go together to a brother at Kent
(Farnborough) for Xmas & Eric comes up here for his holidays.
They wanted to have us all together but I thought it better not on
account of Frances as for long she must be our only
consideration...explain to our friends how anxious we are just
now & how impossible cheerful letter writing is just now.

She signed off with best wished for 1903 then crammed in a few
more words:

Frances has been wonderfully patient & brave & that is greatly in
her favour. She [on front page by address] *does everything &*
takes everything prescribed & has never given way, but always in
every way tried to save me from pain, she is a plucky girl. Tell Sir
Robert for I write to no one just now.

Frances died of appendicitis on 15 December. Her second Newcastle
uncle, Evans Fawcus, was with her and the informant on the death
certificate. One can only hope that her mother also saw her before the
end.

CHAPTER TEN

THE GIRLS SETTLE FOR MARRIAGE

The letters the Carralls wrote to Hart after their arrival in England show them meeting the challenges of an unfamiliar home country, home-sickness for China and reduced circumstances. Frances now had to make decisions about her children's futures as a lone parent. Kath is the most interesting daughter to follow because of her unusual career interests and the survival of Hart's letters to her. The girls were lucky to have an understanding grandmother in Emma Sampson, whom they usually mentioned in their letters, and an astonishing number of Fawcus relatives.

Arriving in a New World

Uncles Jack and Arthur Fawcus, the executors of Jim Carrall's will, had met the girls at the London docks on 24 September 1902 and taken them down to Kingston-on-Thames. Kath gave Hart their first impressions in a letter dated 2 October.

> We found Grandmother, Muriel and Eric very well, and we were
> so glad to be together again. Grandmother is wonderful and
> perfectly in love with Baby, I'm afraid she spoils us all fearfully.
> Of course she is frail and easily tired, but she is very active indeed.
> We are all living close together, though being so many, not all in
> the same houses…
>   This week has been most bewildering what with new sights
> and new relations! The number of the latter that we have seen is
> surprising; they turn up on all sides and are so kind and
> thoughtful. As for the sights, everything is strange from St. Paul's
> Cathedral to a barrel organ! I could write sheets on what we have
> seen already, but there is so much to do still in the way of

*unpacking and winter shopping; it feels so cold after the tropics
through which we have just passed that you will be mercifully
spared having to wade through them this time! I only meant these
few lines to show you we have by no means forgotten you or any
old China friends, and often speak of our life there. I wonder if
any of us will ever return...*

Emma Sampson wrote one of her brief little notes with enclosures,
and Hart would have been pleased with her description of Kath:

*Just a few words to let you know that my dear son's family arrived
yesterday week, except their dear Mother...I have five of the
family with me, the others are near.... Kathleen came this
morning & told me she hoped to write to you, she is kept very
busy, a most industrious & willing girl. I enclose in this two
papers which will I am sure interest you. I am unable to write
more because my cough is too severe.*

Maude wrote to Hart on 5 November to report the arrival of her
mother and sister. She had been amused by the preparations for Guy
Fawkes Day, and especially by one guy which, like a theatre advertisement
she had seen, gave a funny idea of the Chinese:

*...the dresses & faces not a bit like the supposed originals. Really,
those living always in England have very little idea of the ways &
likes or dislikes of any other nationality! The amount of motor
cars & cycles one sees is astonishing, especially the motors,
considering how recently they have been introduced.*

Meanwhile Kath had gone to Hamburg with her Uncle Arthur. She
did not see her mother and sisters again till the summer of 1903. She
had to adjust to a new world and yet another death, with an uncle and
aunt who, however kind, could not share her memories of lost loved
ones and a happy life in China. She told Hart on 14 November that
she was sad not to have heard from him, though she had read the news
item about his guests' visit to the Dowager Empress. She was finding
the noise and speed of life astonishing:

*...Here everything was at first very strange, but I am feeling much
more at home now than I did.... This is such a fine large town,
and a very busy and noisy one too! I can't even now get used to the*

continuous noise of the traffic, the electric trams, the heavy wagons, etc. What strikes one first I think is the way in which everything is adapted to save time. In the houses, in the streets, everywhere, are appliances for speed, & how the people make use of them, how they rush to catch the trams, the steam boats across the lake or canals, how they press and jostle one another when the train comes in! Another unusual sight to me was that of poor white people, every white man in China was someone, however small; but here there are many, in almost rags, and yet they seem to belong to us, they all wore the same kind of clothes! You can imagine how every sight and surrounding is new, no longer any coolies to fetch & carry for one, but a system of local post offices instead of messengers, of electric trains, motors & carriages instead of sedan chairs!...I have been to my first two public concerts on the Exchange (the buzz of voices was extraordinary, like the roar of the sea), to a number of picture galleries, and to museums and other public institutions. There is a fine lake, the Alster, in the middle of the town, the views around it are lovely...

I am to stay here over Christmas.... Today I began a course of German lessons in exchange for English ones...I am also keeping up my music. It seems to be very difficult indeed for girls to find something to do for themselves...when I know more German perhaps I shall find a post as companion to some girl who wants to learn English, a situation which would give me an opportunity to keep up some of my own studies so as to train for something higher.

A sudden opportunity necessitated an urgent letter to her mother on 4 December, which Frances must have forwarded to Hart.

I have to give an answer by December 13th. If I had had longer time to decide, I should not have bothered you now [with Frances ill]*...The lady principal of a German Girls' School applied to Miss M.* [MacDonald] *for an English teacher to the 2nd & 3rd classes beginning from Easter. Miss M. at once thought it would be a good beginning for me, & though I am quite inexperienced suggested I should apply for the situation. If I consent, Miss M will do her best to get the Principal to take me, & she says, if I once get into a school like that, I shall soon be given more* *lessons…. I must not consent to take it up unless I am prepared to carry it on for at least a year. It would mean living here for that time and practically taking up the teaching of English as my profession. In the event of anything happening or of my changing my mind later, I could after six months, give notice, but I shouldn't like to do so, as Miss M. stands, as it were, my guarantee that I shall keep it up. I would be expected to give a lesson of an hour to each class once a week (the 2nd class are girls of 14 & on, and the 3rd of 12 & on) and for it I would receive 6 marks a week, that is £12 a year…. I should like to take it up very much, and think it is just what I should have chosen. If you approve…please will you write at once. It is not definite yet if the Principal will have me, but the first step is to ask you…Uncle and Aunt are prepared to have me…*

Before her next letter to Hart, Kath had heard of her sister's death. She tried to keep the expected stiff upper lip, but her grief and loneliness show in her brevity and her difficulty in approaching the subject.

Hamburg

9th January 1903

My dear Godfather

I am just writing to wish you many happy returns of your birthday. I had lately an account of your autumn house party from the Drews, it seems to have been a great success. That is the latest news I have heard of you. I hope you are keeping well.

You will know of our fresh great trouble. It is difficult to speak of it. I felt it very much as I was not able to be there with Mother & the others at the time. Mother writes to me almost daily, she is wonderfully brave.

She continued with the news of the family. Muriel had decided to train as a lay worker in slums, and was doing three months probation at an Anglican institution in Clapham. My mother and Eric were at local day schools. After telling about the teaching post she had obtained Kath ended: *'My uncle and aunt…are very good indeed to me, but at times, I miss our large household. However I shall get over that…I should be very glad to hear from you, if you ever have time to write me a few lines.'*

The strain of the bottled up emotions showed on Kath's face in a photo taken when she finally met her mother again in August 1903. Figure 10.1 shows her mother still wearing the full mourning and 'weeping veil' expected of a widow for two years, but she has recovered her calm. Children mourned for one year, and girls might wear white instead of black.

Frances wrote to Hart from Newcastle as her brother had made yet another query on the Retirement Allowance. Unlike Kath, she did not hide her sorrow: *'It has been a dreadful blow to me & it is hard to take up life again & get on with it. Sometimes it seems beyond my courage even, but there is no use making a moan of it.'*

She wrote again on 15 January as she had forgotten to include birthday wishes. She despatched these by the more expensive route via the new Trans-Siberian railway.

> *...I should be sorry to be late with my good wishes for the day, seeing since we were with you in Peking I have always written to you for your birthday...*
>
> *I have not had the heart to write much to anyone of late. It was but a month yesterday since I lost Frances, but it seems far longer. I am going down south on 17th & shall live with Mrs. Sampson till our affairs are in order & I have a definite idea of my income. Meantime we are all more or less separated & after so many years being all together it seems unnatural & difficult to keep from rebelling against fate. My people have just done everything for us and I am glad that I acted on your advice & returned to them.*
>
> *...I went to see Emily at Berwick and was much pleased with her new relations & home.* [She was anxious about Muriel's choice to work in the slums.]*...She had set her heart on it, & it seemed best not to oppose it. I do hope she is strong enough for such a life.... Maude is...studying shorthand & typing.... Both she & Kath took the first thing that offered & seem determined to do all they can to help themselves so as to help me & yet since Frances died Kath offers to come back for fear I can't manage alone with Jim, but I have written her not to do so. The brother she is with said, were she to do so, as long as she lived with me, he would allow her £60 a year, so you see they don't hesitate in any way to try to make things comfortable for me & for the girls, but*

*if I can help by letting them help themselves it will be better for
their future it seems to me.*

Her years in China had led her to approve of women gaining salaried
work.

Back in Kingston with her mother-in-law, Frances wrote again on
25 February 1903 to thank Hart for his New Year letter. Family disasters
were continuing but China was still much in her mind.

*I am afraid of late I have quite neglected China letters, not that we
are not glad to have them, for the one question in letters written to
each other is "any news from China"? but our troubles have been
coming thick and heavily. I sent you a paper to tell you of our
having lost Frances. It seemed dreadfully hard for all of us, but, if
she were to go, I am glad that she lived to make the journey home
with us and that I saw so much of her. Only a year ago she
returned from Shanghai & I was so proud of yet another daughter
to take around with me & now she is buried & the rest
scattered...*

*This year has not commenced any brighter for our family. My
eldest brother died last month & on Monday I was at the funeral
of my youngest brother's daughter, who died from the same
operation as Frances underwent unsuccessfully. They had the best
surgeon in London but the Fates seem against us. You must excuse
therefore dull stupid letters...Kathleen is still in Hamburg...The
two lads are still prime favourites with their grandmother & she is
quite wonderful in the way she gets about & sees to things, & the
English air & life agree very well with the young ones.*

*...I am so often asked if you are ever coming home. It seems
wonderful your not even taking a holiday after all you have been
through in Peking. The Drew girls wrote & told ours what a
happy time you had made for them in the autumn.... I hear Mr.
Carl was to go into the old house at Xmas. I hope the garden did
not suffer from no-one living there. My husband used to take such
pride in pointing out his different improvements. The USA consul
sent us batches of Chefoo Expresses in which I see the bund
reclamation is still to the fore.... I don't want you to forget us.
After living so long in the East one does not quickly look to make
new friends...*

She did not give details about Henry's death. He had shot himself, in Harley Street. The location might suggest unpleasant medical news, but events showed that his business was in deep trouble. This, Frances now realised, was why he had strongly urged her to get Eric into the Customs, rather than to hope he might go into the family business. Henry's failure meant his brother, Evans, who had worked for him for thirty years, lost his job. Evans' eldest daughter was still at Girton College, Cambridge, but could continue as Uncle Jack paid her fees. The Fawcus family stuck together, but money was becoming tight.

Hart was modern enough to encourage Kath and her sisters to strive for independence until they married, writing:

25th Feb 1903

Dearest Kathleen

I have rec'd three or four letters from you since you left, but, till now, c'd not find time to answer. You know how sorry I was that you had to leave China under such distressing circumstances, and I am again deeply grieved by the news of the death of poor Frances; and I take such interest in all of you that I am only too glad to hear from you. I think you are all doing the right thing when you aim at working & being self-supporting: work is honourable & independence is a good thing to strive for. I hope your endeavours will be crowned with success, but I trust, too, that, for each, "Prince Charming" will in due season appear & lighten your labours & also brighten your lives.

Nothing special has happened to me here since your departure except that I moved back to my rebuilt house at the end of May. I am now very comfortably installed, but I miss the old things, the dear surroundings I was accustomed to in my rooms before the siege. Everything is new, but the house stands on exactly the same foundations, & all my old servants & the Band boys are with me again. Work has grown frightfully and I peg away from morning to night day after day. My health holds out wonderfully well & the idea of going home has to be kept in the background. Next year I complete fifty years in China, & the year after I shall be seventy: so I look forward to going home in either 1904 or 1905 if I live: at my age the machinery is wearing thin & I may break down any day. Since Xmas I have been very quiet, neither going out nor entertaining: my poor brother died last year, &, as we were great friends, I was very sad over his death...

You remember Mr d'Anjou: he & Miss Myers, his sister's companion, were both bitten by a mad dog three weeks ago & are now at S'hai for the Pasteur treatment. The Drew girls & Esmé Simpson came up 1st September & stayed six weeks with me: there were also three girls from Tientsin: Effie, Winnie [Stewart] and Gertie McLeish): we had great fun & the house was very lively! This year I expect Grace Campbell & the von Möllendorffs for a visit, & some others.[1] I think, too, I shall go to Peitaiho for a month as my house there is also rebuilt. I got out a fine fiddle (Villama) & good 'cello (Dodd) & every morning, as before, I have an hour's music before the office. Do you keep up your practice? I hope you do, for it is a consolation to have such a friend as a violin can become. Hamburg must be a very interesting spot: I suppose you know many people now & are quite at home there. I hope you will like it, keep your health, & be happy.

Finding a Home

Hart finally satisfied Frances' legal brother with a short memo on the Retiring Allowance. She was delighted that he followed this up with a private letter, which gave her courage to broach a difficult issue:

Thirlmere

April 16th 1903

...just before we left Shanghai for England, Mr Hobson read me a cipher telegram from you asking whether I had had the retiring allowance, if not I was to have it & that on reaching home there would be something additional. What with the long delay in Marseilles & never hearing further from you or the London office I did not like to say anything about it, but now settling up the estate & closing the accounts in China I asked Mr Hobson if I were right about the contents of your telegram...& he has written suggesting my reminding you. The fact is my people here will not let me be harassed in any way for money & I feel often that just because I

am a sister that I and mine have more than our full share of things as they are now.

In March my invalid brother died & we are to move into "Over Dinsdale" where he and my brother Jack lived together. [Jack had been employing a live-in nurse to care for Robert Speciall Fawcus at home.]*…Unless I consent to move my brother says he will give up the house & live in lodgings. I feel I can be a help to keep the house there & be ever ready to welcome all that come. It is hard to put things in a letter but it is very touching to have them all thinking of me, not in words but in the way they do things & therefore I think it would be but silly pride on my part, if you deemed a year ago that my husband's services justified you in promising something further for his children, that I should hesitate to remind you now… . Perhaps if I personally or my children had to suffer any consequences then I could much more easily have just let the thing slip, but now, when money is really a consideration to so many of us, for me calmly to take from them rather than like to remind you seems want of trust in you & I know you will not say anything stinging to me, even if you are of the opinion that I might have just left the question alone.*

My mother Gwen had caught whooping cough, reminding Frances that just a year earlier this daughter had caught the fatal scarlet fever. Frances gave Hart better news of Emily, being well looked after by her husband's relations. She now had to handle alone another daughter's love affairs.

Maude lately received a proposal from a young man, now in Peking! She would not say decidedly "no". I do not know, though, if anything will come of it. After our experience with Muriel I get so puzzled what to do about such matters, but she is open & frank & tells me everything. She sticks to her work at Pitman's, and has already one certificate for proficiency, but often she says to me, when she looks at the lady type writer who has been type writing for 15 years & still works away, she wonders if it is worth it all. [Secretarial work then offered no prospect of advance.] *A great thing is that we have about us so many young people, they were lately counting up, there were 19 cousins about the same ages within 20 miles & with their bicycles, meeting is very easy!*

The girls had evidently used some of Sir Robert's parting gift to get bicycles. The young man 'now in Peking' could have been the one who had proposed in Shanghai. Maude's eventual husband was Julian Ridout, a young officer in the Royal Artillery, in Shanghai and later in Peking, 1902–3. They married in 1909, but Maude had perhaps learnt from Emily's experience that it was better to avoid lengthy official engagements.

Kath wrote from Hamburg on 7 May to thank Hart for his letter of 25 February:

> It sounds like old times to hear of the band & your violin & 'cello! I was very glad to read your encouraging words and thank you for your wishes for my success. I began my work after Easter and already begin to feel used to it and to like it…
>
> It seems much longer than just a year since our troubles. It is very sorrowful remembering them, but we have much to be thankful for that we have been so kindly helped through them.

She told him that she was very happy with her uncle and aunt, though she never talked or wrote of Hamburg as she did of China. Even in spring it was not as beautiful as Chefoo:

> Hamburg is looking lovely just now. Every street is lined with lime trees and they are all just in leaf. I have made several tours these last warm days, one to Friederichsruh, Bismarck's country seat, now belonging to his son. The woods round are beautiful. I went in a penny steam-boat on the Elbe the other day to see the harbour! But it is nothing compared to Chefoo's. There are no hills here at all.

With the move to Uncle Jack's house, the worst of the family's troubles were over. 'Over Dinsdale' (Figure 10.2) provided them with a centre and refuge until their mother's death in 1929. Fortunate indeed was the Victorian family that had an unmarried but financially successful brother ready to help those in trouble. All the girls, my mother Gwen included, remembered Uncle Jack with great affection as a kind, wise man with solid principles. (Figure 10.3 shows him with the family this bachelor had adopted.)

Kath wrote to Sir Robert soon after her first visit to the new family home.

24th July /03

My dear Sir Robert,

…You can imagine how glad I was to see Mother and all again. They are looking so well, and Baby is much grown & has quite forgotten his Chinese!…This is such a comfortable house, it is very nice to have our things from China around us again. The family seems to have quite settled down here…

Emily and Maude were holidaying with William and Ada Fawcus near Falmouth. Uncle William also worked in Germany but had a cottage in Cornwall. Muriel was home on holiday from the 'Deaconess Institution'. Kath meanwhile was exploring London.

This is really my first long stay in England…. How fine the Houses of Parliament, Westminster Abbey and St. Paul's are! The Abbey is my favourite, a few days ago we went to Evening Service there, it was most impressive. I hope to visit the Tower, Academy and National Gallery next time. We have also been boating on the Thames. What a number of pretty parts there are along it. I already think my time far too short to do and see all there is to be done and seen! My holidays end on August 22nd and I return to my English teaching in Germany, which I find quite interesting.

She sent love from her mother and grandmother. Frances added a note with good financial news on 30 July:

…Mr Hobson sent me (or rather my brothers) the accounts to home and you will be glad to hear that they come out, even with the exchange as it is, much better than they had expected. I just had a letter from Maude from Falmouth this morning, in which she says "things are looking up a bit!" She has quite decided that her "Prince Charming" was not to be found as yet in the East! I almost wish they were not so heart-whole, for their sakes, but it is nice to have them still all belonging to me. Emily came down from Berwick to spend the holidays with the girls, and her Father-in-law had tea here last week. I like him very much and Emily is just as if she were his own daughter & seems so happy!

Maude's Christmas letter of 29 October 1903 told Sir Robert that despite the wettest summer on record, with the Thames overflowing several times, they were all keeping well and getting to like England. Frances enclosed her usual 'line' to hope that rumours of trouble between Russia and Japan would not cause him extra work. Eric's future was her constant preoccupation, for a boy must be fitted for independence with the capacity to earn a decent living, whereas the girls only needed pocket money. Muriel's return home was not a worry:

> *When the year turns I am sending him [Eric] to a boarding school to be away for a while from petticoat government, but I shall miss my lad. Muriel & Maude both live at home now, it is very nice for me. Muriel has given up slumming & is going in for a course of book binding. Maude has finished her shorthand & typewriting studies & is now going to try & get work at home to do to keep her in pocket money. We are seeing about a good second-hand machine...*

Kath, however, was still determined to earn a decent living, and told Hart on 15 November:

> *...I have six German lessons a week and give four English lessons and two in the school. Two of my "pupils" are ladies of sixty, it is quite amusing teaching them! The work is not always easy, but it makes the days go quickly! A piece of luck came my way the other day, an English teacher here is leaving, and offered me her four classes in schools next year, which I agreed to take, so I shall be earning quite a salary then! The only drawback is that I shall be kept so long away from Mother and the family. They seem to be getting on very well, and have met quite a number of China people lately, the Bowras live quite near...*

Sir Robert now despatched news for which he got several letters of thanks. The first was from Frances.

January 10th 1904

My dear Sir Robert,

This morning's post brought me your welcome letter of Dec 11th...telling me of a supplementary retiring allowance for £1000,

*it seems a very handsome one to me.... Thank you most sincerely
for it. Only this morning I was...wondering if I was really
justified in adding to our expenses by sending Eric...to boarding
school. Your letter seemed like an answer.... I have to thank you
too very much for noting our wish that Eric should later join the
Customs' service...*

*Again thank you, not only & entirely for the extra allowance
you have granted, but also for your kind chatty letter, telling me so
much of the service which is still dear to us. I never can quite
realise that we now no longer belong to it.*

Kath sent her thanks in her birthday letter of 21 January 1904 from
Hamburg. She was worried by the potential impact on him of the
situation between Russia and Japan. Her first English Christmas had
surprised her:

*How people enjoy Christmas in England! The poultry shops with
rows on rows of turkeys, the plum puddings, mistletoe and holly
everywhere, were new to me, and the "waits" who sang carols
every night from Dec 2nd were amusing...*

Frances wrote again on 26 January to thank him for his New Year
letter, and hoped the Siberian mail link would survive the tension
between Russia and Japan. For herself:

*The last six months, since we have been settled here, have been
very homelike, but then I can do nothing wrong in my brother's
eyes & nothing is too good for me. I am often afraid of being spoilt
should reverses come & still it is better to live in the present and
do the best that one can & my best just now seems to be taking
things very easily!*

On 29 January the promised cheque arrived, reviving memories of
her husband's hard work:

*I feel more glad than I can say that my husband's staying on as he
did in China has met with this recognition, not so much for the
sake of the money, though that is very acceptable, but because it
does not seem quite as if he worked in vain & I more than anyone
else know how constantly he thought & worked for the good of the
service and for the future of his family. There was much rejoicing*

when the cheque came today. Muriel & Maude impressed on my
brother to invest it well for us and to try for 3½%.

An extra £35 per year was enough to make a difference.

The outbreak of the Russo-Japanese war made her write again on
8 February, showing how well she knew his care for his staff:

> *I know, as long as things are unsettled in the East, you will just*
> *stick to your post & there will be no seeing you at home in 1905! I*
> *am afraid too this war will affect your plans in many other ways*
> *and probably delay the return of your staff to headquarters, for*
> *though not considerate of yourself, I know how careful you are*
> *where women & children are concerned. I have often wondered if*
> *I did wisely in leaving the East & bringing the girls home, but*
> *now…I cannot say how glad I am we are all here away from the*
> *war, the rumours and the anxiety & yet withal how sad to think*
> *we can never again now be all together as we were in China, both*
> *in 1884 and in 1900. It seems almost wrong to rejoice at being in*
> *England, away from it all, while we have a cherished spot there in*
> *the cemetery, but you will understand there are still others & the*
> *fact of having so lately lost some, more especially of being the only*
> *surviving parent, makes anxiety for the safety of the others more*
> *pressing —*
>
> *Goodbye dear Sir Robert — May you have no such experiences*
> *as in 1900 but rather may this war help to strengthen your*
> *position in China. I believe 1904 is your 50th year in China? I*
> *hope it may be a jubilee year in every respect for you, and that*
> *your lifetime's work will not be thrown away but that your*
> *children will reap the benefit of such long & untiring devotion to*
> *China and the Chinese Customs Service.*

As we shall see, Hart's children gave him little satisfaction. He next
wrote to Kath on 14 February against the background of war. The
Siberian link made a real difference to the speed of communications.

> *Your kind letter à propos of my birthday came this evening; it is*
> *dated 21 January & so has been only 24 days en route. I wonder*
> *how long such rapid travelling will be possible! The Siberian link*
> *is still open & working, but the despatch of troops may interfere*
> *with carriage of mails and warlike doings may even smash the*

Manchurian railway — for we are now having wars at our doors and Japs & Russians have been busy all the week hammering each other on the other side of the Gulf. The news we get is not of a very reliable kind, but, so far as it goes, it shows the Japs can fight & Russia will not quite have a walk over.

I am glad you got your holiday & enjoyed it at home. I am often very sorry for you all, your poor father's death having made life so changed for you: but you are meeting it pluckily and I hope all will go well.

The winter has been a very quiet one as far as I am concerned, but it has been also a very busy one for myself: the work grows enormously not only in volume but also — and that is good — in interest, and I quite enjoy it. Just now I am helped by a sore foot: I have not been out of doors for four weeks, and the necessity for staying in gives more time for work. The foot or rather toe — inflammation resulting from a broken chilblain — is now mending & I trust to be fine again in a week. Other people enjoy the winter, which is colder than most, & paper hunts, rink skating, club Cinderella, and Legation theatricals have been in full swing. We have had three falls of snow all of which seemed to purify the air, but on the 9th & 11th, the days when there was heavy cannon-fire over at Port Arthur [Lüshun], we had two horrible storms here: they lasted on each occasion only a few hours, & were evidently the result of the atmosphere disturbance caused by the firing — the sky was awfully wild and angry and the dust swept about fiercely.

I am still alone. Lady Hart & Nollie had some idea of paying me a winter visit, but I put them off with the war likely — and now we have it — I thought I w'd be better alone and they w'd be far away from the scene of any possible trouble. So I told them to hold on at home till I wired them to come along. There's no saying how long the war will last & I am just considering whether I shall be able to either get away during it or live through it. I shall be 69 on the 20th and naturally must be near "the end of the tether". Thanks for your good wishes: I don't know that they'll help me live longer, but they'll make the birthday this time all the pleasanter.

...Most of the I.G. Staff are still at Shanghai under Mr

Bredon, but unless war makes it impossible I hope to have them all back here by June, when two new houses & offices will be ready.

With love,

Affectionately yours

Robert Hart

P.S. I wonder did you get many Valentines today, & what you'll make of Leap Year!

Kath's reply on 29 May 1904 showed that her sympathies were with Japan:

The war near you is going on in good earnest now, we follow it with interest, what awful destruction these mines work. I hope plucky Japan will win! The German press, needless to say, in view of the Anglo-Japanese alliance, is very pro-Russian & predicts a great yellow peril if Japan wins! Do you think there is any danger of it?

...Doubtless you have heard of Muriel's engagement, which happened at the end of March. We all like him & funnily met him first in Chefoo as a boy the first time we were there, which makes it very romantic! The marriage will not be for some time yet. Emily's husband is on his way home which is delightful for her. Maude often writes me and seems to make the best of everything...

I am going to Goslar in the Harz Mts at the beginning of July to stay with a German family for my six weeks summer holiday, simply to learn the language better. It will be quite an amusing experience as their manners & customs are so different from ours! I then return here for a term and finally leave for good at Michaelmas to try & begin training in England. At present my teaching is getting on well & I am so proud as I have been making £1.5s. a week [about as much as the £60 her uncle would have given her if she had returned to her mother, but it signified independence].

On my birthday Uncle & Aunt took me to the opera, we saw "Lohengrin", I thought the music beautiful. Do you still play the violin at times?

> *Mother…has been bothered about servants lately & is not*
> *suited yet, everyone complains how hard they are to get now. One*
> *escapes that in China!*

The Carrall girls were too independent-minded for many men, and
Maude as well as Muriel eventually married men with experience of
life in China. Women too could disapprove, as their lack of domestic
skills showed up when servants were absent. A female cousin thought
they were

> *mostly not very good at anything — just lounged about and let*
> *Uncle Jack clean their shoes for them. We were rather scornful of*
> *the Carrolls' [sic]. Another disagreed. 'The Carrolls…did not*
> *just sit about drinking tea — they were very energetic, interesting*
> *and amusing people.'[2]*

Kath's later memories were of Uncle Jack voluntarily helping out,
showing his love and care Fawcus fashion, not in words but in deeds.
'*When mother had no help, it was Uncle Jack who came down early to light*
the fires and brush out the dining room and after evening dinner it was he
who washed up.'

Kath Trains as a Teacher, and Muriel and Emily as Wives

Kath had now determined to get a Teaching Certificate in Britain. She
explained her plans in a note with one of her mother's letters to Hart
on 21 October: '*I am home again…for good…I am now going to begin studying*
for the Cambridge Higher Local Examination, which takes place next June.
[This was the examination she had missed in 1900, and which her sister
took in 1901 in Shanghai.] *Later I hope to have a year's training, and then*
I ought to be ready to teach at any school in England!'
   Maude told him:

> *We have become quite reconciled to England, its people & climate*
> *by now, though the latter can sometimes be very disagreeable… .*
> *Muriel generally spends her week-ends at Putney where her future*
> *mother-in-law lives. I do not know when she is thinking of getting*
> *married, as it all seems rather vague. Emily & her husband are in*
> *Scotland, shooting and fishing. She sends letters full of minute*

details as to the number of head shot by Charlie, & is evidently frightfully proud of his doings...

Charlie was now on leave awaiting his next posting, and Emily was finally having a proper married life.

Kath sent Hart her Christmas letter from 'Over Dinsdale' on 24 November 1904, where winter had begun early. As in Chefoo, the snow-covered trees entranced her. The family were gathered together, as Charles Forbes and Emily were staying a week, and Muriel's fiancé and sundry cousins were often in. Kath enjoyed the Christmas shopping and visits to the theatre. Women now also had their clubs — useful, as it was not the done thing for "ladies" to go to a restaurant without an accompanying man.[3]

I went to a Ladies' Club in town for the first time last week; it was tea-time & such cosy tea-parties were going on (one can invite gentlemen friends) & some violins were playing.

...In January I am going to the Winchester High School...[This is now known as St Swithun's. Her fees were paid by Uncle Jack.] *At present I take History lessons twice a week & give a few lessons to the lowest form in the Surbiton High School.*

When Frances visited Kath in Winchester, she found a China connection. She told Sir Robert in her birthday letter on 19 January 1905:

...one of the ladies, who keeps the boarding houses for the High School girls there, knows you well by name & spoke very feelingly of your kindness when her brother Cyril Farrar died in Peking, 21 years ago...& as you may guess I could agree with her in her opinion about you. She could hardly believe you were still out there & that nothing (Boxer troubles) brought you home for a holiday & rest...I left [Kathleen] in the middle of a German & French examination! I hope she will not find it too difficult to settle down to regular school routine again.

Hart replied to this deluge of letters on 28 January 1905. Although the war was indeed causing extra work, he was amused by the doings of the girls.

Dearest Kathleen,

I have before me yours of the 21st Oct and 24th Nov, Maude's of the 22nd Oct, & Mama's of the 21st & 25th Oct... . I was very glad to hear from you all, but I am overtaken with work, and so pressed for time, that a quick reply (although Eric does wind up with a PS WRITE SOON) is out of the question...

It must be nice for you to be at home again & to have so many friends around you with such a big family party, & with so many relations & acquaintances assembling from time to time, there must be much enjoyment for all...Maude...tells me Muriel was going to her mother-in-law, having marriage (a somewhat vague sort of thing) in prospect: I thought mother-in-law came after marriage & not before — although in China, when a girl is betrothed, they say "mother-in-law has been fixed on for her". [In the family Muriel is remembered as witty, amusing and extravagant; so her intended would have to do well as a diamond trader to earn enough to keep her!]

I am glad to hear that Emily & her good man are having such a fine spell together: she must be a capital "retriever" by this time, looking after all his game — and games. [The cultured, musical Emily that he had known was adapting to life with a hunting, fishing and shooting Scottish family - Figure 10.4.]

Thank your Mama for the photos she sent me...the boys are both thriving well. I wish I had one of you: I lost what I had before the siege troubles, and I was specially sorry to lose the one I had of poor Frances — she looked so bonnie! But, as for you other girls, I had met you all & had your likenesses by heart — & in my heart too, & don't require pictures to bring you before me, for I often think of you all: I remember your christening so well and the days when I used to carry Muriel round the garden on my shoulder — I sh'd not like to have to do that now!

We had a great day on the 21st when Walter Richardson married Miss Otterwell: all Peking was at the wedding & the day was splendid. Just now we have perishing cold winter weather with a hard frost, & blue sky, & a cutting wind. I hear crackings in every direction, for the ante-New Year holidays have begun, and today the 'God of the kitchen' has gone to heaven for a week's frolic at leisure with the other deities. I applied for home leave a month ago, but was told I must wait till the war is over. Port Arthur has since fallen & I hear Oyama & Kuropatkin are having a fierce struggle today over Moukden [Shenyang]. It is thought the Japanese success out here & the internal troubles now coming to a head in Russia may soon end the war: so perhaps I'll get away this year. As I shall be seventy on the 20th February I am half anxious to be off: I want to see home & friends once more after such a long absence (I was last in England in 1878), & the work is now so heavy it wants a younger ??? & more active man. But I don't intend to bolt so long as I can work & the Chinese want me to stay, for they have always treated me well & the new developments are all so interesting. Staff all returned & work all back in Peking now.

Kath wrote to him on his birthday, 20th Feb 1905, with apologies for being late.

I have thought of you such a lot lately for I have been reading a book with many references to you — "The Memorials of Cyril (Lipton) Farrer,"…the description of your Christmas dance recalled our visit to you & the happy days Maude & I had with you…

[She was, as her mother feared, finding the adjustment difficult.]…*I have only been here a month & I feel inclined to beat an ignominious retreat & go home, though all the time duty tells me to stick at it! It is quite like school again & after being so free the last years it is hard to be under restraint…. There are eight school-girls in this house, it is presided over by a widow lady & her two daughters. We go to school every day, returning for meals here. At present I am busy with History (French, English & Constitutional), French & German, and History of Education. Most of the girls play the violin or 'cello but they are all in the elementary stage.*

She appreciated the fine buildings of Winchester (though on later acquaintance told him that like most cathedral towns it was sleepy and dull compared to Hamburg). She ended apologetically with news about her sisters' doings. '*I am sure you must be wearied with all these details, but I have only got ourselves to write about.*'

Hart picked up the despondency in her tone and responded quickly.

4 April 1905

Dearest Kathleen

I am overwhelmed with work! I am like a juggler standing between half a dozen tables on each of which I have some hundred plates in motion which I have to keep whirling, without fall or collision, and I cannot give over the care of any to another for I am responsible for all & awfully afraid of a mischance from a wrong touch or a moment's neglect: & their number keeps on rising & their size & importance varies, while some are nickel, others good strong delf [sic], & others of the most fragile glass! I assure you it is very hard to attend to so much, & that I have done it so long, so continuously, &, so far, without mishap, is really almost too good to be true — and yet it is fact! And here I am stuck, although in my 71st year, as gay as ever, busier than ever, and with no prospect of being unharnessed before 'the old man with the scythe' comes along & whips my head off!

Your delightful letter of the 20th Feb came today and it makes me happy to think you had me in your mind that day so lovingly. The people here are all very kind, and I was just overpowered with compliments & good wishes from all quarters & all sorts of folk. [These included the 70th birthday tribute from his staff quoted in the Prologue. Seventy is a very important age in Chinese culture.]

It is curious you should have just met poor Farrer's sister and got his book: I too had a copy before the siege, but alas! it went off in the burning house with all my other valuables. He was a very nice promising youth & his death was a loss to us: I never saw anybody looking lovelier in death. His head was turned slightly to one side, & the faintest of smiles gave the face quite a happy appearance: it did not sadden one, for it said "Where is thy victory?" [He probably expected this to be passed on to Farrer's sister.] *The number of people who have died out here & under me is frightful, horrid to contemplate, and it often allows me to reflect that I have been spared so long*

I sympathise with you in your loneliness, but study is such a delight that I also envy you — long ago it was my intention, if I ever were home again, to go in for another course of study — in science chiefly — at Cambridge, so as to reach heaven with fuller & better prepared mind, but now I give up the idea, for I am too old & eyes grow weak & memory begins to take a fitful hold of the new. Curiously enough, the days of my childhood, three score & more years ago, are coming back clearer & clearer, but I already forget some things I was occupied with yesterday!

Your details did not worry me at all for I take such an interest in you dear girls — your mother included — that the very smallest detail is pleasant to read about.

We had great doings last Sunday when Li Hung Chang's memorial Tablet was put in the ancestral Hall, & today all Peking was at the Railway Station at 7 a.m. to say goodbye to Mr & Mrs. Conger who were transferred from the U.S. Legation here to the Embassy in Mexico. [He was the American Minister, and both had endured the siege with their children.] *On Friday 7th we are all bidden to a quiet dinner at the German Legation, at which "Son Altesse Royale le Prince Fréderic Léopold de Prussia deigneron [sic] assister". What with work, official entertainments, & other calls on my time, I have few minutes to spare, & have to leave undone hundreds of things I'd like to do for every ten I put through! Don't think I forget you if I don't write, for you all come in to my head often enough, being already in my heart, and I always am, with love, affectionately yours, Robert Hart.*

P.S. Elsie Drew is to marry Mr Mackintosh of the H.K. Bank, & Grace Capstick is engaged to Mr Hobart, 2 Wiltshire Regiment.

Kath replied on 19th April when she was back at Over Dinsdale for the Easter holidays. After enthusiastic thanks for the photo he had enclosed, she gave him important family news in a circuitous fashion:

Emily is here, her 'good man' is now on H.M.S. "Queen" in the Mediterranean Fleet, she talks of joining him at Malta in the autumn after a certain event which will have the curious effect of making mother a grandmother! Muriel, Maude & I hope to take some good bicycle rides these holidays if only the weather is fine, but it is so changeable & at present quite cold. We often wish for a

China sky, but here at any rate the spring is lovelier. The first
green is just out everywhere, & the birds are making such a noise,
the primroses are lovely. Today being "primrose day"⁴, omnibus
drivers, "cabbies", butchers etc are wearing bunches… . We heard
from the Drews the other day, Elsa naturally full of her
engagement & very happy.

Frances wrote to Hart in June to thank him for Volume 1 of the Decennial Report, as already quoted. As well as reminding her of her husband's winter illness, it brought back her own past, as a loyal Customs wife.

I do not remember ever hinting to you or to anyone else in the
service how wishful I was to see how the report read as a whole &
after so long a lapse of time I had quite…concluded the report a
thing of my past…thank you sincerely for having had it sent on to
us. I will take it round to show to Mrs. Sampson. It is wonderful
how the China years of her life seem yet so fresh in her memory &
anything connected with China & more especially with the son
buried there will appeal to her very much…

She wrote to Hart again on 12 July 1905 to tell him of the safe arrival of her first grandson, born on 30 June. '*I have been with* [Emily] *since but am soon returning home to give place to Maude as Mother & son are both doing well.*' Charles was at sea, on his way to Malta. The family support Emily received on the birth of her first child is a contrast to Kath's later fate.

Kath wrote after success in her examinations.

I am glad to say I passed both in History & Logic. My next
subjects are German, French, & English Literature in June 1906
which will complete my certificate…I was much interested in the
Peking news; we still get the "North China Herald" and always
look for any news of our old friends. Mother has just taken the
latest "North China" over to Emily…

Maude & I were in town the other day and went to the South
Kensington Museum. We saw the wonderful skeleton of some
antediluvian animal which has lately been unearthed.

This must be the dinosaur which still has pride of place there.
After her half-term break she wrote again on 12 November 1905.

The family gathering was small as Maude was with Emily in Malta and Muriel's engagement continued its unusual course: *'Muriel and her fiancé and his mother spent a fortnight at Exmoor, in the Lorna Doone country last month'.* Kath went with her mother and the younger children to Bexhill for a fortnight in the summer.

> *We all much enjoyed being at the sea again, though I don't think the sea-side places in England half come up to Chefoo.*
> *I am now working pretty hard for my finals next June, after which I have yet another examination, the Cambridge Teacher's Diploma. All this training takes a long time...*

Frances added Christmas wishes and her hopes that in Malta. *'Maude may meet with some congenial spirits, the more I see of life the more I hold in people marrying.'* She continued with her worries about Eric, who was wondering whether he really wanted to be so far away as China. *'Boys are problems & I do not want them to fail in life.'*

Maude sent her Christmas wishes from *106 Strade S. Francesco, Floriane, Malta* and an account of her enjoyments. Hart annotated it: *'Ans'd with an Easter Egg £20, 19 Jan 06'.* As he addressed it to 'Miss Maude Carrall, Malta' the money took a long while to arrive. She may not have needed new dresses as Kath explained:

> *Jan 10th 1906*

> *Unfortunately Emily has been very unwell since they have been in Malta and Maude is housekeeping for her, and helping to look after the baby. Charlie has been with them all the time, and is immensely proud of the boy. Maude was enjoying herself amongst all the naval and military people...but since Emily has been so poorly, she has had a quieter time.*

She gave him news of the rest of the family, then continued with her first experiences of politics.

> *Uncle took me to a most interesting meeting at the Queen's Hall in London the other day. The object was to express public indignation at the Russian outrages on the Jews,[5] so of course there were many Hebrews present. Lord Rothschild was in the chair & the speakers were the Bishop of Ripon, a Cardinal, & the*

President of the Scottish Free Church, representing the Anglicans, Roman Catholics, & non-conformists respectively… . The General Election has now commenced and rouses great excitement everywhere. This is the first time I have ever experienced one & the posters are very amusing, but the abusive and unjust epithets on rival candidates make one quite indignant. I long to go to a meeting, but Uncle thinks they are too rowdy.

Kath would have no vote in the forthcoming election, as politics were still a male preserve. She showed no interest in the suffragette movement, but press cuttings she kept show that the economic handicaps of her gender did concern her.

For most of the family China was fading into the past. Frances wrote as usual for Hart's birthday in 1906, but *'I am so taken up with home affairs & correspondence that gradually I have dropped writing to the East. It is not that I forget but time is wanting'*. Her letter is mainly about Eric, approaching seventeen but *'I get more puzzled than ever about his future career'*. She was also *'much worried about Emily's health…or I should say rather her nerves — she is ordered the rest cure and Maude is meantime looking after things for her'*. Nobody seems to have realised that Emily was pregnant again, and her second son was born fourteen months after the first.

The family still had to be careful about money, and Maude's next letter on 24 June 1906 showed that Hart's delayed gift made a most desirable replacement possible.

Your letter of January 19th has at last reached me after many travels! I was so glad to hear from you & thank you very much for your "Easter Egg"…I must tell you what the "chick" is like. It is going to be a bicycle. You do not know how I have wanted to replace my former one…I slipped on the tram-lines & a large van following me ran over me & the bike. I escaped with bruises but my machine was not so fortunate & proved beyond repair. [She told him about Emily's illness.] As you can imagine my time was too fully occupied for such vain frivolities as capturing or being captured by the present "Knights of Malta".

In her next letter on 12 July 1906 Frances told him how the loss of the freedom-giving bicycle had distressed Maude. *'There seemed no chance*

*of replacing it so that your unexpected present raised her to the seventh heaven
of delight.'* She reverted as usual to Eric. *'Without influence I can find nothing
at home that will advance him in life as his father hoped.'* A newspaper picture
of Sir Robert sent by her brother William in Falmouth prompted a
further desperate letter about Eric on 23 August, when she also thanked
him for the second volume of the Decennial Reports. These reminded
her that his father had always hoped:

> *the boy would go to College but that we cannot now attain to, still
> a little influence exercised by a good friend may do much for him.*
> [Eric, she acknowledged, was no good at exams.] *So I needs
> must be very importunate to get something good for him without
> an exam…I am sure if only he gets well started he will succeed in
> life.*

His school masters had said he was very good at music and shooting.
The first would have interested Hart, but was not the only qualification
required for a Customs career! He told Campbell to put him on the
1908 list, but by that time he had retired and Campbell had died.

The End of Kath's Story

Kath was now near to qualifying, and facing the reality of what was
open to her. The High Schools were by this time well stocked with
women teachers who had obtained a degree. Competition meant starting
salaries had fallen to £70-80 for non-residential graduates and £40-60
for a college-trained teacher like Kath (compared to the £60 her uncle
had offered her if she helped her mother at home.[6] Though compulsory
education ended at thirteen some higher elementary schools were
opened after 1900 to provide education for children aged ten to fifteen.
These were under the Local Education Boards and their Inspectors. Kath
did not relish the prospect of teaching in these. Present-day teachers
may sympathise with the reasons given in her next letter to Hart on
December 2 1906:

> *…I completed my certificate in June, & am now doing my final
> year's training for teaching and working up for the diploma in
> June 1907 — after which I shall at last begin "to labour truly to
> get my own living" — but I wish it needn't be in England where*

*there seems to be nothing but drudgery & competition &
overcrowding among teachers. I have vague dreams of going to
Canada & being a '"schoolmarm" in a log-hut "far from the
madding crowd" of inspectors & Board of Education regulations,
for I have come to the conclusion that I don't want to teach
children anything but how to enjoy life and to live in the widest
sense of the word — & perhaps a school-inspector mightn't agree
quite with my point of view.*

*In a fortnight I shall be home again for four weeks holiday. I
have been thinking that this may be our last Christmas together for
— who knows — Muriel will be married next year! Eric will have
left school — & I will have begun teaching perhaps in Canada!*

What had put Canada into her mind? The only known connection
is the man Maude was to marry, with whom she was probably
corresponding, Julian Ridout, a Canadian by birth. Hart's reply, in his
last known letter to Kath, was sympathetic, but advised her to seek a
Man not a Mission. Women should have equality with men, but they
were always going to face disadvantages imposed by their biological
role. He did not mention his temporary reunion with his wife in 1906,
which had eaten into his letter-writing time, but her sad tone now
prompted a rapid reply.

13 January 1907

Dearest Kathleen,

*Yours of 2 December came today — Sunday. Do not blame me for
silence, much less reproach me with forgetfulness! You often come
into my mind, and are always in my heart, but that tyrant Work
has me in its grip: it is like opium — I can't give it up & I enjoy
it, but it occupies me all day & every day and goes on growing &
growing in both volume and importance, and also fortunately in
interest, and the result is that I am more of a recluse than ever —
seldom going out, & so fully engaged that correspondence and
private affairs are for the most part neglected.*

*I am glad to get all your news and I am wondering whither you
will wing your flight once your pinions are fit and your opinions
sufficiently formed to decide your course. Some good man's loving
arms would be the best nest for you! I am quite of the idea that*

women should have equal status, equal advantage, & equal opportunity: but sex is against adequate result in most cases, and the original idea of a "help-mate" for man cannot be improved on. Here a charming girl & devoted infirmary Doctor-ess (Dr Lily Saville)[7] learnt the language, established a women's hospital, took over the female practice of the Mission, started a nurses' training school, and was going ahead famously — doing so well in fact that another girl doctor (Doctor Norah Linwood) was sent out to assist her. The latter arrived, studied Chinese over a year, and then, wooed & won, went off elsewhere! Meanwhile Dr Saville's health had broken down under her work & anxiety, & she had to go away. Thus all she did falls to pieces & it besides makes practice harder for the male doctors of the Mission. Indeed the great deficit of all Protestant Missions is want of continuity, & the possession of that quality is one of the strong points of the Catholics. But woman — unless she takes vows & lives & dies a nun — is out of her place in men's work, & her success only accentuates subsequent failures. So, go in for a Man rather than a Mission!

I hope your Xmas was as jolly as you expected. Mine was solitary: I have not accepted invitations nor entertained the last two months, for age is telling on me & has found out one or two weak spots in my armour, so the house & office are the best places for me to keep well in and make mischief. I have had a very busy & a very worried year: I planned to go home in May 1907, but something has just occurred to upset this & I am "marking time" & not "marching", though smothered in work — happily successful work.

Kath took his advice to settle for a man, but not immediately. A brief diary shows that she taught at Boscombe after leaving Winchester, and 'broke up' on 23 July 1909, evidently finding it as unsatisfactory as she expected. On 3 August an 'interview with Miss Penrose' led to a post in Florence at the latter's finishing school that autumn. Besides teaching, she accompanied the girls to concerts, operas, galleries, etc. She loved the art, the music, and the walks — 'down by the Arno. The moon was full and the whole scene was such as one dreams of'. A brief Christmas holiday in Rome, where she met the Drews, was a hectic round of sightseeing. On 24 May she saw King Edward's funeral on the 'cinematograph' and on another occasion saw her first aircraft. She then had a month at a similar school in Paris in July 1910, with another round of sight-seeing. After the holidays she spent another term in Paris but returned to be bridesmaid at Maude's wedding to Julian Ridout in January 1911. Even for Kath, family came before career.

The spring of 1911 was full of family doings. She, Maude and their mother paid a final visit to Sir Robert on his birthday 'at home', on 20 February. *'He has much aged & is not able to get about easily, after his stroke.'* They left after chatting with him for a quarter of an hour — the regulation time for a call. He had returned from China in 1908.

She then applied successfully for a post in Canada, at Havergal College in Winnipeg,[8] leaving on SS *Canada* on 31 August 1911. Her diary shows plenty of socialising with other teachers and people she met at the churches she went to [Figure 10.5]. She gave a talk at the German club, in German, on the 'Boxer Krieg' on 28 March 1912 and joined the Literary Club. The diary stops abruptly on Palm Sunday, 31 March 1912. The next three entries are brief: *'24 August 1912. Marriage to J. O. Newton. 6 Aug. 1913 birth of Keeve, daughter. 1929 J. O. Newton died'.*

The marriage was a disaster. Keeve told me her parents were both intellectuals, and this brought them together in Winnipeg. John Newton was a lawyer from Dungannon, Northern Ireland, who hoped to make money in Canada in land development. He made his second visit to Winnipeg in April 1912. He must have courted Kath rapidly, for they married on 24 August 1912. She had no family witnesses. Marriage then meant resigning from the school so she also lost her easy contacts with her fellow teachers. A daughter, Kathleen Frances Newton, always known as Keeve, was born a year later on 6 August 1913. Unlike Emily, Kath had no female relative to support her. However, her brother Eric spent two years in Winnipeg 1912–14. If this was in hope of finding a permanent post, it was unsuccessful. He returned on 23 September 1914, first class, but with no occupation stated, to join the army in the war that had just started.[9]

It seems likely that Kath suffered acute post-natal depression after the birth, and ship's records show that her daughter, aged six months, was sent home with a domestic to her Newton relatives in Ireland, in January 1914. John Newton returned to Britain in January 1915 with the Canadian Overseas Expeditionary Force. In 1916 my mother was helping to look after Kath and Keeve at 'Over Dinsdale'. After the war,

Kath, with Keeve, went back to Winnipeg and her husband, but the reunion was a failure. Her husband put her in a lunatic asylum from which Christian Scientist friends rescued her. She never rejoined her husband after her final return to England in November 1924.

> It was Uncle Jack who came up to meet my train in London from Liverpool, where I landed. He sat beside me in the suburban train we took for Kingston, very quietly, never referring to the tragedy, but he took my hand and gently pressed it and he stood by me till I found a teaching post.[10]

She obtained a post at a good school, Croham Hurst School, then in Croydon, in 1925, which Keeve also attended.[11]

When I first met my aunt in 1946 she was sixty-four, retired from teaching but still tutoring foreign students. I immediately liked her. Much later, on 22 June 1965, she could still fascinate a reporter, John Sinclair of the Belfast *News Letter*, by her account of Sir Robert Hart and the Boxer siege. He wrote:

> Mrs. Newton has retained a deep affection for China and the Chinese people and continues to take a lively interest in all that goes on there nowadays. To talk to her is not only to find oneself brought face to face with a slice of the past but to be diverted and enriched by a mind which has absorbed a great deal of experience and remained fresh, youthful and unprejudiced. [He regretted the absence of a portrait of Sir Robert Hart in the Belfast Gallery.] Instead I...had his portrait painted for me...by a lady who seemed unaware that she herself was an admirable and fascinating subject.[12]

Changing families?

The Carralls, like all in Britain, were sorely tested by the shattering Great War of 1914–18. In addition to the huge number of deaths, it left many survivors physically and emotionally wounded. Charles Forbes had retired from the navy in 1909 to become an Inspector for the Lifeboat Institution. Aged forty-one, he was recalled to service in 1914, and after a relatively quiet war in Portsmouth, became Transport Officer for the British Salonika force from January to August 1918. This was part of a disastrous, bloody, little-known allied campaign against the Bulgarians in which the British land forces were defeated. He was mentioned in despatches for his distinguished services and gallant conduct and awarded the C.B.E., but was so mentally scarred that he committed suicide in November 1918, leaving Emily to bring up three sons on a widow's pension.

Muriel married Henry Constable Roberts in March 1907. She divorced him in 1926, but with sufficient alimony for a comfortable lifestyle till her death in 1940. Maude's marriage to Julian Ridout of the Royal Artillery was happy and durable. Their child, my cousin Frances, preserved her mother's photo albums and other relics of the China years.

My grandmother's worries about Eric were justified. During the war he became a captain, on secondment to the Indian army, and took part in the Mesopotamian campaign in which the Turks inflicted heavy losses on the British forces. He married in August 1919 and was unsuccessful in various business ventures. His wife divorced him in 1929. I remember him as a jobless alcoholic failure but Kath always had a soft spot for him. He died shortly after her, in 1971. Young Jim also disappointed. On 24 March 1918 he joined what was then the naval air arm with a war-time commission. He died young, attempting to become an artist in Paris.

Until she died in 1929 Frances, with Uncle Jack, provided a home and refuge to any family member who needed it. Figure 10.6 shows her and visiting children and grandchildren at Over Dinsdale in 1925. After her death Uncle Jack took a room at the Cambridge Mission in Camberwell Road, London, continuing to walk daily to Lincoln's Inn. Every evening he helped in a club for poor boys, and gave up one evening a week to provide free legal advice. He died in his office in 1937, aged eighty-six. Kath helped clear up his belongings and preserved the Fawcus and Speciall family letters and diaries which he had kept.

Frances would have been saddened by the divorces in her family. When Kath wrote her diary in 1900, divorce, although possible on limited grounds since 1857, had been rare enough for a remarried divorced woman to merit a comment in her diary. By the 1920s it had become relatively common in the middle classes, though still an expensive route to take for less well-off families. The self-discipline which both partners need to maintain a lifelong bond was, as Hart recognised, strengthened in the nineteenth century by religious beliefs in the sanctity of marriage. By the 1920s the failure of the churches to come to terms with modern sciences and technological advances in birth control were undermining also, as Hart as a young man could recognise as a danger, aspects of social morality. But in many respects the role of women had changed comparatively little, except that families were smaller. The norm for my female cousins, a decade or two older than me, was to work for a few years before marriage, and then become full-time wives and mothers, with one to three children. With jobs scarce in the depression years of the 1930s, they did not resume paid work as their children grew up, though they might contribute to society by voluntary work. The 1914-18 war had brought the vote for women, but comparatively little change in their main role, if they had been fortunate enough to marry despite the loss of male life.

My mother, Gwen, married in 1916, but I was not born till 1931 and my contemporaries followed a different pattern to my cousins. Emerging from university in the 1950s, with still very little equal pay or equality of opportunities for advancement on offer, we mostly married early, but found opportunities to work again as our children grew up. The married women returners, as we were called, were welcomed back into the professions in the 1960s. By then, society really was changing, not only because equal pay was becoming more common, but also because women younger than us were given new sexual options by the pill. In the 1950s, female contraceptive devices were fitted in family planning clinics only to the married or about to be married. Children before marriage were still a shame and disaster.

It is time to return to Hart, and to see how he was dealing, amidst increasing frailty and loneliness, with his own two families, and with the many political problems of the new century, causing the work and worry which he mentioned in his letters to Kath.

CHAPTER ELEVEN

HART: THE END

When Hart started his correspondence with my Aunt Kath, he was conscious of being at the height of his powers. In 1893 he had received the long-hoped-for baronetcy from the Queen, an honour from his home country that would pass to his son. In China, he could tell Campbell on 9 August 1896 that:

> *I am stronger than ever and about to be made use of over a far wider field... . I have seemingly reached a height that the whole eighteen provinces can see, and that gives a prestige, and lays open ground, which nobody else can hope for right off... . Apart from work I have worries that I dare hardly acknowledge to myself — and yet these ghosts <u>will</u> walk occasionally. The worst of it is I am utterly <u>alone</u> and have not a single <u>friend or confidant</u> — man, woman or child...there come <u>spasms of loneliness</u> which hit hard.*

Friends were important to Hart, as we have seen in the time given over to them on his busy but brief first leave in 1866. He kept in touch with old friends, and employed their sons when he could, as with the Brazier family. Making new friends was more difficult. He was naturally a sociable man, and his dinner parties, dances and musical evenings were popular. Through them many Customs students came to know and trust him, but he remained their boss. He could also befriend the wives and daughters of his staff and associates, but their stays in Peking were generally temporary, and the relationship had to be maintained by correspondence. His ability to do this and the financial and emotional support he gave to female friends has been demonstrated in his relationship with the Carrall girls and their mother. However, the kind of intimate conversation he had had with Mrs Glover in Shanghai could never be entrusted to a letter.

The worries that he dare not acknowledge must frequently have concerned his children, legitimate and illegitimate, but could not be discussed with his associates in Peking. He could write of them to his friend Campbell in the London office, but they could not safely be discussed in a letter to Frances or any Customs wife in China. His son Bruce ticked him off for sending a telegram regarding Nollie via Bredon's office in Shanghai, with the result, he said, that it had become public property on the China coast. He had no family with whom to share his worries. His younger brother, Jem, was away for much of this time, based in India on a long mission concerning Tibet. Jem's growing addiction to alcohol was another source of secret sadness. Hester was in London, and as he had acknowledged in his diary in 1885, their attitudes to the bringing up of their children differed. Proximity meant she was the prime influence on them. Her example was that of a woman who enjoyed luxury without having either to work for it herself or to play any part in supporting her husband's work. She and her son felt entitled to a high status lifestyle by virtue of their relationship with Hart — but Hart wished his son to develop self-reliance.[1]

The Illegitimate Children in the 1890s

During the 1880s Hart's dealings with his wards were conducted mainly through his lawyer, Hutchins, but on 10 August 1890 he told Campbell that he had not had news of Herbert and the others for a long time, and he repeated his query on 19 October. This crossed with a series of replies Campbell sent in October. Hutchins was making some arrangement for Herbert and his sister to live together. This suggests that Anna had at some point returned to Britain, but that at thirty-one she was not married. Herbert was making about £150 p.a. in a decorator's business (a decent, if not large, income). Arthur was married and not turning out so well. A second letter said that Hutchins had tried without success to persuade Anna and Herbert to go abroad, for Herbert was planning to marry. Campbell later enclosed a cutting from the *Daily News* of 22 October 1890 with the marriage notice. Hart was pleased. He had probably received more details from Hutchins, who, he told Campbell in December 1890, had done excellently for the young people.

The 1891 census carries no information on any of them, though Herbert, his wife, and their son, another Robert Hart, reappear in the 1901 census. They were then living in Leyton, Essex, not very far from West Ham where Herbert had spent his childhood. He described himself as aged thirty-five, an architect, employed, not a partner. In a legal declaration Sir Robert made in 1910 he stated that Anna had died 'some seventeen years ago' but I have been unable to find a British death certificate for her around 1893. (There are many for women named Anna Hart but none fit her age and circumstances.) Possibly she returned to Miss Peile and died in Switzerland. Her death was not mentioned in letters to or from Campbell, so Hutchins probably dealt with any issues arising from it.

The difficult child was Arthur who, according to Hart's 1905 declaration, went to Canada about the same time as Anna died. Hart told Campbell in a letter in November 1893 that he had had a letter from him 'asking for £1000!' which may have been in connection with his departure. He left it for his lawyer to answer. This was at an embarrassing time, when the offer of a baronetcy was on the table, but could still be upset by a scandal. (The time had passed when a temporary relationship with a Chinese girl was regarded as normal for young men; they were instead expected to find a wife from the more plentiful supply of expatriate women in China.) There was also a problem of an impostor 'John Hart' about whom on 6 May 1894 Hart told Campbell he had already spent enough money, thanking Campbell for his efforts in this matter a fortnight later. However, it was the legitimate son and heir, Bruce, who had been *a sore trouble and constant worry* during the previous twelve months (letter to Campbell, 8 April 1894).

The Legitimate Children

In November 1891 Hart was making plans for his twenty-three-year-old daughter Evey to visit him. Hester decided not to accompany her, and she came out on the same ship as one of Campbell's sons. She arrived in Peking at the end of April 1892 and within a month was engaged to William Beauclerk, in the British consular service, at the British Legation. Hart could not object on the grounds either of his position or his lineage, but he was distressed that he was twenty years older than her, a widower with three children. His sister Teresa and Mrs Glover had both shown him the perils of marriage to an older man. He had to make the best of it, however, for Evey was of full age, and he found himself plunged into wedding preparations for the daughter he was already losing. On 3 July, he told Campbell

> *Evey as an unengaged girl was a delight in the house and garden, but since she has said "Yes" to B., I have lost her completely...'*
> [and on 21 August] *'the young lady is so much more his fiancée than my daughter that I am becoming a sort of hotel-keeper.*

The wedding preparations were rushed as Beauclerk wanted the marriage on 5 September, as he was to take charge of the Legation at the end of the month, in the Minister's absence. Evey's dress (for which she had two spares made in China) arrived only the day before. Hart had chosen from a catalogue five diamonds of 'the purest water' each fit to use as a brooch, hair pin and pendant, and together to form a tiara for the wedding. They arrived on 8 September, when the couple were honeymooning in the hills. Hart wrote brief business notes on the engagement to Campbell, asking him for other necessary items, such as new clothes for himself, and to act as trustee for her marriage settlement for which he provided £10,000. He also decided that he must stay in Peking for a year or two longer rather than go on leave, in order to be near her. The young woman was soon to be a 'hotel-keeper' herself, helping her new husband in October to host a visiting British MP who was to become the future Lord Curzon.

Hart told Kath in his letter of 17 December 1896 that he had always been alone except for short visits from Evey in 1892 and Bruce in 1895. This suggests he did not see much of her after her marriage. His dealings with an acting head of the British Legation who was also his son-in-law could not have been easy, though a letter to Campbell of 10 November 1895 shows he thought well of Beauclerk's work as Chargé d'Affaires. The only references to Evey in his letters to Campbell were to the birth in China of her daughters in 1894 and 1896. In 1896 Beauclerk was sent to Hungary for two years and then to Peru. Evey and her children were back in London in 1901, where, according to a letter from Bruce, she was minding her spending carefully. He thought her marriage was rocky. Like her mother she enjoyed travelling. At various times Hart enclosed letters for her or her daughters with his messages to Campbell, but the only direct reference to her is on 15 May 1904, when he told Campbell that he had just had a letter from her from Paris — 'What a wanderer she is!' Nothing suggests that he recovered a warm relationship with the little daughter he had once so much loved. Evie's husband died in Lima in 1908.

Bruce, born in 1874, was legally under parental control till 1895. Just before Evey's wedding, on 28 August 1892 Hart asked Campbell to look him up, as Bruce had not been writing during his first year at Oxford and his father feared he was harming his health by dissipation. He also wrote himself, advising Bruce not to conceal any ill health, but to go at once to a first-class doctor. Bruce evidently replied frankly that he had some genital problem. Hart sent this and his reply to Campbell on 4 December, advising Bruce to get to London to see Dr Macrae as soon as the 'Mods' were over — an examination taken by classicists at Oxford in their second year — and at the same time asking Macrae to be fatherly with him rather than stiffly professional. 'You see I really don't know what Bruce now is and I hardly know how he is to be taken: but his letter shows right feeling and I want him to be properly treated without delay.' His own youthful misfortunes in Belfast would have been in his mind, but on 12 February 1893 Campbell telegraphed that Bruce had returned to Oxford well and jolly, after a small operation, but that he had failed his Mods, which he would have to retake.

Bruce then caused further parental consternation. The nineteen-year-old had engaged himself to marry the twenty-two-year-old Caroline (Carrie) Gibson — a binding promise, as we have already seen. On 12 March 1893 Hart asked Campbell to tell Bruce his father was in favour of a man marrying young, provided he could support himself and his wife, but that a father ought to be consulted before a son faced him with the choice between bearing the cost of a new family or of standing completely aloof. '_Men who marry must support themselves_ — get this idea into his head and let yeast work!' He was worried that the Gibson family would hold Bruce to his promise when the news of the baronetcy came out, and got Hutchins to make him a Chancery ward, which would prevent any marriage without the Court's consent. He hoped the delay would give both young people time to change their minds.

Bruce evidently wanted to visit his father and Hart telegraphed him to come out to Peking via the USA after he had retaken his examinations in June, and to bring his College books and a violin. Bruce arrived in September, and took a close interest in the question of arms for the new baronetcy. Hart told Campbell that he was a pleasant youth, but like his father in having a will of his own. He remained obstinately constant to Carrie Gibson. He studied Chinese a little (there was no more talk of a return to Oxford, so his father had to provide a job) and failed to take any interest in Peking society. In April 1894 Hart was alarmed when Bruce had an illness of a nervous type, and began to think he must allow the marriage, though he was anguished that his son showed no sign of a work ethic. This coincided with his trouble with Arthur and 'John Hart'. Bruce returned to England that summer. He joined the Customs in November as an assistant in the London office, Hart telling Campbell to make him earn his pay. Bruce caused a final disappointment by marrying Carrie privately on 19 December 1894, without informing his mother or Campbell, instead of doing it in the proper style for the heir of a distinguished father.

Bruce and his bride arrived in Peking in May 1895, Bruce to work as Hart's Personal Secretary. Hart was favourably impressed by his new daughter-in-law, and felt that she would be a good influence. On 2 June 1895 he could tell Campbell that Bruce was working '*cheerfully and well enough, but he has a deal to learn*'. In the summer Bruce was taken ill and went to the hills to recover. In April 1896 heart trouble occurred, and he went home in May. It is this second visit that was mentioned in Hart's letter to Kath; he evidently preferred, as with Evie after her marriage, to black out the unsatisfactory parts of his children's visits.

For the rest of his brief career Bruce worked in the London office, taking plenty of time off to recover from various ailments, which required holidays and cruises to treat. His worst period seems to have been between October 1901 and summer 1902, when he was drinking too much and causing Hart agony by threatening to go the same way as his brother. Jem had died on leave in England in November 1902 after a long illness caused by cirrhosis of the liver. With much help from Campbell and Carrie and this example of the consequences before him, Bruce seems to have got his drinking under control. (The bad spell could have been a delayed reaction to strain caused by the danger his father was under the year before.) The ever-threatened breakdown never occurred, and he lived to a normal old age. Hart's letters to Campbell show that he felt partly to blame for the way Bruce had turned out, since he had not been there to give guidance when he was young, but it is also clear that he felt that his mission in China had priority. Bruce was not without ability, and delighted Hart by a good report on the Postal Congress in Rome, as he told Campbell in a letter of 22 July 1906.

Hart's younger daughter, Mabel (Nollie to the family), caused an upheaval in 1900–1, while Hart was trying to deal with the aftermath of the siege of the Legations. Her engagement to the American, J. H. Perry (Jack), on leave as Third Assistant in the Customs, was the subject of ten letters now at Queen's University, Belfast. According to one from Perry to Hart in January, Hester had initially approved of him, but became cooler in October when she heard that one of Campbell's daughters had become engaged to a very wealthy man. Hart told Campbell in February 1901 that Nollie's letters were some of the nicest, but that prudence was against the match. He might not have thought the letter Nollie sent him on 1 May 1901 quite so nice as in it she raged at length against her mother, accusing her of unkindness, inconsistency and hypocrisy. She contrasted this with her father's more sympathetic letter, even though he had refused outright approval. She appealed to him at least to say that they could marry after a year if they were still of the same mind, a delay which she would try to bear while Jack, whose leave was nearly up, returned to China ahead of her. (She said that Bruce had suggested that their father might agree to this.) In law, she was old enough to marry without her father's consent, but Hester had told her that in that case she would not get the type of settlement Evey had received. (The income from £10,000 would provide a useful supplement to Perry's earnings, and would also give her, like Evey, some independence.) She followed this with a telegram on 9 April: 'Do wire consent miserable last appeal Mabel.'

The reply did not come and soon after she broke off her engagement. She wrote to her father on 26 May that she was in two minds whether she had done the right thing — feeling miserable about losing Jack, but confessing to not being sure that she would be happy in China. Bruce took the credit. According to him, Perry had frightened her out of giving him up months before, but Carrie and he had managed to pull her out of the affair, and now she was bright and happy, going to dances night after night, and looking a totally different person. Hart had told Campbell on 10 March that he did not approve of the match, firstly because Perry could barely support a wife, secondly, he was Hart's subordinate, and thirdly, he did not want Nollie to make her home in China. These, he added, were not reasons for forbidding it, and if she went ahead and married Perry, he would send her off *'with a blessing rather than a cold shoulder'*. (This implies that if she had married, she would have got a settlement.) It was these events which gave him his intense interest in the romantic dramas of the Carrall family.

The Truth Comes Out

The next unpleasant personal matter was in 1905, the year that saw his seventieth birthday on 20 February and the warm address from his staff quoted in the Prologue. He sent Kath a photo taken to commemorate the occasion (Figure 11.1). He was also well received by the Empress Dowager, though he complained to Campbell that she did not want him to take leave, although he was tired and bothered by headaches. Part of the problem was who was to succeed him, as Bredon was still not acceptable to several parties.

It would have been an unpleasant shock to get Campbell's letter of 25 June 1905, enclosing a letter from Foss, who had replaced Hutchins as his lawyer, telling him that Herbert intended to go to Canada and was asking for assistance. Still worse, on 30 June the *Morning Post* reported in its Court and Personal column that Mr Herbert Hart, eldest son of Sir Robert Hart, Bart. of Hong Kong, had left Liverpool the day before for Ontario, Canada. Lady Hart had promptly visited the newspaper, which issued a correction the next day, to say that this did not refer to the only son of Sir Robert Hart, Bart., Inspector-General of the Chinese Imperial Customs, Peking. Hart replied on 11 August from Beidaihe, where he was taking a much needed holiday, saying he was willing to help Herbert, if it could be done judiciously. However, Foss must have considered his demands unacceptable. Campbell's confidential letter to Hart on this does not survive but it seems that Herbert, backed by his lawyer, Anderson, had tried to obtain a fairly large sum by claiming that he was Hart's legitimate eldest son. Hart would have preferred to let the story die a natural death and felt that Lady Hart's actions risked adding to the 'conflagration'. He wrote:

> My principle...is to "face the music" and pay no "blackmail" — but this has to be whittled...to cause as little worry as possible to others. I wish you had dipped deeper into my purse and sent off Herbert with £100 instead of only a "Five Pound Note".

Hart also said that he had had a letter the year before from an E. B. Hart (Bruce's initials) saying a young man, possibly Arthur, was moving about Canada using his name. These events prompted a return of previous reflections on the difficulty of disposing of the products of the past and the recognition that his worst troubles had come from his own initial mistakes. He told Campbell that he had proffered information to Hester in 1866 but was told the past was the past, so he said no more. Hart's recollection of what he said to Hester in 1866, as reported in Chapter Two, might well be hazy, for only a month earlier in a letter of 9 July 1905 he had complained to Campbell that the doings of 1900 had swept away not only his personal archives, but also a lot of things out of his memory, so that things recalled by others he could no longer remember crisply and in detail.

Eight days later he wrote the declaration quoted in part in Chapter Two, on headed paper, describing his relationship with Ayaou as the common practice of the time, detailing their children and the payments he made her. He still refused to speak evil of her: *'She was a very good little girl & well behaved, but we were not married, and she was not my wife, and her children were illegitimate.'* He then stated clearly that his and Hester's son Edgar Bruce was his only legitimate son and the heir to the baronetcy. He asked Campbell to get this lodged with his lawyers. (He pushed Arthur's birth back to 1864, rather than the 1865 suggested by his letter to Campbell in 1875. Whenever it was that he finally told Hester about these children, he probably wanted to increase the distance between the relationship and the marriage.) On 27 October Campbell was able to reassure him that he did not think either Herbert or Arthur would cause trouble. Herbert might ask for some pecuniary help to establish himself, and if he did, Mr Foss would see that it was properly used. Although it seems certain from her prompt response to the *Morning Post* notice that Hester was fully aware of the 'wards' this may have been the first time his relationship with Ayaou was revealed to Bruce and possibly also to his daughters. All were now adult, but it could not have been easy for Hart, hitherto a respected if distant father, to have the sins of his youth brought into the open.

Herbert, described as a draughtsman in his death certificate, died on 28 April 1906, at 65 Elm Grove, County of York, Ontario, after a week's illness with a tubercular oesophagus. (He probably had long-standing pulmonary tuberculosis which had advanced to a stage where there was pressure on the tube conveying food from the mouth to the stomach.) Hart received this information in a letter from Herbert's lawyer, Mr Anderson, who evidently again referred to Herbert as Hart's eldest son. Hart told Campbell to pass the letter to his lawyers, asking them to inform Anderson that he had not described the deceased correctly, but that, as his widow and child were poorly off, some aid would not be refused, say £50 p.a. In October he heard that Foss had seen and corresponded with the widow and her friends, hinting that there would be money for the boy's education as a matter of charity, but insisting that Mr Anderson's letter must be withdrawn. The widow again raised the question of Herbert's legitimacy, and Foss closed the interview. Hart replied that he would rely on Foss to do the right thing — what that was is not known.

Little is known about Arthur. There are references in ships' passenger lists to a Mr Arthur Hart making crossings of the Atlantic up to 1930. Despite the references to his small size in youth he may have been the longest survivor.

After a stroke, Hart made more formal declarations in December 1910 in London, the first on his children by Ayaou and similar to the 1905 one, the second dealing with his children by Hester and their marriages. He wanted to make sure that when he died there was no doubt about his legitimate heirs.

The End of Hart's Career

During the family upheavals and the sad deaths of 1901–2 (Mrs Brazier and Jim Carrall as well as his brother Jem), Hart had been preoccupied with the negotiations over the Boxer indemnity. His aim was above all to preserve China from a scramble for its land, and he was working for the last time with Li Hongzhang. (Li died two months after the negotiations were concluded in September 1901. Hart mentioned his last memorial ceremony in his letter to Kath of April 1905.) The result was a scatter of new concessions and 'spheres of influence' but the large indemnity gave the powers an interest in maintaining a central government that could pay it.[2] The indemnities that the victorious powers demanded caused an expansion of the responsibilities of the Customs to create the necessary revenue flows. As he told Campbell when Bruce and Jem were ill, he had had to put personal grief aside, to concentrate on the matters in hand. He was also writing a series of articles aimed at securing better understanding in Britain and Europe of China's position and general philosophy, to counteract the horror aroused by the Boxers. These were collected in his book *These from the Land of Sinim*. He had few staff with him, for he had delegated most administrative matters to Bredon as his Deputy in Shanghai, while reserving policy issues for himself. He hoped this would ease Bredon's path to the succession. He knew that Bredon was opposed by the British Foreign Office and others, but felt under an obligation to him. Policy issues were plentiful, as new ports were being opened over which Japan or Russia wanted special privileges, France wanted the same in postal matters, and the take over of the native customs often buffeted against strong local interests. It was not till December 1904 that sufficient houses and offices were rebuilt to bring the main office back to Peking. The absence of staff and students reduced his social life, in which we saw them playing an important part in 1883 and 1900. If he had intermittently felt lonely before, he was more isolated than ever after the Boxer Rebellion, and this comes out clearly in his letters to Kath.

The Empress Dowager had finally returned to the capital in early 1902 and the modernisers in the regime were now given greater rein. The Empress herself began to invite foreign women and children into the Palace. More importantly, education was being reformed and expanded, and other measures were taken to encourage trade, railways and industry. By this time there was a growing group of young Chinese who had obtained a better knowledge of the world and western science through mission education, contact with Japan, or stays in Hong Kong and the international settlements. They were beginning to be influential in seeking to modernise China's governmental institutions. As part of this modernisation, on 9 May 1906 Hart heard, not directly but via the British Legation, of an edict by which the Chinese had introduced a Board to which Hart was to report, an intermediary between him and a reorganised Yamen for foreign affairs. It was a shock to which he had to adjust.

Nollie and Hester were then in Peking, having finally made an overdue visit from March to May 1906. (They got no mention in his last letter to Kath.) Hart told Campbell on 6 May 1906 that he was glad to see them, but found it difficult to accept the way they ate into his time. Meal times expanded, and his usual hour for letter-writing before dinner had to be given over to them. They also altered his housekeeping arrangements, opening the windows beyond the 4 a.m. to 7 a.m. which was his practice, and allowing in the flies! He told Campbell that he would feel a bit lonelier after having had their company for three months, but work would give him little time for moping. The worries over the new Board were enough to make him glad to have the end of family distractions, and as he told Campbell on 26 May 1906, there was also internal unrest and the possibility of trouble ahead.

Although suffering from increasing problems with eyesight and memory, he felt obliged to stay on (as the Chinese wished), to reassure his staff that their work and conditions would not be substantially changed under the new arrangements. The smooth transition to what was a more logical place for the Customs in the official hierarchy was his last major achievement. Tired, lonely and dispirited, he finally left in April 1908, after the death in December 1907 of his friend Campbell in the London office. Officially, it was leave for three years, with Bredon taking over as Acting DG till a successor could be decided, but Hart knew that it was the end of a long career. The Manchu dynasty he had served had finally taken the modernisation path that he had tried to promote, but too late to maintain its power. The sickly reforming Emperor, who had remained in the shadow of the Dowager Empress, died in November 1908, to be followed shortly by Cixi herself. The revolution took hold in August 1911, just before Hart's death in September, and a republic was declared in 1912.

Hart arrived back in Britain in June 1908 and was immediately in demand to make speeches and to receive honours, Hester generally accompanying him. The honours included the freedom of London, Belfast and Taunton. He spent much of the autumn of 1908 in Ulster, and became one of the first Pro-Chancellors of his old college when it received its charter as a university that year. He presided at the first meeting of its Senate. Queen's was grateful for the generous support he had already given, for example, towards a building for the Student's Union, twenty years previously, and to its Better Equipment Fund ten years before.[3]

Though he remained keenly interested in Queen's (which still annually offers a scholarship founded in 1914 in his memory), London was his main base. He saw Nollie suitably married on 20 November 1909 to Major Cunningham Brodie, a Liberal MP. Hart died, not at Hester's

London house in Cadogan Place, but in a country residence that he had acquired in Marlow, Buckinhamshire, on 20 September 1911. He was buried nearby, at Bisham Parish Church, his pall being carried by six Commissioners, including three known to the Carralls — Hobson, Hannen, and Reis. Other Customs men on leave and representatives of China also attended. *The Times'* account mentions no women mourners — sad given his fondness for female company.

Hart died, honoured in Britain and China in his time, but strangely forgotten now except by specialists in Sino-British history. *The Times* paid him the tribute of a long and perceptive obituary, calling him as romantic a figure as General Gordon, Rhodes, or any other great Englishmen overseas. While Gordon and Rhodes have had several biographers, no-one has yet been able to do Hart full justice. Perhaps this is due to what *The Times* writer called his complex personality, in which a tolerant acceptance of life derived from his reading and experience of Chinese ways had been grafted on to his early training as a Presbyterian Ulsterman. He was, as the obituarist says, a man able to sympathise with a wide range of people, a man who combined deep learning with the poetic imagination which is shown in some of his letters to Kath, a man who endeared himself to a very wide circle of friends and acquaintances. His generosity is also clearly demonstrated in the Carrall letters, as well as in those to Campbell.

Hart left what might be termed a standard upper class will. As reported by *The Times* of 22 November 1911, his estate was valued at £140,000 and he left Hester for life all his household and personal effects, and an annuity of £2,000 p.a.[4] Hester died in 1928. The rest went to his son, Bruce. His daughters had already had their settlements.

Hart and his Staff

We now know that the Customs Service which Hart built up gave sufficiently valuable service to China to survive the 1911 revolution, the 1914–18 war which deprived it of its German staff, the transition to greater recruitment of Chinese to its upper levels while retaining is reputation for honesty and efficiency, and the civil wars into which the new Republic floundered. It kept going in a format Hart would have recognised even after the Japanese attack on China in 1936 and the 1939–45 world war. The last foreign Inspector-General resigned only in 1950, soon after Mao Zedong had established himself and the Communist Party in October 1949 as the clear victors in the civil war, ending some thirty years of conflict and inaugurating a new isolationist regime.

Hart himself could not take the survival of the Customs for granted but he strove to ensure the future of its staff by ensuring its usefulness to China as a nation, rather than to a particular ruler. He was well aware of the weakness of the Qing dynasty and that his own position was tenuous.[5] Though he could maintain good relations with the Tsungli Yamen, that body had only limited influence within a divided Imperial Court. In 1898, stimulated by the Japanese victories, the fragile Emperor Guangxu was pushing for some modernisation. During most of the Hundred Days of that summer of 1898, when the Emperor issued a spate of reforming decrees, Hart was on holiday in Beidaihe. The conservative Empress Dowager Cixi resumed power in September. Hart's first audience with her was only in 1902, with the girls of his house party.[6]

While Hart gave preference to recruits he knew and liked, they had to be competent, as this, together with honesty, was vital to the survival of the Customs. In a letter of 20 January 1874 he had to agree with Campbell that one of Hance's sons did not measure up, though he would dearly have liked to help that family. The same letter shows he thought Paul King, recommended by an uncle who was an old Customs employee, had written a poor paper (*Elementary education seems nowhere nowadays!*) but took him on as Campbell had passed him. In a letter of 30 October 1882 Hart disapproved of King's long-running quarrel with a colleague over a trivial matter which Campbell then had to sort out. He thought King had shown a lack of the common sense required from *'men who have to stand fire and face the public'* as Carall did in Foochow and Chefoo. He valued men with enough common sense to react appropriately to special circumstances. On 14 June 1896 he told Campbell that he was surprised to hear that King felt 'let down' by being recalled to China after four years in the London office following sickness while on leave. He had thought he was energetic and was disappointed to hear he was *'in a nervous state'*. King's slow progress was not due to a despot's prejudice against his uncle, as King implied in his memoir, but was measured by fitness for post. By February 1897 Hart could describe him as a good man, and promoted him to Deputy Commissioner. As he showed with Jim Carrall, he could revise his opinion of men he did not personally like if they did well in their posts. It helped if he liked the wife, but competence came first. He tried to provide decent accommodation for those old enough to marry (if young, they had to take what they could in lieu of the bachelor accommodation normally provided), and looked into housing personally on his trips up the Yangzi when new ports were opened, and in Peking. And according to Frances, he was known for his care for women and children. The widespread Victorian belief in the frailty of women was balanced by a strong sense that it was the duty of men to protect the weak, as the young men did in the siege of the Legations.

Hart's personal knowledge of so many of his senior staff came from the time the best of them spent in Peking as students, often supplemented by spells on the central staff. It provided the basis for the friendship so many felt for him. Personal observation was supplemented by the reports of his commissioners, while he got the background of port life from women such as Frances in Chefoo and Emma Carrall in Canton. Hart was unashamedly an old-fashioned patron rather than a new model civil servant. He would have promoted his brother Jem further if he could, but even in 1877 he had decided that Campbell should take charge of the Paris Exhibition. *'I should have liked to name James H. Hart for the post and its chances, but he is fond of fun and I can't depend on him for all the work I see there's to be done'* (letter to Campbell of 7 December 1877). Usually his judgement was good, and many of those whom he had selected as students went on to become Commissioners under his successors.

Hart, Women and Family

Hart's genuine concern for staff and families has been illustrated here, but in the constant battle between his work ethic and his emotional needs, work had always won, and had always been well done. The cost had been high. A gulf had opened up between himself, his wife and his legitimate and illegitimate children which caused him immense personal pain.

While maintaining a distance between himself and them, he treated his illegitimate children and Ayaou generously by the expatriate standards of the time, and accepted financial responsibility. As with JCW2, the father of Emma's first husband, this could include help for a grandson.

He never considered treating Ayaou as a wife. Unlike Meadows, he kept her hidden, but when he had to reveal her, he praised her. Once he had seen their photographs and read their letters, some warmth crept into his letters to Campbell about their children, with the one exception of the letter dated 24 August 1879. It is unlikely that he ever corresponded with them directly, for he would have felt his prime duty was to the woman he had married, and her children. His conscience, even as a young man, would have told him that it was wrong to give a woman children without accepting the full responsibilities of a father, whatever the common practice, and he never blamed anyone else for his 'mistake'.

He had needed a wife who would be a 'help-mate' in his work — the word he used in his last letter to Kath. His over-hasty selection of a wife in 1866, understandable in the circumstances of the brief time available to him, had consequences as long-lasting as those of his illegitimate relationship with Ayaou. His ability to empathise with amiable or able women is clear in his relationship with Mrs Glover and the Carralls but Hester, immature when he first met her, never developed the qualities he needed for a close friend. That misfortune separated him also from his daughters and his son, so that he failed as a father as well as a husband. His legal children appreciated his understanding letters, which were surely as kind and insightful as those he wrote to Kath, but this did not balance out the greater influence on them of the mother with whom they lived.

As a husband and father he failed, to his own lasting regret, but as a loyal friend, as well as in his career, he succeeded. By the 1880s Hart's primary need was for women as friends who understood his passion for his work and his enthrallment with China. To the younger ones he offered kindly avuncular affection. In this he was unusual by the standards of our sex-fixated times, but not unique. The journalist Mary Sieghart felt that the older Bill Deedes had a similar need, taking young female journalists under his wing when his wife had no interest in his work. She wrote "I adored him, but in an utterly chaste way".[7] I am sure Emma Carrall and my Aunt Kath would have said exactly the same. When Kath and Maude visited he probably occasionally felt sparks of sexual attraction, and he enjoyed kissing them, but he knew how to keep the relationship at the level of friendship.

But while an older friend like Frances could write freely to him of her problems with her daughters, he, as her husband's boss, could not tell her about Evie and Nollie. Even in friendship, his position impelled him to keep a certain distance, making for the loneliness he expressed to Kath and to Campbell. Nevertheless his warmth and generosity to the women and girls who became his friends are clear from the letters. His friendship with young girls may seem strange to us, but their fathers would certainly have forbidden these visits had they felt their daughters' innocence and reputation were in any danger. Young Effie Ragsdale's father was American consul in Tientsin and could have refused permission without feeling any threat to his career. Maude and Kath could joke about his kisses, and their grandmother, Emma Sampson, no innocent herself with her three husbands, and who had known him since 1858, was grateful for his attentions to her grand-daughters. In one of the last letters of her life, in 1909, she sent Kath 'some scraps about that kind and noble man Sir Robert Hart', scarcely the description of a suspected seducer. The Times journalist, Morrison, had plenty to say about Mrs Bredon's alleged lover[8] but made no accusations of this sort against Hart. It is our own current attitude to the dominance of sex and the publicity now given to perverts that causes doubts.

Personal Postscript

Western media now seem to value women mainly for their sexual attributes. Whether this is better than valuing them mainly as mothers and the centre of the family is certainly open to question. I hope that both women and men, with or without children, can come to be judged by the totality of their character and achievements. I am glad that the limitations on jobs open to women, which I still faced in the 1950s, and the huge differences in salaries then offered to male and female graduates outside teaching no longer exist. We can now choose to have only two or three children and take their survival for granted. There is time before and after child bearing and rearing to do much else.

The churches no longer play the same role as in the nineteenth century in sanctifying marriage and parenthood and, fortunately, there are no longer the same penalties for children born outside of marriage. Nevertheless, the task of passing on to the next generation values that will sustain a good society remains important, and society suffers when parenting fails. A difficult task can be helped by society's support, and, for me, by religious belief, but it also helped by the commitment of both parents, as Hart learnt to his cost. How parents divide the shorter time that this now takes between the need to earn and the need to care is up to them.

Though Hart seldom went to church by the end of the century, his niece Juliet Bredon said he remained deeply religious.[9] The second last entry in his diary was *'Easter Sunday 19th April 1908: Christ is risen.'* The Bishop of North China said at his Memorial service:

> Those who value the Christian faith, in whatever form, can thank God that here in [Peking]…there has been for so many years a man in high position and of commanding influence who kept his faith in the Christian revelation, and who…set a high tone of administrative purity and devotion to duty, while leading an exemplary and blameless life.[10]

Hart knew his successes and failures could not be measured only by the outward wealth and fame that he had earned. For me, that adds to his stature.

ACKNOWLEDGEMENTS, NOTES AND SOURCES

I have tried to keep notes to a minimum, while making them useful to both the general reader and the scholar. Everyone who works on Hart owes a great deal to the team at Harvard University who deciphered and published the early years of his journal and his letters to his friend and colleague, James Campbell, who headed the London office of the Customs. I am very grateful to the Harvard University Asia Center and the Harvard University Press for permission to use extracts from:

John King Fairbank, Kathleen Frost Bruner and Elizabeth MacLeod Matheson, eds. *The I.G. in Peking: Letters of Robert Hart, Chinese Maritime Customs, 1868-1907*, The Belknap Press of Harvard University Press, Copyright © 1975 by the President and Fellows of Harvard College.

Kathleen F Bruner, J K Fairbank and R J Smith, eds. *Entering China's Service: Robert Hart's Journals, 1854-1863*, Council on East Asian Studies, Harvard University, Copyright © 1986 by the President and Fellows of Harvard College.

Richard J Smith, J K Fairbank and K F Bruner, eds. *Robert Hart and China's Early Modernization: His Journals, 1863-66*, Council on East Asian Studies, Harvard University, Copyright © 1991 by the President and Fellows of Harvard College.

The exact citation can be traced by the date of the diary entry or letter which is always given in the text. An endnote is used only when the source is the Harvard authors' commentary or notes.

Campbell's replies to Hart have been transcribed by Chen Xiafei and Han Rongfang, *Archives of China's Imperial Maritime Customs: Confidential Correspondence Between Robert Hart and James Duncan Campbell 1874-1907*, and are similarly treated. A few originals are in Queen's University, Belfast (QUB), MS 15, and these are annotated as such.

Hart's diary extracts for the years after 1866 are my own transcriptions from the original volumes held at QUB. All letters to Hart from members of the Carrall family are in the Hart archive (MS 15) held at QUB, and I am immensely grateful for the help given by the Senior Librarian, Deidre Wilde and her staff on my visits and for permission to use them. Hart's letters to Aunt Kath (Kathleen Newton, née Carrall) were donated to QUB by her daughter, Keeve Irons, together with photographs Hart sent to Emma Sampson or to Kath. The Irons gift is in MS 15.

Files on Jim Carrall in the Customs archive in the **Second Historical Archive of China,** collected for me by Catherine Ladd, are referenced by their location, **Nanjing** and file number. Quotations from the British National Archives at Kew simply have their file reference.

The **Notes** sometimes provide additional detail about minor characters mentioned. Information on Customs staff was generally found either in John K Fairbank et al., op. cit. or from the Imperial Maritime Customs staff pages on the Bristol University website. Some of the women were found in the Biographical Details that Susanna Hoe provided in *Women at the Siege of Peking 1900*. R G Tiedemann is a good source for missionaries. Google was also useful!

Other notes explain a term or practice which I think may be unfamiliar to some readers.

Prologue

1. <http://www.contemporarywriters.com/authors/profile/`?p=auth119>
2. Wonderful comment by Robert Nield, President of the Hong Kong Branch of the Royal Asiatic Society.
3. Amah was the word used by expatriates in China for a nurse or nanny, ayah in India.
4. At the time of the gift Keeve, née Newton, and widow of David Acheson, was married to her second husband, Jack Irons.
5. Frances *Wood, No Dogs and Not Too Many Chinese: Treaty Port Life in China 1843-1943*, pp. 144-5 and Robert Bickers, 'Purloined Letters: History and the Chinese Maritime Customs Service', p. 696 are amongst those who quote King's memoir to characterize Hart's personnel policy as in part influenced by long-lasting prejudice. This is not apparent in Hart's remarks about King in his letters to Campbell, which are discussed in Chapter Eleven.
6. The photos can be seen at <http://chp.ish-lyon.cnrs.fr/

Image.php?> – use key word Carrall. They were scanned by Jamie Carstairs, Bristol University. The original albums have now been gifted to QUB.

7. Niall Ferguson, *Civilization: The West and the Rest,* Chapter Six and especially pp. 277-88, has an interesting discussion on the contribution of the work ethic to Western economic success, its relationship to Protestantism, and the growth of Christianity in China since the fall of ideological communism.

8. QUB, MS 15/8, J.

9. Paul Wilcocks, on his father's reaction.

Chapter One

1. The surgeons only separated from the Barber-Surgeons Guild in 1745, gaining their Royal Charter in 1800. The Royal College of Surgeons conducted examinations for membership (MRCS) but has no record of John Wakeham Edwards. Country surgeons in the 1810s often still learnt by apprenticeship.

2. Their defeat prevented the French from attacking Jamaica. Emma thought it had to do with the conquest of Bermuda! Her grand-daughter Kath took copies (now with me) and donated the originals to the Maritime Museum at Greenwich.

3. The MRCS required four years study, under teachers with recognised qualifications, including six months each for the study of practical pharmacy and physics, and three years of lectures, demonstrations and dissections studying anatomy, physiology, surgery, and pharmacology etc., followed by examination (1839 Regulations, supplied by the Royal College of Surgeons).

4. Judith Summers, *Soho, a History of London.*

5. A memorial plaque in St John's Cathedral says he was resident in Antigua for fifty-seven years, dying in 1899, and had been Senior Medical Officer for twenty-one years.

6. E M *Swift, The Zinzan Families,* found that Zinzan had sent his son to live with Webb as his medical assistant at the time of the 1861 census. Robert Webb is a common name but not when associated with Poplar, surgeons and an isolated part of south Devon. Like Zinzan, Webb had a Licentiate of the Apothecaries Company (LCA), as well as the MRCS.

7. Wilcocks descendants adopted this method of distinguishing fathers and sons by number. I am grateful to Paul Wilcocks, who has created a huge database of Wilcocks descendants, and to his fellow Wilcocks researchers, Karen Johnson, Karin Groves, Janet Kral, and Gillian Selley, for their serious and successful detective work on Anna Sess. It was difficult because the Victorian capital S is easily confused with capital L, see Figure 1.4.

8. Information from Dr R G Tiedemann, Centre for the Study of Christianity in China, Oxford OX2 5TN. He also guided me to the Carl Smith cards (now on the archival site of the Hong Kong government). Tsang Shun Fai of Hong Kong University later pursued relevant references for me.

9. Emma's third husband was later to argue that *fan* could also be translated as 'stranger', and *kwai* as 'ghosts', and that Europeans had unnecessarily demonised the combination *fan-kwai* as meaning 'foreign devils' (Sampson, 'A Plea for "Fan-Kwai"').

10. J Doolittle, *Social Life of the Chinese*. Chapter Twelve.

11. Jonathan Fenby, *The Penguin History of Modern China: The Fall and Rise of a Great Power, 1850-2008*, pp. 15–19.

12. James D Johnston, *China and Japan: Being a Narrative of the Cruise of the US Steam-Frigate Powhatan, in the Years 1857, '58, '59 and '60*, Chapter Seven.

13. Fa-ti Fan, *British Naturalists in Qing China: Science, Empire, and Cultural Encounter*, pp. 24-5. This created difficulties for 'gardeners' sent out to collect plants for Kew, unless they had a local patron, who could upgrade them socially.

14. G S Graham, *The China Station: War and Diplomacy, 1830-60*.

15. Quotations on Whampoa from consular files are from FO 228/157, FO 228/189, FO 228/190, FO 228/214. and FO 682/1987. P. D. Coates, *China Consuls: British Consular Officers, 1843-1943*. gives details of conditions for vice-consuls. Ernest John *Eitel, Europe in China: The History of Hongkong From the Beginning to the Year 1882*. was also useful.

16. The exchange rate varied, but Hart noted in his diary for 24/11/1854 that 'Meadows gave me $5, or £1.0.10d.' (There were 20 shillings in the £.) On the same day Hart paid his teacher $7 as his salary for the month. Hart's annual salary then was £200, so Buckton's claim was substantial.

17. P D Coates, *China Consuls: British Consular Officers, 1843-1943*, pp. 192-3 on Robinson (who also thought that in dealing with rebellions the Chinese government was the most oppressive in the world). Douglas Hurd, *The Arrow War: an Anglo-Chinese Confusion, 1856-60*, p. 14, on Alcock and Parkes.
18. J Fenby, op. cit., p. 15.
19. Kathleen F Newton, *My Grandmother, Emma Spry Edwards, 1829-1909*.
20. Jardine Matheson archive, Cambridge University.
21. Lorchas were fast sailing ships built in Macao, using a combination of Western and Chinese technology. They were often registered in Hong Kong, entitling them to protection by the British navy, and were often used for opium smuggling.
22. Though there are later works, Douglas Hurd, *The Arrow War: an Anglo-Chinese Confusion, 1856-60*, gave me the most useful account of the Anglo-French campaign since it incorporated eye-level comments and descriptions, including many from Lord Elgin's private papers and the Bishop of Hong Kong's comment. E J Eitel, op. cit. provides opinion in Hong Kong.
23. Bruner, K F et al., *Entering China's Service*, p. 212, transcribe her name as 'Brickton'.
24. Bapna, N, Swarankar M, and Kotia, N, 'Genital Tuberculosis and Its Consequences on Subsequent Infertility'.

Chapter Two

1. Stanley Bell, *Hart of Lisburn* and R O'Leary, 'Robert Hart in China: The significance of his Irish roots', provide information on his background.
2. The quote and comments are by Henry Inglis, cited by K F Bruner et al. in *Entering China's Service*, p. 3-5.
3. R A Jones, *The British Diplomatic Service, 1815-1914* describes a service in which ambassadors were appointed by the political leaders (and rose and fell with them). They then appointed most of their own staff, except for a Foreign Office secretary. It was only in the later 1850s that a transition began from personal missions on behalf of the sovereign (like that of Lord Elgin) to a system where senior diplomatic appointments were made from a cadre of career diplomats. The young Hart's seniors, Alcock,

Wade and Parkes became examples of this in China.

4. Brazier's career is recorded in his obituary, Royal College of Chemistry, 1889.

5. John Meadows had joined his elder brother, Thomas, who was in the regular consular service, in Canton in 1845. John learnt Chinese, and progressed to a variety of freelance jobs as translator. In 1850 he had come to Ningbo as Acting Interpreter.

6. The 'German rational views' probably refers to *The Life of Christ Critically Examined,* 1840, by David F Strauss, of Tubingen University. It was translated into English by George Eliot in 1846 and may well have been known at Queen's College. Strauss applied logic and dialectics to examine the four Gospels, and to establish his 'mythical' interpretation of parts of the Bible. By this he meant the representation of an event or idea in a historical form with the 'pictorial and imaginative thought and expression of primitive ages'. This challenged accepted beliefs in the literal truth of the Bible.

7. P D Coates, *China Consuls: British Consular Officers, 1843-1943,* p. 93–4.

8. The name was Bemvindo in the consular records. Hart must have misheard the Chinese version of his name.

9. Juliet Bredon, *Sir Robert Hart: The Romance of a Great Career Told by His Niece* provides the information on Patridge.

10. P D Coates, op. cit. p. 98 suggests that the young lady jilted him for another, behaviour disgraceful to her and hurtful to his pride.

11. K F Bruner et al. *Entering China's Service: Robert Hart's Journals, 1854-1863,* pp. 153-4.

12. Lan Li and Deirdre Wildy, 'A new discovery and its significance: The statutory declarations made by Sir Robert Hart concerning his secret domestic life in 19th century China'.

13. Quoted by K F Bruner et al., op. cit., p. 244.

14. E B Drew, 'Sir Robert Hart and his life work in China', lists 11 ports where Hart opened offices between 1861 and 1864, and 'became acquainted with his men — chiefs and juniors — and arranged matters by personal interviews with the local Chinese officials [who] had but a dim comprehension of his purposes'. Edward Bangs Drew was an American who joined the Customs in 1865, straight after graduating from Harvard, and we shall meet him in Chapter Eight as Commissioner for Tientsin.

15. E B Drew, op cit. and Catherine Ladds, 'Youthful, Likely Men, Able to Read, Write and Count'.

16. Charles Gordon was an officer of the Corps of Royal Engineers in the British army, and had taken part in the Allied Expeditionary Force which attacked Peking in 1860 (Chapter One). Afterwards, he took the place of an American who was leading the 'Ever Victorious Army'. His exploits earned him the nickname in England of Chinese Gordon, and this abstemious, religious man became a popular hero. He returned to the British army, and his varied career included being Governor-General of the Sudan, 1874-9. Popular clamour forced Gladstone to send him back to the Sudan, in 1884, with orders to conduct an orderly evacuation of troops being harassed by the rebellion led by a religious leader, the Mahdi. These besiegedhim in Khartoum. Gladstone delayed in sending a relief mission, and Gordon died, still a hero, when the city fell to the Mahdi in January 1885.

17. Richard J Smith, et al., *Robert Hart and China's Early Modernization: His Journals, 1863-66*, pp. 34-36.

18. He wrote this down, he said, because that day a man had died suddenly. If that happened to him at least his friends and relatives would know from his journal that there was some hope of meeting him again in heaven. This shows that he knew his diary might not remain private.

19. Juliet Bredon, *Sir Robert Hart: The Romance of a Great Career*, p. 31.

20. From Henry Longfellow's poem *A Psalm of Life*. Hart refers to this poem on several later occasions in connection with his children with Ayaou.

21. James Hart (Jem in the diary) joined the Customs as a 4th Class Clerk in 1867. He was dear to Hart, very clever, but unlike his brother, he remained something of a playboy till late in life.

22. First and third quotes from R J Smith et al., op. cit., second is my own reading of the 1868 diary.

Chapter Three

1. J Needham, *Science and Civilisation in China*, refers to him as 'the great Bretschneider', and Fa-ti Fan, *British Naturalists in Qing China*, gives him an important role. The biography of Sampson is an

extract from Needham's 1898 book, *History of European Botanical Discoveries in China*, published in St Petersburg., but is quoted from a collection of material: Theophilus Sampson, *Botanical and Other Writings on China, 1867-1870; With a Biographical Sketch by Emil Bretschneider*, edited by H Waltravens.

2. P D Coates, *China consuls: British Consular Officers, 1843-1943*, pp. 113-4.

3. FO 228/223 contains his application and the testimonial from Winchester already quoted which he used to support it.

4. P D Coates, op. cit., p. 90.

5. Fa-ti Fan, op. cit. p. 69.

6. Archives, Royal Botanic Gardens, Kew, *Director's Correspondence, Chinese and Japanese letters*, Vols. 150 and 151. 6 Oct 1886. Letter sent after Hance's recent death.

7. Information for this section comes from P D Coates, op. cit., Ong Jin Hui, Chinese Indenture Labour: Coolies and Colonies, W L Lai, *The Chinese in the West Indies, 1806-1898: A Documentary History*. p. 152, Arnold J Meagher, *The Coolie Trade: the Traffic in Chinese Laborers to Latin America 1846-1874*. and T Sue-A-Quan, *Cane Reapers: Chinese Indentured Immigrants in Guyana*. Dr Trev Sue-A-Quan, a Canadian, is a descendant of great-grandparents who went to Guyana in the last shipment organised by Sampson. He has tracked others, who like them, made good use of new opportunities.

8. Wilhelm Lobscheid came to Hong Kong for the Rhenish Missionary Society in 1848 and after a leave 1850–53, returned for the Chinese Evangelisation Society. From 1855 to 1859 he was Inspector of the thirteen Government schools in Hong Kong giving a Chinese education. From 1861 to 1868 he worked with the Netherlands West India Emigration Co. He was the author of an English-Chinese dictionary published in Hong Kong in 1866 and 1869, which Sampson must have found extremely useful in his later career. He left China in 1870, becoming a pastor in the USA (Tiedemann, <http://ricci.rt.usfa.edu/biography> and E J Eitel, *Europe in China: The History of Hongkong From the Beginning to the Year 1882*.

9. Two other clauses in Sampson's proposed contract showed equal treatment for men and women, unusual for the time. Each adult was to sign a contract for agricultural labour, and each was to receive the same embarkation bonus. There is an article in *The*

China Review, Vol. 1 No. 2, 1872, concluded in Vol. 1. No.3, on the subject. It is not signed but I suspect it to be by Sampson because of its style, and the intimate knowledge it shows of the actualities of Chinese emigration. The author contrasts the well-supervised British-sponsored emigration with what 'we may briefly term Spanish emigration' where the emigration agent was an independent merchant speculator, selling his cargo on arrival for pecuniary gain. This, in the author's opinion, rendered the guaranteed return fare after five years meaningless; such a man might go bankrupt, quit China, etc., and could not guarantee payments to be made in five or ten years time. He also pointed out the difficulty of policing Chinese brokers, even if licensed, since they recruited through agents. He thought the regulators lacked 'practical acquaintance with the business they sought to regulate'. The writer acknowledged faults and difficulties in the Canton system, but thought it the best available.

10. T Sampson, *Sketches of the Botany of Kwangtung*, ms.
11. Kathleen F *Newton, My Grandmother, Emma Spry Edwards, 1829-1909*.
12. George Piercy, *Love for China, Exemplified in Memorials of Mary Gunston, the First Female Teacher in Connection With the Wesleyan Methodist Mission at Canton.*
13. Eitel worked for many years in Kwantung, first for the Basle Mission and later for the London Missionary Society, resigning in 1879 to become Inspector of Schools in Hong Kong. He wrote books on Chinese Buddhism and Feng Shui as an example of Chinese natural science, as well as on Hong Kong's history.
14. Bowra papers, SOAS.
15. From the Preface of Hance, *Adversaria* (in Latin, published in Paris), quoted by Bretschneider in Sampson, op. cit. and kindly translated for me by the Rev. David Newman.
16. T Sampson, *Sketches of the Botany of Kwangtung, ms.*
17. Royal Botanic Gardens, Kew, Archives, *Director's Correspondence, Chinese and Japanese letters*, Vols. 150 and 151.
18. Fa-ti Fan op. cit., p.1.
19. P D Coates, op. cit.
20. Royal Botanic Gardens, Kew, Archives, *Director's Correspondence, Chinese and Japanese letters*, Vols. 150 and 151. Hance to Hooker, 21 June 1867.

21. Mrs John Henry Gray, *Fourteen Months in Canton*.
22. T Sampson, 'Whirlwind at Canton'.
23. Both letters are in Royal Botanic Gardens, Kew, Archives, Misc. Reports.

Chapter Four

1. Helen Brazier died after childbirth, at the age of twenty-eight in Scotland. This was her fourth child, so this was not expected. She was born and brought up in China, being the daughter of Dr Myers who was a medical officer attached to the Customs. Her husband James was Chief Secretary, IMC. She, her husband and her sister all endured the 1900 siege of the Legation with Sir Robert (Susanna Hoe, *Women at the Siege of Peking 1900*).
2. Thirza's letter is in Charles Drage, *Servants of the Dragon Throne: Being the Lives of Edward and Cecil Bowra*. A family history note on the Web says her sister Mary spoke Cantonese fluently.
3. J K Fairbank, et. al, in a note to this letter, trace the reference to Sam Weller's father in the *Pickwick Papers,* on the dangers of marrying widows and acquiring stepchildren.
4. Hart made no comment on Ayaou's children in his diary but they feature in his correspondence with Campbell and Campbell's replies. His letters about them to his lawyer, Hutchins, are not available. In the 1871 census the Davidson family were living on the Manor Houses Estate, in West Ham, a part of Essex which had become a London suburb. Anna twelve, Herbert eight, and Arthur five, all born Pekin [sic] overlapped in age with their own children aged nine, seven and two.
5. Elizabeth Buettner, *Empire Families: Britons and Late Imperial India*, discusses this in relation to expatriate families in India.
6. P D Coates, op. cit., p. 165.
7. H van de Ven, 'Robert Hart and Gustav Detring during the Boxer Rebellion'.
8. E B Drew, *Sir Robert Hart and His Life Work in China*, p. 21.
9. Hart refers to Ayaou having married a Chinese man in a later declaration (Lan Li and Deirdre Wildy, *A New Discovery and Its Significance*). Richard J Smith et al., *Robert Hart and China's Early Modernization*, p. 367, note that his diary shows he received letters

from Ayaou in on 2 July 1870 and 20 May 1872. The comment on the latter was "Will this ever end?" If the November 1875 letter should be read as implying she was dead, she must have died at some point between 1872 and then.

10. This probably refers to the Tartar General, a high Manchu military officer, whose civil duties included keeping a watch on Chinese officials, and receiving the revenues derived from trade. He could report directly to the Emperor, whereas other officials reported through the Viceroy (J Doolittle, *Social Life of the Chinese*, Chapter Twelve.)

11. Lan Li and Deirdre Wildy, op. cit.

12. Martha Vicinus, *Independent Women: Work and Community for Single Women, 1850-1920*.

13. For Charles Gordon see footnote 18, Chapter Two. He had been killed at Khartoum on 26 January 1885. The Almacks, like many others, grieved at their hero's death.

14. QUB, MS 15/2/11.

Chapter Five

1. Jim's superior in Foochow in August 1883 said he had one and a half years of study in Peking (Nanjing, 679(2)). When Edward Bowra was studying in the 1860s he listed his four fellow students as American, French, Prussian, and a Britisher (Bowra papers, SOAS). Hart wrote to Campbell in December 1871 *'The Students' Court is full now: headed by Hammond* [an American] *and composed of all nationalities, they're a rum lot, but nice lads withal'*.

2. J K Fairbank et al. *The I.G. in Peking : Letters of Robert Hart*, Letter 130, n. 2.

3. I C Cannon, *Public Success, Private Sorrow: The Life and Times of Charles Henry Brewitt-Taylor (1857-1938)*.

4. The description of the school, and the quotation on Rachel Speciall, is taken from Maude Robertson, 'Child Life in the 'Sixties', reprinted from *The Sussex County Magazine*, and collected by David Hitchins, on a cd, *Quakers in Lewes*, 2003, which seems to be no longer available. I am grateful for his earlier help.

5. Kathleen Newton, *Notes on my Father J.W. Carrall*.

6. A two-person gambling card game originating in Paris.

7. The descriptions of events in Fuzhou in 1884 are based on L E

Eastman, *Throne and Mandarins :China's Search for a Policy During the Sino-French Controversy,1880-1885*; and Nicole Tixier 'La Chine dans la Stratégie Impériale: le Rôle du Quai d'Orsay et de ses Agents'. on the French consular activities. Customs reports from Hannen and Carrall are in Nanjing, 670(2) 732 and Hart's replies in Nanjing 679(2) 721. Sinclair and Warren's reports are in FO 228/752 and FO 228/753.

8. Washington State University, Manuscript Archives. *George W. Woods Journals, 1883-6.*

9. The whole kingdom was often referred to by contemporary observers as Annam, its southern and most important province.

10. M de Bezaure, the French vice-consul, had returned from leave in April 1884, replacing Frandon (personal communication from Nicole Tixier). In 'La Chine dans la Stratégie Impériale', Tixier describes how Bezaure ensured that the French Admiral could maintain telegraphic communication before and after the battle, despite the danger and personal discomfort involved.

11. P D Coates, *China consuls*, p. 211.

12. The writers were J F Boche and L L Cowen, *The French at Foochow.*

13. L E Eastman, op. cit., p. 162-4 thinks the Chinese were aware of the importance of a legal declaration of war. However, there were advantages to them as well as to the French in the ambiguous situation. As Sinclair had pointed out to them, it had enabled a German ship to refuse the French Admiral's request that they stop a delivery of rifles to the Chinese, and other arms supplies were also en route. If war was declared, neutrals should not provide arms to either side. It was, however, useful that their own people should think that their government was responding to the attack by a declaration of war.

14. Ibid, p. 162.

15. Nanjing, 679(1) 31993.

16. Catherine Ladds, *Empire Careers: The Foreign Staff of the Chinese Customs Service, 1854-1949.*

17. Hart to Campbell on 21 June 1884 gives this equivalent for Dr Martin's identical salary in Peking, after a fall in the value of the tael the previous month.

18. S F Wright, *Hart and the Chinese Customs.*

19. I C Cannon, op. cit.

Chapter Six

1. Catherine Ladds, *Empire Careers: The Foreign Staff of the Chinese Customs Service, 1854-1949.*

2. All descriptions of Chefoo and its economy in 1900 and the map on p. 147 are from Carrall, 'Chefoo'.

3. Jonathan Fenby, *The Fall and Rise of a Great Power, 1850-2008.*

4. George Steinmetz, *The Devil's Handwriting: Precoloniality and the German Colonial State in Qingdao, Samoa and Southwest Africa.*

5. SOAS: CIM/CSP, 1795, Annals, 1930 of the CIM, Chefoo. The author of the quote is not clear, but it is dated August 14, 1890.

6. E. Buettner, *Empire Families: Britons and Late Imperial India* points this out in relation to British children from India.

7. Nanjing, 679(2) 589).

8. P D Coates, *China Consuls*, pp. 205-6 mentions the big game hunting there.

9. Poem by Ann Lych Botta, 1848.

10. Nanjing, 679(2) 636 No. 2726.

11. Hart is referring to G W Steevens, *With Kitchener to Khartoum*, Blackwoods, 1898.

12. This must have been the Weihaiwei road, in the map on p. 147, which was intersected by the road passing Filanda 27 (a weaving factory).There was no road along the coast to the schools, and a note in the diary shows the land route could take more than an hour.

13. Her typescript of a broadcast she made in 1943.

14. Frances Osborne, *Lilla's Feast: A True Story of Love, War and a Passion for Food* is an entertaining biography of Lilla Eckford, the author's great-grandmother. Lilla and Vyvyan were both in Chefoo in 1939, so they may have helped my mother locate her father's steward and her amah on our visit. Osborne thought Vyvyan had forgotten his real father, but Kath mentions that on one of their walks he showed them the grave of his real father in the cemetery on Temple Hill above the town.

15. Diana Preston, *The Boxer Rebellion: China's War on Foreigners. 1902*, p. 31.

16. Mabel Fawcus's upper class in-laws looked down on her was because she retained the short North country 'a'. (family correspondence retained by her descendant, Lindsay Stilwell, and

also in a memoir by Victor Bonham-Carter, *What Countryman, Sir?* They also despised her brother's failure to appreciate good wine!

17.   ADM 196/43.

Chapter Seven

1. The Gipperichs feature in the diary in Peking, Tientsin and Chefoo. There was a French trading house of this name, but they also met a Miss Elspeth Gipperich at the Austrian legation in Peking. The diary show that those in Chefoo spoke German, which they helped Kath practise.

2. Harry Bristow was a student at the British Legation. His father, Henry Barnes Bristow, was Consul at Tientsin 1893–7, and seems to have retired there, for Kath met him on their return trip. Bellingham and Jamieson are not mentioned again. A G Bethell, British, went on to be a Commissioner. Ulick Wintour, also British, had joined the Customs in 1895. He was now 4th Assistant B, Postal.

3. Miss Brazier was Daisy Brazier, daughter of Professor Brazier (Chapter Two). Annie Myers was her sister-in-law. Annie's father was a doctor to both the Customs and the British consular service. Both women went through the siege of the Legation bravely and helpfully (Susanna Hoe, *Women at the Siege of Peking 1900*).

4. Newton, Kathleen, *It Happened to Me.* All references to her later memoir refer to this.

5. A mis-spelling for Paula von Rosthorn, whose husband had been in the Customs, but later joined the Austrian consular service and was acting Chargé d'Affaires at the Austrian legation at the time. She played a brave part in the siege (Susanna Hoe, op. cit.)

6. Edward Wagner was French, at this time 2nd Assistant (B) Postal, and had joined the Customs in 1892. Ferguson, despite his name, was Dutch. I have not identified Strauch's nationality. De Luca was the younger of two sons of a former Italian Minister to Peking, who both joined the Customs.

7. Lucy Ker was a Canadian, married to William Ker, then Asst Chinese Secretary at the British Legation. She was to lose her two-year-old son as a result of the siege.

8. Despite his name, he was a Russian member of the Customs, whom Hart had noted in 1896 as very promising.

9. It is evident that Jim Carrall did not like Bredon, so there could have been a family prejudice operating here. Robert Bredon seems to have been kind to the girls in Peking, and Juliet later became well known as an author, writing books on Hart, Peking and China, well into the 1920s. She is said to have been born in Peking, so after Robert's arrival there in 1873, making her possibly in her twenties at this time. Though there are many references to her books, I could not find her birth and death on Ancestry.com or Google.

10. Constantin von Hanneken was Detring's son-in-law, a former German army officer who was helping Li Hongzhang modernise the northern section of the Chinese army.

11. Postal Secretary for the Customs. Hart valued his ability in this field though he disliked his temper.

12. Baron M von Babo was Austro-Hungarian Consul in Chefoo, a wine connoisseur and wine maker.

13. The burning of the stations was known to the British Legation on 28 May (D Preston, op. cit. p. 54) but Father must have heard of the murder of the missionaries from the China Inland Mission in Chefoo, for it was protested to the Yamen by Sir Claude Macdonald (head of the British Mission in Peking) only on 4 June.

14. Walled city fourteen miles from Peking, later to be the last stop of the relief force.

15. A French member of Carrall's staff, who later became a Commissioner.

16. K F Newton. *Incredible 8 weeks ordeal*. No date.

17. J W Carrall, *Events in the North of China, 17th June 1900 to September 3rd.*, Irons gift, MS15, QBU.

18. The First Chinese Regiment had been raised eighteen months earlier (D Preston, op. cit. p. 126).

19. Nanjing 679(1) 31993- No. 2901, 5 July 1900.

20. Nanjing 679 (1) Chefoo S/O, 1900–06.

21. George Morrison was *The Times* correspondent in Peking. During a temporary 'half-truce' in July those in the Legation had been able to send some messages to Tientsin and onwards to their governments (D Preston, op. cit. p. 180).

22. As Campbell was happy to tell Hart in his next letter.
23. Carrall wrote to Bredon about it, *'The whole business is a shameful exhibition to the Chinese of "how these Christians love one another".'* Nanjing, 679(1) 31993. One costume of the time consisted of a short belted dress, knee-length knickers, and dark stockings, all in wool. The dress might have short sleeves. It gave considerably more freedom to swim and dive than the corsets and long skirts worn earlier — <www.fashionencyclopedia.com>
24. Interestingly this confirms the opinion of George Morrison which Susanna Hoe, op. cit., thought might be his prejudice.
25. Andrea Jacobs, 'Examinations as cultural capital for the Victorian school girl'.
26. Illegible, but identified by Susanna Hoe, op. cit. Hart probably wrote the informal name for its mess.
27. Ibid. p. 179.

Chapter Eight

1. Gwen Steele-Perkins, *Sacrifice,* circa 1937.
2. From 'Lucretius' by Alfred Lord Tennyson.
3. One of the first powdered infant foods. As it was a substitute for mother's milk, it is more likely that it made up Baby's milk than that it was added to it.
4. In 1919 a newly arrived policeman described it as 'the best city I have seen and will leave any English town one hundred years behind' (R Bickers, *An Englishman Adrift in Shanghai,* p. 39).

Chapter Nine

1. Carrall's Customs correspondence is from Nanjing, 679(1)31993.
2. Gwen Steele-Perkins, *Sacrifice,* circa 1937.

Chapter Ten

1. His letter to Campbell of 11 October 1903 says Lily Foley and Winnie Stewart were the two other guests. He enjoyed their music and company after 6 p.m., though it ate into his time for reading and writing. It seems the last party of this type.

2. I am grateful to Lindsay Stilwell, descendant of Mabel Fawcus, for these comments in his family letters.

3. Martha Vicinus, *Independent Women: Work and Community for Single Women, 1850-1920*, p. 297 describes their usefulness for female sociability.

4. Then held annually in remembrance of Queen Victoria's friend and Prime Minister, Disraeli: she had sent primroses, his favourite flower, for his funeral wreath.

5. There had been massacres of the Jews in Russia, which was in a generally unsettled state, not helped by its defeats by the Japanese.

6. M Vicinus, op. cit., p. 176 discusses teaching salaries.

7. Dr Saville, 1869–1911, studied at the London School of Medicine for Women and was appointed to Peking by the London Missionary Society in 1895. She left Peking in 1905 through ill health. She later went to Tientsin under the Chinese Government and died there (Susanna Hoe, Women at the Siege of Peking 1900, pp. 386-7).

8. It later changed its name to Rupert's Land College to avoid confusion with Havergal College, Toronto.

9. On Eric's next visit to Winnipeg in 1919 he stated that he had spent two years there previously. His return journey in 1914 has been found from Ancestry.co.uk, but not the outward one. (Thanks to Karen Johnson for finding these.)

10. Unlike her other trips, the manifest has been found, listing her as Kathleen Newton, tutor, travelling with other members of the Overseas Education League from Montreal to Liverpool on 1 July 1924. Kath recorded that Uncle Jack met her in her memoir of him. This is also the source also for his later life and death.

11. Uncle Jack helped to get Keeve back from the Newton cousin who moved her around between Switzerland, Brittany and Ireland for three years, 1922–5. Despite a remarkably disjointed childhood, Keeve managed to get her Higher Oxford Certificate, and to bring up three children in a stable home. She died in January 2011 in Dungannon near her son, Peter Acheson. (She had met her first husband, David Acheson, while visiting her father's relatives in Northern Ireland.)

12. The cutting is part of the Iron's Gift, MS 15, QUB.

Chapter Eleven

1. The main sources for Hart's relations with his legitimate and illegitimate children are the correspondence between him and Campbell, and Lan Li and Deirdre Wildy, 'A New Discovery and Its Significance'. His family correspondence in regard to Nollie are in MS 15/2/1/2, QUB, which also contain Bruce's remarks on his elder sister Evie.
2. Jonathan Fenby, *The Fall and Rise of a Great Power*, p. 93.
3. Letter to *The Times*, from a correspondent in Belfast, 23 September 1911.
4. *The Times*, 22 November, 1911.
5. Descriptive phrase used by Robert Bickers, 'Purloined letters, History and the Chinese Maritime Customs Service' *Modern Asian Studies*, 40,3, p. 694.
6. Jonathan Fenby, op. cit., pp. 65-74.
7. Mary Sieghart, 'A Perfect Gentleman'. *Times 2*, 11/03/2008.
8. Susanna Hoe, *Women at the Siege of Peking, 1900*.
9. It could have been behind the deaths of both John Wakeham Edwards in 1854 and the invalid brother that Jack Fawcus was caring for in 1901-3. Family rumour suggests the young Jim Carrall and his French wife shown in Figure 10.6 were 'riddled with some dreadful disease' (Keeve), caught, according to my mother, from a maid at his school.
10. Juliet Bredon, *The Romance of a Great Career*, Chapter Eight.
11. Both quotations are from Bell, *Hart of Lisburn*. (The last entry, on Easter Monday, was 'Slept badly'.)

BIBLIOGRAPHY

Libraries, archives and other collections

UNITED KINGDOM

Private collections of family papers and correspondence

Papers and notes by Mrs K F Newton (née Carrall) and passed by her daughter Mrs Keeve Irons to Mary Tiffen. These include:
Diary for 1900.
Diary and notes, 1909-12.
Hanger with Chefoo and Peking photos.
Portraits of family, including Emma Spry Sampson and Emma
    Carrall. (Photographs not given a source are from this
    collection, or, if modern, were taken by Mary Tiffen.)
Newton, K F *Going to school in North China*. Northern Ireland Home
Service, BBC 16 February 1943. Typescript.
Newton, K F *John George Fawcus, Barrister*.
Newton, K F *My grandmother, Emma Spry Edwards, 1829-1909*.
Newton, K F *Notes on my father J W Carrall*.
Special family letters and diaries, including those of Anna Maria
    Fawcus.
Steele-Perkins, G F *Sacrifice*. Memoir (née Gwendoline F Carrall).

Frances Harvey Jamieson (Maude Carrall's daughter). Two albums of photos, passed by her son Lennox Harvey Jamieson to Mary Tiffen. Originals are now deposited at Queen's University, Belfast, after digitisation by Bristol University, and uploading to the site <http://chp.ish-lyon.cnrs.fr/>. These are identified in the text as Ca01 and Ca02. The scrolls, gown, cap and order are now in his possession or that of his brother Rodger or his nephew Rudolf Ridout-Jamieson.

William Forbes Newton. Three pages of photos from an album of Emily Forbes, née Carrall.

Peter Acheson (Kath's grandson). Certificates, Kath's marriage, birth of Keeve.

Queen's University, Belfast, Special Collections

Irons' Gift, now in MS 15

Four letters (Hart to Kathleen Carrall).

Letters to his god-daughter (Hart to Kathleen Carrall) (19 letters)

Carrall, J W *Events in the North of China, 17th June 1900 to September 3rd.* ms.

Newton, K F Folder headed *Pageant of Five decades,* containing::
Childhood in China. Northern Ireland Home Service, BBC 16 February 1943.
It happened to me. 1960.
The man who conquered adversity.
Incredible 8 weeks ordeal.
Sinclair, J. 'Sir Robert Hart in China'. Cutting from Belfast Newsletter, Belfast, 22/06/1965.

Sir Robert Hart Collection

MS 15/1 Hart's diaries.

MS 15/2. Correspondence.
Letters to Hart from Frances Mary Carrall, Maude Fawcus Carrall, Kathleen Fawcus Carrall, Frances Fawcus Carrall, Emily Fawcus Carrall (later as Mrs Forbes), her husband Charles Forbes; and from Emma Spry Sampson. These are in various bundles in Boxes 1, 2, 3, 4, 6, 7, 9, 10, 12b, 14 (139 letters).
15/2/8 letters re Nollie Hart and Perry,
15/2/11 letters from Campbell.

MS 15/6 Three photographs originally in Irons Gift, now filed with other Hart photographs.

MS 15/8 J Address to Hart on his 70th birthday, 1905.

Borthwick Institute, University of York. Parish records. York.

Bristol University: <www.bris.ac.uk/history/customs> Customs personnel and other data.

Cambridge University
Jardine Matheson Archive.

School of Oriental Studies (SOAS) Special Collections
Bowra Papers.
Letters, Hart to Campbell.
China Inland Mission: Chefoo schools.

London School of Economics (LSE)
North China Herald.
Decennial reports, Chinese Maritime Customs.

National Archives, Kew, Surrey
Foreign Office (FO) consular files for Canton, Foochow, Chefoo, 1853-1900.
Admiralty (ADM 196/43) officers' confidential files.

Royal Botanic Gardens, Kew, Archives
Director's Correspondence, Chinese and Japanese letters, Vols. 150 and 151.
Miscellaneous Reports: China Index Florae Sinensis, 1883-1905.
T Sampson: *Sketch of the Botany of Kwantung*. Dated 1880, presented by a relative in 1927.

General Register Office Certificates of Birth Marriage and Death.

Probate service <www.hmcourts-service.gov.uk>, probate and wills of Theophilus Sampson, Emma Sampson, Frances Carrall (probate only).

Geological Society of London J W Carrall membership application and paper.

Friends of Highgate Cemetery: Burial records.

Lambeth Palace Library Shanghai marriages and baptisms.

Royal College of Surgeons *Lives of the Fellows*, *Medical Register*, *London Medical Directory*.

CHINA

Nanjing. Second Historical Archive of China. Reports and memos by J W Carrall, from Foochow and Chefoo (collected by Catherine Ladds).

Hong Kong Public Record Office. Online Catalog of the Carl Smith Collection (Buckton and Sampson cards followed up for me by Sammy Tsang).

Hong Kong University Library. Hong Kong Journals on line *The China Review, or notes & queries on the Far East.* <http://sunzi.lib.hku.hk/hkjo/> Articles by Sampson after 1872.

Hong Kong, St **John's Cathedral.** Marriage certificate, Theophilus Sampson and Emma Buckton.

Yantai: Buildings Archive. Record of grave inscriptions, former Temple Hill cemetery.

UNITED STATES

Washington State University, Manuscript Archives and Special Collections. George W Woods Journals,1883-6.

Pittsburgh Theological Seminary, USA. Clifford E Barbour Library. T. Sampson. *Progressive Lessons in English.*

Other family historians

Dawn McKonkey: Correspondence on Edwards family.
Lindsay Stillwell: Correspondence and photograph on Fawcus family.
Dr T Sue-A-Quan. Correspondence on Sampson and Chinese emigration to Guyana.
Mike M Swift *The Zinzan families.* CD.
Paul Wilcocks, Karen Johnson, Karin Groves, Gillian Selley. Correspondence on descendants of James Carrall Wilcocks I.

Internet family history resources

Ancestry.com Census data, Immigration records, London, births and baptisms,1815-1906, Marriage and Banns, 1754-1921, Edwards family tree.

Findmypast.com Census, birth, marriage and death data

genuki.org.uk Devon, Kingsbridge 1850, from White's Gazetteer, and other records.

RootsWeb.com ENG-DEV-SOUTHHAMS—LArchives Edwards family in South Hams.

R. G. Tiedemann, <http://ricci.rt.usfa.edu/biography>

Books, Journals and Theses

(Some of the older books listed here were accessed from the Internet. Some are also available in SOAS and LSE libraries.

Bell, S, *Hart of Lisburn*. Lisburn Historical Press, 1985.

Bickers, R, 'Purloined letters: History and the Chinese Maritime Customs Service', *Modern Asian Studies*, 40. 3 (2006).

Boche, J F & Cowen, L L, *The French at Foochow*. <www.archive.org/stream/frenchatfoochow00rochrich>, 1884.

Bonham-Carter, V, *What Countryman, Sir?* B-C Press, 1996.

Bredon, J, *Sir Robert Hart: The Romance of a Great Career Told by His Niece*. Hutchinson, 1909 (now available at <www.gutenberg.org/files/12344>).

Bruner, K F, Fairbank, J K, & Smith, R J, *Entering China's Service: Robert Hart's Journals, 1854-1863*. Council on East Asian Studies, Harvard University, 1986.

Buettner, E, *Empire Families: Britons and Late Imperial India*. Oxford University Press, 2004.

Cannon, I C, *Public Success, Private Sorrow: The Life and Times of Charles Henry Brewitt-Taylor (1857-1938), China Customs Commissioner and Pioneer Translator*. Hong Kong University Press, 2009.

Carrall, J W, 'Chefoo'. In *Decennial Reports on the Trade, Navigation, Industries...of the Ports Open to Foreign Commerce in China, 1892-1901*, Inspectorate General of Customs,1905.

Carrall, J W, *The Tourist's Guide for the City of Canton*. J M da Silva, Macao, 1877.

Cheng, Pei-kai, Lestz, M and Spence, J D, *The Search for Modern China: A Documentary Collection*. W.W. Norton & Co. 1999.

Coates, P D, *China consuls: British Consular Officers, 1843-1943*. Oxford University Press, 1988.

Davidoff, L & Hall, C, *Family Fortunes: Men and Women of the English Middle Class, 1780-1850*. Revised 2002 edn, Routledge, 1987.

Doolittle, J, *Social life of the Chinese*. <http://books.google.com/books> edn, Sampson Low, Son & Marston, 1866.

Drage, C, *Servants of the Dragon Throne: Being the Lives of Edward and Cecil Bowra*. Peter Dawnay, 1966.

Drew, E B, 'Sir Robert Hart and his Life Work in China', *Journal of Race Development*, 4. 1, 1913.

Eastman, L E, *Throne and mandarins: China's Search for a Policy during the Sino-French Controversy, 1880-1885*. Harvard University Press, 1967.

Eitel, E J, *Europe in China: The History of Hongkong from the Beginning to the Year 1882*. Luzac & Co, 1895.

Fairbank, J K, Bruner, K F, Matheson, E M, ed. *The I.G. in Peking: Letters of Robert Hart, Chinese Maritime Customs, 1868-1907*. Belknap Press of Harvard University Press, 1975.

Fan, Fa-ti. *British Naturalists in Qing China: Science, Empire, and Cultural Encounter*. Harvard University Press, 2004.

Fenby, J, *The Penguin History of Modern China: The Fall and Rise of a Great Power, 1850-2008*. Allen Lane, 2008.

Ferguson, N, *Civilisation: The West and the Rest*. Allen Lane, 2011.

Graham, G S, *The China Station: War and Diplomacy, 1830-60*. Clarendon Press, 1978.

Gray, M J H, *Fourteen Months in Canton*. MacMillan, 1880.

Hoe, S, *Women at the siege of Peking 1900*. Holo Books, 2000.

Hui, O J, 'Chinese Indenture Labour: Coolies and Colonies'. In *The Cambridge Survey of World Migration*, ed. R. Cohen, Cambridge University Press,1995.

Hurd, D, *The Arrow War: an Anglo-Chinese Confusion, 1856-60*. Collins, 1967.

Jacobs, A, *Girls and Examinations*, Ph.D., University of Winchester, 2003.

Jacobs, A, 'Examinations as cultural capital for the Victorian school girl: "Thinking with Bourdieu"', *Women's History Review*, 16. 2, 2007.

Johnston, J D, *China and Japan: Being a Narrative of the Cruise of the US Steam-Frigate Powhatan, in the Years 1857, '58, '59 and '60, including an*

Account of the Japanese Embassy to the United States. Charles de Silva; Cushings & Bailey, 1861.

Jones, R A, *The British Diplomatic Service, 1815-1914.* Wilfrid Laurier University Press, 1983.

Ladds, C, 'Youthful, Likely Men, Able to Read, Write and Count': Joining the Foreign Staff of the Chinese Customs Service, 1854-1927', *The Journal of Imperial and Commonwealth History*, 30. 2, 2008.

Ladds, C, *Empire Careers: The Foreign Staff of the Chinese Customs Service, 1854-1949.* Ph.D. thesis, University of Bristol, Department of Historical Studies 2007.

Lai, W L, *The Chinese in the West Indies, 1806-1898: A Documentary History.* The University of the West Indies Press, 1998.

Li, L. & Wildy, D, 'A New Discovery and its Significance: The Statutory Declarations made by Sir Robert Hart concerning his Secret Domestic Life in 19th Century China', *Journal of the Hong Kong Branch of the Royal Asiatic Society*, 13. 2003.

MacKenzie, J M, 'Empire and the Global Gaze'. In *The Victorian Vision*, ed. J. MacKenzie, Victoria & Albert Publications, 2001.

Meagher, A J, *The Coolie trade: the Traffic in Chinese Laborers to Latin America 1846-1874.* Xlibris corp, 2008.

Needham, J, *Science and Civilisation in China.* Cambridge University Press, 1986.

Neelam, Bapna, Mohanlal, Swarankar and Namita Kotia, 'Genital tuberculosis and its consequences on subsequent infertility', *J.Obstet.Gynaecol.India*, 55. 6, 2005.

O'Leary, R, 'Robert Hart in China: The Significance of his Irish roots', *Modern Asian Studies*, 40. 2006.

Osborne, F, *Lilla's Feast: A True Story of Love, War and a Passion for Food.* Doubleday, 2004.

Piercy, G, *Love for China, Exemplified in Memorials of Mary Gunston, the First Female Teacher in Connection with the Wesleyan Methodist Mission at Canton.* Hamilton, Adams & Co., 1865.

Preston, D, *The Boxer Rebellion: China's War on Foreigners. 1900.* Paperback edition, Constable & Robinson Ltd., 2002.

Robinson, M, *A South Down Farm in the Sxties.* Dent, 1938.

Sampson, T, 'Whirlwind at Canton', *The China Review*, 6. 6. 1878.

Sampson, T, *Botanical and other Writings on China, 1867-1870 with a biographical sketch by Emil Bretschneider.* Ed. H. Waltravens, C. Bell, 1984.

Sieghart, M, 'A Perfect Gentleman. *The Times, Times 2,* 11/03/2008.

Smith, R J, Fairbank, J K, & Bruner, K F, *Robert Hart and China's Early Modernization: His Journals, 1863-66.* Council on East Asian Studies, Harvard University, 1991.

Spurling, H, *Burying the Bones: Pearl Buck in China.* Profile Books, 2010.

Steinmetz, G, *The Devil's Handwriting: Precoloniality and the German Colonial State in Qingdao, Samoa and Southwest Africa.* University of Chicago Press, 2007.

Sue-A-Quan, T, *Cane Reapers: Chinese Indentured Immigrants in Guyana.* 2nd edn, Cane Press, 2003.

Summers, J, *Soho, a History of London.* Bloomsbury, 1989.

Tixier, N, 'La Chine dans la Stratégie Impériale: le Rôle du Quai d'Orsay et de ses Agents'. In *L'esprit Économique impérial (1830-1970). Groupes Réseau du Patronat Colonial en France et dans l'Empire.* Société Française d'Outre-Mer, 2008.

van de Ven, H, 'Robert Hart and Gustav Detring during the Boxer Rebellion', *Modern Asian Studies,* 40. 3, 2006.

Vicinus, M, *Independent women: Work and Community for Single Women, 1850-1920.* University of Chicago; Virago, 1985.

Willis, R, 'Testing Times', *History Today,* August 2005.

Wood, F, *No Dogs and not too many Chinese: Treaty Port Life in China 1843-1943.* John Murray, 1998.

Wright, S F, *Hart and the Chinese Customs.* William Mullen and Son, 1950.

Xiafei, C & Rongfang, H, *Archives of China's Imperial Maritime Customs: Confidential Correspondence Between Robert Hart and James Duncan Campbell 1874-1907.* Foreign Languages Press, Beijing 1990.